1994

Rules and Conventions

Parallax Re-visions of Culture and Society

Stephen G. Nichols, Gerald Prince, and Wendy Steiner

SERIES EDITORS

Rules
and
Conventions

Literature, PHILOSOPHY, Social Theory

EDITED BY METTE HJORT

The Johns Hopkins University Press
Baltimore and London

THE JOHNS HOPKINS UNIVERSITY PRESS
701 West 40th Street
Baltimore, Maryland 21211-2190
The Johns Hopkins Press Ltd., London

Library of Congress Cataloging-in-Publication Data

Rules and conventions : literature, philosophy, social theory /
edited by Mette Hjort.
p. cm. — (Parallax)
Includes bibliographical references.
ISBN 0-8018-4394-4. — ISBN 0-8018-4395-2 (pbk.)
1. Canon (Literature)   2. Literature—History and criticism— Theory, etc.
3. Literature—Philosophy.   I. Hjort, Mette.
II. Series: Parallax (Baltimore, Md.)
PN80.5.R85   1992
801'.95—dc20   92-6641

Contents

Acknowledgments

With the exception of "Literary Conventions," by Thomas G. Pavel, the chapters in this volume were all written especially for *Rules and Conventions*. I would like to thank the contributors for their warm cooperation and support. Pavel's essay was first published in his *Fictional Worlds* (1986) and is reprinted here courtesy of Harvard University Press. Comments by David Bell and an anonymous reader for the Johns Hopkins University Press helped improve the manuscript. I am grateful to the Social Sciences and Humanities Research Council of Canada for a postdoctoral fellowship and precious time to work on the anthology. Finally, I would like to thank our editor, Eric Halpern, and our manuscript editor, Carol Ehrlich, for good treatment.

Introduction

METTE HJORT

One of the most salient features of the contemporary literary-critical landscape is a widespread tendency to explore interdisciplinary connections, especially theoretical ones. As a result of this trend, the traditional "canon" of primary literary works has been joined by a new canon of theoretical sources. For example, literary scholars frequently draw on Sigmund Freud's *Beyond the Pleasure Principle* and Ferdinand de Saussure's *Course in General Linguistics,* and do so without feeling any need to justify this mobilization of works from "another field." Surveys of critics' citations reveal that texts by Karl Marx, Freud, Friedrich Nietzsche, and Martin Heidegger figure among the most frequently cited references. This broadening of the literary critic's sources has in many ways been an exciting and promising development. At the same time, however, the formation of a second canon does raise issues that echo the well-known critiques of the selective and restrictive nature of the traditional literary canon. Not only have literary scholars often failed to make an adequate survey of the fields from which they have borrowed, but their "creative appropriations" of work from other disciplines have also led to misleading and fruitless analogies. Although no one should call for a return to traditional forms of disciplinarity in literary studies, it is time for critics to develop and strengthen the bases of their interdisciplinary efforts, especially in those cases in which there is a large body of relevant work in other disciplines.

In such a context, concepts of rules and conventions are of particular significance. Rules and conventions are of indisputable historical importance and occupy a privileged place within contemporary theory across the disciplines. What is more, both notions have long played a central role in traditional literary-critical discourses and remain fundamental to the new poststructuralist canon. Although traditional critics have placed a great deal of explanatory weight on the notion of convention, they have repeatedly failed to provide any detailed elucidations of the term and of its implications. Conventions, it would appear, are what make literary explanations possible, and do not themselves need to be explained. The poststructuralist approach is quite different, but it too is inadequate: critics have converged on one highly speculative understanding of convention, which they have generalized across a wide range of contexts and practices. The favored idea is that a phenomenon is "conventional" whenever it is "arbitrary" and historically contingent. It is further assumed that all natural and social phenomena — as we know them — are conventional. Yet, this insistence on the conventional nature of *all* human experience ultimately renders the term meaningless and deprives the concept of any real explanatory power, a situation that is only exacerbated by the belief that conventions by definition are unknowable. The poststructuralist conception of rules and conventions is no doubt of genuine interest, particularly in the context of an ongoing critique of German idealist philosophy, but the fact remains that a number of alternative accounts have been developed that literary theorists would do well to consider seriously.

The present volume explores some of the interdisciplinary connections that have been absent from the literary-critical landscape, introducing readers to the various avenues of inquiry that they make possible. Reference is made to both Anglo-American and Continental traditions, a strategy that helps to correct one of the major imbalances of the poststructuralist canon. More specifically, the reader will find here a sustained dialogue surrounding David K. Lewis's groundbreaking and by now classic work, *Convention: A Philosophical Study*. Responding to Willard Van Orman Quine, Lewis drew on game-theoretical insights in order to argue that language is conventional in the sense first expressed by David Hume. The linguistic and game-theoretical backgrounds of Lewis's account are further explored in essays drawing on work in Anglo-American philosophy of language by such major figures as Donald Davidson, Michael Dummett, Saul Kripke, and Quine. Not only do these essays contribute to key debates over the nature of convention in analytic philosophy of language, they also enhance our understanding of rules and conventions through dialogue across the disciplines. Thus, for example, Paul Grice's distinction between linguistic meaning and speaker's meaning calls attention to the lack of nuance characterizing current literary-critical accounts of meaning and intentionality. Similarly, the complexity of literary texts and history usefully identifies the areas in which current philosophical conceptions of rules and conventions are in need of further work.

Although the topic of language is undoubtedly central to literary studies, many critics are rightly motivated by a desire to study the sociohistorical conditions and political consequences of literary phenomena. They will find in this volume contributions that draw on a refreshing variety of theoretical sources, including systems theory, analytic Marxism, liberal political philosophy, rational choice, and the ideas of such classic and contemporary thinkers as Thomas Hobbes, Friedrich von August Hayek, Alasdair MacIntyre, and Pierre Bourdieu. Together the contributions establish a range of philosophical options that will allow critics successfully to avoid the prevalent false choice between an apolitical aestheticism and anachronistic forms of Marxist orthodoxy.

This anthology is motivated, then, by the perceived need for a new and rigorous form of interdisciplinarity grounded in issues of common concern. As a result, the contributors to this volume were not only encouraged to contact work outside their own disciplines but were themselves drawn from a diverse number of fields. What they all share is the assumption that rules and conventions are explanatory categories permitting insight into language, social interaction, creativity, cultural change, aesthetic practice, social order and disorder, rationality, and agency. The contributors further believe that rules and conventions are complex phenomena requiring a combination of empirical and conceptual analysis. Although these shared assumptions give unity to the various chapters, they do not entail some monolithic perspective, and the reader will thus find real differences here. Indeed, the volume embraces positions as diverse as strong conventionalism, pragmatism, deconstruction, constructivism, realism, and methodological individualism.

Rules and Conventions: Literature, Philosophy, Social Theory was designed, not simply to build bridges between disciplines, but to convey what I take to be an important message, which runs something like this: "Conventionalism is dead, long live conventionalism." Although this slogan cannot possibly capture the scope and detail of the various contributions, it does begin to evoke at least two of the goals motivating the project. The aim, more specifically, was to provide an alternative to the inadequate conceptions of rules and conventions mentioned above, while at the same time establishing the centrality and significance of the phenomena in question. There are, I believe, many good reasons for endorsing the proposed line of inquiry. Some are primarily methodological but have a definite bearing on issues of real substance. Others go directly to the heart of how we construe our lives together as human beings.

In social science, it is common to distinguish between *methodological holism* and *methodological individualism*. These terms have a long and tangled history, and many thinkers have sought to resolve the opposition by refining the original claims made by orthodox methodological individualists. In general, what separates these two schools of thought is a basic disagreement over the kinds of explanations that are appropriate to social action and, by extension, individual action. Methodological individualists contend that social realities do not exist in their own right and are reducible to the intentions, deliberations, and actions of individual agents. Methodological holists, on the other hand, claim that social phenomena have a certain autonomy and cannot simply be viewed as an aggregate of individual actions: the whole is more than the sum of the parts. A classic example of methodological holism can be found in Marcel Mauss's (1968) anthropological theory, which was meant to explain social action in terms of general structures and collective representations. Now, what is striking is that, over the last two decades, literary critics have eagerly embraced a form of methodological holism that has led to a systematic preference for holistic conceptions of language, writing, and convention, as well as to a series of ominous pronouncements concerning the death of the subject and the impossibility of practical rationality. More recently, however, there has been a growing awareness of the shortcomings of holism, and critics are now looking for ways of incorporating concepts of agency into their critical paradigms. I believe that the present volume on rules and conventions has much to offer along these lines. Not only have many of the contributors written extensively on questions of agency, but their approach to rules and conventions mediates successfully between social and individual levels of description. As defined here, rules and conventions call attention to the complex interplay between individual intentions, anticipations, and inferences and shared practices, habits, and traditions.

To explore rules and conventions is to explore what agents have in common. It is to focus on what brings human beings together, on what is known in French as *le lien social* — the social bond. On this score, too, *Rules and Conventions* is usefully at odds with current critical practice. It is fashionable today to foreground the warlike or strategic dimensions of human behavior at the expense of all cooperative or communicative forms of interaction. Indeed, some critics even go so far as to insist that *all* actions necessarily are (equally) strategic. Insofar as critics attempt at all to articulate the shared dimensions of human experience, they evoke the idea of a community that serves as a framework fact and that cannot as a result be described in any detail. The contributions to *Rules and Conventions* are quite different in this regard, for they focus on how, in certain contexts, the social bond originates, is sustained, and changes. The anthology thus contains crucial insights about the shared realities that make possible social order, communicative action, and human agency as we know it. The importance of this contribution should not be underestimated, for as is well known, theories may function as self-fulfilling prophecies. To sacrifice all concrete instances of community on the global altar of strategy may very well be to contribute to the reality of the war-like universe that is boldly depicted in theory. Having evoked something of the significance and timeliness of *Rules and Conventions,* I shall in what follows provide a brief characterization of each of the contributions.

In the first chapter, George Wilson brings the issue of rules and conventions to bear on the complex question of linguistic and literary meaning, providing a critical examination of some recent and highly influential claims made by Steven Knapp, Walter Michaels, and Stanley Fish. According to Wilson, the view that the meaning of a literary work is simply what its author intended it to mean hinges on a largely unexamined, unargued, and wholly theoretical rejection of the twofold idea that expressions mean something in a particular language, and that these meanings involve rules and conventions. Wilson goes on to identify the undesirable consequences entailed by a failure to consider important distinctions among speaker's meaning, utterance meaning, word meaning, and sentence meaning. Linguistic meaning, then, is not a matter of purely formal derivations based on abstract or mechanical rules but of conventional meanings that may be intentionally mobilized within a given context of use. Wilson claims that Fish's statements concerning literal meaning provide no support for the stance adopted by Knapp and Michaels. Indeed, "Against Theory" (1982) is shown merely to repeat the failings already inherent in Fish's arguments. Wilson's discussion of linguistic meaning establishes the context for his concluding remarks about the thorny issue of literary meaning. Wilson distinguishes between a restricted and an unrestricted conception of the intentionality of literary texts. Whereas the former is limited to the level of verbal meaning, the latter concerns the work's meaning as a whole. Wilson argues that if Knapp and Michaels hold the restricted view, then their position is uncontroversial and contributes little or nothing to the discussion of intentionalism. If, on the other hand, they intend to embrace the unrestricted view, then they fail to provide the arguments needed to make their position cogent and persuasive.

Jon Elster approaches artistic conventions from an interdisciplinary perspective, drawing on game theory, analytic Marxism, and philosophical psychology. He defines such conventions as constraints and suggests two distinct ways in which they may be construed, namely, as inculcated social norms entailing sanctions if violated, and as equilibria providing arbitrary solutions to coordination problems. Following Elster, both conceptions belong within a full account of aesthetic conventions. Elster discusses a number of different functions assumed by such constraints, attributing particular importance to the manner in which they enhance, rather than obstruct, creativity. Elster goes on to broach the difficult problem of change and innovation that has proven so intractable to many theorists of convention. In an attempt to account for the emergence of new conventions, Elster examines and rejects what he refers to as the "exhaustion argument," the idea that conventions change when the various forms of creativity that they make possible have been explored in full. A more convincing solution, claims Elster, may be found in the Marxist critique of capitalist relations of production. New forms of art emerge, then, not as a result of stagnation, but because new conventions simply are more effective in promoting creativity. Inasmuch as originality is a concept associated with untrammeled freedom, it should be distinguished from genuine creativity, which presupposes constraint. Contemporary society, suggests Elster, wrongly privileges originality over creativity.

Thomas Pavel takes issue with the particularly radical form of conventionalism entailed by the structuralist doctrine of language and related literary theories. In the structuralist view, arbitrariness, necessity, and inscrutability are the defining features of conventions. According to Pavel, this definition has a number of unappealing consequences: the necessity of regarding all literary forms as equally conventional; the rejection of all notions of literary reference; and the necessity of espousing a constructivist epistemology. He thus goes on to propose an alternative conception of conventions, based on the game-theoretical model of Lewis. The advantage of this model is that while it retains the emphasis on arbitrariness, it considerably weakens the element of necessity, substituting conditional preferences, beliefs, and mutual expectations for the black box of unconscious and inescapable mechanisms. The game-theoretical approach also recognizes the importance of distinguishing between various kinds of regularities. Pavel thus emphasizes the crucial differences separating the constitutive conventions, preconventions, and social conventions embedded in literary texts. The nature of the reading experience will to a large extent be determined by the reader's ability to participate successfully in these different coordination games. Much like Elster, Pavel sees the role of full-blown constitutive conventions as being one of imposing constraints or limiting strategic possibilities. He also raises the question of change, suggesting that conventions evolve as a result of the gradual displacement of the coordination problems to which they provide solutions.

Paisley Livingston's central claim is that Lewis's concept of convention does indeed have value for the study of literature, but not in any straightforward way. The assumption that autonomous textual features may be described as conventions in Lewis's sense, is, following Livingston, inaccurate. Instead, the advantage of Lewis's game-theoretical model is that it proposes a type of action explanation that may be usefully extended to the domain of literary research. For a literary account to be properly explanatory, some of the preferences, expectations, and beliefs of the agents involved in the process of literary interaction have to be successfully identified. In appropriating Lewis's concept of convention, literary scholars need to modify the model somewhat, while keeping a number of the original distinctions clearly in mind. Thus, the assumptions of rationality underwriting Lewis's model should be weakened in order to account for literary communication. On the other hand, Lewis's view that conventions are recurrent rather than one-shot solutions to coordination problems should be retained. Having examined the pertinence for literature of Lewis's *Convention* (1969), Livingston goes on to discuss the implications of the modified account presented in "Languages and Language" (1975).

In the second part of his chapter, Livingston substantiates his theoretical points in a discussion of what he takes to be an exemplary instance of literary explanation, Lars Lönnroth's analysis of *Njáls Saga*. The composition of this saga is shown to have involved two sets of constraints, for while the desires of the patrons called for the public rehabilitation of a notorious ancestor, the expectations of the rest of the audience required conformity to the established tradition of saga telling. Livingston concludes that the pragmatics of *Njáls Saga* involved conventional, pseudoconventional, and unconventional dimensions. Inasmuch as the saga provided a one-shot solution to the problems of bard and sponsor, it is not, properly speaking, conventional. Whether this solution might be defined as preconventional in Pavel's sense would depend on whether it was considered arbitrary by the agents involved. At the same time, many of the regularities of the saga form are properly conventional. These conventions cannot alone provide the basis for literary explanations; as arbitrary solutions to coordination problems, they do not tell us anything about why the coordination problem emerged in the first place, and only a holistic action explanation could do so.

Paul Dumouchel's contribution is at once historical and theoretical. He focuses on Thomas Hobbes's concept of rules and conventions and on its specific contribution to recent debates over the nature of social regularities. Dumouchel begins with a brief overview of the ways in which conventional phenomena were defined prior to the seventeenth century, thereby establishing a context in which the specificity of Hobbes's views can be properly grasped. The novelty of Hobbes's position, claims Dumouchel, is its fusion of two previously disjoined elements: arbitrariness and rationality. Dumouchel goes on to consider the implications of Hobbes's view of conventions as rational agreements between agents. More specifically, it is a matter of determining whether Hobbes believed that such agreements had to be explicit and not merely a form of spontaneous or emergent coordination. Dumouchel then turns to Hobbes's statements concerning the rules of epic poetry, which have rarely been examined in the light of the latter's more general claims about conventions. Nor has it been recognized that Hobbes's view of poetic rules provides counterexamples to recent criticisms of his account of conventions, which has been seen as too closely linked to notions of explicit agreement and a fully fledged rejection of tradition. Based on nuances in Hobbes's discussion, Dumouchel develops a distinction between conventions and highly abstract rules. Whereas these general rules are invariant and directly related to the basic goal of epic poetry, conventions are simply the arbitrary ways in which these rules may be applied in accordance with the ever-changing expectations of historically situated agents. The two-tiered system evoked by Hobbes has the distinct advantage of providing a plausible explanation of how conventions change. In his concluding section, Dumouchel compares Hobbes's rules to Hayekian rules of conduct, and Hobbes's literary conventions to Lewisian conventions. Hobbes is applauded for having stressed an element of rationality that Hayek will later sacrifice and for having confronted the problem of change that Lewis circumvents.

In a contribution that surveys the basic role played by concepts of convention in a range of disciplines and historic traditions, Alain Boyer begins by establishing the philosophical richness of the notions in question. Yet, his argument is also polemical, for it challenges the well-entrenched view of Lewis and others that conventions necessarily involve arbitrariness. Boyer claims that the restriction of conventional phenomena to what is arbitrary has the effect of excluding a wide range of practices that nonetheless correspond to our everyday understanding of what is involved in conventions. The scope of the Lewisian model is limited to the arbitrary equilibria that emerge as a result of a complex interplay of conditional preferences. Contracts and any number of institutional regularities that fail to meet the criterion of self-regulation are, as a result, excluded from the theoretical picture. Boyer's attempt to attenuate the importance attributed to arbitrariness is further developed in a suggestive consideration of the temporality of conventional phenomena. "Difference," claims Boyer, "emerges from indifference," for what was once arbitrary is less so as a result of the weight of effective history. Yet, at the same time, it is also important to recognize that the passage of time may bring to light the arbitrary nature of conventions. This point is aptly illustrated in a discussion of the romantic rejection of neoclassical conventions. Finally, Boyer addresses himself to the difficult question concerning the origin of conventions. Boyer suggests that ultimately the motivational bases for conventions are to be sought in the desire to contain violence and to inhabit a social space in which reality is experienced as something more than an endless series of unexpected events.

Joseph Margolis argues in favor of a pragmatic conception of regularities such as genres, laws, canons, and principles, as well as of the inductive processes by which these regularities are grasped. Margolis skillfully negotiates a middle course between the two poles of what he perceives as the false choice of realism and a fully fledged skepticism.

Most generally, the realist position on natural and social regularities tends to be supported either by a metaphysical argument of Aristotelian inspiration or by an epistemological argument characteristic of Descartes and the modern period. While these two traditions involve different conceptions of induction—what Margolis calls "essentialist induction" and "regularity induction"—the two conceptions are shown to be similar in crucial regards. The Aristotelian view presupposes the existence of natural regularities and is undermined once the changing nature of reality is recognized. The modern attempt to discover invariant nomic universals falters once the existence of an unchanging set of axioms is called into question. The pervasiveness of these two basic approaches is documented by detailed discussions of figures such as Heinrich Schenker, Northrop Frye, Hayden White, Paul Ricoeur, E. D. Hirsch, John Rawls, and David Lewis. Margolis's critique of essentialist and regularity induction prepares the ground for an alternative conception that is based in part on arguments proposed by Bas van Fraassen and Nelson Goodman. What distinguishes Margolis's "equilibrative induction" from rival accounts is the attendant recognition that induction is an activity that necessarily remains rooted within social contexts. Induction, then, is subject to ideological interests and determinations, as are the regularities it produces. While equilibrative induction denies regularities their "essentialist bite," it by no means, says Margolis, commits us to an undiluted form of skepticism. The skepticism in question here is purely second-order, focusing not on the "plausible recovery" of arbitrary regularities but on the arguments by which they are legitimated and passed off as objective, necessary, and invariant.

Charles Taylor squares off against the intellectualist conception of rule following that is a major feature of modern culture. On Taylor's view, monologic and intellectualist theories of agency have two salient features: a definition of the subject as first and foremost a vehicle of representations; and a view of knowledge and moral action as hinging on the possibility of disengaging all mental activity from the distorting influences of the human body and other agents. Taylor begins his argument by focusing on Ludwig Wittgenstein's critique of foundationalist views of rule following. Most generally, the alternative proposed by Wittgenstein is to see rule following as a practice presupposing the existence of an unarticulated background. According to Taylor, the concept of background holds genuine promise, yet its importance is largely undermined by an influential line of interpretation. More specifically, in *Witt-genstein on Rules and Private Language,* Kripke construes this background as a series of systematic, de facto connections inculcated by society, a position that Taylor considers monologic and wholly consistent with the intellectualist tradition. Taylor argues that an adequate account of the role of rules in human practice presupposes a quite different view of understanding and agency, one capable of acknowledging the fundamental importance of the dialogic and embodied dimensions of social existence. What is needed, then, is an account of the unarticulated background as a form of tacit knowledge and as a kind of embodied understanding. Following Taylor, Bourdieu's notion of "habitus" makes a major contribution along these lines, for it underscores the impossibility of separating rules from the practices they animate. This is not, says Taylor, to deny the need for a concept of rules within the anthropological disciplines, for much of human life clearly reveals important regularities that may best be described in terms of rules. What must be avoided, however, is the typical intellectualist mistake of attributing causal efficacy to these rules.

In a wide-ranging discussion of rap music, Richard Shusterman demonstrates the extent to which conventions play a role in sustaining social division and conflict, in circumscribing the boundaries of cultures of taste, and in upholding or undermining the legitimacy of certain aesthetic products. Rap music, claims Shusterman, is a postmodern art form that poses a serious challenge, not only to the conventions characteristic of modernism, but to the related doctrine of philosophical modernity and its radical differentiation of the cultural spheres of art, politics, and knowledge. In its postmodern emphasis on recycling, eclecticism, citation, and appropriation, rap music openly flouts the norms and ideology underwriting attempts to distinguish rigorously between high and low art. The idea that properly aesthetic artifacts have a unity and integrity that is at once permanent and inviolable is called into question by the self-confident affirmation of open-ended creative practices that privilege process over product. Traditional conceptions of originality and genius are replaced by a quite different understanding of creativity, while the view that genuine or great art should have a universal appeal is explicitly challenged by rappers, who emphasize the local and partisan dimensions of their music, appealing directly to clearly identifiable social groups. In the case of rap, the disinterested attitudes that are believed by many to be essential to a properly aesthetic response give way to a form of involvement that bridges the gap between politics, knowledge, and art. Having established the many ways in which rap self-consciously violates the conventions of modernism, Shusterman goes on to consider the issue of rap's aesthetic value, his claim being that the systematic attempts to deny that rap really is art are unfounded. This point is demonstrated at great length in a close reading of a particularly popular piece that is also a "rap manifesto in rap," "Talkin' All That Jazz," by the Brooklyn crew Stetsasonic.

The concept of convention is a central element in Siegfried Schmidt's empirical and sociological account of the emergence and persistence of aesthetic autonomy. Drawing on systems theory and constructivist epistemology, Schmidt argues that, from the eighteenth century onward, literature in Germany has functioned as a self-referential, self-organizing social system embracing a range of distinct action roles. According to studies conducted by Schmidt and his colleagues, the boundaries of this literary system are constituted by two basic conventions, namely, an "aesthetic" convention and a "polyvalence" convention. Whereas the former suspends all considerations having to do with the truth or falsehood of literary representations, the second lends legitimacy to a plurality of interpretive responses. Having defined these two macro conventions, Schmidt goes on to describe the historical context that made possible the transformation of literary discourse into an autonomous social system. Thus he explores a number of the social and political changes that occurred during the course of the eighteenth century, paying particular attention to the following issues: the decline of feudal society and the emergence in its place of a functionally differentiated society, the transition from natural to positive law, the separation of state and society, the specialization of knowledge, the secularization of education, and structural transformations at the level of the family. Schmidt then examines the changes that directly affected the action roles and institutions associated with literature. He discusses the professionalization of authorship, the development of a book market organized along capitalist lines, the modified self-understandings of authors, the development of new reading practices and modes of reception, and the growth of a more general and anonymous reading public. Schmidt finally suggests that doctrines of aesthetic autonomy ultimately prevailed over competing conceptions because they attributed to literature, and to art more generally, a capacity to resolve the kinds of tensions and oppositions entailed by the historical process of functional differentiation. Schmidt concludes that if literature is to fulfill its historical role, then it must retain its autonomous character, forgoing all forms of unmediated political engagement, as well as the pursuit of cognitive or scientific goals.

In Peter McCormick's contribution, literary and philosophical discussions of convention are contrasted. McCormick begins by considering the interpretive complexities of a passage from *Romeo and Juliet* that serves as his primary example. In answering key interpretive questions concerning meaning and sense, or truth and significance, literary critics frequently have recourse to a notion of convention. Yet, representative statements by Frye, M. H. Abrams, and R. S. Crane provide little or no clarification of these issues, for it remains unclear how the proposed notions of conspicuous stylistic features, implicit agreements, and nonperceptual and noninferential background information are to be understood. Given this situation, McCormick's strategy is to turn to analytic philosophy of language and, more particularly, to Davidson's influential discussion of deviant expressions and their implications for current debate concerning the role of conventions in language. McCormick subsequently goes on to endorse aspects of Dummett's and Ian Hacking's critiques of Davidson's argument. More specifically, Davidson's account is said to reduce language to overlapping idiolects and to rely on an overly monologic conception of communication. Finally, McCormick brings the analytic accounts to bear on the literary case, pointing first to the insights they make possible: formalist and pragmatic concerns need to be balanced in an interpretive approach that gives privileged status to textual regularities, as well as to the intentions of writers and readers; an adequate interpretation must satisfy the criterion of inductive verifiability; and basic terms, such as "meaning" and "truth," stand in need of critical analysis. Yet, it is by no means a matter of proposing a fully fledged appropriation of the analytic views, for the latter are also problematic in a number of respects: the central concept of theory remains vague; the crucial distinction between deviant and normal linguistic usage seems nonsensical in certain literary contexts; and the question of whether a theory of truth has primacy over a theory of meaning, or vice versa, has yet to be resolved.

Claudia Brodsky Lacour focuses on two related and difficult ques-

tions: the origin of conventions, and their changing or properly historical nature. Most generally, her argument is that the origin of conventions necessarily eludes all theories of convention. The context for her
discussion is provided by a dual perception: whereas influential analytic theories of convention tend to be insensitive to the historical dimensions of the phenomenon, historical work on the topic frequently lacks
conceptual rigor. Brodsky Lacour's response is to mobilize a range of
materials, for she underscores important similarities and differences
between the positions on convention adopted by Lewis, Quine, Kripke,
and Stendhal. Brodsky Lacour begins by considering the Lewisian theory of convention, a theory that attempts to explain, not how conventions originate, but how they are maintained. She identifies a number
of problems associated with the notion of common knowledge, emphasizing in particular the role played by reciprocal expectations in engen-
dering distorted or incorrect expectations and beliefs. Brodsky Lacour
also suggests that Lewis's account is circular, claiming that his concept
of tacit agreement presupposes the very linguistic conventions it is
meant to explain. Following Brodsky Lacour, a more adequate approach
to conventions may be found in the work of Quine and Kripke, and thus
she turns to the former's discussion of truth and its relation to convention, and to the latter's theory of rigid designators and its rejection of a
theory of names as hidden descriptions. Finally, Brodsky Lacour articulates some of the insights of Stendhal's *Racine et Shakespeare,* in which
romanticism is defined, not as a set of identifiable conventions, but as
the moment when conventions change. Any attempt to imitate romanticism leads inevitably to a conventional result, classicism. Conventions
can arise and change if and only if conventions always already are in
place. And in trying to identify the unconventional within the conventional, we contact and produce only conventions.

Göran Hermerén's contribution is a response to two related questions. First, to what extent is our understanding of works of art tradition-
or convention-dependent? Second, if our understanding of art is tradition-dependent, then to what extent is rational debate over art possible
between critics rooted in different traditions? In response to the first
question, Hermerén argues that an "adequate or good understanding"
of works of art, as well as of the interactions between agents participating in the art world, presupposes familiarity with certain conventions
and traditions. Understanding, says Hermerén, is a pragmatic notion,

for our various cognitive endeavors may be motivated by a wide range of goals. For example, critics may seek a historical, social, or aesthetic understanding of a given work. Hermerén distinguishes between six different kinds of conventions, arguing that their importance varies with the cognitive goal in question. Thus, for example, familiarity with "life-style traditions" pertaining to the artist's ideological dispositions would be irrelevant in the context of a purely aesthetic understanding but would figure centrally in the case of social or historical understanding. In response to the second question, Hermerén argues that rational debate over art is possible between agents who are part of commensurable traditions. Drawing on the vast literature on the problem of commensurability within the philosophy of science, Hermerén argues that commensurability in the arts is not a matter of overlapping claims or beliefs about individual works but of a shared standard of rationality.

CHAPTER ONE

Again, Theory:
On Speaker's Meaning,
Linguistic Meaning, and
the Meaning of a Text

GEORGE M. WILSON

"But I shall keep Wildfire, now I've got him; though I'd a bid of a hundred and fifty for him the other day from a man over at Flitton—he's buying for Lord Cromleck—a fellow with a cast in his eye and a green waistcoat. But I mean to stick to Wildfire; I shan't get a better at a fence in a hurry. The mare's got more blood, but she's a bit too weak in the hindquarters."

Bryce of course divined that Dunstan wanted to sell the horse, and Dunstan knew that he divined it (horse-dealing is only one of many human transactions carried on in this ingenious manner).

—George Eliot, *Silas Marner*

Late in the *Philosophical Investigations*, Wittgenstein makes the following famous comment:

In the use of words one might distinguish "surface grammar" from "depth grammar." What immediately impresses itself upon us about the use of a word is the way it is used in the construction of the sentence, the part of its use—one might say—that can be taken in by the ear.—And now compare the depth grammar, say of the word "to mean," with what its surface grammar would lead us to suspect. No wonder we find it difficult to know our way about. (1953, no. 664, 168e)

Whatever we may think of (or, for that matter, understand by) this remark about the "depth grammar" of the verb "to mean," it is obvious enough that even the "surface grammar" of the word is complex and potentially confusing. The syntactical liaisons that "to mean" has established in English are notably diverse. For example, we say,

Fire means smoke,
The heirloom means something special to its owner,
The agent means to perform a certain type of action,
The speaker means such-and-such (a content) in uttering his words,

and

A lexical expression (a word, phrase, or sentence) means so-and-so in language L.

One could easily add other constructions to this list, but as an opening reminder, these examples will suffice. Many will feel that there is a larger conceptual unity hidden behind the surface dissimilarities of these forms. Thus, it seems plausible that if a speaker means some content by his utterance, then this fact is closely tied to what the speaker means (intends) to *do* in uttering the sounds in question. And many have believed that what lexical expressions mean in a language must *somehow* be determined by what speakers of the language mean when they employ those expressions. These and related hypotheses have been much studied by philosophers of language and linguists, but it has proved a difficult and subtle matter to work out the supposed connections in a clear and convincing way.

I have opened with these platitudes about the vagaries of "to mean" and about the theoretical issues that these vagaries generate because it is my impression that they are still too little considered and weighed in the investigation of another topic in which *a* concept of "meaning" also takes center stage. I have in mind discussions of what it is for a literary work or literary text to mean something. Broadly speaking, the conceptual inadequacies that trouble me take one or both of two forms. First, fairly obvious points about differences between the concepts of "speaker's meaning," "utterance meaning," "word meaning," and "sentence meaning" are either ignored or flouted. Second, the notion of "the meaning of a text" is too closely assimilated to one or another of the concepts of linguistic meaning mentioned above.

In this space, I cannot even begin to substantiate my impression that these sins are widespread. What I do intend is to show that they are deeply implicated in recent and very influential investigations of the problems and prospects of "theory" in literary studies. I consider in some detail one central line of argument in the article "Against Theory," by Steven Knapp and Walter Michaels,[1] and, in pursuing this, I look at some supplementary considerations presented by Stanley Fish. Fish's work seems to have inspired some of the crucial argumentation in "Against Theory," and Fish has emphaticallv endorsed the chief con- clusions that Knapp and Michaels reach. I argue that the grounds that these writers offer against theory in literary studies depend essentially upon their unargued dismissal of a range of substantial theoretical questions and developments within the philosophy of language. In the absence of a genuine theoretical engagement with the questions and developments that they bypass, the morals that Knapp/Michaels and Fish wish to draw are, it seems to me, completely vitiated. Because the structure of their proposals and the reasons that purportedly support them are not easy to make out, it is necessary to start by paying careful attention to the text of "Against Theory" itself.

In the opening sentence, Knapp and Michaels explain, "By 'theory' we mean a special project in literary criticism: the attempt to govern interpretations of particular texts by appealing to an account of inter- pretation in general." A little later, they continue,

> Theory attempts to solve — or to celebrate the impossibility of solv-
> ing — a set of familiar problems: the function of authorial intention,
> the status of literary language, the role of interpretive assumptions,
> and so on. . . . In our view, the mistake on which all critical theory
> rests has been to imagine that these problems are real. In fact, we will
> claim such problems only seem real — and theory itself only seems pos-
> sible or relevant — when theorists fail to recognize the fundamental
> inseparability of the elements involved. (11–12)

There is much in these remarks that remains unclear, and other com- mentators have in fact complained about their terse and obscure char- acter. In particular, the intended domain of "critical theory" is con- siderably underspecified. However, rather than tackling that question directly, it seems more fruitful to pursue the definite hint that the characteristic mistake of theory is to separate elements that cannot be separated.

In the paragraph that follows the exposition just quoted, we are offered a key example of the mistake of separating the inseparable:

> The clearest example of the tendency to generate theoretical problems
> by splitting apart terms that are in fact inseparable is the persistent
> debate over the relation between authorial intention and the meaning

of texts. Some theorists have claimed that valid interpretations can only be obtained through an appeal to authorial intentions. This assumption is shared by theorists who, denying the possibility of recovering authorial intentions, also deny the possibility of valid interpretations. But once it is seen that the meaning of a text is simply identical to the author's intended meaning, the project of *grounding* meaning in intention becomes incoherent. Since the project itself is incoherent, it can neither succeed nor fail; hence both theoretical attitudes toward intention are irrelevant. The mistake made by theorists has been to imagine the possibility or desirability of moving from one term (the author's intended meaning) to a second term (the text's meaning), when actually the two terms are the same. One can neither succeed nor fail in deriving one term from the other, since to have one is already to have them both. (12)

Now, on first inspection, these claims seem quite surprising. What we *appear* to have is merely the reaffirmation, without argument, of a standard and controversial theory concerning the nature of the meaning of a literary text, namely, that the meaning of such a text is whatever the author intended that text to mean. How can the authors hope, one might wonder, to rest a systematic attack upon critical theory by dogmatically adopting one such theory against its various competitors?

Nevertheless, I think that the appearances here are, to some extent, misleading. In context, it becomes clear that we still have not grasped the kind of theorizing that Knapp and Michaels oppose. As they themselves note, the strong intentionalism about the meaning of a text that they endorse is shared with, for instance, such recent theorists as E. D. Hirsch, Jr. (1967, 1976), and P. D. Juhl (1980). And yet, these writers are immediately singled out as theorists who have paradigmatically committed the type of illicit "separation of elements" that Knapp and Michaels think they have discerned. Hence, we cannot have identified the crucial issue that they are trying to raise. So what *is* the fatal assimilation that Hirsch, Juhl, and other intentionalists have committed?

In a summary statement, Knapp and Michaels inform us that "in debates about intention, the moment of imagining *intentionless meaning* [my italics] constitutes the theoretical moment itself. From the standpoint of an argument against critical theory, then, the only important question about intention is whether there can in fact be intentionless meanings. If our argument against theory is to succeed, the answer to this question must be no" (15).

In outline, the situation seems to be this. Knapp and Michaels contend that Hirsch holds or is committed to holding that there are "intentionless meanings," and he therefore can plausibly adopt the (correct) intentionalist view of literary texts only by demonstrating that such texts cannot or should not be interpreted in terms of intentionless meanings. Hirsch's mistake, characteristic of theory in general, seems to be his supposed acceptance of intentionless meanings, and this engenders the further illusion that interpretation of literary texts in terms of intentional or intended meanings requires a theoretical defense. This illusion, or variants of it, defines for Knapp and Michaels the misbegotten domain of theory.

Indeed, it is precisely the charge made against Juhl that he suffers from a variant of Hirsch's illusion. It is not that Juhl, at least in the first instance, is supposed to countenance intentionless meanings; rather, according to Knapp and Michaels, he commits himself to "intentionless language." Having so committed himself, he also is forced to mount a theoretical defense of the position that literary texts cannot be interpreted as (or, as if they were) stretches of intentionless language: "Like Hirsch, but at a further level of abstraction, Juhl ends up imagining the possibility of language prior to and independent of intention and thus conceiving intention as something that must be added to language to make it work. Like Hirsch, and like theorists in general, Juhl thinks that intention is a matter of choice" (19). Hence, believing in either intentionless meanings or intentionless language constitutes the ground-level mistake from which the "ontological" confusions of critical theory are produced. Within the taxonomy of "Against Theory," there are still other variants of the same mistake. There are theorists who both accept intentionless meanings and maintain that interpretations of texts *can* be derived from such a basis. The New Critics apparently are supposed to exemplify this version. There are theorists who accept the existence of intentionless language but hold that language of this ilk is essentially meaningless. This seems to be the position that Knapp and Michaels attribute to Paul de Man (21–24).

I think that this specifies the structure of the issues that Knapp and Michaels wish to pose. But, of course, all of this does not take us very far until we understand what intentionless meaning and intentionless language are supposed to be. It is at this juncture that the argument of "Against Theory" takes a puzzling turn. That turn leads to a complete dead end, and the true subject of dispute is hiding down a different alley.

Using their example of a poemlike set of inscriptions that have been etched by waves upon a beach, Knapp and Michaels argue for the following two theses: Any inscription, no matter how much it physically resembles a possible or actual inscription of an expression in a language, is not itself a meaningful inscription unless that inscription, or some earlier inscription to which it is suitably related, was produced in the right way by an agent with the right kind of semantic intentions. (Call this the thesis of the intentionality of meaningful inscriptions.) Further, no such inscription is actually an inscription of a genuine linguistic expression (a word, phrase, sentence, etc.) unless that inscription, or some earlier inscription to which it is suitably related, was produced in the right way by an agent with the appropriate kind of semantic intentions. (Call this thesis the intentionality of linguistic expressions.)[2] The Knapp-Michaels discussion gives the impression that Hirsch must accept intentionless meanings because he is supposed to deny the first of these theses, and Juhl must accept intentionless language because it is claimed that he denies the second thesis. Finally, on the assumption that these authors do deny the claims in question, they are thereby held to be convicted of, at a minimum, vast implausibility.

Whatever we may think about the truth or falsity of the two targeted theses, there is factual trouble about trying to arrange the debate in these terms. In his comments on "Against Theory," Hirsch (1985) strongly affirms his belief in the intentionality of meaningful inscriptions and accuses Knapp and Michaels of constructing a straw man in arguing against him in this way. As far as I can see, looking over Hirsch's discussions of the relevant topics, he seems justified in his response. Similarly, Juhl seems to be fully willing to affirm the intentionality of linguistic expressions. Discussing his own version of the "wave-poem" example, he says, "Would it be possible to interpret a series of marks on a rock which closely resemble the words of an English sentence if we knew that they had been produced by water erosion? Could one even call them 'words'?" And, in the footnote that accompanies these lines, he adds, "Construing a text even on this most basic level appears to involve the assumption that it has been produced by a being capable of language" (84). On the other hand, Juhl grants that the "text" formed by the waves does have a kind of limited and derivative interpretability. That is, because the accidental inscriptions *resemble* possible inscriptions of genuine linguistic expressions—expressions that have a meaning or meanings in the language to which they belong—it is possible to "interpret," that is, assign meanings to the intrinsically meaningless inscriptions on the basis of their resemblance to the genuine words and sentences.

This last observation about Juhl's actual position provides a clue to the true source of disagreement between Knapp/Michaels and all of the positive theorists they consider. Hirsch and Juhl, like most other writers on the subject, plainly do subscribe to the commonsense idea that words, phrases, and sentences mean something (and, often, mean several things) as expressions in a language, for example, in English, French, Swahili, and so on. Somewhat surprisingly, it emerges that this is precisely the idea that Knapp and Michaels reject.

Their rejection of this view is stated most expressly in their footnotes. In the main text, they say rather murkily that "for Juhl, the words continue to mean even when devoid of intention. They mean *'in abstracto'* and thus constitute the condition of language prior to the addition of intention." Then, in an appended footnote, they add,

> Juhl's motives are, in fact, not far from Hirsch's. For both theorists, meaning *in abstracto* is indeterminate or ambiguous ("indeterminate" for Hirsch, "ambiguous" for Juhl): both appeal to intention in order to achieve determinate or particular meanings or, as Juhl says, to "disambiguate" the text (*Interpretation*, p. 97). This theoretical interest in the problem of indeterminacy derives in part from the widespread notion that words and sentences have a range of "linguistically possible" meanings, the ones recorded in dictionaries and grammar books. But a dictionary is an index of frequent usages in particular speech acts—not a matrix of abstract, pre-intentional possibilities. (20–21, n. 12)

A little later, they summarize their criticism: "For Hirsch and Juhl, the goal of theory is to provide an objectively valid method of literary interpretation. To make method possible, both are forced to *imagine* [my italics] intentionless meanings or, in more general terms, to imagine a separation between language and speech acts" (21). A footnote to this remark begins as follows: "This distinction, in one form or another, is common among speech-act theorists. H. P. Grice, for example, distinguishes between 'locutions of the form "U (utterer) meant that . . ."' and 'locutions of the form "X (utterance-type) means . . ."'" (21, n. 13). Presumably, the point of the footnote is to indicate that Paul Grice and other speech-act theorists are supposed to share the illusion of Hirsch and Juhl. But, for Grice, when the given utterance is an utterance of an expression in a language, the "timeless" meaning (or meanings) of the utterance-type *just is* the meaning (or meanings) of the expression-type in the speaker's language. Thus, it appears that the Knapp/ Michaels brief against "language *in abstracto*" is a brief against the notion that words and sentences have meaning in the language that contains them.

When Richard Rorty (1985, 133–34), in a comment on "Against Theory," reaffirms the significance of the distinction between what an expression means in a language and what a speaker means, on a particular occasion, by uttering that expression, and when he questions whether Knapp and Michaels have provided grounds for doubting the import of the distinction, they offer this reply:

> According to Rorty, there is a "useful" "logical space" between "what sentences mean and what a given utterer means by them on a given occasion." . . . This is what Rorty glosses . . . as the distinction "between two sets of intentions—the ones normally had by users of a sentence and some special ones had, or possibly had, by an individual user." . . . But what makes some intentions normal and others special? Rorty seems to be thinking of the distinction between special and normal intentions as if it were a distinction between *particular* intentions and some other kind. . . . In our view, however, normal intentions are just frequent particular ones. The "space" between these two sets of intentions is not logical but empirical. (141–42)

These and similar comments may suggest that Knapp and Michaels occupy a position weaker than the one that I have ascribed to them. For here they *may* be allowing that statements of the form

Word *W* means——in *L*
Sentence *S* means . . . in *L*

can count as intelligible and true *if* they are understood simply as reports of what speakers of *L frequently* intend in and by their use of *W* or *S*. However, it is a commonplace in the linguistics literature that this conception is untenable.

Two observations illustrate the basic difficulties. First, for all I know, the words "Your spouse will think you look very sexy in mauve" are most frequently used by clothing salespeople who have the intention of selling mauve sportswear to their customers. If this were to be so, it would not have the consequence that the specified sentence has, as part of its meaning, "You ought to buy some mauve sportswear." Second, it has often been stressed that there are an unbounded number of perfectly meaningful sentences in any natural language that have *never* been uttered, and, out of these, there are many that will never be. Intuitively, these merely "available" sentences have perfectly definite meanings, and grammatically competent speakers who know the senses of the lexical constituents can recognize what these meanings are. Obviously, considerations about the frequency of accompanying intention can play no role in fixing the meaning of such uninstantiated forms. This second point is one basic reason that the task of reaching an adequate conception of sentence meaning is so hard. In any event, I conclude that Knapp and Michaels are committed to denying that words and sentences have meanings in a language in anything like the way we usually conceive this to be the case. As we saw earlier, they sometimes seem to assert that proposition pretty directly.

If I am right in thinking that Knapp and Michaels' rejection of language *in abstracto* is ultimately the rejection of our commonsense belief that words, phrases, and sentences have meaning in, for example, English, then the position they have chosen to occupy is a radical one. In light of this, one would expect to find some argument or some marshaling of evidence in support of the bold hypothesis. But it is one of the confusing features of "Against Theory" that it is hard to locate clearly any such argument or evidence. However, I mentioned earlier that the essay does include considerations in favor of the thesis of the intentionality of meaningful inscriptions and the thesis of the intentionality of linguistic expressions. In addition, the essay recurrently suggests that if someone believes, as Hirsch and Juhl do, that lexical expressions have linguistic meanings, then that person is committed to denying either one or both of the intentionality theses. Further, this consequence will be, for Knapp and Michaels, a *reductio* of the belief that generates it. Thus, for example, an invocation of such a *reductio* seems to be found in the following passage:

> But this prescription only makes sense if its two terms (language and speech acts) are not already inseparable in the same way that meaning and intention are. Juhl is right of course to claim that marks without intention are not speech acts, since the essence of a speech act is its intentional character. But we have demonstrated that marks without intention are not language either. Only by failing to see that *linguistic meaning* [my italics] is always identical to expressed intention can Juhl imagine language without speech acts. (21)

Moreover, the salience and centrality that the authors accord to the intentionality theses within their article as a whole square with the present interpretation of how they mean their argument to run. Loose deployment of the unfortunate coinages "intentionless meanings" and "meaning *in abstracto*" render these connections difficult to trace out, but if these are not the implications relied upon, then, I believe, there is simply no relevant argument to be found.

If the argument of "Against Theory" is to demonstrate that expressions do not have established or conventional meanings in a language, then the would-be case against the view is extremely weak. Suppose that I hold, as I do, that the word *slumber* means (roughly) "sleep" in English. In holding this, I suppose that there is an established and widely known practice among speakers of the language of using the relevant sound sequence and/or inscription with certain intentions, that is, with the intention that the given token count as an instance of the word *slumber* and with the further intention that the word be understood as applying, in the particular utterance, only to cases of sleep. No doubt this supposition presupposes that the relevant sound and inscription types are employed with some considerable regularity by English speakers who have the indicated intentions. But none of this entails that *each instance* of the sound or inscription types connected with the word *slumber* must itself be an instance of the word nor that it must mean "sleep." For that matter, the token may not mean anything at all. In particular, if a receding wave leaves a pattern of marks that resembles a genuine inscription of the word *slumber,* one is completely free to deny that these marks really constitute an instance of the word or of anything meaningful. In short, it is simply false that the idea that words or sentences mean something in a language is in any way incompatible with the intentionality theses that Knapp and Michaels emphasize so much.

There is, at the heart of this important section of "Against Theory," a void. What we have accomplished is painstakingly to trace out Knapp and Michael's conception of what they call "the theoretical moment itself" — the crucial juncture at which the mistaken demand for a certain sort of critical theory supposedly arises. By their lights, the nascent theorist, at that juncture, postulates the separation of inseparable elements. What does this amount to? The theorist has accepted what they take to be an illusory distinction between the meanings of a sentence in a language and what the speaker means by uttering the sentence on a particular occasion. Why is this distinction the product of an illusion? At this juncture in "Against Theory," it seems to me, we come upon the void.

It is symptomatic of a certain insouciance in the article that the writings of Paul Grice are mentioned in passing in a footnote and mentioned there only as a purported instance of the error in the philosophy of language which Knapp and Michaels believe they have identified.[3] It is, in fact, a distressing symptom for several reasons. Grice is the philosopher who has done the most to draw our attention to the variety of ways that we talk about meaning in connection with our use of language. It is he who has delineated the nuanced but important distinctions we make when employing these different forms of "meaning talk." It is sheer conceptual regression to ride roughshod over those distinctions when we have every reason to know better. Further, Grice and others following his lead[4] have attempted to develop a motivated, systematic theory of some of the key semantic and pragmatic concepts that he, in the first step, has analyzed. This work includes a careful account of both speaker's meaning and the meaning of expressions in an ideolect and in a language.

Finally, the perspective from which Grice has sought to carry out his program is similar, in several respects, to the perspective that Knapp and Michaels appear to hold. First, in a certain sense, the concept of speaker's meaning is the basic concept within his larger program. Second, this concept is to be analyzed in terms of the speaker's intentions in producing the utterance. Third, for Grice, facts about the meaning of sentences in a language do *supervene*, in a complicated way, upon a wide range of interconnected facts about what speakers of the language mean in using the relevant terms and constructions. In at least some versions of Gricean theory, this supervenience relation is mediated by the global fact that the widespread, cooperative practice of meaning something by one's utterances in communicative exchanges establishes a set of implicit conventions or mutual understandings about what is to be meant (normatively) if and when a given term is deployed.[5] The connection between speakers' meanings and linguistic meanings is necessarily mediated in some such indirect way—and, however it goes, the mediating relations are complex—because, as Grice is fully and deeply aware, the idea that, for example, what a sentence means is determined by what speakers "frequently" mean when they utter it simply cannot get off the ground.

So, as Knapp and Michaels observe in their footnote, Grice *does* accept the notion of the linguistic (in his term, "timeless") meaning of a word and of a sentence, and he takes these notions to be important. Since he has also tried to provide us with a theoretical understanding of them and to exhibit their interconnections with other useful concepts, it is a travesty of reasonable discussion of the issues for Knapp and Michaels to dismiss, out of hand and with no argument at all, both the letter and the spirit of Grice's work in the area. It is one thing to be "against theory" on the principled grounds that it can be shown that there is some fundamental weakness in the theoretical enterprise in question. It is quite another thing to be "against theory" by blankly setting one's face against the theoretical work that others have carried out. It is true that what Knapp and Michaels oppose is a kind of theory in the area of literary studies, and they believe that they do have principled grounds for rejecting that. But my objection has been that the grounds they offer rest, in the long run, upon a rejection of theory in the philosophy of language, a rejection that takes the less happy form of pretending that it does not exist.

Although there is no contribution of substance to the topic of meaning in "Against Theory," the essay, even in the sections I have been investigating, seems to resonate with the influence of Stanley Fish. Fish, both prior to and after "Against Theory," has also argued against the standard conception of linguistic meaning, so it is possible that Knapp and Michaels have meant to rely upon arguments adduced by Fish. I, therefore, wish to turn in a moment to a brief inspection of some of Fish's relevant claims. However, to do this effectively, it will prove useful to rehearse some of the main distinctions, referred to above, which Grice has stressed and which, following his precedent, most current work in philosophy of language and semantics relies upon.

Consider this sentence:

(A) No woman will ever bear my children.

Intuitively, this sentence has *at least* two distinct linguistic meanings in English. It can mean either

(A₁) No woman will ever be the mother of my children

or

(A₂) No woman will ever tolerate the presence of my children.

Unlike, for example, "Flying airplanes can be dangerous," which is grammatically ambiguous, the linguistic ambiguity of (A) arises in virtue of the linguistic (lexical) ambiguity of the verb "to bear." In general, when particular speakers utter (A) in a context, they intend their utterance to express only one or the other of the linguistic meanings represented by (A₁) or (A₂). Hence, we need to distinguish between

(i) the linguistic meaning or meanings that a sentence S has in a language L

and

(ii) the linguistic meaning that an utterance of S expresses on a given occasion of use.

The latter will be determined by the intentions of the speaker in uttering S on that occasion.

Moreover, (A) can also be used to illustrate anther familiar point. Suppose that two speakers, Willy and Wally, have each uttered an instance of (A). It may well be the case that the linguistic meaning that each of their utterances expresses is the same, namely, the intended grammatical structure of their utterances and the intended lexical meanings of the words they use are identical. Let us stipulate that the expressed linguistic meaning of both utterances is given by, say, (A₂). Despite all this, there remains a clear sense in which each speaker has used his words to say or express something different. Because of the indexical pronoun "my" in these utterances, Willy has said about his children that no woman will ever tolerate their presence, while Wally has said the same about his own children. One utterance might well be true while the other is false. What we have here is the banal but important point that the semantically evaluable (e.g., the truth-evaluable) content of an utterance tends to be context-dependent. Such content depends not only on the expressed linguistic meaning of the utterance but on specifiable features of the speech-act context. These features are employed to fix, in a rule-governed way, the particular values (usually referential values) of parameters that the expressed linguistic meaning leaves open precisely for such a required occasion-relative determination.

This phenomenon occurs most blatantly in connection with indexical terms and phrases and with markers for tense and aspect, but it is well established that it is also found in subtler and less explicit forms. For instance, the pronoun *she*, used deictically, is another indexical term, but we also have uses like

> Each woman in the club owns a TV, and *she* also owns a video recorder.

In the second conjunct, the occurrence of *she* is not used deictically, and that conjunct, in its context, says

> Each woman in the club also owns a video recorder.

It is not at all obvious that this use of *she* expresses a distinct linguistic meaning, even though it is functioning differently than in deictic uses, and the contribution from the speech-act context is quite different. Thus, even a minimal consideration of just the third-person pronouns illustrates how variable the modes of semantically relevant context-dependence can be. One final example. If a speaker asserts, "Every napkin is frayed," it is likely that the domain of the generalization is meant to be restricted to some salient domain like "napkins in the house," "napkins on the table," or whatever. Notice again that we may often have two utterances of such a sentence, where the linguistic meanings expressed by the utterances are the same, but where the specific content expressed by each utterance is different. To have a way of marking distinctions of these kinds, let us say that the linguistic meaning that S expresses on an occasion is not, as a rule, sufficient to determine

(iii) the *context-loaded* linguistic meaning that S expresses on an occasion of utterance.[6]

As mentioned above, it is this notion that applies to the semantically evaluable content expressed by the utterance.[7]

Finally, I turn to the crucial concept of

(iv) what the speaker meant by uttering S on a given occasion.

Imagine a situation in which Wally utters (A), with the expressed linguistic meaning of (A_1), and with all of the context-dependent parameters fixed in an obvious way. For present purposes I need to tell a more extended story about the circumstances in which Wally says what he does. Therefore, I add that Willy knows (and Wally knows that he knows) that: Wally is desperately in love with Milly and wants to marry her; the romance has recently been shaky, and Milly has been threatening to break it off; Wally, as he speaks, has just returned from a confrontation with her about the subject; and Wally has strong reactions to his romantic troubles and tends to melodramatize his life. Given all this, Willy recognizes that, by uttering (A), Wally means

(B) Milly has terminated our relationship.

That is, (B) represents a part, although, in this case, the chief part of what Wally means as he says (A). And Wally means this in the sense that this is a part of what Wally means to communicate or convey to Willy by producing his utterance. At the same time, (B) is clearly *not* any part of the (contextually loaded) linguistic meaning of (A) as it is used in this speech act. That meaning, here, as in other cases, is represented by (A_1). Of course, it is partly by grasping that the linguistic meaning expressed by (A) on this occasion *is* (A_1) that Willy is able to make out that it is (B) that Wally means here to be communicating. This example, and innumerable others like it, shows the necessity of distinguishing (iv) from (i) through (iii) above.

There is a lesson to be drawn from these observations that will have special relevance when I turn to Fish. The lesson is this: the phrase "the meaning of such-and-such an expression (utterance, form of words, statement, etc.)" is, as it is ordinarily used, an extremely treacherous one. It can be and is used to refer to any of the "meaning" concepts (i) through (iv). We have only ourselves to blame if we fail to be careful about what the phrase signifies in any given case.

Some of the usefulness of these distinctions in a specifically literary context can be hinted at by reflection upon a passage from Cleanth Brooks's "The Heresy of Paraphrase."

> He [Yvor Winters] goes on to illustrate his point by a brief and excellent analysis of the following lines from Browning:
> *So wore night; the East was gray,*
> *White the broad-faced hemlock flowers.*
> "The verb *wore*," he continues, "means literally that the night passed, but it carries with it connotations of exhaustion and attrition which belong to the condition of the protagonist; and grayness is a color which we associate with such a condition. If we change the phrase to read: 'Thus night passed,' we shall have the same rational meaning, and a meter quite as respectable, but no trace of the power of the line: the connotation of *wore* will be lost, and the connotation of *gray* will remain in a state of ineffective potentiality."
> But the word *wore* does not mean *literally* "that the night passed," it means literally "that the night *wore*" — whatever *wore* may mean, and as Winters' own admirable analysis indicates, *wore* "means," whether *rationally* or *irrationally*, a great deal. Furthermore, "So wore night" and "Thus night passed" can be said to have "the same rational meaning" only if we equate "rational meaning" with the meaning of a loose paraphrase. (1947, 200–201)

Restated in the terms lately elaborated, Brooks is making a couple of absolutely correct points. First, the expressed linguistic meaning of "So night wore" at this juncture is *not* "Thus the night passed," although that *is* a part of what the dramatic speaker means to convey by these words. Rather, the expressed linguistic meaning here is, roughly, "Thus the night erodes." Second, the expressed linguistic meaning of "wore," used as meaning "erodes," is important to the lines in virtue of our general knowledge of what genuine processes of erosion are like. That knowledge is tapped when we generate the various other things (the "connotations") that the speaker means to suggest, evoke, and play upon within the larger context of the poem. In effect, Brooks is warning against conflating two common senses of the adjective "literal." Often, the phrase "the literal meaning of an utterance" simply denotes the linguistic meaning the sentence expresses in that utterance. But suppose that this very utterance, with its expressed linguistic meaning, has been used *figuratively* by the speaker. In such a case, we may wish to have a nonfigurative paraphrase of what the utterance, as used figuratively, was meant by the speaker to imply and evoke. And, if we accept some proffered paraphrase as adequate to its purpose, we may say that it gives "the literal meaning" of the figure. But, that just means that it gives or purports to give in explicit, literal terms what the speaker meant by using the utterance as a figure of the sort in question. Brooks is quite right in thinking that a fair amount of confusion could be avoided if we were to keep these notions straight.

We are now in a position to examine some of the objections that Stanley Fish has made against the concept of the linguistic meanings of words and sentences. I am assuming and will continue to assume that this is the concept that Fish rejects, but it is extraordinarily difficult to find a reasonable, settled formulation of his views. He informs us that expressions do not have meanings *"in the abstract,"* stable and determinate meanings, *clear and obvious* meanings, meanings that are *"beyond or below* interpretation," and *"self-sufficient and self-declaring"* meanings (my italics). Indeed, these are but a few of the characterizations that are cheerfully put on parade.[8] In the introduction to his new book, there is a passage that seeks to clarify and consolidate his position which provides a taste of the problems Fish's readers face. He asserts that he will defend

> the thesis that the meaning of a sentence is *not* a function of the mean-
> ing of its constituent parts; or to put it another way, that meaning can-
> not be formally calculated, derived from the shape of marks on a
> page; or to put it in the most direct way possible, that there is no such
> thing as literal meaning, if by literal meaning one means a meaning
> that is perspicuous no matter what the context and no matter what is
> in the speaker's or hearer's mind, a meaning that because it is prior to
> interpretation can serve as a constraint on interpretation. (1989, 4)[9]

By "literal meaning," Fish seems to have in mind what I have preferred to call *linguistic meaning* because of the potential for confusion adumbrated in my remarks on Brooks. But Fish, in this one very long statement, says a number of things about the properties that he takes linguistic meanings to have.

On the one hand, he rightly says that it is widely assumed that the linguistic ("literal") meaning that a sentence expresses in a specific use is a function of its grammatical structure and the linguistic meanings expressed by its constituents. On the other hand, he also specifies that linguistic meanings (of words and sentences? of utterances of words and sentences?) are

(i) derived from the shapes of the marks on the page;
(ii) perspicuous no matter what the context and no matter what is in the speaker's or hearer's mind;

and

(iii) prior to interpretation.

Each of these claims about linguistic meaning is either false or wildly misleading. No responsible theorist believes that the linguistic meaning of a sentential utterance or inscription must be easily understood ("is perspicuous") by an audience independently of a host of facts about their epistemic situation, their linguistic knowledge, and their state of mind. Think of reading one of the more elaborate sentences in, say, Henry James's *The Golden Bowl* while under the influence of LSD. No responsible theorist believes that an audience understands the linguistic meaning of a sentence without having, in some sense, interpreted its words and syntactical organization. Finally, the linguistic meaning of an inscription is "derived from the marks on the page" only if derivation includes recognizing the marks as an instance of a natural language expression, knowing at least some of the linguistic meanings that the expression has in the language, and forming a reasonable belief about which linguistic meaning the writer intended the inscription to express. Again, no responsible theorist holds that such a derivation proceeds, as Fish (1989, 316-18) suggests, solely or even primarily in accordance with a set of abstract and purely formal or mechanical rules.[10]

No doubt, these whimsical additions help to make Fish's negative position sound more plausible, but they utterly distort the views he wishes to dispute. Nevertheless, since Fish patently intends to contradict widely credited views in linguistics and the philosophy of language, and since he does sometimes describe his target in a fashion closer to the mark,[11] I will proceed on the assumption that he *is* attacking the concept of the meaning of an expression in a language — the concept that I have heretofore discussed.

Fish's strategy in criticizing the concept of linguistic meaning is to present an example or series of examples of uses of language accompanied by a gloss upon how each example is supposed to work. The gloss is meant to prove that the standard concept of linguistic meaning cannot provide a coherent or, at least, an adequate account of what the examples show to be the case. In a range of his writings Fish has given a number of such examples, and I do not have the space to work through them all. But, this doesn't matter. I have chosen two of Fish's cases — one from a relatively early article and one from the general introduction to his latest book — that are wholly typical of his mode of criticism. We will see that these and similar arguments are subverted by the fact that they simply ignore the basic Gricean distinctions sketched before.

The example in Fish's *Doing What Comes Naturally* concerns John Milton's interpretation of a pronouncement of Christ's as reported in Matthew: "Whosoever shall put away his wife, except it be for fornication . . . committeth adultery." Here is what Fish says about the case:

> In the course of his *Doctrine and Discipline of Divorce* Milton labors at what might seem an impossible task, to read that text as saying that a man may put away his wife for any reason he likes. He does it (or tries to do it) by arguing from intention. He points out that when Christ uttered these words he was speaking to the Pharisees in a context in which they were tempting him to a lax pronouncement concerning the law. It is, says Milton, in response to their provocations that Christ delivers a judgment even more severe than they themselves would have delivered, thus simultaneously escaping their net and undercutting their strictness by overgoing it: "So heer he may be justly thought to have giv'n this rigid sentence against divorce, not to cut off all remedy from a good man who finds himself consuming away in a disconsolate and uninjoy'd matrimony, but to lay a bridle upon the bold abuses of those overweening Rabbies."[5] In other words, since this stricture was intended only for those of pharisaic temper, the freedom of men who are not Pharisees cannot properly be abrogated by invoking a prohibition that was not addressed to them. While Christ might say to the Pharisees, "*You* can divorce only for reason of adultery," he says to us, "to *you* divorce is permitted if, in your judgment, your marriage is not a true spiritual union." (8–9)

The point of all this, Fish adds, is that "meanings that seem perspicuous and literal are rendered so by forceful interpretive acts and not by the properties of language" (9).[12]

We might notice, first of all, that Fish's account of Christ's statement is underdescribed. The quantifier phrase, "whosoever shall put away his wife," calls for a contextual determination of the range, here of people, to whom the generalization applies. One possibility is that Christ intends the range to include only the Pharisees or, perhaps, those of "pharisaic temper." On this option, or so it seems, the context-loaded linguistic meaning expressed by this use of the sentence is

Anyone who is of pharisaic temper who intends to divorce his wife . . . ,

and what Christ has hereby said is narrower than the message he wanted his immediate audience to suppose that he had stated. Moreover, the specific content of his words on this occasion is something that he, according to the proffered interpretation, believed, although he did not intend the Pharisees to whom he spoke to recognize the restricted character of that content. On the second option, Christ did intend the generalization to be unrestricted so that now the context-loaded linguistic meaning his words express is

Any man, whoever he may be, who intends to divorce his wife . . .

This interpretation has the consequence that Christ "literally" says something he does not genuinely accept, but he intends his immediate audience to suppose he does, while expecting members of the wider nonpharisaic class to realize that he does not. In either event, if we keep the dimension of context-dependence in view, there is no reason to think that Christ's utterance does not express one of the established linguistic meanings of the sentence that it instantiates. What is more, the linguistic meaning expressed by the utterance, *modulo* the variable context-loading, is the same on either option.

The case is complicated by the fact that Milton's interpretation postulates that the utterance is directed, in a differential way, toward two different audiences, to the Pharisees addressed and to everyone else who encounters the pronouncement. It seems that what Christ means to convey or imply to each of these audiences is significantly different. But this fact has no bearing on what context-loaded linguistic meaning the utterance expresses. This factor is operative, more simply, in certain cases of irony. Suppose I am returning a paper to a student in the presence of one of my colleagues. I believe that the paper is a terrible piece of work, and my colleague realizes that this is my assessment. But, because I do not want to hurt the student's feelings in the circumstances, I say, "This is a very good paper," while accompanying my utterance with a grimace and a wink that I expect my colleague, but not the student, to pick up. The sentence, as I use it, has a perfectly definite context-loaded linguistic content. It is just this content I mean to communicate to the student. By contrast, while the linguistic meaning expressed by the utterance is the same for my colleague, I intend that she grasp that these words, with their normal linguistic meaning, have been used ironically. To her, I mean to convey the message "This is an awful paper." But, of course, what I hereby mean to convey to her is no part of the context-loaded linguistic meaning of the statement. Since the same observations apply to Christ's pronouncement (according to Milton's account), with the two audiences to which it is directed, I see no reason at all for thinking that there is any problem about what literal or linguistic meaning it expresses. We have only to sort out the factors of context-loading and speaker's meaning and correctly assess their different contributions to the total speech-act content.

In a paper published in 1978, Fish introduced a different sort of example. Affixed to the door of the Johns Hopkins Faculty Club is a gnomic string of words, "PRIVATE MEMBERS ONLY." As Fish points out at some length, it is easy to conjure up various more or less plausible meanings for these words to bear. And, in different contexts, the same words could be used to convey any number of different messages. Fish had asked his students to conspire with him in dreaming up the possibilities. What was the point of this exercise? Fish says, "What they [the students] did was move the words out of a context (the faculty club door) in which they had a literal and obvious meaning into another context (my classroom) in which the meaning was no less obvious and literal and yet was different. What they did not do was move away from a meaning that was available apart from a context to the various meanings contexts confer" (275). A few paragraphs further, Fish notes, in effect, that the word *private* has a number of established senses, any one of which might be relevant to some use of the designated string of words. Trying to explicate the upshot of all this, Fish advises the reader,

It may seem confusing and even contradictory to assert that a text
may have more than one literal reading, but that is because we usually

reserve "literal" for the single meaning a text will always (or should always) have, while I am using "literal" to refer to the different single meanings a text will have in a succession of different situations. There always is a literal meaning because in any situation there is always a meaning that seems obvious in the sense that it is there independently of anything we might do. *But that only means that we have already done it,* and in another situation, when we have already done something else, there will be another obvious, that is, literal meaning. (276)[13]

Hence, Fish presumably holds that there is nothing that corresponds to what I have called "the linguistic meaning of the words," a meaning that runs through all these cases.

If this is the conclusion Fish wishes to reach, we should first remember that the defender of linguistic meaning is not committed to the idea that there is always a single linguistic meaning, which the words will express on every occasion of use. It is obvious that the word sequence (qua type) is multiply ambiguous. (Of course, Fish denies the existence of this kind of ambiguity, but we are still looking for his arguments). First, the sequence is grammatically ambiguous. It may exemplify, among other things, either of the forms

(Private members)$_{np}$ only,

in which "private" modifies "members," or

Private! Members only!

in which two separable "contents" are conjoined. Moreover, each of the words in the sequence has more than one linguistic meaning in English. It is not controversial that any of the potential linguistic meanings of the word sequence could be expressed in a suitable context.

The new wrinkle that the present example adds is the fact that we are considering a string of words that does not constitute a complete English sentence. This serves to remind us that we often do use such nonsentential sequences to perform determinate speech acts, speech acts that communicate a specific content. However, it is hard to understand how this observation, important as it is for other issues, bears on the present dispute. Consider the following simpler case. We imagine that each of three doors in an office building bears a sign that says, simply, "OUT." On the first door, the sign is meant to signify that the occupant of the office is away. The second sign is meant to indicate that the door on which it is posted leads out of the building. The sign on the third door is supposed to be a warning to keep out of the area behind the door. It seems to me that the word, as it appears on each sign, expresses the same, standard linguistic meaning. It means, as we may boldly put it, "NOT IN." This is fully compatible with the further fact that the people who posted these signs meant (probably successfully) to convey or communicate three very different things. In fact, I have just described what they meant, in each instance, to convey by the posting of their signs. Here, as before, we have only to separate the question of the linguistic meaning of the expression from the question of what speakers mean by using the expression. The novelty in this example and in Fish's is that the (context-loaded) linguistic meaning expressed by the word or word sequence on an occasion of use does not determine a full statement, injunction, warning, or whatever. But this does not prevent a speaker or a sign poster from using the expression to perform a speech act that serves to convey the intended speech-act content.

I mentioned earlier that the question "What do these words mean?" is treacherous because it is commonly and properly used to ask after either linguistic meaning or speaker's meaning. Fish seems to have succumbed to this particular piece of semantic treachery. Indeed, in the quotations set out above he equates, as he does so often, the "literal" (i.e., the linguistic) with the "obvious" (sometimes the "perspicuous"). This strongly hints that Fish is committing a version of the error that we found Cleanth Brooks trying to disentangle. Fish assimilates the meaning that the sign posters "obviously" meant to convey with the linguistic meaning expressed by the words that they used to convey it.

For these reasons I doubt that Fish's work can shore up the line of thought in "Against Theory." In fact, what we find in Fish is an extension of the pattern discovered in Knapp and Michaels. We are given arguments that purport to expose errors involved in making certain distinctions between varieties of "meaning," but the arguments proceed from the outset by misunderstanding or otherwise obliterating the force and utility that those distinctions have. It is not my claim that the concept of the meaning of an expression in a language is invulnerable to challenge. On the contrary, legitimate doubts and objections have been raised. Willard Van Orman Quine and some other philosophers have argued against the viability of the concept no matter how it might be refined and qualified.[14] The longstanding and substantial problems that have been encountered in attempts to give a clear, systematic account of linguistic meaning and of associated concepts are grounds, at a minimum, for serious concern. Lexicographers, translators, and critics of literature have a lively awareness of the shakiness of prospective criteria for what does and does not pertain to the meaning of a word, phrase, or sentence. What I *do* claim is that questions about the nature and ultimate status of the semantical concepts is a theoretical question par excellence. Whether these concepts are to be accepted and developed, or whether they should simply be scrapped, turns upon whether they, or some better version of them, have a central role to play in our best theories of linguistic knowledge, use, and comprehension. The complaint I have made against Knapp and Michaels and against Fish is that they fail to make a real contribution to the relevant theoretical issues, and they seem to pay little attention to the conditions that a truly cogent contribution would have to satisfy.[15]

In concluding this discussion, I would like to return to a thesis of Knapp and Michaels that I mentioned at the outset but did not there try to assess. That thesis, as they state it, is that "the meaning of a text is simply identical to the author's intended meaning" (12).[16] Let us dub this "the thesis of the intentionality of the text." It is this claim that they share with Hirsch and Juhl, and I examined their attempt to dissociate their understanding of it from what they see as Hirsch and Juhl's misguided "theoretical versions." I argued at length that their attempt has failed. However, it may also appear that the considerations about meaning that I have sketched and endorsed commit me to agreement about meaning with Knapp and Michaels, Hirsch, and Juhl on this matter. After all, I have virtually reproduced a kind of argument that Hirsch and Juhl deploy in their defense of a version of the thesis.

A fundamental but minimal part of what is involved in understanding a literary text is the reader's understanding of the sentences it contains as expressions of definite linguistic meanings and as bearers of particular illocutionary forces. But I have agreed that an utterance or inscription does not express a definite linguistic meaning unless the utterer so intended. More narrowly, the referential and other values that anchor a context-loaded linguistic meaning are also largely fixed by the utterer's intentions in this regard. Finally, I would add that the illocutionary force of an utterance centrally depends upon the utterer's speech-act intentions. Thus, when we claim to understand a segment of a literary text even at this rock-bottom level, we thereby claim to have made out the relevant linguistic and speech-act intentions. Now, it is true that we are normally concerned, in the first instance, with the meaning and force of the utterances in inscriptions of the work's narrator or dramatic speaker. So our judgments have this form: it is fictional in the work that the narrator, in producing his or her words, had such-and-such intentions. However, with qualifications that are not essential here, what makes it correct to judge that fictionally the narrator uttered these words with those intentions is the fact that the author, in composing the text, intended to make it fictional that the narrator performed that speech-act. It is fictional that Roderick Random, qua narrator, expresses what he does in a segment of the novel in virtue of Smollett's intention that the words in question were to mean what they do. Hence, as a rule, what Hirsch calls "the verbal meaning" of the text is determined by the author's intentions.[17] What I have just outlined is the argument *for* the intentionality of the text *from* the requirement that meaning of the text or work be "determinate," an argument that Hirsch and Juhl elaborate extensively. In my view, the argument is fundamentally sound.

What puzzles me is the controversy that surrounds this conclusion, and my puzzlement has two related sources. First, the thesis of the intentionality of the text is an extremely weak claim *if* it is restricted, as here, to the verbal meaning of the text. Understood in that way, it leaves wholly open the broad issue of whether "correct" answers to the wide range of other types of interpretive questions we ask about a text are likewise settled by the author's relevant intentions. Most of the interpretive questions that are posed by a reasonably complex work remain unresolved even after everything about the verbal meaning of the text has been ascertained. Hence, the role of the author's intentions in relation to these questions is not prejudged by the present restricted thesis of the intentionality of the text. I suspect that a fair amount of the controversy is generated by conflicting assumptions about what is and is not subsumed by the phrase "the meaning of the text (or: the work)." I shall come back to this. Second, despite many suggestions to the contrary, it is hard to find a historically significant theorist who clearly and unequivocally denies the restricted thesis.

Take this second point first. This is plainly not the place to try to document my impression that it is true. Many important poststructuralist theorists frame their characteristic concerns and contentions in terms that make it difficult to measure them against the baseline I have drawn. In any event, the main historical source of the disputes about intentionalism in literary criticism has been the doctrines and the practice of the New Critics. And yet, as far as I can see, neither Brooks, Warren, Eliot, Ransom, Tate, Blackmur, nor Winters (if, indeed, the last two *were* New Critics) denied explicitly or implicitly that the verbal meaning of a text is determined by the author's intentions. Somewhat unfortunately, it has been standard practice to cite Wimsatt and Beardsley's (1946) famous paper "The Intentional Fallacy" in this connection. The practice is unfortunate because this rather short and quite polemical piece does not represent the most careful, nuanced statement of either writer's position — let alone, of some "New Critical" consensus. However, even this paper does not in any definite way repudiate the restricted thesis. In the following passage, Wimsatt and Beardsley are delineating types of data, much of which, if properly handled, they will count as admissible evidence for an interpretation.

> There is (3) an intermediate kind of evidence about the character of
> the author or about private or semiprivate meanings attached to words
> or topics by an author or by a coterie of which he is a member. The
> meaning of words is the history of words, and the biography of an
> author, *his use of a word, and the associations which the word had for* [my ital-
> ics] *him,* are part of the word's history and meaning. (10)

Even within their larger context these remarks are less than pellucid, but these are not the thoughts of writers committed to the view that the verbal meaning of a text is exhausted by the grammar and public linguistic meanings of expressions in the language.[18] Given that "The Intentional Fallacy" is such a paradigm of intentionalism, this illustrates the difficulty of finding an outright denial of the intentionality of the verbal meaning of the text.

This point need not be surprising if we look back to my first point: that the restricted thesis is actually very weak. It will help to understand this if I briefly review some of the elementary meaningful dimensions of a literary work that the restricted thesis does not cover. Such a review will simultaneously heighten one's sense of the often subtle and complex "meaning" attributes that an *unrestricted* version of the thesis purportedly subsumes.

A poem or work of literary fiction is a more or less extended discourse, and the structures and strategies of a discourse have meanings that outrun the meanings of its component inscriptions. Here is a trivial example. I may know the linguistic meaning expressed by each of these sentences: "All men are mortal; Socrates is a man; Socrates is mortal." And I may know that each utterance has the force of an assertion. But, if I do not grasp that this short discourse constitutes an *argument* from which the conclusion is supposed to follow, then I have missed a key aspect of the set of utterances taken as a whole. Although this example is indeed trivial, we should reflect upon the discourse structuring that goes on in descriptive exposition, elaboration of a cumulative narrative segment, depicted conversational exchanges, and stretches of psychological and moral explanation. If a reader has grasped the verbal meaning of a text without understanding much of these or similar discourse enterprises, then his or her sense of the work is dim indeed.

In a poem or work of literary fiction, a reader is confronted with, more specifically, a *fictional* discourse. That is, the reader of the text is to imagine that it represents the speech acts of a fictional or fictionalized narrator or dramatic speaker. As a rule, the character, personality, sensibility, and intelligence of the narrator are implicitly dramatized to some extent by the way in which the activity of narration is conducted. One consequence of this is that there generally will be questions about what the narrator meant to imply or suggest by framing the narration as he or she does. In addition, the narrator will stand in various possible epistemic relations and relations of truthfulness to the narrative states of affairs which he or she presents. A reading of a work that misunderstands all or much of this will not be competent. Further, such a fictional discourse will be significantly *conventionalized* in terms of specifically literary conventions. I have in mind the myriad actual and possible conventions of, for example, style, genre, prosody, dramatization, and closure; conventions whose meaningful functions in the context of the discourse they help to organize are often both distinctive and important.

Finally, a fictional discourse is *about* the fictional history of people, objects, events, actions, and circumstances. It describes the denizens of the work's fictional world. These agents and items of the narrative or dramatic subject will themselves be positioned in a range of meaningful configurations. Actually, I suspect that when readers are perplexed by "the meaning of a work," it is most often the nature and "meaning" of these narrative configurations that concern them. They do not understand the psychology or the role of an enigmatic character, the import of some crucial action or event, or the function of some apparent gap in the development of the plot. Typically, readers hope to arrive at a global meaning, a pattern of narrative-based explanation, that fits the set of configurations as a whole. Clearly, mere verbal meaning falls far short of providing them with any of this.

Any or all of these topics (and more besides) may be in question when "the meaning of a work" is being investigated. One should be struck by the diversity of these topics and by the very different concepts of meaning that come into play in connection with them. *All* of the uses of "to mean" exemplified in the sample sentences on the first page of this chapter are activated when we speak of the components of the meaning of a text. We already have had adequate exposure to the problematic features of phrases like "the meaning of this sentence (or: this utterance)," but those problems are literally multiplied when we discuss, without adequate guidance, doctrines about the meaning of a text or work.

Even in Juhl's generally thoughtful work, he portrays his overall enterprise in the following way: he aims at providing an analysis of locutions of the form

Literary work W means [or: has meaning] M

He seems to have in mind a project analogous to the attempts of Grice and others to analyze, for example,

Sentence S in language L means N.

But, as I have suggested before, it seems obvious that the phrases "the meaning of a work" and "the meaning of a text" serve as very rough umbrella terms that point indistinctly at a host of varied concerns that readers may have in trying to construe a given work or text. It may sometimes be a convenience to have such terms, denoting, as they do, a loosely connected cluster of topics, but the fact remains that they have approximately the same degree of precision as kindred phrases like "the consequences of war" or "the importance of the nightly news." Juhl does not ever make it plausible that he is dealing with a concept that has enough unity and determinateness to be subject to the kind of analysis he envisages. Of course, this particular stricture applies only to

Juhl, but too many theorists (and, for that matter, antitheorists) are content to elaborate their positions in terms of sweeping theses about the meaning or meanings of a literary text. Their readers are then left to fend for themselves in figuring out just what facets of "meaningfulness" in literary works are supposed to be subsumed by the grand hypotheses. I feel sure that no serious student of literature would disagree with me concerning the egregious vagueness of talk about the meaning of a work. And yet, as we have seen, theoretical discourse about literature seems to tempt some of these same thinkers into formulations that they would otherwise eschew.

Inspection of my short list of dimensions of meaning in a literary work reminds us why a relatively unrestricted thesis of the intentionality of the text has been and remains so dubious. It surely demands further argument to maintain that correct answers to questions concerning these topics are necessarily grounded in the author's pertinent intentions. For example, even the query "What is happening here in the story?" has an answer that transcends the facts of verbal meaning. Suppose we know that certain sentential inscriptions express the meaning "things are so-and-so," and suppose we know that this proposition fictionally has assertive force. We cannot conclude from this, without further inquiry, that, in the work, things *are* so-and-so. We will require, for instance, the assumption that the work's narrator is to be counted as reliable about matters like things being so-and-so.

When John Dowell, the narrator of Ford Madox Ford's *The Good Soldier* (1915, 106) tells us, "So that was the first knowledge I had that Florence had committed suicide. It had never entered my head. You may think that I had been singularly lacking in suspiciousness; you may even consider me an imbecile," can we safely infer that the time referred to *is* the first time he had known of her suicide? Surely not. Dowell gives us a hundred reasons for mistrusting his declarations of this sort. Any reasonable judgment about this would have to be carefully supported on the basis of a larger reading of Dowell's character, his performance as a narrator, and the detailed development of events in this saddest of all stories. I choose this example because Ford's biographer, Arthur Mizener, claims that Ford himself actually viewed Dowell sympathetically and intended us to take pronouncements like the one above to be largely accurate. "But the Dowell who is telling the story knows everything that Ford does and thinks all the things that Ford did about human affairs" (1971, 265).[19] And yet, even if Ford, in writing the novel, did intend us to accept all such statements from his narrator, the fact remains that this is hard for the attentive reader to do. Ford *also* intended the reader to draw likely inferences from the representations of the text and to do so on the basis of plausible assumptions about the workings of the world and human affairs. When such inferences point sharply away from the fictional fact that the author, by hypothesis, intended to create, then we are confronted with conflicting intentions, and we are likely, with considerable justice, to conclude, "The author meant it to be fictional that things are so-and-so, but, in the work, things really are thus-and-such." In any event, this much is clear. Even a strong intentionalist must concede that, when an author's intentions are conflicting in this manner, then nonintentionalist considerations must be brought to bear if there is to be a fact of the matter as to what is fictionally happening at the specified point in the work.

Similarly, the verbal meaning of the text cannot determine what the narrator meant to convey or suggest when he or she puts matters in a certain way. Here also the same potential conflict between intention and realization can arise. A well-known paragraph from Herman Melville's *Billy Budd* (1924) yields a particularly strong example.

> But shrewd ones may opine that it was hardly possible for Billy to refrain from going up to the afterguardsman and bluntly demanding to know his purpose in the initial interview, so abruptly closed in the fore-chains. Shrewd ones may also think it but natural in Billy to set about sounding some of the impressed men of the ship in order to discover what basis, if any, there was for the emissary's obscure suggestions as to plotting disaffection aboard. Yes, the shrewd may so think. But something more, or rather, something else than mere shrewdness is perhaps needful for the due understanding of such a character as Billy Budd's. (281)

Especially in the last lines of the passage, the narrator clearly means to imply that Billy's "nature" is to be construed in some special way. But what specifically does the narrator fictionally imply? (The text is studded with suggestions that the story of Billy Budd is to be read in some less than obvious mode.) To answer this question in this case turns out to be roughly equivalent to giving a well-supported interpretation of the novella as a whole. The complexity of that task does not need arguing, and to suppose dogmatically that Melville's intentions, general and specific, would prove definitive is to beg every interesting question that the long debates about intentionalism have raised. And certainly, the issues are not going to get simpler if we look at interpretive cruxes that are, on the face of it, of a more elaborate and sophisticated variety.

Naturally, I do not imagine that my remarks on the last few pages show that a relatively unrestricted thesis of the intentionality of the text is false. The possible replies and counterreplies are too many and varied for such a quick resolution. What I have wished to bring out is how much an unrestricted version is committed to compared to the minimal thesis of the intentionality of the verbal meaning of the text. In other words, I have wished to stress the great importance of distinguishing the different versions in general discussions of intentionalism. Unfortunately, this obvious methodological precept is very often not observed. Thus, for example, to return to my original point of departure, "Against Theory," I find it impossible to be sure whether Knapp and Michaels have the restricted or a relatively unrestricted version in mind. But, either way the authors face a dilemma. If they intend the version that is restricted to verbal meaning only, then they simply have taken no position at all concerning most of the topics that have made intentionalism a vexing and contentious stance. Moreover, we have absolutely no reason for supposing that the issues connected with these untouched topics can be resolved in the absence of a good deal of literary theory of a more or less traditional stripe. On the other hand, if "Against Theory" advocates a relatively unrestricted version of the notorious thesis, then its authors offer no serious defense of that position at all. The Knapp/Michaels essay, despite the radical character of its rhetoric, leaves everything, including "theory," exactly as it was before.

Conventions, Creativity, Originality

JON ELSTER

Artistic conventions are constraints on the artist, since they limit his or her freedom. They are, moreover, constraints of a peculiar kind, as may be seen from a brief survey of the other constraints that artists face. First, there are the constraints that flow from technology, as illustrated by silent movies, movies in black and white, and the 78 rpm record. Second, there are constraints due to lack of money and of what money can buy. Sculptors may have to do without marble; novelists may have to adapt their chapters for serial publication; and film directors may have to take the big battle scenes out of their script. Third, there are temporal constraints. The play has to be in shape by opening night; and the stadium must be ready for the opening of the games. Last, there are freely self-imposed constraints. If Woody Allen made *Manhattan* in black and white, it was not because he lacked the technology or the money for using color. When George Perec wrote *La disparition* without using the letter *e* a single time, it was not (or so I presume) because his typewriter was defective.

Conventions constrain for different reasons. If playwrights in seventeenth-century France wrote in alexandrines and respected the unity of space, time, and action, the explanation is not to be found in technology, money, time, or choice. Instead, it obviously had something to do with the expectations of other artists or of the public. I believe there are two main ways of looking at the matter. On one view, artistic conventions are like social norms — noninstrumental rules of behavior maintained by internalized emotions and by the sanctions that others impose on violators. Social norms, in this conception, range from the

I am indebted to G. A. Cohen, H. F. Dahl, and S. H. Olsen for their comments on an earlier draft of this chapter.

apparently trivial to matters of life and death; they include the rules of etiquette described by Pierre Bourdieu and Marcel Proust no less than the codes of vendetta still in effect in some Mediterranean countries.[1]

On another view, an artistic convention is a special kind of equilibrium, often referred to as a "convention equilibrium" and characterized by two features. First, as in all equilibria, when all follow the convention, nobody wants to deviate. Second, when all follow the convention, nobody wants anyone else to deviate either. The choice between driving on the left side and the right side of the road illustrates this situation. A more fanciful example is provided by the rule that governs the night life of Brooklyn mafiosi: "Everybody who had a girl friend took her out on Friday night. Nobody took his wife out on Friday night. The wives went out on Saturday night. That way there were no accidents of running into somebody's wife when they were with their girl friends" (Pileggi 1987, 90). Clearly, all that matters is coordination on one rule. Taking girlfriends out on Saturdays and wives on Fridays would do just as well, as long as everyone did the same. Social disaster would strike, however, if people followed different conventions, because then one might risk meeting a friend with his wife when taking one's girlfriend out. As Harold Macmillan complained, "In the old days you could be absolutely sure that you could go to a restaurant with your wife and not see a man that you knew having lunch with a tart. It was all kept separate but this does not seem to happen these days."[2]

An argument for seeing conventions in art as convention equilibria might go as follows. Art, like other forms of self-realization, requires competent judges; otherwise it becomes a private language, a morass of subjectivity.[3] If art were to vary widely in form and subject matter, quality would be hard to evaluate and appreciate. Even if each artist were to work under tight, self-imposed constraints, intersubjective standards would be weak if different artists chose different constraints. However, if all artists were to work under the same constraints, their works could be compared and standards established by the community of artists and critics. Hence, conventions in art possess both features of convention equilibria. Since each artist wants to be judged by others, he has no incentive to deviate from the common framework that makes competent appreciation and self-realization possible. Since he wants his judges to be competent, he has no reasons for wishing others to deviate either.

An argument for seeing conventions in art as social norms might go as follows. As a matter of fact, people do not see conventions as arbitrary but useful coordination schemes. On the contrary, conventions are viewed as normatively compelling. Playwrights or painters who violate the conventions are not simply neglected: they are booed, ostracized, and persecuted. If people who buy unfashionable paintings are subject to sanctions by their peers, so are those who make them. On both sides of the market, in fact, we find the same interminable ballet of conformism and one-upmanship, with some individuals making the conventions ever more elaborate and others desperately trying to keep abreast.

For my purposes here, I do not have to choose between these views. In many cases, we shall probably find that each explains part of what is going on. Instead, I shall go on to discuss constraints and their role in art more generally. Later, I return to the more specific issue of conventions, to suggest a reason why artists benefit from working under shared constraints. The general premise for my discussion is that artistic creation is the exercise of choice within constraints, based on a prior choice or espousal of constraints. The goal of the choice within constraints is to create a *local maximum* with respect to aesthetic value.[4] In a good work of art, nothing can be added, nothing subtracted, without detracting from the value of the whole. Creativity is the ability to reach or approach high-level local maxima.[5] The idea of a global maximum is meaningless: there is no such thing as the best of all possible novels, any more than there is a greatest number. Needless to say, I do not want these mathematical metaphors to be taken literally. I only want to draw attention to the twin properties of *fullness* and *parsimony* that in my opinion represent the ideal for artistic strivings. This is partly a factual, partly a normative claim. Here I shall not try to defend it in either version.

The idea of choosing one's constraints might seem more puzzling. Why would anyone prefer having fewer options to more? Why add avoidable constraints to the unavoidable ones? What made Perec write a whole novel in which the letter *e* was never used, and then another in which no other vowel was used? I believe that his decisions were extreme cases of a normal practice in art, that of limiting the feasible set for the purpose of being able to make meaningful choices within it. It is certainly debatable whether the deliberate expansion of the feasible set in *Finnegans Wake* was accompanied by an artistic gain; at the very least, it seems safe to say that James Joyce's method, in other hands, would be disastrous. Where there are too many possibilities, the artist's search for a local maximum by experimenting with small variations becomes unfeasible.

I believe that the first to formulate the problem of creativity in this way was Henri Poincaré, in his essay "L'invention mathématique." In a key passage he writes:

> Inventer, je l'ai dit, c'est choisir; mais le mot n'est peut-être pas tout à fait juste, il fait penser à un acheteur à qui on présente un grand nombre d'échantillons et qui les examine l'un après l'autre de façon à faire son choix. Ici les échantillons seraient tellement nombreux qu'une vie entière ne suffirait pas pour les examiner. Ce n'est pas ainsi que les choses se passent. Les combinaisons stériles ne se présenteront même pas à l'esprit de l'inventeur. Dans le champ de sa conscience n'apparaîtront jamais que les combinaisons réellement utiles, et quelques-unes qu'il rejettera, mais qui participent un peu des caractères des combinaisons utiles. Tout se passe comme si l'inventeur était un examinateur du deuxième degré qui n'aurait plus à interroger que les candidats déclarés admissibles après une première épreuve.[6]

> Discovery, as I have said, is selection. But this is perhaps not quite the right word. It suggests a purchaser who has been shown a large number of samples, and examines them one after the other in order to make his selection. In our case the samples would be so numerous that a whole life would not give sufficient time to examine them. Things do not happen in this way. Unfruitful combinations do not so much as present themselves to the mind of the discoverer. In the field of his consciousness there never appear any but really useful combinations, and some that he rejects, which however, partake to some extent of the character of useful combinations. Everything happens as if the discoverer were a secondary examiner who had only to interrogate candidates declared eligible after passing a preliminary test.[7]

He then goes on to argue that the first, preliminary selection is made at an unconscious level, while the final selection is made by the conscious, deliberating self. The criteria of selection used by the unconscious or subliminal self are essentially aesthetic.

On peut s'étonner de voir invoquer la sensibilité à propos de démonstrations mathématiques qui, semble-t-il, ne peuvent intéresser que l'intelligence. Ce serait oublier le sentiment de la beauté mathématique, de l'harmonie des nombres et des formes, de l'élégance géométrique. C'est un vrai sentiment esthétique que tous les vrais mathématiciens connaissent. (57)

It may appear surprising that sensibility should be introduced in connexion with mathematical demonstrations, which, it would seem, can only interest the intellect. But not if we bear in mind the feeling of mathematical beauty, of the harmony of numbers and forms and of geometric beauty. It is a real aesthetic feeling that all true mathematicians recognize, and this is truly sensibility. (59)

He recognizes, however, that this leaves a difficulty:

Est-il vraisemblable que [le moi subliminal] puisse former toutes les combinaisons possibles dont le nombre effrayerait l'imagination? Cela semblerait nécessaire néanmoins, car s'il ne se produit qu'une petite partie de ses combinaisons, et s'il le fait au hasard, il y aura bien peu de chances pour que la *bonne,* celle qu'on doit choisir, se trouve parmi elles. (59)

Is it conceivable that it [the subliminal ego] can form all the possible combinations, whose number staggers the imagination? Nevertheless this would seem to be necessary, for if it produces only a small portion of the combinations, and that by chance, there will be very small likelihood of the *right* one, the one that must be selected, being found among them. (60)

To solve the problem, he suggests that not all possible combinations are generated and presented to the sieve of the unconscious. Certain elements are more likely to be used as building blocks than others: "ce sont ceux dont on peut raisonnablement attendre la solution cherchée" (61) ("those from which we may reasonably expect the desired solution" [61–62]). Jacques Hadamard, expanding on Poincaré's idea, suggests that the trick is to generate and combine elements that are optimally dissimilar. "It is well known that good hunting cartridges are those which have a proper scattering. If this scattering is too wide, it is useless to aim; but if it is too narrow, you have too many chances to miss your game by a line" (1949, 48).

Artistic creation differs in many ways from mathematical invention. In mathematics, beauty is a good but imperfect indication that the goal — truth — is in sight. In art, beauty is the goal. This and other differences notwithstanding, the two processes are similar in that both require a delicate balancing of variation and selection. The artist, however, solves the problem (or the problem is solved for him) in a way that has no analogue in mathematics. His problem of selection is made more manageable and more focused by the fact that he works within constraints that reduce the initial myriad of combinations to some radically smaller subset. In science or technology, creativity is never enhanced by the creator's pulling his punches or tying one hand behind his back. In art, however, less can be more. In other contexts, the reason for restricting one's opportunities can be weakness of will[8] or the desire to gain a strategic advantage.[9] In art, the reason for imposing constraints or welcoming them is, as I said, the need to concentrate the creative powers on a task of manageable size.

Consider first the constraints imposed by technology. Before the advent of the long-playing record, jazz recordings were limited to about three minutes' duration. A solo rarely lasted more than a minute, which may be about the maximal time a continuously inventive flow of improvisation can be sustained. Unless I am mistaken, jazz has never again attained the levels of perfection it reached in the studio recordings by Louis Armstrong, Lester Young, and Charlie Parker. The rise of the sound engineer, and in particular the technical possibility of splicing tapes to combine parts of several takes into one, probably also had a negative impact on the quality of recorded music. There are those who think the quality of movies deteriorated steadily as sound and then color became available.

Consider next financial and temporal constraints. Not all low-budget movies turn into cult objects and ultimately into classics; and some high-budget movies acquire lasting value. Yet the stories told about some low-budget movies suggest that necessity can be the mother of creativity. Although there are many problems that cannot be solved by throwing money at them, the availability of funds makes it tempting to go for this quasi solution. Although all architects want a larger budget, an unlimited budget would paralyze rather than liberate their creative powers. Although they always want an extension of the deadline, having no deadline at all would leave them dangling without support. In bargaining experiments, it has been found that in a large number of cases, agreement is reached just before the deadline.[10] The knowledge that time is running out concentrates the mind wonderfully.

Self-imposed constraints can serve the same purpose. Fred Astaire insisted on his dance scenes being shot in one continuous sequence or, at least, in a small number of uninterrupted chunks. Why did he adopt this unusual practice, which necessitated each scene being shot as many as fifty times? Partly, I suspect, because the flow itself is artistically valuable; partly out of professional pride; and partly perhaps to impose a constraint on himself that, by making his art more difficult, would enable and force him to concentrate harder. Even before the invention of the word processor, I knew a writer who typed his manuscripts with justified right-hand margins. Perhaps his behavior was compulsive rather than freely chosen, but the benefits from being constrained may still have been forthcoming.

Consider, finally, purely conventional constraints, such as orthography, grammar, and tone scales; the rules defining a sonnet; the iconography and color schemes to be used when painting traditional religious topics; the number of acts in a play or of movements in a symphony; and so on. Earlier I discussed a couple of mechanisms that might sustain such conventions. Here, I want to suggest an additional benefit of conventions, analogous to that of membership in a Weight Watchers club. One way of coping with obesity is to impose constraints on oneself, such as substituting low-fat margarine for butter or never eating between meals. These strategies are notoriously vulnerable to manipulation; in particular, it is always easy to persuade oneself that it is all right to violate the current regime because another holds out more promise. At any given time, the dieter follows a set of constraints, which, however, are constantly modified so as to have no purchase on the current situation. The best way out may be to join a group of other people with the same aspiration, for the purpose of providing mutual support and, more importantly, control. If the group rule is to eat no butter, the individual cannot plausibly tell himself and the others that another regime will be more effective.

In a similar fashion, conventions may stabilize self-imposed constraints. There is nothing natural or compelling about the sonnet form. If the scheme had been 3-3-4-4 rather than 4-4-3-3, the verses would have been just as good. Imagine, however, a writer who starts out composing a sonnet and then runs into difficulties that he could solve by using the 3-3-4-4 form. He may then easily persuade himself that the unorthodox form is no less effective as a vehicle for self-discipline and concentration than the orthodox form — unless he is deterred from doing so by the community of writers and critics. Rather than making the charitable assumption that he chose the unorthodox form ahead of time and stuck to it, they will assume that he started out the orthodox way and then changed out of laziness and self-indulgence. At least, this is what they ought to assume if they are to provide an external check on his weakness of will. The artistic process can be frustrated by a "shortage of scarcity," in George Ainslie's (1986, 156) wonderful phrase. Because rationing oneself is difficult, we need others to impose the constraints that we might try to escape were we left to our own devices.

I am not claiming that these benefits of conventions explain why they are in place. Weight Watchers and Alcoholics Anonymous were deliberately set up as a collective control of individual backsliding. It would be absurd to argue that conventions arise out of a social contract in a similar way. Nor do I think that the stability of conventions owes much to their restraining effect on individual akrasia. It is more plausible to explain their stability in terms of social norms or equilibrium reasoning, as explained above. Yet once a convention has arisen (for whatever reason) and is kept in place (by one or both of these mechanisms), it can also provide invaluable rationing functions.

Whatever their nature and origin, the effect of constraints is to reduce the amount of variation that goes into the next stage, that of selection. Here, the two-stage selection process posited by Poincaré seems plausible. Some unconscious selection takes place before the conscious refinement and fine-tuning can begin. I know this from introspection, and it is hard to see how it could be otherwise. Even though the constraints have the effect of limiting the number of possible combinations of the basic elements, the number that remains is still more than can be consciously surveyed. First, an unconscious or intuitive process somehow puts together combinations of elements that promise to have aesthetic value, rejecting other combinations (virtually all, in fact) as worthless. Next, the conscious part of the mind takes a hard look at the products of the intuitive part, discarding or accepting according to deliberate, intentional criteria.

The picture bears a strong resemblance to the views of Carl Sagan, put forward in *The Dragons of Eden* and summarized as follows by Sally P. Springer and Georg Deutsch (1981):

> Sagan describes the right hemisphere as a pattern recognizer that finds patterns, sometimes real and sometimes imagined, in the behavior of people as well as in natural events. The right hemisphere has a suspicious emotional tone, for it sees conspiracies where they don't exist as well as where they do. It needs the left hemisphere to analyze critically the patterns it generates in order to test their reality. (192)

This description matches that of Poincaré (1908a), in suggesting that the criteria of beauty and harmony can be misleading.

> Quand une illumination subite envahit l'esprit du mathématicien, il arrive le plus souvent qu'elle ne le trompe pas; mais il arrive aussi quelquefois, je l'ai dit, qu'elle ne supporte pas l'épreuve d'une vérification; eh bien! on remarque presque toujours que cette idée fausse, si elle avait été juste, aurait flatté notre instinct naturel de l'élégance mathématique. (59)

> When a sudden illumination invades the mathematician's mind, it most frequently happens that it does not mislead him. But it also happens sometimes, as I have said, that it will not stand the test of verification. Well, it is to be observed almost always that this false idea, if it had been correct, would have flattered our natural instinct for mathematical elegance. (1908b, 60)

Yet there is a difference between the processes described by Sagan and Poincaré and those at work in artistic creation. It would be strange to say that an artist can be misled by beauty or patterns. Sagan hits the nail on the head when he suggests that scientists can be misled by patterns into finding conspiracies where none exist. Social scientists may be particularly prone to this fallacy,[11] but in earlier centuries natural scientists also fell victim to the fallacious search for meaning in all things.[12] Obsessional works of art, however, like Alexander Zinoviev's *The Yawning Heights,* Joseph Heller's *Catch 22*, or the paintings of Hieronymus Bosch and Francis Bacon, are not in any way vitiated by their one-sidedness. On the contrary, we appreciate these works (perhaps reluctantly) because they isolate and purify strands of experience that we usually fail (or do not want) to acknowledge.

A further difference between art and science is the following. According to Poincaré, mathematical invention involves three kinds of acts: the generation of variation, the preliminary selection, and the final choice. In the arts, I have argued, the deliberate choice or espousal of constraints must also count as a separate part of the creative process, limiting the amount of variation on which the subsequent selection can operate. The two differences work, as it were, in opposite directions. In art, variation is artificially limited, but the selection criteria are less stringent. On the one hand, some combinations are excluded on formal grounds from the outset. On the other hand, no combinations are excluded on grounds of falsehood.

So far I have approached the analysis of conventions in art from the point of view of "normal art," analogous to Thomas Kuhn's "normal science." I have argued that conventions and other constraints are conditions for, rather than obstacles to, creativity. The creativity may be of the highest order. Whereas normal science is often thought to be a vehicle for mediocrity, the examples of Mozart and Jane Austen show that normal art is as capable of perfection as are rebellious or revolutionary forms. By a rebellious work of art I mean one that knowingly flouts established conventions. A revolutionary (or original) work is one that creates a new set of conventions, which eventually may become commonly accepted. I shall focus on the latter category of nonnormal art, but first a few words about the former.

The deliberate violation of a convention to create some special effect is really parasitic on the convention. Consider two conventions of mid-nineteenth-century theater. One is that the final resolution of the action does not occur before the very end of the play. The other is that characters in the play must never appear to be aware of the fact that they are nothing but characters in a play. Towards the end of Henrik Ibsen's *Peer Gynt,* when Peer is afraid of drowning, the strange passenger tells him that "one does not die in the middle of the fifth act," simultaneously violating the second convention and exploiting the first. This rebellion differs from Luigi Pirandello's revolutionary "characters in search of an author," since Ibsen's exuberant departure from the convention presupposes, for its effect, that readers and spectators take it for granted. Although any rebellion, by showing that the convention is artificial and contestable rather than natural and self-evident, contains the potential for a revolution, it need not have this further effect.

In characterizing a work of art as revolutionary, original, or innovative, there is an implicit comparison with an earlier form. I shall consider innovation as a change in conventions relative to the immediately preceding period. The new conventions need not be historically unprecedented. The return to a much earlier period can amount to innovation, a self-conscious break with the tradition by which one has been shaped. But I shall limit myself to innovation in the more radical sense, the invention of new and unprecedented forms. The emergence of free verse, nonfigurative art, and atonal music are well-known, dramatic examples, but innumerable smaller innovations could be cited.

What explains artistic innovation—the emergence of new conventions? Why cannot artists remain content with the medium within which they have been trained? One answer is that "if artists were concerned only with making beautiful pictures, poems, symphonies, etc., the possibilities for the creation of aesthetically pleasing works of art would soon be exhausted. We would (perhaps) have a number of lovely paintings, but we should soon grow tired of them, for they would all be more or less alike" (Lessing 1983, 75). As illustrated by this passage, the "exhaustion argument" can take the form that after a while there are no more beautiful works of a certain kind to be made, or that after a while beautiful works of a certain kind lose their power to please. In my opinion, the argument is implausible in either form. It is absurd to argue that the realistic novel went out of fashion when and because all good plots, characters, and dialogues had been invented, and equally implausible to assert that at some time in the second half of the nineteenth century readers got tired of realism. Nor do I think that realism went out of business because novelists got tired of it.[13]

An alternative account could take off from the Marxist critique of capitalist relations of production.[14] Among the many things Marx found wrong with capitalism was its alleged inefficiency or suboptimality in developing the productive forces or, in non-Marxist language, technology. In this conception, technical change is a function both of the intensity of the search for new techniques and of the efficiency of selecting among the techniques generated by the search. Capitalism, Marx argued, is inherently inferior to communism with respect to the selection of new techniques, being motivated by profit rather than by the desire to reduce human drudgery. At a low level of development of the productive forces, however, capitalism is superior to communism in the intensity of the search for new techniques. Communism, to be viable, presupposes a high level of material welfare, at which people can spontaneously engage in creative activities, such as artistic, scientific, and technical innovation. By providing the profit motive as a spur to search, capitalism enables mankind to reach that level; but once it is reached, capitalism becomes the ladder it can kick away. The general idea underlying this analysis is that a mode of production remains in existence as long as it is historically progressive, that is, as long as it generates new techniques at a higher rate than any other mode could do. It disappears when and because another mode becomes superior.

The "exhaustion argument" has a certain resemblance to Marxist theory. The theory asserts: Relations of production change when and because they cease to promote technical change. The exhaustion argument says: Conventions change when and because they cease to promote creativity. The value of the comparison is that it suggests an alternative to the exhaustion argument. To see this, note that the Marxist theory compares the actual rate of development of the productive forces with the hypothetical development under another regime, not with their earlier development under the same regime. What induces change is suboptimality, compared to what could be, not stagnation, compared to what has been. The exhaustion argument, as stated and rejected, invokes stagnation as the explanation of new forms of art. The comparison with Marxist theory suggests that new conventions come into being when and because they promote creativity to a higher extent than the earlier form could do.

We then have to ask a further question: what has happened to make the new conventions more fertile than the earlier ones? One answer (the analogue of the Marxist answer) could be that the very achievements attained within the old conventions make other conventions the optimal vehicle for further development. Perhaps one could cite the relation between Paul Cézanne and cubist painting in support of this idea. Another could be that extra-artistic events, such as the Industrial Revolution or class conflict, create a need for new forms of artistic expression. The confused cliché that a "fragmented society requires a fragmented art" expresses this view.

I do not feel able to carry the discussion much further. The subject matter is amorphous and vast, and it does not easily lend itself to precisely formulated hypotheses and generalizations. Instead, I want to conclude on a different note. It is obvious to the most superficial observer that the rate of change of conventions is much higher today than in any earlier epoch. At the same time, I do not believe that the rate of production of works that will be seen as having durable value is any higher than before. It seems to me that much of contemporary art and art criticism is laboring under a fundamental misconception — the overevaluation of originality at the expense of creativity. Some further questions along these lines are the following. Does one have to be a great artist to make a radical break with the past? How much time does it take for the artistic community to adjust to a new set of conventions? Could the very effort of innovating distract and thus detract from the power to create? Could there be an analogy in this realm to the tales of inventors who go bankrupt only to see their inventions successfully exploited by others? Does the "penalty for taking the lead" exist in the arts? How could one identify premature innovations and premature decay of conventions?

CHAPTER THREE

Literary Conventions

THOMAS G. PAVEL

In literary theory, conventionalism is most noteworthy for its rejection of mimetic approaches to fiction. Its most radical manifestation can be found in the structuralist doctrine, but it also can be met in nonstructuralist contexts.[1] Literary texts, under a structuralist-conventionalist view, cannot be taken to speak about states of affairs outside themselves, since any such apparent referring is regulated by rigid conventions that make those states of affairs behave like effects of a perfectly arbitrary illusionistic game. It would not make much sense to examine the structure of fictional worlds, nor the interplay between these and actual worlds; reality in fiction is just a textual convention, not so different from the compositional conventions of the rhyme pattern in sonnets, the five acts in tragedies, or the alternation between main and secondary plots in Renaissance drama and eighteenth-century epistolary novels. The literary trend that strove most conscientiously toward minute referential adequacy, realism, has repeatedly been described as a mere ensemble of discursive and textual conventions. And since language and discourse cannot copy reality, the realist convention is just as arbitrary and nonreferential as any other.

A claim like this rests on an implicit notion of semiotic conventions that includes the traits of arbitrariness, obligatoriness, and unconscious character. In the Continental semiotic tradition, these features can be traced back to Ferdinand de Saussure's theory of the linguistic sign. According to this theory, the phonetic side of the linguistic sign (the signifier) and its semantic content (the signified) are linked together by an arbitrary connection: the sound *tri:* does not relate to the concept "tree" by virtue of any inner causality; in addition, the meaning "tree" should be distinguished from the object tree. Prima facie, this stand seems innocuous, since the conventionality of the bond between sound and meaning as well as the distinction between concept and object have been accepted ever since Aristotle's philosophy of language. The novelty of the Saussurean approach consists in the synthesis between a classical conventionalist thesis and the romantic Humboldtian conception that sees language as a field of energy expressing the world-view of the speech community. The classical component guarantees the formal organization of the semantic content of a language into an arbitrary yet systematic network of oppositions that remains independent from the world of objects by virtue of the distinction between object and concept. In accordance with the romantic component, the formal network projects itself into the world and organizes it in conformity with the linguistic a priori. In the act of naming a tree *tree*, we do not merely apply the appropriate linguistic label to an object, as common sense wants it; rather, we isolate the object tree in the natural continuum only inasmuch as the sign *tree*, whose signified belongs to a chain of formal oppositions, forces us to do so.[2]

The Saussurean synthesis was further developed by Louis Hjelmslev, who proposed a universal distinction in natural languages between the expression plane (the phonetic level) and the content plane (the semantic side), each of these planes being in turn constituted of form (the structural principle) and substance (the phonetic and, respectively, the semantic matter, as organized by form).[3] In each natural language the form of expression and the form of content arrange and systematize two amorphous *purports:* the phonetic continuum at the level of expression and the universe at the level of content; these, Hjelmslev adds, do not enjoy any kind of semiotic existence outside the form that raises them to the status of substance. The two forms, expression and content, each carrying along its correlative substance, adhere to each other in an arbitrary solidarity called *semiosis.* Since, moreover, in the Saussurean tradition opposition is the main principle of form organization, the universe amounts to an amorphous purport organized into a substance by a linguistic network of oppositions. The shape of the language-bound network obeys only its internal logic; hence its arbitrary and conventional character. This network is unconscious as well, since we are deceived by the mechanism, do not perceive its functioning, but believe instead in nature's independence from language.

Hjelmslev's four-term structure has since been widely applied to various systems of signs, literary texts included. From a semiotic perspective, various forms of content obey only their internal oppositional logic, imposing it on the purport in order to structure it as the substance of the content. In simpler terms, autonomous semiotic principles variously organize the world, rendering any notion of reference, representation, or adequacy to reality ornamental, if not superfluous. Seen as governed by semiotic conventions, literary texts do not describe real or fictional worlds, but merely manipulate an amorphous purport on which they impose their arbitrary rule. Mythic and realist discourse are equally conventional and unmotivated; Honoré de Balzac's novels do not resemble reality any more than do chivalry novels; they just make use of a different semiotics, as conventional and artificial as any.[4]

This argument, and along with it a widespread practice of textual analysis, rests on two theoretical moves: it entails first a definition of conventions as systems arbitrary with regard to the domain they govern; second, it assumes that semantic structures are born in some prior unexplained way, independent of the field of reference that they entirely determine. Severe conventionalism, combined with linguistic apriorism, repels empirical doubts; and, since semiotic systems *constitute* reality, no empirical evaluation of the argument would ever be possible.

It is perhaps interesting to notice that while the semiotic trends chose the conventionalist path of development, the debate inside linguistics itself took a different turn. Contemporary linguistics has gradually abandoned its earlier apriorism and conventionalism and shifted its attention from semiosis — the arbitrary link between meaning and sound — to language universals, innate grammars, and the links to cognitive psychology.[5] This shift has failed to make itself felt in literary theory. Still, it indicates the difficulties experienced by the conventionalist approach in one of its traditional strongholds, the theory of language.

Classical Conventionalism

If by convention one understands "an agreement between persons, nations; general agreement on the usages and practices of social life; a customary practice, rule, method, etc." (*Webster's New World Dictionary,* 1970), traditional thinking about literature perennially has hesitated between conventionalist and nonconventionalist stands. The theoreticians of classicism believed that literature obeys a set of rules, but these rules mirrored the order of nature, be it through norms established by the ancients or through direct observation of nature by the moderns.[6]

In spite of their acute awareness of literature's dependence on norms, the classicists did not develop an autonomous theory of convention; since literary norms did not differ from the laws of nature, literary practices different from theirs were simply discarded as erroneous. It was only with the advent of romanticism, when classicist rules began to be felt as artificial, that a theory of literary conventions developed which condemned conventions as exterior, fallacious norms preventing nature from speaking in its own voice. Closer to us, Russian formalism rejected convention again, on grounds not all that different from romantic historicism. The notion of defamiliarization is designed to contrast the new artistic work with the established literary conventions of a given historical moment: a good writer renders familiar objects and situations strange by presenting them from an unexpected angle and by breaking with the accepted perceptual and cognitive conventions.

But the classicist idea of literature as obeying a definite set of textual norms has not failed to make new appearances; and some of our century's theorists, notably T. S. Eliot (1957), Ernst Robert Curtius (1948), and Michael Riffaterre (1978), have made claims surprisingly similar to those of the seventeenth-century partisans of the ancients. Eliot's statements about the synchronic nature of world literature amount to a variation on a classicist theme; textual interdependence is precisely what partisans of the ancients emphasized, as opposed to the velleities toward textual independence showed by the moderns. The stress on textual interdependence may lead to undervaluing referential power and to concentrating instead on texts and their formal properties. Devotion to the ancients reveals a strong attachment to ornament and decorum: Eliot believed that poetry is essentially music, of sound or ideas; its social function consists in keeping language alive. But since the music of poetry is a music of ideas, ideas in poetry are there mainly in order to make music. And, if the social function of poetry is to keep language fresh, the efforts of poetry should be linguistically oriented.

Also related to the ancients is Curtius's description of European literature as a texture of topoi that travel from one period to another and from one text to another, independent of historical determinations. A given literary text provides for a meeting place of recurrent themes and figures deriving in most cases from the classical age. While Eliot's antimodern maneuver evacuates referential strength by replacing ideas with music and language, Curtius achieves a similar result by reducing texts to their lowest common denominator: the commonplace.

In Riffaterre's intertextual theory of poetry, the poetics of Aristotle meets Saussurean semiotics in a most remarkable synthesis: Riffaterre denounces what he calls "the referential fallacy" by suggesting that, just as victims of the intentional fallacy mistake the authors for the text, the new fallacy causes critics to substitute reality for the representation thereof. In everyday language, words appear to refer vertically to the objects they represent, but in literature, in which the meaningful unit is the entire text and not the isolated word, lexical elements lose their vertical semantic force and act upon one another contextually, producing a new effect of meaning, *significance*. Significance differs from dictionary meaning; it is generated and governed by the properties of the text, by the ambiguities and the overdeterminations of the poetic language. The naive referential view, Riffaterre claims, fails to account for poetic effects, since the mechanisms of the latter involve constant reference to other words and texts. But this is the only referential link of literary works: self-sufficient, poetic texts do not speak about the world, they only refer to other texts. Dependence on the texts of other writers blends, in Riffaterre's theory, with semiotic rejection of the real world's referential autonomy. Classicist confidence that the ancients once and for all captured the rules of nature in their texts is lost; in its stead we are offered a Saussurean view that separates the semiotic systems from their unattainable referents, replacing poetic worlds by ever-changing conventions of intertextuality.

Hume-Lewisian versus Saussurean Conventions

That language has conventional aspects has long been accepted as one of the familiar philosophical verities, periodically called into question by some restless thinker but soon reinstated as unquestionably valid. In a relatively recent occurrence of this vacillation, Willard Van Orman Quine (1936) has argued that since the term *convention* entails the notion of conscious contract, linguistic conventions could not possibly have been established by overt agreement, for such an agreement must presuppose some form of already existent language. The development of language must rather have proceeded by slow evolution, trial and error, leading to the behavioral conglomerate we all know and which in no accepted sense of the term resembles conventions. Leaving aside unwarranted assumptions about conscious contracts, Quine argues, we should limit ourselves to the study of linguistic regularities. Language does not belong to the family of conventions but to that of customs; and about these the only appropriate response is careful observation.

As a response to Quine's position, David Lewis (1969) proposed an analysis of conventions that includes nonexplicit contracts. Lewis's position comes close to David Hume's definition of convention as "a general sense of common interest, which sense all the members of the society express to one another, and which induces them to regulate their conduct by certain rules."[7] As the ensuing lines suggest, Hume does not assume that the expression of the common interest must be explicitly linguistic, though it can occasionally take such a form. The crucial element in Hume's account is that conventions do not derive their validity from explicit promises but from reference to the actions of others:

> I observe that it will be to my interest to leave another in the possession of his goods, provided he will act in the same manner with regard to me. When this common sense of interest is mutually expressed and is known to both, it produces a suitable resolution and behaviour. And this may properly enough be called a convention or agreement betwixt us, though without the interposition of a promise; since the actions of each of us have a reference to those of the other, and are performed upon the supposition that something is to be performed on the other part. (490)

In Lewis's account of convention, reference to the actions of other people is modeled on coordination behavior and games. Two of his examples indicate the kind of gentle attention to the acts of others that the theory assumes to underlie conventional behavior:

> (1) Suppose you and I are rowing a boat together. If we row in rhythm, the boat goes smoothly forward; otherwise the boat goes slowly and erratically. . . . We are always choosing whether to row faster or slower; it matters little to either of us at what rate we row, provided we row in rhythm. So each is constantly adjusting his rate to match the rate he expects the other to maintain.
>
> (2) Suppose several of us have been invited to a party. It matters little to anyone how he dresses. But he would be embarrassed if the others dressed alike and he dressed differently. . . . So each must dress according to his expectations about the way the other will dress: in a

tuxedo if the others will wear tuxedos, in a clown suit if the others will wear clown suits (and in what he pleases if the others will dress in different ways). (1969, 5-6)

Although expressed agreement is often the basis of coordination, Lewis stresses the frequent absence of explicit communication in coordination behavior and games. If the problem posed by the situation is familiar, the solution will be tacitly found on the basis of precedent; but even in the case of new problems, sophisticated subjects may solve them without communicating, and may achieve coordination in accordance with the criterion of conspicuous novelty or saliency: in order for the other subjects to notice and expect one another to notice it, the solution has to be strikingly unique.

The definition of convention generalizes the analysis of coordination problems. In solving such problems we learn how to handle future coordination situations, each precedent contributing to our ability to address new coordination problems. Extrapolation of past successes leads in turn to "the general belief, unrestricted as to time, that members of a certain population conform to a certain regularity in a certain kind of recurring coordination problem" (41); the experience of general conformity leads to the expectation of it, which reinforces the community, since all members of the group have similar expectations. The group reaches thus "a metastable self-perpetuating system of preferences, expectations, and actions capable of persisting indefinitely" (42). This phenomenon Lewis calls *convention,* the definition of which will include a regularity in behavior, a system of mutual expectations, and a system of preferences, all of which must be common knowledge within the population:

A regularity R in the behavior of members of a population P when they are agents in a recurrent situation S is a *convention* if and only if it is true that, and it is common knowledge in P that, in any instance of S among members of P,

(1) everyone conforms to R;
(2) everyone expects everyone else to conform to R;
(3) everyone prefers to conform to R on condition that the others do, since S is a coordination problem and uniform conformity to R is a coordination equilibrium in S. (58)

In light of this definition, the horizon of expectations within which writers and their public operate can be seen as the background of various coordination games involving tacit cooperation between the members of the literary community. The author and the reader must understand each other and be able to coordinate their moves in a fashion not too different from that of the two people rowing a boat in Hume's and Lewis's examples. And just as expressed agreement is not necessary for the implementation of an equilibrium of coordination, one does not need the actual presence of the other participant(s) in the game in order to reach the desirable conclusion. One can imagine a coordination game — finding a hidden object, a letter or a treasure — in which the participants are not allowed to come in touch with one another and must decipher signs left behind by the coplayers. Is the absence of the other participants an insuperable obstacle to finding the letter or the treasure and, consequently, to the obtaining of equilibrium? To further dramatize the question, is the death of one participant an obstacle? In Edgar Allan Poe's "The Gold-Bug," the treasure is found in spite of Kidd's death: the game of conspicuous novelty succeeds across generations. Absence does not necessarily affect the game, nor does the game require absence.

The Hume-Lewisian perspective leads to conclusions opposed to those developed within a Saussurean paradigm. Games in writing are but a particular type of coordination problem, even though, based on Saussure's doctrine of the differential character of any linguistic system, Jacques Derrida has argued that linguistic exchange, even in an oral form, bears the mark of what could be called "primordial" writing. The Saussurean doctrine, as expressed by Derrida, assumes that every linguistic sign is but a trace of the absence of all other signs. Since this is an important feature of alphabetical writing systems, wherein the optimal differentiation between signs requires that no sign possess its own features but that these be economically distributed throughout the system, Derrida concludes that spoken language is structured like writing. Still, a sign also points to the absence of the object it stands for: the sign "I" functions in the absence of the signified ego, as if it were an inscription of its death. Again, this is a feature of writing systems, whose operation does not require the signatory to be alive. Hence, Derrida argues, speech allows, even presupposes, the death of the subject: like writing, speech excludes the presence of the living voice from its act (1967, 88–104).

The above definition of convention might, however, help counter to some extent the philosophical portentousness of the death of the subject. Modeled as a coordination game, linguistic exchange can sometimes dispense with the copresence of the participants. Since coordination can be achieved in spite of absence, the death of one or more participants does not create insuperable obstacles for the game. Therefore, absence does not have to be elevated to the rank of a paradigmatic rule of linguistic coordination. It offers only an example of a coordination game in which, depending on the purpose of the coordination, the participants put a special emphasis either on the unexpectedness of the clues or on their familiar character. The transmission of traditions, beliefs, rites, or texts across generations depends on strategies of stability involving the use of iterability as a source of mutual expectations; the establishment of new artistic trends, realism among others, calls for strategies of novelty, based on conspicuousness as a key to equilibrium. In religion, two types of strategies lead respectively to ritualistic systems and mysteries; in social behavior, to sophisticated politeness versus casualness; in education, to repetitious versus problem-solving methods; in poetry, to formulaic versus innovative patterns. Formulaic literature functions by virtue of the assumption that poems closely respect a set of preestablished formulas known to both the poet and his public. Encoding and decoding Homeric poems, Serbo-Croatian folk narratives, or the poetry of the troubadours proceeds via reference to familiar schemata, as sources of mutual expectations.

The un-Saussurean perspective of the Hume-Lewis approach extends to the normative and unconscious aspects of conventions. Those who assume social conventions to be governed by a languagelike system are inclined to stress their obligatoriness and unconscious character; since in the Saussurean paradigm linguistic structure formally organizes our understanding of the world, there is no possibility of avoiding its constraints, nor can we render it transparent to the intuitions of the native speaker. A most severe conception of artistic and literary conventions ensues: their obligatoriness and secrecy is such that literary texts appear to be woven by an invisible conventional hand in the absence of the author, whose disappearance Barthes celebrated (1968). Conversely, in a Lewisian world, where conventions are stabilizations of coordination games, they are obligatory only in a weak, de facto sense; that brides at some periods in history dress in white is obligatory (when it is) only because this particular solution tends to become stabilized; other solutions remain possible, however. Likewise, in systems based on novel solutions, literary games change incessantly: the mobility of artistic conventions suggests their weak obligatoriness. This entails a considerable amount of choice, hence the need for awareness and deliberation: the irremediably unconscious aspect of Saussurean conventions is therefore inadequate. True, in Lewis's definition a convention becomes such only when the community forgets to deliberate about its appropriateness. But the memories of its implementation can easily be recalled and the same game, or a modified one, can start again, leading to new solutions and new conventions.

Conventions of Fiction

The literary theorist who comes closest to Lewis's sense of freedom and contingency is Barbara Herrnstein Smith, who has described a set of principles of cooperation followed by readers of fictional discourse.[8] By virtue of the *convention of fictionality*, literary utterances are perceived as representations of linguistic structures, representations that generate their own semantic content. This convention regulates the behavior of the readers by requiring from them a maximal participation oriented toward the optimal exploitation of textual resources. The convention of fictionality warns the readers that usual referential mechanisms are for the most part suspended and that, for the understanding of the literary text, outside data mean less than in everyday situations; so every bit of textual information must be carefully examined and stored.

I would add that Herrnstein Smith's convention functions as a more general constraint on reading and interpretation: maximal decoding is required of readers of history as well, especially when dealing with remote periods. The very popularity of history and biography indicates that many readers who are prepared to cooperate with the narrative-descriptive text also desire genuine historical information in return. On the other hand, archaic formulaic works, which usually presuppose a heavy battery of known prescriptions, do not direct the attention of their readers toward the same kind of effects as a modern text: reading strategies based on precedent differ from those searching for novelty, and it may well be that this distinction cuts across the conventions of fictionality.

A further important distinction entailed by a Lewisian approach sets apart *conventions proper,* which are stable, well-entrenched patterns of solutions to problems of cooperation, from *social games of coordination,* which require cooperative solutions but do not necessarily lead to their entrenchment as conventions. In contrast, the semiotic approach tends to assume that every regularity of semiotic behavior reflects a rule of the semiotic code. Roman Jakobson's poetic analyses, for instance, treat every detectable pattern in a given poem, be it accessible to the reader's attention or subliminal, as an expression of the poetic grammar that governs the text in question. But the typology of literary convention needs to distinguish between *constitutive conventions,* which establish the very texture of the communicative process, and mere coordination regularities, or *preconventions.* A taxonomy of literary conventions that takes this distinction into account would find at least four quite diverse kinds thereof.

First, constitutive conventions set the main rules of social activities: in natural languages, grammar assumes this role; in a football game, the rules according to which it is played. The existence of these rules in the literary exchange is subject to doubt, and many writers deny that art can fruitfully be compared to language. But supposing that literary activity, though not a language *stricto sensu,* can be conceived as a complex coordination game, there certainly are numerous constraints outside which the game could not take place. Entrenched coordination equilibria, such as metrics, the form of a sonnet, the five-act division of a tragedy, appear to constitute the very frame whereupon literary exchange is meant to rest.

An example from metrics can be instructive. When reading or reciting the first of the two following lines:

> Not from the stars do I my judgement pluck;
> And yet methinks I have astronomy . . .
> (Shakespeare 1609, Sonnet 14)

We face several choices. Read like prose, the stressed syllables will probably be the following:

> Not from the stárs dó I my júdgement plúck

A more theatrical reading can in addition stress the first syllable:

> Nót from the stárs dó Í my júdgement plúck

The sequence "do I," moreover, can be pronounced as "dó I" or "dó Í"; and extra emphasis can be placed on "my," and, provided it leaves enough time between words, a highly emphatic reading could add a stress on "from":

Nót fróm the stárs dó Í mý júdgement plúck

In spite of the diversity of possible scansions, after reciting the entire sonnet (and perhaps many more sonnets as well), one discovers several general regularities: for instance, the last but one syllable is virtually always unstressed; or, more often than not, the even syllables are stressed, while the odd ones are more likely to remain unstressed. A tacit metric scheme takes shape, that of the iambic decasyllable — to which every competent reader of English poetry conforms and expects others to conform, since rhythm is a coordination problem, and conformity to the metric scheme provides the guidelines for the coordination equilibrium.[9]

Similarly, the efforts of modern narratology have been directed toward the discovery of the constitutive conventions of narratives. How do we know that a certain discourse or textual development is a narrative? In a similar way, the answer runs, to our mechanism for accepting that a certain sequence of words is a sentence, that is, by checking it against an internalized grammar. Narrative grammars contain information on narrators, on the content of narratives, on events and their organization. Most of these elements can be seen as entrenched solutions, which by tacit agreement become constitutive conventions. Not unlike the fixed sonnet form, there are narrative patterns that require from the reader knowledge of the established conventions: first-person narrations, epistolary novels, and detective stories are recognized and enjoyed by virtue of an entrenched agreement whose cooperative nature makes it quite similar to Lewis's conventions.[10]

But not all predictable narrative effects qualify as conventions proper. A contemporary well-trained reader, as well as her nineteenth-century counterpart, knows quite well that large-sized novels published in England in the first half of that century most often deal with matrimonial questions, especially when the author is a woman and the tone is serious. In such novels, marriage will be actively sought as the optimal state of affairs for the protagonists, under certain social and sentimental constraints. A good reader knows that this regularity is part of the novel's background and that the right expectation makes the game possible. One understands what *Pride and Prejudice* and later *Jane Eyre* are about only when one expects, or realizes, that matrimony and the condition of women are central topics and that an intimate relationship links them to the novel as a literary form. However, such a regularity does not qualify as a proper convention, since uniform conformity to it does not obtain: not only do many nineteenth-century novels have nonmatrimonial topics, but those dealing with matrimony handle the subject in very diverse ways. The situation resembles coordination games, in which the strategies for cooperation are not yet ossified into conventions: each particular instance of the game, while sharing some of its features with other games, asks for specific skills and idiosyncratic solutions. Preconventions will thus include those literary regularities that do not reach the high uniformity of conventions and can therefore be understood as local rules or hints in a particular group of literary games. At the level of narration techniques, a similar situation arises in connection with, say, the embedded narrative (*Wuthering Heights*): in order to play the game well, one has to be aware of the romantic technique of embedding a story difficult to believe into a first-person narrative told by a reliable individual. That this awareness has to be learned is not an obstacle to the argument, since, as with many games, we may start with a simple set of rules and gradually come to discover more and more complex strategies.

The distinction between naive and more sophisticated reading becomes essential, therefore. In a game-theory perspective, literary texts are assumed to be built around a few basic rules that give access to the text; while a naive reader knows these and only these rules, more advanced strategies can gradually become available through training and practice. Just as good chess players not only master the elementary rules of the game but are capable of applying such strategic laws as the principle of intermediary goals, or the principle of controlling the central squares, good readers know how to detect regularities that are invisible to less-trained readers. Advanced readers may know in advance the matrimonial outcome of *Jane Eyre* and enjoy the tortuous progress toward it, or they may have understood that Balzac's novels always turn on financial catastrophes, or that in *Remembrance of Things Past* virtually every character has an ambiguous sexuality.

The Lewisian dichotomy between solutions based on precedent and those based on novelty can be applied to one and the same literary text, depending on the background of its readers. The embedding of a core narrative into a frame narrative can be perceived by a naive reader as a surprising innovation, whose rules and reasons he has to uncover by carefully observing clues planted by the author. A reader ignorant of this particular game does not know whether the first frame of *Wuthering Heights* is meant only as a transition toward a more substantial account or if it is destined to become the main thread of action, to which, after the presentation of the manuscript, the story will return. A more sophisticated reader, or the naive reader at a second reading, will replace the strategies of discovery with strategies of recognition. During a second (or sophisticated) reading, the transition from novel solutions to solutions based on precedent helps to emphasize an important component of aesthetic pleasure, which the romantic and modernist traditions, with their insistence on spontaneity, innocence, innovation, and surprise, unfortunately neglect. Like all games in which skill improves with training, literary games enhance the pleasure of taking fewer and fewer risks, of feeling oneself more and more in control. As with the student of chess, the practicing reader senses the growing of his power and dexterity; he enjoys his progress and loves to continue the practice. So the abrupt romantic and formalist opposition of innovation to ossified conventions should be modified to include the gradual assimilation of new games, the prolonged training of readers, and the progressive gain of control over new kinds of coordination problems.

To turn back to preconventions, it is not always easy to discern regularities that belong to the literary game from those engendered by the representation of social conventions established outside the literary exchange. That revenge tragedies contain ghosts who often play a major role in the revelation of the crime (*Hamlet*) may be no more than a literary device — although it can also be argued that most of Shakespeare's contemporaries believed in ghosts. But the maxims of power in force in Renaissance tragedies ("An earthly crown is the most desirable thing," "Any limitation of supreme power is an adversary to that power") undoubtedly describe social beliefs and practices contemporaneous to the texts. In the Spanish theater of the Golden Age and in Pierre Corneille's tragedies, the code of honor respected by the characters is such that indeed each conforms to the code, each expects the others to conform to it, and each prefers to act according to the code, on the condition that the others do the same. But obviously the theatrical code of honor more or less faithfully represents a social convention in force in the aristocratic milieu contemporaneous to the play. To further complicate the situation, it must be noted that reference to social reality outside the text does not change the conventional status of the code inside the play, since a public belonging to a different period is perfectly capable of understanding *represented conventions,* even when these lack an effective social counterpart. Utopian and science fiction make us familiar with the technique of inventing nonexistent social conventions. Literary texts and myths, but also biographies, history, hagiography, often spell out conditions for social coordination.

Victor Turner has noted the interdependence between what he calls *social dramas,* which are spontaneous units of social process involving a crisis and its redress, and genres of cultural performance: "life, after all, is as much an imitation of art as the reverse" (1981, 149). Although the representation of social dramas lies at the origin of literary narratives, "some genres, particularly the epic, serve as paradigms which inform the action of important political leaders . . . giving them style, direction, and sometimes compelling them subliminally to follow in major public crises a certain course of action, thus emplotting their lives" (149). More generally, represented conventions often display a normative role: they operate as hints of the ideal behavior required from members of the community. Hence the strongly idealized appearance of some of these representations, both in classic and romantic literature. Conventions of courtship, for instance, as typified by *Astrée* or, more than a century later, by *Werther, The Elective Affinities,* and the prolific succession of romantic novellas and novels on the theme, concluding with the parodic *Tristan* of Thomas Mann, possess a distinctively normative ring: too severe to be faithful reproductions of social practices, these texts exerted nevertheless a lasting fascination on their public in the same fashion as the medieval lives of saints secured the attention of theirs: as models impossible to follow literally, but giving social behavior orientation and meaning.

Sometimes preconventions tacitly implement peculiar characteristics of the fictional world. Fifty years ago, in a strong rejection of psychological interpretations of Shakespeare's tragedies, Elmer Edgar Stoll described the "convention of the calumniator credited," which requires the good characters to believe the lies and calumnies of villains (1933,

6–8). According to Stoll, since Othello's gullibility lacks a psychological basis, it can only be understood as an instantiation of the calumniator credited, like Gloucester's credulity in *King Lear* or Arden's giving credit to his wife's confabulations in *Arden of Feversham*. It can be added that at the end of the nineteenth century Henrik Ibsen's *Doll's House* was built upon a complementary variant of this convention, according to which innocents never manage to make themselves heard. August Strindberg's *Father* thematizes the impossibility of not believing the calumniator, even when his or her malice is apparent. *The Dance of Death* by the same author is constructed around several kinds of calumny and gullibility. In Anton Chekhov's *Cherry Orchard*, the heroine lets herself be persuaded by the lies of a distant character, presumably wicked. Clearly, the rule of the calumniator credited, which in its generalized form requires the success of every deception, does not govern the literary behavior of the audience. Nor is it a represented convention, since the deceived character does not know about the rule and therefore does not conform to it willingly. But it is not a constitutive convention either, since the literary competence of the audience does not necessarily include it. A competent spectator who senses the rule of the calumniator credited will expect on the one hand that Othello believes Iago's insinuations but, on the other hand, as a witness of disloyal behavior, he will hope that the Moor does not trust the calumniator. In other words, this regularity occasions unusual expectations of a higher order that contradict the more current expectations. Yet new hypotheses and theories represent the regularities of the universe in an unexpected way; the content of a theory increases proportionally with its unexpectedness. Regularities like the calumniator credited do not proceed otherwise: to show consistently the success of deception is to submit that the world is governed by unexpected laws, or rather by laws that are surprising at one level but predictable at a higher level. Functioning as a set of *hypothesès* about the fictional world, this type of preconvention constitutes an important part of the referential mechanisms of literature.[11]

The Semantics of Tragedy

Semantic threads of this kind can be found in constitutive conventions as well: literary genres, for instance, often carry along strong hypotheses about their fictional worlds. These are less visible in the current definitions of genre, usually based on a mixture of criteria pertaining to the structural aspects of the literary text, its semantic characterization, and the conditions of its reception. The Aristotelian notion of tragedy includes the imitation of an action—a semantic notion; the change of fortune with its two components, reversal (*peripeteia*) and recognition (*anagnorisis*), which can be seen as a set of structural plot constraints. Catharsis, understood in a ritualistic framework or in a more modern psychological interpretation, refers to the process of reception.

A multiplicity of criteria leads to flexible definitions. In a classic paper, Morris Weitz (1956) argued that aesthetic concepts have an open-textured quality; although their instantiations offer Wittgensteinian family resemblances, they stubbornly resist attempts to fix their definition once and for all. To "close" an aesthetic concept is ludicrous, Weitz maintained, since this would contradict the built-in potential for innovation that we feel to be a central characteristic of art.

Weitz's argument expresses in a strong way a familiar doctrine, often found in relativistic contexts: the orthodox historicist believes that cultural categories do not possess transhistorical essences because they depend for their definition on particular historical periods; similarly, the Whorfian anthropologist relativizes these notions to the cultural context in which they are used. But need the rejection of essentialist definitions lead us into severe relativism?

Let us assume for a moment that the meaning of aesthetic notions such as "art," "tragedy," or "portraiture," to use Weitz's own examples, may be represented in terms of their extension. The notion of art would thus be represented by the class A of individual works of art. The extension of tragedy would consist of the class T of individual tragedies. Weitz's argument rightly intimates that one cannot attach to these classes sets of properties shared by all potential members of the class. Indeed, if a set of universal properties existed, it would mean that every new object claiming to belong to the class in question would have to possess these properties. Such a requirement would closely resemble the position of neoclassical criticism, which embodied a narrowly circumscribed point of view. In contrast, the relativist proposal amounts to breaking up the sets of tragedies into mutually exclusive subsets historically or culturally indexed. Thus, the set T of all tragedies would divide into, say, the sets T_g of ancient Greek tragedies, T_m of medieval tragedies, T_r of Renaissance tragedies, T_c of French classicist tragedies, and so on.

This extensional definition requires an ideal reader/spectator acquainted with all the tragedies ever written before an arbitrary date, say t, but who is unable or unwilling to formulate a clear definition of the genre. But does this reader/spectator know what a tragedy *is*? When presented with a certain text or performance, is he capable of giving the correct answer to the question "Is this text or performance a tragedy?" Assume that the ideal reader/spectator has a perfect memory, that the texts/performances submitted for his judgment have been produced before the arbitrary date t, and that he is aware of this chronological detail. In order to decide whether a certain text/performance is a tragedy or not, all he has to do is check it against the set of tragedies he is acquainted with. If he recognizes the text/performance as one of the list, the answer is affirmative; if not, the text or performance is not a tragedy. If, however, the text or performance has been produced after the date t, the case is undecidable, and according to Weitz the essentialist model is refuted.

Yet would a relativist model fare any better? We can imagine a set of ideal readers/spectators, each acquainted with one of the sets of tragedies written before the arbitrary date t. Reader Rg is acquainted with the set Tg of Greek tragedies, reader Rr with the set of Tr or Renaissance tragedies, and so on. A certain text (or performance) written before t qualifies as a tragedy if at least one of these ideal readers recognizes it as belonging to the set of tragedies within his domain. Again, the decision is impossible for a text produced after t. The restrictions entailed by a relativist model are so strong that some of its consequences are clearly undesirable. One of the assumptions of the model is that the sets of tragedies Tg, Tm, or Tr do not intersect: thus, each reader being acquainted with only one set, he cannot recognize as a tragedy a piece belonging to a different set. For instance, according to the model, the ideal reader acquainted with the French classical tragedies will not recognize as a tragedy Euripides' *Iphigenia in Tauris*, a highly counterintuitive conclusion. In the same vein, how would the model account for texts belonging to some set Tj and which, as a consequence of a revival, Renaissance or Renascence, come to belong also to some other set Ti? More generally, how does the model account for transhistorical phenomena?

The committed historicist would certainly object to the proposed model as being oversimplified, even distorting: to represent historical periods in an extensional way as unqualified sets to which individual texts irreversibly do or do not belong is to miss the entire point. Cultural phenomena, he would argue, are subtle, fuzzy. A Wittgensteinian point in his favor would be that readers who have called "tragedy" various texts are as a matter of fact able to go on and guess which other texts are tragedies, without having grasped a property that all and only tragedies possess. Blunt extensional characterizations are bound to be false. But then how should we represent the fuzzy nature of cultural phenomena if not by using multiple criteria and flexible characterization? Genres are constitutive conventions, enjoying a relative stability but sensitive to historical movement as well. Some, like tragedy, are semantically homogeneous and posit strong hypotheses about fictional worlds. In such cases, semantic criteria play a privileged role in the establishment of the convention. As we shall soon see, however, not even in such well-defined cases are semantic criteria the only ones that contribute to the definition of genre.

Semantically, tragedy can be characterized in contrast with mythical ontologies and epic sequences of events. Myths, being narratives, are composed of chains of events; by virtue of their privileged ontology, they serve as models of intelligibility for events in the profane world. The user does not need to question myths: it does not make much sense to ask, for instance, why Theseus abandons Ariadne and why Dionysus falls in love with her. For their users, myths do not need *explananda,* since as paradigms of sense they furnish explanations for profane events. That such-and-such a real-life woman has been abandoned by her lover and later marries someone else becomes intelligible in the light of Ariadne's myth. To be understood and justified, precarious existence needs the support of archetypical chains of events.

As long as the users strongly adhere to their myths, mythological religion offers a considerable advantage over other world-views — nonmythological relations or scientific models — since it organizes the world in a remarkably detailed and durable way. When the adhesion to mythological constructions begins to weaken, the withdrawal of community support removes from myth its absolute truth, and what has been the very paradigm of reliability changes into fiction. But the ontological structure displayed by myths does not vanish. Like the sacred universe, the world of fiction is separated from the real (or profane) world; the nature of the distance, however, has changed. While the sacred worlds enjoy a plenary reality that does not allow for questioning and needs no explanation, fictions dwindle to a secondary reality. Even if fictions continue to provide explanatory models for chains of events, the users of fiction can claim the right to assess their pertinence and appropriateness. One does not measure the truth of a myth; rather, the truth of the world is measured against the myth. In contrast, one can evaluate tragedies; as the dramatic competitions in Greece show, one cannot avoid evaluating them. Hence the flexibility of fictions: explanatory models being constantly judged, fictions must struggle in order to have their truth recognized and accepted. Therefore fiction feels free to explore hypotheses, to construct models deliberately offered for public appreciation.

When adhesion to mythical systems declines, what suffers most is the intelligibility of events in the profane world. Formerly related to sacred events in a salient structure, human destiny tends to lose its explanatory principles once the mythical link weakens. From imitation of divine patterns, the sequences of human events turn into autonomous chains, which obey their own inner logic. Then it becomes necessary for the fictional activity to produce strong, striking sequences of events, in order for the weight of the fictional models to replace successfully the worn-out mythical explanations. It is as if a mythical theory of the profane world had to be replaced by another theory or group of theories proposed by fictional works.

As shown by Claude Bremond (1973) in narratology and Georg von Wright (1966) in the logic of action, events obey a logic of possibility. Notably, the logic of epic poems develops according to a system of choices and decisions so that at every stage the protagonists enjoy a certain amount of control over their action. Clearly this is only an incomplete control, since the moves of other protagonists and the intentions of the gods constantly thwart the projects of each actor. However, the constraints on the freedom of the agents derive mostly from the strategic situation in force at each moment of the story, a situation determined by previous decisions and by the intentions and capabilities of the rival forces. In this respect epic poems represent a kind of "degree zero of the narrative," in which no constraint belonging to a higher level affects the concatenation of the actions.

In epic conflicts, the two parties ideally have the same chances of winning, and victory belongs in principle to the antagonist who uses more skillfully the rules of the strategic game. But, as critics have always known, in a tragic conflict the dice are loaded, most often from the very beginning: thus Agamemnon entering without hesitation into Clytemnestra's trap, Antigone fighting with her back to the wall against the authorities, Oedipus looking for a truth destined to destroy him. The nature of the deceit is often linked to the strategic configuration. Jean Racine uses conflictual patterns in which one of the parties has no chance to win. In *Bajazet,* the death sentence against the protagonists is sent to Byzantium before the beginning of the tragedy; in *Britannicus,* the spectator witnesses the decrease in the fortunes of one group of antagonists (Britannicus and Agrippina); the tragic in *Bérénice* originates in the fact that Titus's decision is irrevocably made and remains unshaken.

Other means, only indirectly linked to the strategic configuration, can serve equally well as filters for possibilities, distorting the chances of the players. Shakespeare often stresses the strategic idiosyncrasies of the failing heroes: the way in which Hamlet, Macbeth, Lear, and Othello make their decisions cannot but radically weaken their chances of success, even if at the beginning of the conflicts they stand on a par with their opponents. Christopher Marlowe's tragic heroes, disposing of a matchless force, have the game distorted in their favor: thus the invincible Tamburlaine, the Jew of Malta, Doctor Faustus. Their fall originates in this incomparable force, which prevents them from correctly assessing the final strategic configuration. They end in disaster for having set themselves impossible goals.

Among other characteristic ways of limiting the chances of the heroes, one should mention heredity (Ibsen's *Ghosts*), the structure of personality (Strindberg's *Dance of Death*), the nature of the adversary (Beckett's *Waiting for Godot*). Perturbations in the structure of time often accompany the tragic distortion of chances: Barthes, for example, noticed the circularity of time in Racine's tragedies; other critics have commented on the structureless time in Beckett's plays.

More generally, the tragic protagonist either has no feasible choice of action or disposes only of an illusory choice: tragic plots thus suggest higher-order constraints on the chains of events, which eliminate a considerable number of strategic possibilities. Since the strength of a hypothesis is in proportion to the number of possibilities it excludes, the tragic hypothesis proves to be particularly strong. It presents the image of a universe in which the possible chains of actions are drastically limited: compactness and closure meet the tragic heroes.

But drastic limitation of strategic possibilities is not the only means of characterizing tragedies: like all literary genres, and more generally like any convention, tragedy is a self-regulating system. A local fault will be compensated by overdetermination in other areas. The compactness of the universe can be indicated by means other than the filtering of possibilities or the distortion of chance. With the usual outcome resulting in predicament or catastrophe, less skilled authors try to develop tragic themes the other way around, starting from the consequences. The plays of John Webster or Cyril Tourneur overflow with poorly motivated murders, as if a certain saturation of catastrophes were an equivalent of the tragic hypothesis. Solutions miming tragic compactness sometimes employ the exterior features of the tragic tradition. The distortion of chances is better perceived at those social levels on which the characters can devote all their energies to the process of decision making: for a long time, the use of this social level served as a substitute for the tragic proper. Corneille's *Le Cid* is called a tragedy mainly because the characters are kings and princes.

Nonetheless, in spite of its flexibility, tragedy seems to be losing its strength as a literary convention. The reason may be found, as with any weakening convention, in a displacement of the coordination problem: if my proposed characterization of the tragic hypothesis is correct, then it becomes apparent that proving the compactness of the world has been the main direction of the efforts made by philosophers, scientists, political thinkers, and even theologians. The tragic hypothesis enjoys such prestige, spreads with such celerity, that it is perhaps natural that dramatic works are no longer its privileged medium. Does this mean that tragedy is dead? Perhaps yes, in its original core, the tragic text; certainly not in the irresistible proliferation of its strategic hypotheses. This suggests that fictional hypotheses about the world are not forever confined within a given fictional genre. Since their circulation involves the entire cultural space, theory of fiction cannot be isolated from the general economy of the imaginary.

CHAPTER FOUR

Convention and
Literary Explanations

PAISLEY LIVINGSTON

That "convention" has long played an important role in literary scholarship cannot be the object of any reasonable doubt: critics often claim
that some aspect of a literary work is conventional or unconventional,
just as they frequently apply the term "convention" to patterns they
have discerned in some corpus. Yet critics employ the term in highly
divergent ways.[1] For some, conventions are constitutive of all literature, and without conventions there would be no specifically literary
discourse. Others believe that the realm of convention extends even
further, embracing not only literature but all of culture. "Convention"
would in that case be applicable to any nonnatural and nonnecessary
regularity discernible within human practices or artifacts. Other critics
work with more restricted senses of the word. In their view, descriptions of the conventional dimensions of literary history only set the
stage for an examination of the features of those original and creative
literary works that break with convention in one way or another. Yet
critics of the latter persuasion often disagree rather sharply over the
nature and scope of the conventions in question: for some, it is a matter
of a limited set of artificial and unrealistic devices; for others, the term
is virtually coextensive with whatever is rational and comprehensible
in discourse, in which case the break with convention is imagined to
require the emergence of some sort of radically disruptive singularity.

Given such divergent applications of the term, it seems crucial to
maintain that arguments over the conventional or nonconventional
nature of literary discourse can only succeed if we have a reasonably
precise and accurate concept of convention to work with, which is quite
obviously what has been lacking. If a literary convention is any nonuni-
versal pattern or regularity that a critic may happen to discern in some
corpus of literary works (and this given some very broad understand-

ing of "literary works"), then it would be folly to deny that the history of world literature abounds with conventions. What is much less obvious, however, is whether critics should be credited with genuinely explaining anything by describing such regularities and by subsuming—or deciding not to subsume—particular cases beneath them. A general lack of clarity and agreement about the cognitive goals of literary research contributes greatly to the chaotic nature of a good part of critical debate. Having a better idea about what would constitute a genuine explanation of a literary phenomenon would help us to decide whether some notion of convention has a chance of making an important contribution to such explanations. Similarly, having a better idea about what constitutes a convention is the first step to being in a position to decide whether conventions can reasonably be granted any such explanatory role.

Recently some literary theorists have explored the possibility of adopting a precise definition of "convention" that has been developed in another field, namely, the Humean conception as it was elaborated by David Lewis in his 1969 study *Convention*. Some have argued that Lewis's notion is highly applicable to the case of literature, while others have denied this, claiming instead that in such a context the definition can only serve as a negative analogy that makes it possible to grasp what is different about literary conventions. In what follows I address myself to the question of whether Lewis's notion of convention has any value in the context of literary research. Very generally, my conclusion is that it certainly does, but not in any simple and straightforward manner. Although it is clear that one way to attack the problem is to set out immediately to identify literary items that do and do not appear to correspond to Lewis's definition, my view is that to adopt such an approach is to fail to grasp the more significant issues—issues having to do with the nature of literary explanations, and more specifically, with the role of certain concepts of action and interaction in a literary context. I think it crucial to stress the fact that Lewis's definition of convention is couched in terms of game theory and corresponds to a very particular class of situations identified therein.[2]

It is important to understand that a viable application of game-theoretical intuitions in a literary context would require reference to a broad range of situations, including a number of complex variables and factors that game theorists have only recently begun to incorporate in their formal models. Consequently, what needs to be considered is not simply whether Lewis's concept of convention, taken in isolation, has any instantiations in the history of literature. What should be asked instead is whether a more basic conceptual and explanatory framework, which finds one of its expressions in mathematical game theory, has any pertinence to literary research. Game-theoretical thinking has had a tremendous impact in a number of the social sciences and is considered by many to provide their unifying microfoundations.[3] Yet literary scholars rarely evoke this material and typically assume it to be wholly irrelevant to their field.[4] In such a context, attempts at applying Lewis's theory of conventions have at the very least the merit of drawing attention to an interdisciplinary connection that is long overdue. Moreover, even if we may conclude that not all, or even few, literary conventions are Lewisian conventions, the fact remains that there may be important explanatory gains to be had by applying concepts of strategic interaction and interdependence in a literary context.[5]

At the outset, I set forth some key aspects of the Hume/Lewis definition of convention, situating it within the context of some of the basic game-theoretical assumptions upon which it relies. Basically, I show that Lewis's notion of conventions is one among a variety of solution concepts discussed in game theory, and I evoke some of the other variables and possibilities. I then turn to the question of analogous models in literary research, identifying some general theses about literary explanations that would have to be adopted in any application of the intuitions of game theory. I entertain one way of applying Lewis's concept, discuss its explanatory status, and then take up Lewis's own discussion of the role of conventions in linguistically coordinated communication. After that, I discuss what I consider to be an example of a highly successful literary explanation, and I use this example to illustrate and develop some of the issues introduced earlier.

I

I shall begin with a very broad characterization of the notion of convention advanced by Lewis, for although this theory has been competently set forth by a number of commentators, many literary scholars remain wholly unfamiliar with it, and a fairly standard account should be presented before any more controversial points are hazarded.[6]

To grasp the basic idea behind Lewis's notion of convention, we must first understand the nature of the "coordination problems" that conventions are supposed to solve according to his theory. The example of the Modern Language Association's annual convention can be used to illustrate this category of problems. For a variety of personal and professional reasons, thousands of members of the association choose to attend a few days of meetings in the hotels of a major North American city. Although any number of problems may be accurately associated with such gatherings, a basic and nontrivial one is the difficulty of thousands of academics managing to meet at the same time and place. This is a coordination problem first of all because it is an example of what game theorists call a "strategic" game or situation, that is, one in which the best course of action for each player depends on what the other players do (Schelling 1960, 1, n. 1). In such a situation, the decisions of rational players are interdependent and involve reciprocal expectations about what the others are going to do. Game theorists distinguish between such cases and those in which the individual's skill or luck determines the outcome of a particular situation. Thus, in relation to the example, I might have an extremely clever idea about why the MLA convention should be held in a particular city in a given year, but if what I want most is to attend the convention, my decision to go to a particular city will not be a good one unless I have sufficient reason to believe that the others will make a similar decision. According to the game-theoretical definition, this kind of interdependence of decisions and outcomes is characteristic of all strategic situations.

Coordination problems constitute a proper subset of such strategic situations, namely, those situations in which the interests of the parties involved coincide. In Thomas Schelling's apt examples, keeping a rendezvous and the game of charades are coordination problems, while chess and chase are games of conflict: in the former, players strive to achieve a meeting of minds, and in the latter, they strive to avoid one (1960, 85). Interactions such as bargaining and negotiation lie somewhere in between the two extremes, for here the players share goals that cannot be realized independently (such as the goal of making an exchange or agreeing to a contractual engagement), but their interests do not perfectly coincide (buyers and sellers have different preferences about the final price, even though they share the goal of making a deal).

If we look at an MLA convention as a totality, it is clear that it is not a pure example of a coordination problem because many of the people who attend the meeting have conflicting goals: some of them compete, for example, for jobs and prestige. Yet there remains a nontrivial sense in which those who decide to attend the conference initially share at least one coordination problem, which is that of meeting at the same time and place, even if their other interests do not coincide. What is more, although the individuals attending the conference may have had some personal preference for a different meeting place, such preferences were overruled by their dominant preference for attending the meeting. Several different places were possible, and each member had only a conditional preference for any one solution, preferring most of all to go where the others would be going. In Lewis's view, talk of the "arbitrariness" of a conventional solution to a coordination problem must be understood in terms of the conditional nature of the agents' preference for conformity to a particular solution. Thus it is "arbitrary" to prefer to attend a meeting being held in New York in the sense that one would also have preferred Chicago or any other place where one thought the others would be meeting.

Coordination problems, then, are situations in which two or more people have goals that coincide, and in which the successful realization of each person's goal depends on there being the right kind of relation between what everyone in the situation does. Moreover, these people's common goals can be realized in more than one way. For Lewis, conventions are solutions to a broad range of problems of the type just delineated. In a nutshell, Lewis defines a convention as a regularity of behavior produced by a system of expectations (1969, 118). More precisely, conventions are solutions to coordination problems, as defined above, realized by the right kind of mutual expectations about the actions, preferences, and rationality of the other parties in the game. In Lewis's scheme, conventions are solutions to a range of complex types of interdependence because they are essentially a matter of repeating the "meeting of minds" that once occurred in some earlier, analogous situation. According to Lewis, then, a convention is not simply any regularity of action or belief that may be observed to hold within some population, for the following additional conditions must also hold (1975, 5–6). Not only must everyone conform to the regularity, but everyone must believe that the others conform to it, and this belief is what gives everyone a good and decisive reason to conform to it. Everyone prefers this conformity to a situation where some minority would not conform to it. Moreover, the conventional regularity in question is not the only possible one that could meet these conditions: some alternative could have perpetuated itself as a convention instead of the one that did so. Finally, the conditions just specified are matters of "common knowledge" to the members of the population: at least potentially, they are known to everyone, it is known to everyone that they are known to everyone, and so on.

Before we move on to the question of how this concept might be applied in a literary context, it is important to introduce a few remarks about some of the more general assumptions that have to be in place for this kind of approach to be viable. In the light of some of the extreme theses of recent critical theory, it may be necessary to point out that talk of "problems," "decisions," "expectations," and so on places us in a conceptual framework that is by no means neutral with regard to a number of fundamental issues in the philosophy of the human sciences. For example, game theory—and therefore Lewis's notion of convention—requires that we make certain minimal assumptions about the capacities of the "players" or "agents" who figure in a given game or situation. It is fashionable today to reject these assumptions as excessively "rationalistic," but such charges are ill-informed: game theorists do not contend that we should always assume that all players adopt optimal strategies based on perfect knowledge of the situation. In some game-theoretical models, for example, a single player is composed of a number of agents that are not even aware of one another's moves and strategic rationales (Harsanyi and Selten 1988, 30–33). Interpreted psychologically, such a model amounts to describing a game played by someone with multiple personalities that move in turn, each of which is oblivious to the others. It should be clear then that there is no requirement in game theory that we have to assume that players are perfect philosophical Subjects.

Even so, it is necessary to adopt some modest theses about the players' ability to engage in intentional action based on practical reasoning. We must assume first of all that we may attribute to the players certain mental states having semantic content. Moreover, it must be assumed that these states figure in genuine explanations of the behavior of the players: for example, what a player does can be explained in terms of action descriptions in which the player's doings are linked to decisions, which are in turn linked to the player's preferences and beliefs. In short, the game-theoretical framework implies that we describe players or agents whose behavior can be explained in terms of "reasons"— including a variety of attitudes. As I point out in more detail below, these theses will be accompanied in any particular model by other assumptions chosen from among a variety of possibilities, ranging from very strong to very weak constraints on the players' rationality. Thus Lewis (1969) speaks of "ancillary premises regarding our rationality" (53) and of the player's knowledge that another player possesses "a modicum of practical rationality" (57). Both of these statements about rationality assumptions could be specified in a number of significantly different ways in descriptions of different strategic situations.[7] It may be worthwhile to point out, however, that there must be at least some minimal assumptions about the players' practical rationality if we are dealing with a genuinely strategic situation, that is, players must rely on expectations about the other's actions in deciding what to do, as opposed to assuming that the outcome depends uniquely on their own decisions.

The basic assumptions that I have just evoked specify what kinds of items can be viewed as players or agents in a strategic situation, namely, those entities capable of manifesting behavior explicable in terms of reasons. This seemingly trivial point is important to keep in mind in the context of contemporary literary theory, for it implies that it would be misleading to try to apply Lewis's theory to relations be- tween purely textual or discursive entities.[8] If conventions are doings guided by expectations, as Lewis clearly says, then texts and their fea- tures cannot literally be conventions, because texts are not the kind of things that exhibit behavior or that have any of the different sorts of mental states that are grouped beneath the rubric of "reasons." The seeming intentionality of texts is in fact on loan from the agents who make and use them: texts do not expect, believe, or prefer anything, and they do not literally have any problems. Two texts cannot coordi- nate their decisions because they have none to coordinate.

The right way to explain literary texts within the framework in ques- tion here is to perform a pragmatic analysis in which the texts are linked to actual intersubjective relations in which they figure as a form of mediation. In other words, it is a matter of explaining why texts are made and used in one way as opposed to other possible ways, and of couching such an explanation in terms of the purposive behavior of the agents involved, not uniquely in terms of the immanent properties of features of texts. This does not mean that reference to objective textual features can play no explanatory role in such a context, but that this role must be linked in the right way to references to an agent's cognitive or other relations to the text's properties. Thus, we would try to explain a particular textual feature by linking it to an author's reasons (for example, a desire to have this or that impact on a potential reader, etc.), just as we might try to explain a reader's reception of the text in terms of the reader's reasons, reasons that typically include various inferences about the writer's mental states. In short, Lewis's concept of convention and the whole apparatus of the theory of interdependent situations is not applicable to the world of blind, nonintentional textual production. But given that the latter is a romantic fantasy meant to defy explanation, this is hardly surprising.

To resume my argument, I am claiming that any successful literary application of Lewis's theory of conventions and, more generally, of the theory of interdependent decisions, will rest upon certain nontrivial assumptions having to do not only with the kinds of entities that must figure in literary processes but also with the nature of literary explanations. More specifically, the assumption is that literary situations are primarily composed of relations (and interactions) between agents, these relations being mediated by discourse; literary explanations, then, would be a species of action explanation. The implication is that when a critic or scholar identifies a property of a text and describes it as conforming to a convention (in the sense of a property common to some larger corpus), this does not yet constitute a proper explanation, which would require that the critic also make good on some crucial additional claims about the beliefs, preferences, and expectations (of writers and readers) that contributed to the making of those recurrent textual properties. This point is important because many critics assume on the contrary that literary conventions are autonomous "discursive systems" that go about instantiating themselves in the production of individual discourses having certain typical features. Such an assumption sets far too few constraints on the scholar's search for significant regularities and tends to detach description from any cogent explanatory enterprise.

If Lewis's concept of convention is to be applied successfully to literature, then it would be necessary to begin by finding viable analogues for the following key concepts: (a) the players and/or agents in a situation; (b) the goals sought by these agents, and more specifically, the common interests that could be served in more than one way without anyone preferring a different solution; (c) the doings of these agents that may or may not solve the problem of achieving their goals; and (d) the reasons (beliefs, expectations, preferences, etc.) that explain the agents' decisions about what to do in order to realize their goals. If some set of the doings mentioned under (c) become established and maintained as the regular way of solving a type of coordination problem for a given group, this being a conditional preference, the object of common knowledge, and so on, then these doings can be called conventions in Lewis's sense.

Given that it is highly unlikely that all literary situations correspond to Lewis's coordination problems, it would seem advisable to anticipate some of the other variables that may be identified within the general framework of a theory of interdependent decisions before we begin to try to find the right literary analogues for Lewis's notions. To begin, it would seem safe to assume that not all of the goals of agents in literary situations coincide. Consequently, the models should include conflicting goals, some of which could be properly literary goals. What is more, it is important to identify relations between these different goals, especially when the goals stand in instrumental or means-end relations to each other. It seems safe to say that actual literary situations are likely to combine a variety of goals in complex relations, just as the members of the MLA must meet in order to compete.

In the coordination problems and solutions singled out by Lewis, the agents involved share common knowledge of one another's policies, preferences, and payoffs. In a more comprehensive theory, this type of situation will be placed alongside situations of incomplete information, which may result from a number of different conditions. Players may have limited knowledge of any or all of the following kinds of factors: (1) the actual consequences that will result from any particular combination of decisions adopted by the various agents involved; (2) the ways in which the other agents rank different possible consequences in terms of their relative preferences for them; (3) the other agents' attitudes toward risk; and (4) the amount of reliable information other players have about any of the factors just listed. Game theorists refer to these factors in discussing the extent to which the players in a situation have "complete" information. But they also draw a distinction between perfect and imperfect information: situations in which there is "perfect information" are those in which all players know the nature of the game as well as all of the moves that have previously been made within it.

There are, then, various possible assumptions that theorists may make about the players' rationality, for it is not always the case that we should expect the players to make all and only optimal decisions. In mathematical game theory, concern for this issue motivates the distinction between pure and mixed strategies, the latter involving a random element. In an informal context, the same issue could be dealt with by weakening the assumptions about the rationality of the agents' deliberations. These assumptions have to do with the accuracy, coherence, and completeness of the players' background beliefs and information about the situation at hand; they concern the players' ability to draw the right inferences about which move is most optimal in terms of their preferences and information; they also have to do with the ordering of the players' preferences. There is room here for many significant variations; as Martin Shubik has pointed out, there is "no single, narrow view of utility that is forced upon us by the game-theoretic approach" (1982, 81).

Other variables that should be kept in view have to do with objective features of the interactional situations being examined. Do players all move simultaneously or is there a temporal asymmetry of one form or another? In the coordination problems studied by Lewis, the agents make their decisions simultaneously, whereas it is clear that not all literary situations are of this sort. Another distinction concerns whether the situations are "static" or "dynamic," or in other words, whether the game is played only once or whether there is, on the contrary, a repetition of the same type of game with the same cast of players. Game theorists study both types of situations, but the concept of convention as Lewis develops it can only be properly applied in a dynamic context. This point has been overlooked in some of the literary applications of Lewis's views. The idea that should be kept in mind is stated by Lewis himself in the following passage: "A convention is so-called because of the way it persists, not because of the way it originated. A convention need not originate by convention — that is, by agreement — though many conventions do originate by agreement, and others could originate by agreement even if they actually do not. In saying that language is convention-governed, I say nothing whatever about the origins of language" (1975, 26).

Elsewhere Lewis underscores the same point by asserting that conventions are solutions to recurrent coordination problems, the idea being that different situations are similar enough for people to solve them by means of a common solution that, having once emerged, somehow persists. The theory of conventions is a hypothesis about how these solutions persist, not about what brought the solution about on the first occasion, and Lewis in fact points to a variety of different ways in which a particular solution might first arise (including salience, precedent, and agreement). It follows that there can be no conventional solution to a unique or "one-shot" coordination problem. This implies that the concept of convention only has explanatory value in relation to recurrent features of literary phenomena.

Finally, we come to two central and highly difficult concepts of game theory, the notions of "equilibrium" and "solution," which should be of particular interest to us if our goal is not simply a mechanical application of Lewis's notion of convention but the development of a more general and multifaceted analytical framework based on some basic game-theoretical insights. In game theory, an equilibrium (point) is defined as a combination of strategies having a particular property. Namely, each player's strategy is the best reply to all the other players' strategies. To grasp this point, suppose that I am a player in a one-shot game. Everyone has already decided what to do, and the outcome of the game (our respective payoffs) is settled. Let us also assume that I am not particularly happy with that outcome. Suddenly a *malin génie* whispers in my ear that he will let me replay the game if I like, and I can change my decision about what move to make this time around. But just as I am beginning to imagine the huge payoff that I am going to win, the demon adds that the moves of the other players will remain the same. If the previous combination of strategies was an equilibrium, I should at that point decline the demon's offer because I cannot possibly make a more advantageous choice. The same would be true for the others if the demon made the same offer to any one of them.

It should be noted that a single game may have many such equilibria, which is precisely the difficulty in Lewis's coordination problems, where the issue is a matter of getting everyone to settle on one of several possible equilibria. Lewis's notion of convention, then, is a type of solution to a situation characterized by more than one equilibrium. The critic who complains that most literary texts are not conventional in Lewis's sense because the features of literary works are motivated rather than arbitrary is essentially claiming that the majority of literary situations do not have more than one coordination equilibrium and hence do not allow a conventional solution.[9] Instead of asking whether all literary regularities can be explained as conventions, we might better ask what different kinds of equilibria and solutions characterize different kinds of literary situations.

With this range of parameters in mind, I turn now to the specific question of which aspects of Lewis's concept of convention have a direct analogue in literary history. In a seemingly obvious and straightforward application of the model, literary "situations" would be assumed to be a special kind of "communication," which Lewis himself has approached as a species of coordination problem. In that case, one could conceive of the following literary analogues to items (a)–(c) above: (a) the players/agents are writers, speakers, readers, listeners, spectators, etc. of a certain delimited population, or, in other words, those who participate in literary activities (henceforth I shall for the sake of convenience mention only writers and readers); (b) the writer's goal is that of writing a literary work and of having it be understood and evaluated by readers in some preferred way as opposed to other possible ways. We should observe that this clause does not necessarily involve the assumption that the writer always wants to get the reader to understand the work in some particular, highly detailed manner; rather, the writer's goal could be the very broad one of getting readers to respond in some general way. The reader's goal is that of understanding and evaluating a literary work in some preferred way; and (c) the players' relevant activities are the particular practices of writing and reading they adopt, thereby realizing or failing to realize their common goals. Those conditionally preferred discursive practices that prevail in a given population, bringing about coordination, are conventions. Given the right criteria, some subset of the latter could be further identified as properly literary conventions, beginning perhaps with those that enable people to engage in a specifically literary form of communicative interaction.

Yet this apparently straightforward manner of adapting the model is complicated by aspects of what Lewis himself has to say about the application of the theory of conventions to the problem of communication. Most importantly, in Lewis's treatment of the issue, the application requires the mediation of the concept of language, for he specifies that the conventional regularity of verbal behavior in a linguistic community or population, P, perpetuated by a common interest in coordination, is a matter of the use of a certain language, £, as opposed to at least one other possible language, £'. Now, it is of course possible to take up Lewis's definition of convention without accepting any of his statements about language, but it would seem prudent, at the very least, to examine his reasoning before making any such decision. His basic claim is that the solutions to communicational coordination problems are typically (but not always) made possible by the convention of using a certain language. Given that most literary practices are linguistic or include and rely upon a natural language, the literary scholar interested in Lewis's proposals must consider whether the basic linguistic convention that Lewis posits is not alone sufficient to account for whatever literary coordinations may occur; should the response be negative, it would still be necessary to ask whether any of the specifically literary conventions that might be discovered could not be said to function in an analogous manner, in which case it would be a matter of positing the operation of a convention to use a literary language.

Lewis comments that "under suitably different conventions, a different language would be used by P. There is some sort of convention whereby P uses £—but what is it? It is worthless to call it a convention to use £, even if it can correctly be so described, for we want to know what it is to use £. My proposal is that the convention whereby a population P uses a language £ is a convention of *truthfulness* and *trust* in £" (1975, 7). Lewis goes on to explain that to be truthful in £ is to avoid uttering sentences in the language that are not true in that language; trusting in a language is imputing truthfulness to those who make utterances in that language. He comments that the regularity of being truthful and trusting in whichever language is used by one's fellows "neither is a convention nor depends on a convention" (1975, 30).

What is a convention, then, is that in a given population the regularity of truthfulness and trust *simpliciter* happens to take the form of truthfulness and trust in a particular language, £, and not in another logically possible £'. It may hardly seem arbitrary that a particular person uses the particular language employed in the community into which he or she was born and raised, but the individual's preference for this language is conditional in the sense that under certain conditions, the individual would have preferred to employ a different language. Thus, Lewis's many mentions of the convention of truthfulness and trust should always be understood as referring to a convention of truthfulness and trust in a particular language, conditionally preferred to the exercise of the very same attitudes in another possible language. Adopting the attitudes of truthfulness and trust as such is not a conditional preference and is hence not a conventional stance in Lewis's view. I stress this point because it is not emphasized in the pertinent passages in *Convention* (1969), but it is underscored in the later essay (1975) and has important implications for talk of conventions being constitutive of literary discourse as a whole.

Lewis's insistence on conformity to a convention of truthfulness and trust seems especially inappropriate to literature. Here we may usefully refer to Lewis's response to the anticipated objection that such activities as joking, telling tales, and social rituals could be instances of using a language £ without being a matter of any usage that conforms to the convention that he has described. Lewis sketches three possible responses to this objection, each of which is potentially pertinent to a literary adaptation of his model. One response involves constructing a definition of a "serious communication situation" in regard to which the stipulations concerning the convention of truthfulness and trust could be said to hold. Other situations would simply be left unspecified, but the central claim about the importance of the role of convention in language would remain intact insofar as no language could persist for long without any serious communication taking place in it. Another option involves characterizing the nonserious cases as violations of the conventions of language, albeit "explicable and harmless ones." Again, the theory of the conventional nature of language use is defended, but at the cost of a largely negative characterization of categories of linguistic behavior that seem fairly central to literary history.

Lewis's other approach, which is the one he develops in the most detail, is to suggest that the apparent violation of his conventions in so-called nonserious language use is not actually a violation of the language but only of a simplified approximation to it. In fact, the speakers' and hearers' knowledge of £ includes not only the standard attitudes of truthfulness and trust but also the contextual signs and features by means of which "nonserious" uses of language can be recognized. Thus, what would appear to count as a breakdown of truthfulness and trust is not really one. As soon as a hearer or speaker is in one of the contexts of an alternative use of language, the attitudes of truthfulness and trust are altered in an appropriate manner. Lewis says little about the nature of these contextual shifts and merely allows for them by speaking of the possibility of a "polymodal language," in which a number of "mood" operators would be added to the functions that assign meanings to strings of types of sounds or inscriptions (1975, 14; 1969, 185–95). When employed, such operators would alter the behavioral implications of the standard attitudes of "truthfulness" and "trust." In the schematic example that Lewis provides, when a sentence is marked as being in the imperative mood, the former attitude of truthfulness would become the attitude "that we might call *obedience* in £" (1975, 15; 1969, 184). Presumably the sentences occurring in such contexts of usage as "telling tales" would undergo some analogous operation whereby their truth-values would be transformed into the appropriate kind of modalized response.

Those who are tempted to follow this suggestion by constructing a theory of a literary mood (to be based, no doubt, on some combination of aesthetical and fictional notions) should, however, take note of some of Lewis's other remarks. In an example of a contextual modification of the attitudes of truthfulness and trust, Lewis suggests that "what would otherwise be an untruth may not be one if said by a child with crossed fingers." This phrase suggests that literary contexts would be signaled by some kind of array of conventional liminal signs, ranging from the words "Once upon a time" to "A Novel." But Lewis continues: "Unfortunately, the signs and features of context by which we recognize nonserious language use are seldom as simple, standardized, and conventional as that" (1975, 28). Lewis's observation here is quite correct and conflicts directly with the prospect of any straightforward application in which some convention or set of conventions would serve to mark off categories of nonserious usage, including some class of aestheticized or "literary" contexts.

Moreover, Lewis's aforementioned comments about the *nonconventional* nature of the "default" attitudes of truthfulness and trust in £ should be carried over to their modalized variants. The modal attitude of obedience—to use Lewis's own example—is *not* a convention. To paraphrase Lewis's remarks, the regularity of being obedient (or playful, or literary, etc.) is neither a convention nor depends on a convention. What is a convention, then, is that the regularity of obedience *simpliciter* happens to take the form of obedience in a particular language, £, and not in another logically possible £' in a given population. Thus, we are far from having established that the class of specifically literary linguistic behavior, should such a class be imagined to exist, could be marked off by Lewisian conventions. Instead, the various attitudes of playfulness, feigning, truthfulness, trust, and so on precede the entire apparatus of a particular language £, to which they are connected by purely conditional preferences. What is conventional is not being playful, earnest, and so forth, but being playful *in this particular £ and not another possible £'.* If we imagine the existence of a set of alternative possible literary languages that a given community could adopt for the purpose of engaging in literary communication, then the choice between them could be "conventional," provided that these different languages are all equilibria. Of course, no one has ever provided any such model, and even should one be provided, it would not be the literary convention as such that would explain why people adopt the literary mode of language use at any given point or why they ever adopt it at all. We should note as well that Lewis contends that not all communicative coordinations necessarily require conventions (1969, 158), which suggests that at least some instances of literary communication would not have conventions as their conditions of possibility.[10] Yet should a category of literary linguistic communicative behavior be established, it remains possible that conventional coordinations would be a subset of the solutions found within it.

If the use of a language is a conditional preference for one £ as opposed to other possible £'s, involving such attitudes as truthfulness and obedience, whose behavior is being coordinated in this manner? Lewis's (1969) comments suggest that it is a matter of a coordination of the behavior of different speakers, but in another text he provides a broader view, the change in the initial theory having been prompted by suggestions made by Jonathan Bennett.[11] Lewis proposes that communicative coordination has direct and indirect forms. The direct form coordinates the efforts of a truthful speaker and a trusting hearer, both of whom conform to the regularity of using the language £ because they expect the other to engage in a complementary conformity. In the case of the coordination of speakers and hearers in a conversation (or in the case of a relation between writers and readers mediated by written texts), successful communication hinges on some degree of reciprocal or shared understanding. More basically, it hinges on the direct coordination of the intentions of speakers with the belief acquisitions of hearers. Suppose, then, that S wants someone else to believe that S means p and utters u to that end. S wants the hearer, H, to know that S means p by u. In hearing u, H wants to know what S meant by it. Coordination is achieved if S utters u to communicate u, and H does believe that what S means by u is p. So much for the direct form of coordination (although we have hardly begun to fathom here the complexities of the "Gricean" mechanism that is often thought to be at work in such relations).[12]

The indirect form of coordination that Lewis imagines is far more extensive, being described by him as a "four-way affair," extending between present speakers and past speakers, present speakers and past hearers, present hearers and past speakers, and present hearers and past hearers: "in coordinating with his present partner, a speaker or hearer also is coordinating with all those whose past truthfulness and trust in £ have contributed to his partner's present expectations" (1975, 8). It should be clear that a number of issues would have to be dealt with if these remarks were to be carried over to a literary context. For example, it would be necessary to specify how the temporal relations identified in the last passage are concretized in contexts of literary communication where the present speakers and hearers (viz., the writer and the reader) are not necessarily copresent to each other in the same time and place. If I am reading a text by a given author, who exactly is involved in the indirect coordination that extends between the present speaker and past hearers? In principle, the answer would embrace any and all readers who could in some way or other have shaped that author's present expectations, that is, those expectations that he or she had about the future public at the time when he or she was composing the text that I am now reading.

2

In this section I focus on the role of convention in what I consider to be a highly successful example of literary analysis, Lars Lönnroth's *Njáls Saga: A Critical Introduction.*[13] That Lönnroth's work is particularly relevant in the present context is evidenced by the fact that he devotes an entire chapter, "The Language of Tradition," to a description of the many "standard ingredients" that existed before the writing of the saga. Indeed, the critic's emphasis on the concept of convention is established by the following bold declaration at the beginning of the chapter: "The composition of *Njála* was governed by a set of narrative conventions established long before the saga was written" (1976, 42). Lönnroth's frequent use of "convention" and "conventional" is not explicitly Lewisian, for he nowhere proposes a definition of the term and does not refer to the philosopher. Yet one may nonetheless ask whether his usage is compatible with — or could be said implicitly to conform to — Lewis's notion. Answering this question will allow me to illustrate some of the issues involved in applying Lewis's theory in a literary context, and I hope to show that Lönnroth's analysis manifests a very strong position, indeed, an exemplary explanatory model, in regard to the kinds of issues evoked above.

Lönnroth argues that the anonymous author of the saga had heard or read enough sagas to have been highly familiar with their recurrent traits, and as a result was in a position to recall and employ the traditional elements "without having to depend on any particular saga, or even a particular genre" (1976, 42). Lönnroth convincingly demonstrates that *Njála* contains many standardized narrative and stylistic elements that figure in a number of other sagas. Examples include highly formulaic ways of composing such small discursive segments as descriptions (e.g., the introduction of a new character) and scenes (discrete narrative segments presenting a dramatic situation). Among the stock scenes figuring in *Njála* and other sagas are such items as "a hero is presented at a foreign court and accepted as one of the king's men," and "a woman goads her kinsman to take revenge on her enemy by suggesting that he is a coward if he does not" (1976, 47–48). Not only is the inclusion of such scenes in the saga a formulaic procedure, but the saga writer could employ an established way of presenting them, using set phrases and terms. For example, many lexical choices the author made in presenting his characters were conventional: "Here Sigmundr's appearance and character are described in conventional phrases found throughout saga portraits of typical troublemakers. . . . One of the adjectives used to describe Sigmundr is a French loanword (*kurteiss,* from the French *courtois*), but it had become conventional in saga portraits by the end of the thirteenth century" (1976, 49).

Convention, then, is undoubtedly an important concept in this critic's approach. Yet Lönnroth's consistent attention to the originality of the composition, as well as his detailed discussion of the particular features of the writer's pragmatic context, attenuates the claim that the composition was governed by conventions. As we read on, we learn that the author of the saga engaged in a "clerical 'reinterpretation' of tradition" and that this selective shaping of traditional materials was "characteristic of this particular author's method" (1976, 106–7). The formulaic procedures evoked earlier are contrasted to many moments where the author diverges from them. Thus, Lönnroth comments that when Hrútr makes his prophetic remark that the young Hallgerðr has the eyes of a thief, this is a scene "unprecedented in saga literature." The scene is "traditional only in a general sense, for its motif is highly original, even though the presentation follows the general conventions for a saga scene" (1976, 49). Lönnroth's claim, then, is that conventional and unconventional procedures appear side by side in the text, which includes "both traditional and untraditional elements" (1976, 49).

At first glance, in Lönnroth's use of the word, "convention" would seem to be synonymous with "standardized and pre-existing element used in a number of literary compositions." Yet such an impression fails to take into account Lönnroth's systematic reference to the pragmatic dimensions of the literary process. For example, when Lönnroth notes that many saga writers slavishly followed certain conventional patterns, he goes on to sketch a causal account of this behavior, referring not only to the personal motivations of the writers but to their anticipation of the audience's reactions. Thus, he notes that the authors of stereotypical sagas were guided by "a force of habit, strengthened by the conventional expectations of the audience" (1976, 54). In another passage in which he characterizes the functioning of such conventional patterns for the Icelandic audience, Lönnroth comments that "the enjoyment of such a story probably came in recognizing a well-known narrative structure and in measuring this particular hero against the many other heroes who passed similar tests. Each listener would have in mind both the Travel Pattern and a number of traditional ideas of life abroad. A storyteller could count on this and thus would not have to spell out matters in detail — a few hints would be enough" (1976, 75). Similarly, Lönnroth comments that "in each of the feud episodes, the author's exposition thus appears to be ruled by convention, and in most cases the further development of action is determined by the author's choice of conventional opening, just as a chess player's game is determined by his initial choice of 'Queen's Gambit' rather than a 'Sicilian' or 'French' opening" (1976, 77–78).

It would appear that Lönnroth's use of the notion of convention harmonizes with the game-theoretical approach in at least one very important respect, namely, the emphasis on the analysis of situations constituted by complex relations between the author and the audience. As I have already suggested, the first step in every simple and straightforward application of Lewis's notion is to suppose that literary coordination problems and their conventional solutions are a matter of communication. That the author of a literary text wishes to communicate with his audience — in the sense of having certain beliefs be successfully conveyed to the public by his text, and this in the appropriate manner — is indeed an appropriate assumption in many contexts, for even when the author's goals are hardly restricted to that of conveying a precise message to a particular audience, achieving a minimal threshold of understanding is often a necessary means to whatever other ends the literary discourse is meant to realize.

Although there is no reason to assume that all of the author's and reader's goals coincide in the way that the recipe for a coordination problem requires, it is often appropriate to assume that both author and reader need to achieve a certain level of communicational coordination. Yet the assumption about common communicative ends is still far too general; in some instances, it might be sufficient to assume that the degree of communication that this assumption requires could be satisfied by the presence of a basic linguistic convention coordinating the author's and the reader's expectations. If we simply assume that what the author of *Njála* wanted was for his audience to "understand" his text in some blank and wholly general sense, then the fact that he knew that they were fluent in his language would have sufficed; the author would have had no need to follow any more specific conventions as long as he obeyed whatever regularities were involved in the use of the particular linguistic system that we call Old West Norse. It is also clear that in relation to the specific example, it will not do to claim that the relation between the author and the public is coordinated by some set of constitutive literary conventions—conventions that guarantee, for example, that the audience will adopt a "disinterested" attitude toward his discourse.

Lönnroth's analysis is based on more appropriate and detailed assumptions. His discussion of the pragmatic context of the text's creation and reception make it possible to fill in the general assumptions about the agents' goals that necessarily figure in any strategic model of a literary situation. Making sure that these elements are in place is crucial, and Lönnroth's study is rich in this respect. Lönnroth presents a highly detailed hypothesis concerning features of the rhetorical context within which the text was originally composed and received, and he assumes that the author's expectations about the public's response played a major role in guiding the author's compositional strategy. Writing a saga and presenting it to a particular public on specific types of occasions was not an activity determined uniquely by some system of autonomized textual codes, rules, or conventions but by the writer's practical deliberations about literary precedents and about the beliefs and preferences that were most likely to animate the audience's response. Lönnroth's filling in of this general point is masterful, and ranges from synthetic statements about the general conditions of authorship and reception in thirteenth-century Iceland to a detailed hypothesis about the particular occasion of the writing of *Njála*. In what follows, I present only a few of the broad strokes of that analysis.

The saga, Lönnroth proposes, was written in an aristocratic milieu "where the reading of chivalric romance had recently been introduced as a more refined alternative to drinking, dancing, and games. Yet the Icelandic version of this milieu appears to have been more rustic and homespun than its Norwegian equivalent, and it thus includes clerics as well as prosperous farmers and their families" (1976, 174). Sagas were likely to have been read aloud over a period of days on the occasion of ongoing festivities held at one of the larger farms, the entertainment being sponsored and financed by a wealthy chieftain family. In the case of *Njála*, there is good evidence for believing that the Svínfellings, an old and powerful family that held sway in southeastern Iceland at the time, was responsible for sponsoring the saga's writing and for hosting the earliest occasions upon which it would have been presented. Given that some of the central figures in the saga were well-known ancestors of the Svínfellings—including Flosi, infamous for having instigated and led the burning of Njáll—this situation of patronage was anything but a neutral and purely literary context; on the contrary, the author's attempt to write a saga that could be expected to please his audience developed under twin, and to some extent contrasting, constraints: on the one hand, the account proposed by his saga had to be largely faithful to the local tradition, both in its form and in its recounting of historical and legendary facts; on the other hand, the saga had to be flattering to the sponsors and, most of all, "compatible with the ambition of the Svínfellings to be regarded as good Christians and as great and venerable protectors of law and order" (1976, 177). Lönnroth establishes that the Svínfelling chieftains aspired to a particular form of authority, "based not only on their own local chieftainship in the Svínafell area but on a more grandiose legal tradition" (1976, 180).

In such a context, a saga that traced these chieftains' heritage back to certain prestigious historical figures would serve their interests. Moreover, Lönnroth shows that an element of the Svínfellings' ancestry—Flosi's infamous deed—"must have been embarrassing to the thirteenth century Svínfellings" (1976, 176). And thus Lönnroth conjectures that "the entire second part of our saga may, in fact, be described as an attempt to save Brennu-Flosi's reputation: it pictures him as a noble chieftain and a devout Christian who was driven against his will to burn Njáll in his home and who later regained his honor by making full atonement for his deed" (1976, 177).

Lönnroth presents a picture of an author who wanted to succeed at a highly specific rhetorical task, that of convincingly imparting a new significance to a well-established story while staying fairly close to the standard manner of recounting such events, as well as to the standard version of the facts. What is more, Lönnroth's inferences about the motives of the author of Njála include another major dimension, namely, the relation between his "clerical" and largely Augustinian world-view and those pagan attitudes associated with the tradition of the Icelandic sagas. Not only was it necessary for the author to coordinate his efforts with what he knew about the audience's expectations, beliefs, and preferences, but in so doing he had to coordinate two large components of his own background knowledge, components that amounted, in some respects, to mutually exclusive conventions. But what of the goals of the audience? In Lönnroth's account, the desire of the sponsors was to be entertained by a well-crafted yet traditional saga, a saga, moreover, that would portray their ancestors in a flattering light, publicly confirming their sense of honor and social prominence. Thus, the two sets of goals, those of the author and those of the sponsors, overlapped and could have been jointly realized by the action of reading a newly composed saga of the appropriate sort on the right occasion.

Was the successful performance of such a saga a solution to a coordination problem? If we were to assume that the goals of the authors and audiences of sagas were functionally identical across many situations of composition and reading, then we might imagine the existence of a set of conventional stories, any one of which would successfully serve to coordinate the participants' interests on a given occasion. We could even add that the formula for the stories to be told in such rituals could include a requirement concerning the necessity of flattering some of the hosts' ancestors, especially ones with less than spotless reputations. The formula could also specify that each new story should be grammatical (i.e., in conformity to the algorithm) but should also include enough unusual variations to seem fresh or even innovative. As long as a typical saga is told, the needs of those participating in such an occasion would be met. What Lönnroth claims, however, is that *Njála* is not a text that belongs to a larger corpus of stories of this sort — although he does refer favorably in passing to the idea that the conventional aspects of saga composition may be analogous to the operation of a generative grammar (1976, 48). But insofar as the goals that motivated the writing and reception of *Njála* did not define a recurrent situation for the author and his public, the writing of this *new* saga was not in a global and strict sense a coordination problem amenable to a conventional solution following Lewis's definition. Lönnroth consistently argues, then, for a position that amounts to viewing the text as a solution to a problem-situation that differed significantly from other literary occasions.

To say that the situation in question differed significantly from other ones, however, is not to imply that it shared no important features with any analogous situations. That it did is why some of the standard procedures could be incorporated into the composition, and indeed, one should strengthen this thesis by adding that the author would most likely have failed in his task had he departed entirely from the formulae of the saga. Along these lines, Lönnroth suggests that the author does not want his "foreign" sources and clerical attitudes to vitiate the form of the traditional saga: the author's literary education "is only sporadically revealed," and his Christian themes, "though extremely important in the overall structure, are hidden under thick layers of traditional saga motifs" (1976, 200). Weaving the new political themes and emphases into the old texture was an important facet of the rhetorical strategy adopted by the saga writer, for the rehabilitation of Flosi could only be convincing in such a context. Lönnroth conjectures that this rhetorical approach is motivated by the fact that at some points in his narrative, the author of *Njála* overtly breaks with the legends that were common knowledge at the time: Flosi is described as one of the first chieftains to convert to Christianity, and he is transformed from being one of the most active opponents of the Norwegians' Christian mission in Iceland into being one of those who were eager to support the new faith. Lönnroth comments that "to anybody familiar with the older and widespread accounts of the conversion of Iceland, this must have been a radical departure—so radical, in fact, that it could hardly have been accepted unless the author had skillfully integrated Flosi's new role as missionary hero with an otherwise completely traditional account" (1976, 177). We may note as well that the author's goals included avoiding any public perception that the events in *Njála* had been shaped by the author's desire to flatter his hosts, or worse still, by the author's obedience to some specific request made by them. Appearing to remain close to the traditional model of the saga was the way to achieve that end. Such an appearance could only be maintained by actually adopting many of the standard procedures and formulae of saga composition.

One might thus be prompted to speak of *Njála* as having been motivated by a "pseudo-conventional" strategy: globally, neither the problem nor its solution was conventional in a strict sense, but the rhetorical effect desired required an appearance of the conventional, which was in turn only made possible by genuine recourse to conventions at a local level. We should recall here that the reading aloud of a saga and an audience's response to it were linear processes unfolding in time, comprising any number of discrete moments, some of which could have involved an unnuanced delivery and recognition of wholly traditional and standardized saga formulae. At these local moments, then, the author and audience were satisfied with the choice of a particular type of narrative procedure drawn from a set of equally plausible and acceptable choices, all of which could have served as equilibria. It is in this sense that the actual choice of a scene of goading, as opposed to another possible variation, was genuinely conventional. Yet globally, the narrative transaction was not conventional, for there was no other "language" that would serve the purposes of this community's ceremonial entertainment equally well. Viewed as a whole, the desire to recount and to listen to some variation on the traditional saga's phrases, scenes, images, and actions was anything but a "conditional preference" for one possible equilibrium among others.

As I emphasized in the first half of this chapter, any adequate analysis of interaction must rest on claims about the extent to which the parties involved have complete and accurate information about the actions, beliefs, and motives of the others. This is the case because for the parties involved, expectations about the others' behavior are precisely what is required for making decisions about what to do. Although it is possible to assume that none of the agents' decisions is based on expectations of this sort, it is usually more accurate to assume, on the contrary, that agents are in fact guided by the "modicum of practical rationality" to which Lewis refers. Thus, although someone may play chess without thinking very much about what the opponent is going to do next, such a person will be quickly defeated by anyone who is even slightly competent. When I observe that someone plays well, I had better assume that his or her moves are indeed chosen in terms of anticipated responses.

Similar reasons explain why it is appropriate for the literary scholar to devote a great deal of attention to an author's expectations about his audience's background beliefs and preferences, which is precisely what Lönnroth does.[14] Given the nature of the evidence with which scholars are dealing and the historical rift between the contemporary scholar and the affairs and attitudes of thirteenth-century Iceland, there is no guarantee that even the most well-supported hypothesis about the beliefs and attitudes of the author and his audience will be true. Yet sometimes the available evidence makes it possible to give a fairly strong justification for very fine-grained assumptions about what the author thought he could take for granted as common knowledge in a particular literary situation. For example, Lönnroth points out that the text of *Njála* is marked by a revealing, systematic discrepancy in its deployment of place names and topographical information: the text is accurate, but not always very specific, in evoking locations in southeastern Iceland, while it is at once more explicit and less accurate in regard to southwestern Iceland. The inference drawn from these well-established features of the text is that the author was highly familiar with the southeast and took it for granted that his audience would know the precise locations of the farms mentioned; at the same time, the author was less familiar with the southwestern part of the country and expected his audience to be in a similar position (whence the occasional error as well as the effort to give specific and detailed information).

In another example of this point, Lönnroth describes an author who makes various detailed assumptions about what his public would and would not know about the genealogy and kinship relations of members of the audience, local oral traditions, legal and religious institutions, and legendary events. He goes so far as to say about the author that "in dealing with native saga tradition and genealogy, he could scarcely appear too esoteric for his public" (1976, 200). Thus, Lönnroth describes the situation as one in which author and audience enjoyed detailed common knowledge and a coherent network of fairly accurate reciprocal beliefs. As a result, they were in a position to work with highly determinate expectations when making inferences about the communicative process. And as I have argued above, some of these expectations yielded properly conventional regularities of utterance and response.

Lönnroth's remarks about the particular nature of the author's rhetorical situation, however, introduce additional complexities into the analysis, particularly when we try to fathom the attitudes that went into the initial reception of the text. Here our evidence is sparse, but it is fairly safe to conjecture that the saga writer was fairly successful in attempting a subtle balance between the traditional saga form and his more occasional political and genealogical themes. This implies that his sponsors were gratified by the rehabilitation of Flosi, which they could not fail to notice. But at the same time they had reason to feel that the tradition had been suitably respected. The sense of this latter clause is anything but precise, and one may only speculate about the degree to which its filling in would require reference to attitudes of fully fledged hypocrisy or some more or less subtle variety of bad faith or self-deception. Here we may note that the saga writer was not operating with any of the more idealized or extreme assumptions about the rationality of his audience, at least in the sense that he expected that at least some of the contradictions between facets of his message would not be perceived, or at the very least emphasized, by the audience, perhaps as a result of wishful thinking: the satisfaction derived from hearing a tale in which Flosi's image is positively transformed would overwhelm any cognitive scruples about the facts of the matter, as well as any stance about the sanctity and precedence of the legends that had provided a very different account of the infamous ancestor's deeds.

My discussion of Lönnroth's analysis of the pragmatic conditions of the production and initial reception of the text should not lead us to assume that the critic's goal was to reduce the significance of *Njála* to a single, historically remote context. On the contrary, for Lönnroth remarks that the genealogical and political implications of the saga "constitute only a small part of its 'meaning' as a whole — an undercurrent easily disregarded by modern readers, who can enjoy the story of Gunnarr and Njáll without caring at all about the heritage of the Svínfellings" (1976, 187). This last remark raises additional questions about a pragmatic analysis of literature, for we may ask what becomes of an emphasis on the reciprocal expectations and common knowledge linking a writer and the public when we turn to the examination of such long-term and extended relations as those that may be said to exist between the anonymous author of *Njála* and as diffuse a group as that consisting of "modern readers." The author of *Njála* could hardly have many highly *specific* expectations about modern readers, and it is likely that those he could have had would not correspond to many modern readers' ideas about a wide range of issues, including those that directly concern the making and reception of a literary discourse. For example, Lönnroth is probably right in contending that the idea that sagas were primarily vehicles for the self-expression of individual authors is a background belief that certain modern readers bring to the saga, a belief, moreover, that did not figure in the author's motivations and self-understanding. To make this kind of judgment does not entail that one holds the view that the only reasonable, correct, or legitimate interpretations and evaluations of *Njála,* or of any other text, are those that the author sought to arouse in some particular audience. For example, when read in the context of contemporary theories about the nature of cycles of revenge, *Njála* is a text that takes on a value and significance that are hardly wedded to the author's original project.[15] Thus, the point to be kept in mind is that distinct types of explanatory aims may guide scholars' orientations toward a single work.

Reflection on the historical conditions of literary communication does have implications for how we conceive of different kinds of literary explanations and of the role certain concepts can play within them. When a literary scholar guided by the interests and orientations of romantic aesthetics approaches a text such as *Njála,* seeking to rescue from the work a number of particularly modern values and meanings, the interaction mediated by the text is no longer a matter of a coordination of different agents' overlapping goals, unless we construe the latter in such a loose and general way as to invent a possible intersection of ends. What goals does the author of *Njála* have in common with the critic who might today publish a deconstructive reading of the text? It is even less likely that such a case could accurately be presented as an instance of a *communicational* coordination, for fairly obvious reasons. Although *we* might decide to work with some conception of a specifically literary form of communication whereby the intersection of intended and received meanings need not be great (or could even be null) for successful communication to occur, it remains the case that the ancient author had no intention of engaging in any such form of communication, for the simple reason that no such notion of literariness or textuality figured within his system of beliefs. The implication in the present context is that in regard to cases of modern, aestheticized receptions of an ancient text, we can hardly speak of any features of the text as functioning as conventional solutions to a coordination problem in Lewis's sense. Only in an attempt to explain the text's role and significance within some context of genuine, communicational interaction does the notion of convention potentially have any genuine explanatory value, and in such a context, that value is a function of the degree to which the text's standardized features played the right kind of role within a recurrent type of situation.

CHAPTER FIVE

Hobbes on Literary Rules and Conventions

PAUL DUMOUCHEL

Hobbes was a friend of the Muses, and although he wrote little on the subject of literature, he has been credited with having exercised a considerable influence on the development of English literary criticism. Donald F. Bond (1937) saw in him one of the fathers of psychological criticism, as did Clarence Thorpe (1940), who extensively studied his influence on Abraham Cowley and John Dryden. Joel Elias Spingarn (1908) and Basil Willey (1934) argued that Hobbes's mechanical conception of nature shaped Augustan literary thought and played a major role in the movement for a plainer style that culminated in the Royal Society's program to reform language.[1] George Watson (1955) bestowed on Hobbes the uncertain honor of having killed metaphysical conceit, while Theodor M. Gang (1956) and Raman Selden (1974) defended him from this charge. More recently Miriam Riek (1977) challenged Spingarn's thesis. According to her, Hobbes's poetics remains close to older rhetorical texts and contains little that prefigures neoclassical theory. Sascha Talmor (1984) adopted a similar point of view but directed her criticism specifically against Thorpe, denying any relationship between Hobbes's psychological theory and his literary criteria. Beyond the various debates concerning his exact role and the precise influence of his thought, there is overall agreement that Hobbes played a major part in the transition from Jacobean sensibility to neoclassical aesthetics. *The Answer of Mr. Hobbes to Sir Will. Davenant's Preface before Gondibert* (1650) has become a standard item in any anthology of seventeenth-century criticism.[2]

Interestingly enough, very few commentators have attempted to relate Hobbes's poetics to other aspects of his philosophy, with the exception of his psychological theory. And this restricted connection has generally been established by extensively quoting Hobbes's definitions of "wit" and "fancy" in the *Leviathan* (1651a). This situation may be partially explained by the fact that most critics interested in Hobbes's poetics have not been philosophers. The questions they have asked have been historical and have centered on the issue of Hobbes's influence. Conversely, most philosophers interested in Hobbes have given little attention to his conception of literature. Even today, then, the relation between Hobbes's philosophy and his literary conceptions is generally left unspecified, being for the most part subsumed beneath the rubric of the conjunction "also": Hobbes *also* wrote about literature, just as he *also* played tennis and the lute.

Yet an analysis of Hobbes's poetics in relation to his central philosophical tenets could, I believe, provide a major test of his consistency. Hobbes's literary conceptions are presented as a set of conventions, or at least rules, pertaining essentially to epic poetry. The status and nature of these rules or conventions were never clearly analyzed by Hobbes, which is somewhat surprising since convention is one of the central categories of his philosophy. What, then, one might ask, is the status of these literary conventions when compared to the social contract, the laws of the Sovereign, or even the conventions that, following Hobbes, gave rise to language? Hobbes, like all of his contemporaries, believed that one of the functions of epic poetry was to partake in the moral and political education of men. Given his keen understanding of the potentially disruptive effect of literary texts on political order, it is certainly of interest to understand whether, and how, he accommodated his praise of epic poetry to the needs of political stability and to his repeated criticism of classical authors.[3] Finally, Hobbes's concept of convention has recently come under potent criticism, which I shall review more carefully later on. What is noteworthy is that Hobbes's poetics provides clear counterexamples to two reproaches often directed against his idea of convention: an excessive reliance on explicit agreement (Lewis 1969; Watkins 1976)[4] and a total rejection of tradition (Hayek 1973). This again raises either the issue of consistency or that of the validity of current readings of Hobbes, which may well be in need of revision.

The vast research program evoked above by far exceeds the scope of this chapter, which has the more modest aim of covering some preliminary ground. More specifically, I analyze Hobbes's literary rules and conventions in light of his concept of convention. At the same time I wish to provide a measured defense of his approach.

Historical Background

Hobbes simply took convention to be rational agreement between persons.[5] In order to grasp the far-reaching consequences of this apparently innocuous definition, it is useful to establish the main features of the historical context within which Hobbes intervened. My goal is by no means to provide a historical analysis of the concept of convention but to map out some of the uses to which the term had been put, up until the seventeenth century, so as to shed light on the kinds of things that were usually taken to be conventions, and on the ideas that were closely associated with or contrasted to the notion.

Classically, what is conventional is opposed to what is natural. In such contexts, convention is associated with changing customs and local traditions, its characteristic traits being parochialism and mutability in contradistinction to the stability and uniformity of nature. This opposition also indicates the artificial character of conventions. They are human artifacts and not simply the way of nature. Convention is also opposed to reason. To some extent, the grounds of this opposition are the same. Conventions are contingent and changing, while reason yields only universal and immutable truths. The latter distinction emphasizes the unmotivated and arbitrary character of conventions in relation to the firm foundations of what is rational. It also indicates that not all that is artificial is conventional. In the light of this opposition, conventions were conceived historically in two very different ways, which played an important role in the modern development of the concept. On the one hand, the opposition tended toward a clear antagonism; "convention" referred to superstitious traditions and unnatural customs contrary to reason. On the other hand, it tended toward an amiable accommodation. "Convention" came to designate, not what is inimical to reason, but the domain of things indifferent, a region where reason was without prescriptive force and that could thus be abandoned to the arbitrariness of human will and fancy (Manley 1980). It is this domain that Hobbes enlarged to encompass most of social life. He argued that although reason does not determine the content of our conventions, it forces us under pain of war and disorder to agree to one convention or another.

These oppositions were, of course, bound to change with the transformation of our concepts of nature, reason, and tradition. In the sixteenth and seventeenth centuries, "ancient traditions of the land," "immemorial customs," and, somewhat later, "the general practice of mankind" came to be seen as normative ideas through which "use becomes a second nature" (Manley, 90–106). As a result, the arbitrary conventions of human agents came to be contrasted with the very ideas of custom and tradition to which they had previously been closely linked. This shift signaled a new turn in the concept of convention. Because of its intimate relation to the ideas of custom and tradition, convention had generally not been perceived as deriving from an agreement, though explicit agreements were by no means excluded from its domain. Once the age of a tradition was seen as a sign of the general consent of mankind, this universal agreement became proof of its reasonableness. It indicated that the tradition was founded in reason and nature, not in mere human decision. Consequently, traditions lost their arbitrary character. They could not be otherwise than they were. Ancient traditions, then, were not rational, for at some point in time people had agreed to them. Ancient traditions were rational, since all agents concurred in perpetuating them, and since this uniformity of opinion in turn made them akin to some universal law of nature or reason. The classical opposition was maintained, but customs and traditions changed sides.

Hobbes's achievement in this context was to forge a concept of convention that construed its arbitrary character as consonant with, rather than as opposed to, reason. It was the rationality of the agreement itself that made a convention rational for Hobbes, rather than general consent, which often signals nothing more than a blind imitation of the past. The formal aspect of his concept — a convention is a rational agreement among agents — makes it highly tolerant, inasmuch as it says very little about the actual content of the convention. Nonetheless, because there are things to which no rational agent will agree, the concept retains a normative character, which allows Hobbes to use it as a formidable weapon against the claims of tradition.

Hobbes on Convention

When Hobbes speaks of conventions as rational agreements between agents, "agreement" should be understood in a fairly strong sense. Just as there are things to which no rational being would agree, those things in which all human agents concur are not agreed to at all, at least not in a sense that would make them conventions. Agreement is an action or a decision, and there is convention only where such an action is necessary—that is to say, only when alternative courses of action are open to the agents and they have to choose, agree, and settle on one of the options. The fact that they have to choose can also be construed in various ways that need to be spelled out. For one thing, it means that agents are rationally constrained to decide upon a course of action, which is what makes their agreement rational. To forbear decision would entail damage, or failure, and a lack of rationality in view of their interests.[6] Yet, as mentioned above, conventions also imply that reason cannot impose on them only one possible course of action. That is why agents are forced to choose from among a plurality of options. Finally, that they have to choose can mean that their agreement is not spontaneous. If, in a given situation, agents spontaneously and naturally converge on one solution, then it seems that no agreement, choice, or decision is needed. Would such instances of spontaneous "agreement" or coordination be a matter of convention for Hobbes?

It is clear that, in a sense, agreement is spontaneously reached with regard to those things in which all individuals concur. For Hobbes, we know, such concurrence should be viewed as a reasonably clear sign that what we are dealing with is *not* a convention (1656, 13-16). Conversely, spontaneous coordination is not a necessary sign of universal consent. Since at least David Hume (1739), philosophers have drawn attention to extremely local cases of spontaneous coordination, which they have often taken to be paradigmatic conventions. Recently authors like Hayek (1967, 1973), Thomas Schelling (1960), Lewis (1969), Robert Axelrod (1984), and Michael Taylor (1987) have argued that spontaneous coordination plays a fundamental role in social life, and these thinkers have offered sophisticated theoretical models of its possible emergence. Following Hayek (1973), Watkins (1976, 691-93) proposed that Hobbes believed spontaneous coordination to be impossible.

It certainly remains an open issue whether Hobbes thought all agreements should be made explicit, but it is evident that he did think some forms of spontaneous agreement were possible. One example, to which Crawford Brough Macpherson (1962, 62-65) gives perhaps too much importance, is the price of a commodity. In the *Leviathan* (1651a, 208) Hobbes argues that the fair price of a commodity is whatever parties in an exchange are willing to give, and it is clear from the context of the discussion that he did not think any agreement necessary other than the exchange itself. But the other most obvious example is Hobbes's conception of language. Language, Hobbes thought, antedates and makes possible all explicit agreements. He also believed that it rests on the consent of human agents, on conventions concerning the meaning of certain sounds, rather than on the nature of things (1651b, 296, 303; 1656, 13–28). Hobbes, then, certainly did believe spontaneous coordination could occur, at least in some cases.[7]

Did he take these to be conventions, rational agreements between agents? The correct answer, I think, is sometimes. To be more precise, Hobbes thought that some forms of spontaneous cooperation could turn out to be conventions, and that only those that could be seen as resulting from a rational agreement should be retained. As Watkins (1976) and Hans Vaihinger (1924) rightly pointed out, there is a strong "as if" tendency in Hobbes's philosophy. Hobbes did not believe that society was based historically on an original contract in the state of nature, but he argued that it could be seen "as if" it did. He also thought that only those rules that could be seen as resulting from this original contract were just and rational. This, as suggested before, gave Hobbes a powerful tool with which to counter the claims of tradition. In his discussions of the common-law tradition of England, Hobbes put forward two closely related arguments. First, he claimed that it has no legitimacy because it has never been agreed to, and that men should only be governed by laws to which they agree. Second, he suggested that the custom of precedents, which is the backbone of the common-law tradition, should be abolished because it entails rules to which no rational agent can agree. Given that all men are prone to error, says Hobbes, and because past judges have been known to err, the custom of precedents entails that past injustices, at least sometimes, will be imitated by future judges (1651a, 323–25; 1681, 119–20, 175–76, 184). Such a rule cannot be seen "as if" it had been agreed to by rational agents and cannot be a legitimate convention.[8] Hobbes's concept is intrinsically normative.

This creates a certain tension within his philosophy, and it is important to see how he resolves it. For Hobbes, what makes a convention a convention is the agreement from which it stems. This tends to identify a convention with its origin.[9] An agreement is rational if it was agreed to by rational agents, and thus is a convention in Hobbes's normative sense. Obviously, this is true only if the agreement actually took place. Given the arbitrary character of conventions, there are many things to which we could have agreed but did not. These nonetheless can be considered "as if" we had agreed to them. Clearly, these are not our conventions, and we cannot be bound in any way by such "as if" agreements. Yet this is exactly what Hobbes wants to do. He wants us to feel obligated to our government because it can be considered "as if" it resulted from an actual agreement in the state of nature. How is this possible? How can such hypotheses override our actual agreements?

The answer, I believe, has two parts. On the one hand, we should note that Hobbes's "as if" test applies to existing practices. Its goal is first and foremost to evaluate the rationality of the rules by which we already abide, rather than to propose new ones; although, as we shall see in the case of epic poetry, the latter is not excluded should our existing institutions prove to be irrational. The "as if" procedure is an evaluative device that may be applied to existing instances of spontaneous coordination.[10] On the other hand, the procedure is also a means of making our agreement explicit. In order to understand this, we need to remember that for Hobbes political philosophy is not only an explanatory discipline, it is also a political act. Quentin Skinner (1966, 1972a, 1972b) argued that the writing of the *Leviathan* should be considered as a political intervention, on the part of Hobbes, occurring at a crucial moment in the English Civil War.[11] Since then, numerous scholars have insisted on this interventionist dimension of Hobbes's philosophy, among them Sheldon Wolin (1970), Richard Ashcraft (1978), David Johnston (1986), and Mark Whitaker (1988). This is, I believe, the context in which the following oft-cited sentence at the end of the introduction to the *Leviathan* should be read: "Yet, when I shall have set down my own reading orderly, and perspicuously, the pains left another, will be onely to consider, if he also find not the same in himself. *For this kind of Doctrine, admitteth no other Demonstration*" (1651a, 83; my emphasis). Bringing his contemporaries to consider their present government, absolute monarchy, or parliamentary supremacy in 1651, "as if" it resulted from a rational agreement in the state of nature, that is as satisfying the conditions of the social contract, was for Hobbes a means of making their consent to that government explicit and binding, and hence of limiting the very dispute of the sword that plagued his country.

It may seem extremely naive and highly pretentious for Hobbes later on to have credited himself with having had such an influence.[12] But the important point is to understand why he believed the procedure to be efficient. The reason is that Hobbes deemed this procedure to be in use at all times, being at the root of major changes in our customs and traditions. We continually question the rationality of our ongoing practices in view of the ends toward which our agreements tend. Hobbes deemed this rational criticism to be the cause of all changes in religion (1651a, 179–82, 710–11),[13] just as he considered it to be an active element in the transformations impinging on poetics, as we shall see shortly. Hobbes clearly had important reasons for believing that it could serve to refine our political institutions. Conversely, he sought to limit the range of rational criticism in matters of government (1651a, chaps, 18, 21, 29; 1651b, chap. 12). The question of why certain things can be abandoned to spontaneous agreement and rational criticism, while others cannot, is crucial but will not be pursued here. For the present purposes, let us simply note that limits to the criticism of government are always imposed in reference to the purpose of the covenant, which is the protection of the subjects, and that Hobbes's attempts to convince his contemporaries to consider their institutions "as if" they proceeded from a rational agreement always remind them of that very purpose, namely, their protection.

The upshot of this discussion is that Hobbes's concept of agreement among rational agents promises to explain rationally both change and continuity in traditions and customs, while retaining the arbitrary character of conventions.

Literary Conventions

Hobbes's *Answer* (1650) to Davenant's *Preface before Gondibert* (1650) and his *Virtues of an Heroic Poem* (1675), which is the preface to the translation of Homer that he completed at the age of eighty-five, contain the fundamentals of his teaching on literature.[14] My goal in what follows is not to provide a complete analysis of these two texts but to determine the status of Hobbes's poetical rules. Two questions are at issue here. First, are these rules conventions in Hobbes's sense, that is, can they be seen as rational agreements between agents? Second, how does Hobbes's approach stand in relation to the conceptions of two of his modern critics, Lewis and Hayek?

The *Answer* opens with one eye on the audience. After briefly praising Davenant's poem, Hobbes mentions two objections that can be raised against his testimony, namely that he is an incompetent or a corrupt witness: "Incompetent, because I am not a Poet; and corrupted with the honor done me by your Preface" (1650, 45). In order to forestall the first, Hobbes embarks on an inquiry into the nature and species of poetry. From the beginning, poetry is placed under the sign of imitation and is defined by its goal: "by imitating humane life, in delightfull and measur'd lines, to avert men from vice, and encline them to vertuous and honorable actions" (1650, 45). It is important to note that imitation, for Hobbes, is a very broad concept that, as the introduction to the *Leviathan* suggests, encompasses just about all human activities.[15] What differentiates types of poetry is both the form and the object of this imitation, that is, the manners of men. Consequently, poetry is divided into three major forms, corresponding to the division of society into court, city, and country. Heroic poetry is appropriate to the manners of the court, scomatique to those of the city, and finally pastoral to the mores of the country folk. These three forms are each divided into two subgenres, depending on the means of representation (narrative or dramatic performance). In all, then, says Hobbes, there are exactly six forms of poetry: dramatic and heroic poetry, comedy and satire, pastoral comedy and pastoral or bucolic. The activity of the poet is further distinguished by a more precise definition of the object imitated: "But the subject of a Poeme is the manners of men, not naturall causes; manners presented, not dictated; and manners feyned (as the name of Poesy imports) not found in men" (1650, 46). This allows Hobbes to isolate poetry as a subset of all that is written in verse and at the same time, in three antitheses, to compare it to natural philosophy (Lucretius), ethics (Hesiod), and history (Lucian). Fictions written in prose Hobbes will reject from poetry, for, by far, prose is not as delightful as "measur'd lines."

The ground is now established on which Hobbes will evaluate Davenant's *Gondibert*. It is not very novel ground, as most of its elements were current in seventeenth-century criticism. Hobbes's only contribution so far, if there is any, is the manner in which the characteristic traits of poetry are closely related to its goal. On the basis of this definition, Hobbes will derive rules to judge Davenant's success, and these are the rules I intend to analyze in relation to Hobbes's concept of convention. Hobbes's definition of epic poetry I consider as describing a situation of literary communication in view of its goal: to divert men from vice and to encourage them to virtuous and honorable actions by imitating human life in delightful and measured lines. In the *Virtues*, Hobbes is much more succinct in his statement of the goal of poetry. Moreover, aesthetic pleasure there takes precedence over moral education. Nonetheless, in both cases it is in relationship to its goal that the rules of poetry are established. In the latter essay, Hobbes's rules are presented as an answer to the following rhetorical question: "But because there be many men called critics, and wits, and virtuosi, that are accustomed to censure poets, and most of them of divers judgments, how is it possible, you'll say, to please them all" (1675, iii)? The aim of the poet is to please (and instruct) his public, and there is nothing the public would like better than to be pleased. Thus, in literary communication there is a certain coincidence of interest between the writer and his audience. Hobbes's poetical rules are at once criteria with which to measure the success of poetic communication and the means by which it may be achieved. That this is so is clearly evidenced by the fact that Hobbes's criticism is never purely theoretical nor psychological, contrary to the influence with which he has generally been credited.[16] Hobbes is not interested in the psychological process of poetic invention but in the finished product itself, the poem. And he is interested in it from the point of view of the reader.

The first rule mentioned by Hobbes pertains to the form of Davenant's poem. Given that heroic poetry, as we have seen, differs from tragedy solely by virtue of the means of representation, Hobbes cannot but agree to the form of *Gondibert* "consisting in five bookes divided into Songs, or Cantoes, as five Acts divided into Scenes has ever bene the approved figure of Tragedy" (1650, 46). According to Pavel (1986, 124), the five-act division of tragedy is a *constitutive convention*, something that establishes the main rules of a social activity. He defines such rules as entrenched coordination equilibria, that is, as conventions *stricto sensu* in Lewis's (1969) sense. What, at first, makes Hobbes's statement of this very traditional rule interesting in this context is that it is justified by precedent. Hobbes gives no other reason for his approval than a received tradition, which is surprising coming from a man who, two pages later, will condemn "reasonless imitation of custome" (1650, 49). Is this a mere slip of the pen, a deeper inconsistency, or should we believe that, at least in certain circumstances, Hobbes thought that the simple existence of a tradition was reason enough to conform to it? In other words, did Hobbes believe that a conditional preference for a given regularity R can be based on the fact that most members of the relevant population P conform to R, and that this conditional preference is reason enough to accept the convention?

When Hobbes next addresses the question of Davenant's choice of verse and rhyme, he prefaces his judgment with a lengthy historical consideration. Verse among the Greeks, says Hobbes, was originally the style of religion, of the oracles, and of the laws.[17] "When afterwards the majesty of that stile was observed, the Poets chose it as best becoming their high invention" (1650, 46). Further, argues Hobbes, the first poems were destined to be sung "(which custome hath been long time layd aside, but began to be revived in part, of late yeres in *Italy*) and could not be made commensurable to the Voyce or Instruments, in Prose" (1650, 47). Finally, in view of the nature of their languages, the Greeks and Romans found hexameter more appropriate to epic poetry, while the English converged on lines with ten syllables. "And this measure is so proper for an Heroique Poeme, as without some losse of gravity and dignity, it was never changed" (1650, 47).

Because the aim of poetry is to divert men from vice and to inspire virtuous and honorable actions, a goal shared by religion and politics, the style of the latter is also proper to poetry. Inasmuch as poetry is to accomplish its task in a delightful manner, the use of verse may be further stabilized by means of voice and instruments, a custom that, for some unknown reason, was abandoned at one point, but was once again being revived. Finally, given the nature of the English language, epic poets should choose the gravest possible line of ten syllables. The sole justification for these rules would appear to be past success within a definite communicative enterprise in which the profit and delight of the reader were the shared goals of the poet and his audience. What makes these rules rational courses of action, or at least what justifies their acceptance, is that they have been proven successful. Davenant so far is in tune with tradition. Now comes his first departure from tradition and Hobbes's defense thereof:

In that you make so small account of the example of almost all the approuved Poets, ancient and moderne, who thought fit in the beginning, and sometimes also in the progresse of their Poems, to invoke a Muse, or some other Deitye, that should dictate to them, or assist them in their writings, they that take not the lawes of Art, from any reason of their owne, but from the fashion of precedent times, will perhaps accuse your singularity. (1650, 48)

Hobbes then explains that he condemns neither Davenant nor the custom of the heathen poets, "otherwise than as accessary to their false Religion" (1650, 48). The reasons for this balanced judgment are historical and, in a sense, hermeneutic. According to Hobbes, ancient poets were justified in invoking the Muses, because this squared with their contemporaries' religious beliefs. But, for a Christian man, it is improper to do the same. That common beliefs are crucially what is at issue here is sharply brought out by the fact that Hobbes notes that we readily accept claims to inspiration on the part of our own Divines. (Though he immediately goes on to regret this as generally harmful to the Commonwealth.) A similar argument is used, a little later on, to defend Davenant from "those that think that the Beauty of a Poeme consisteth in the exorbitancy of the fiction" (1650, 51). Contrary to those who desire impenetrable armor, enchanted castles, flying horses, and invulnerable bodies in epic poetry, Hobbes rules that "as truth is the bound of the Historicall, so the Resemblance of truth is the utmost limit of Poeticall Liberty" (1650, 51). He then argues that in ancient times "such strange fictions and Metamorphoses, were not so remote from the Articles of their faith, as they are now from ours, and therefore were not so unpleasant" (1650, 51).

Clearly, Hobbes is historicizing his rule concerning poetic freedom, and he suggests that it should be interpreted in the context of our changing idea of nature. But he is also pointing to what, in his mind, makes poetic communication successful, the poet's ability, among other things, to conform to certain expectations on the part of his public, and changing expectations at that. These expectations are partially grounded in precedent and in past success in the communication game, but the poet's intelligence consists in perceiving which precedents should be abandoned because his contemporaries' beliefs, and hence their expectations, have changed. This coordination with the public is made possible by virtue of the fact that the poet shares with his audience numerous beliefs. Christian men should not be expected to invoke the Muses, nor should the sectarians of the English Civil War be expected to appreciate such remnants of paganism. Similarly, a seventeenth-century poet should not expect the educated public of the Age of Reason to believe in flying horses or enchanted castles.

This necessity for the poet to coordinate his actions with the expectations of his public is further underscored by many other rules, especially by Hobbes's rules against the "Indecencies of an Heroique Poem." These fall into two categories. The first is relevant when there is a disproportion between the poem's characters and their actions: "Of the first kind, is the uncomlinesse of representing in great persons the inhumane vice of Cruelty, or the sordid vices of Lust and Drunkenesse" (1650, 53). Not that Hobbes believed that great persons never suffer from such faults, but rather that the readers of poetry, "which are commonly persons of the best quality" (1675, iv), will not expect great lords and heroes to engage in actions that they generally attribute to more common folk. The second category is relevant when there is a disproportion between the poet and the persons of the poem. Essentially it is a matter of the poet's failing in his choice of words, attributing to his heroes the dialect of

> the Inferior sort of People, which is allwayes different from the language of the Court. Another is to derive the Illustration of anything, from such metaphores or comparisons as cannot come into men's thoughts, but by meane conversation, and experience of the humble and evill Artes, which the persons of an *Epique* Poeme cannot be thought acquainted with. (1650, 53)[18]

If poetical rules are a matter of the poet's conforming to the expectations of his public, then we should not be surprised by their socially conservative character. What is more interesting is that Hobbes allows for these rules to change and provides a general mechanism to explain such change. It should be noted first that the origin of the transformation of poetic rules is situated, not in poetry itself, but at the level of larger social changes. New beliefs about the Muses or flying horses stem from religious sources or the growth of knowledge. The input motivating poetic transformations comes from outside poetry. What should also be noted is that the process that explains the modification of literary rules is essentially the same as the one that accounts for the stability and permanence of these rules. In both cases, the poet is trying to conform to the expectations of his audience, and it is because these expectations change that literary conventions are modified.

Are these rules conventions, in Hobbes's sense? Can they be seen as rational agreements between agents? At first sight, it seems clear that they indeed can, at least inasmuch as certain regularities of poetic behavior are to be modified because they would not receive the assent of rational agents, that is, the gesture of invoking the Muses. A closer look suggests that the situation is somewhat more complex, and that our conclusion varies in function of the way in which we describe the phenomena. The two cases in which Hobbes commends Davenant's departures from the fashion of precedents can probably be subsumed under the same rule: resemblance to nature traces the limits of poetic liberty. On this reading, both Davenant and the ancient poets abide by the same rule in different historical contexts. The contexts explain the diversity of the end product, but the rule remains the same. It follows that, for Hobbes, the invocation of the Muses may be a regularity of poetic behavior, and may perhaps even be a literary convention, but is not a poetical rule. The same can be said of just about every case in which change can be explained rationally, an example being metrics or what constitutes the "indecencyes of an Heroique Poeme." In all these cases, we can imagine that it is possible for changing external circumstances to explain a different overt behavior on the part of the poet who conforms to new expectations in his audience, while there is still no departure from the rule of choosing the most grave metrics or from that of avoiding a disproportion between the persons of a poem and their actions.

Under one description, then, we have changing regularities of poetic behavior, metrics, choice of words, or what was called diction, invocation of the Muses, and the "exorbitancy of fiction"; under the other description, we have a compliance with an immutable set of rules. The first description yields something that very much resembles Hobbesian conventions, an arbitrary agreement between rational agents. The second description refers to rules so closely related to the aim of poetic communication that it is hard to see how Hobbes could propose alternative rules without abandoning what for him constitutes the very goal of epic poetry. If such is the case, then these rules are not conventions, for they lack their arbitrary character.

My suggestion is that we should not choose between these two descriptions. Rather, we should consider them as providing together a two-level mechanism that explains changes in literary conventions on the basis of more stable rules of communication. This proposal implies, for the sake of clarity, the following terminological decision: from now on, I shall use "conventions" to refer to the regularities of behavior that emerge in various circumstances as a result of abiding by the more stable rules; the rules themselves I shall, of course, call "rules."

All of Hobbes's rules share an important characteristic. They are negative rules. What I mean by this is not that such rules are necessarily worded as prohibitions but, rather, that they do not prescribe any one course of action only. As Hayek (1967, 68–69) pointed out, such rules are never the sufficient causes of any action. They act as constraints on actions induced by other causes. Hobbes's rules concerning the resemblance to nature or the indecencies of epic poems do not tell the poet what he should write. They limit the courses of action available to him. They impose constraints on his choice of words and metaphors, on the range of his imagination. What is more, they do this in a highly abstract way, involving terms such as "resemblance to nature" or "discretion," which need to be contextually interpreted.[19] Consequently, as we have seen before, compliance with these rules can give rise to very different regularities of behavior in the history of poetry. And these regularities are concrete positive prescriptions, for they indicate to the poet some definite action or gesture of omission — for example, that of invoking or of not invoking the Muses. These, then, are conventions, for they can be seen as implicit agreements among rational agents.

It is not clear that Hobbes clearly perceived the difference between negative rules and conventions. The status of such positive rules as the five-act division of tragedy or the accompaniment of verse with voice and instruments remains uncertain. Nonetheless, his text certainly suggests the distinction. Negative rules appear as a means of explaining changes at the level of conventions, behavioral regularities that can be construed as concrete positive prescriptions.

Hobbes's Critics Revisited

In what follows I shall compare Hobbes's two-tier system of rules and conventions to claims made by two of his modern critics, Hayek and Lewis. More precisely, my intention is to compare Hobbes's literary rules to Hayekian rules of conduct, and his literary conventions to Lewis's concept of convention.

The main thrust of Hayek's argument is directed against what he calls "constructivist rationalism," a view that holds that institutions only will serve certain purposes if they have been consciously designed with these purposes in view (1973, 8, 31–34). This approach to social phenomena, argues Hayek, stems from an intellectual error and is doomed to failure.[20] The error consists in believing that successful action must be based on demonstrated truths, a belief that leads to an inordinate desire completely to reorganize society following purely rational principles. This, according to Hayek, is the impossible enterprise put forward by Hobbes, Jean-Jacques Rousseau, Jeremy Bentham, and Karl Marx, and it is one that can lead only to disaster. Rationally designing an institution to serve a given purpose is naturally conducive to specifying the various steps leading to that goal. This means that an institution will be defined by a set of concrete positive rules dictating the particular actions that would produce the desired effect. Yet, in the context of complex social organizations, argues Hayek, such a procedure is radically vitiated. "Complete rationality of action in the Cartesian sense demands complete knowledge of all the relevant facts" (1973, 12), and this is where the difficulty lies. There is, according to Hayek, a "necessary and irremediable ignorance on everyone's part of most of the particular facts which determine the actions of all the several members of human society" (1973, 12). In designing an institution, we shall certainly fail to take crucial information into account, and thus the result will be contrary to our proposed goal. Hayek's argument is precisely that this ignorance is definitive and ineliminable. It is not associated with the present, limited state of our knowledge, which we may hope to see mended in the future. The ignorance in question is constitutive of complex societies, but it is not universal. These facts are known or will become known to someone as he acts, and through his actions they will determine the course of society, but they will remain unknown to most other agents. What Hayek calls our incurable ignorance is simply the impossibility of anyone's taking into account all the relevant facts that enter into the composition of society. This information cannot be centralized, though it exists as available information distributed over all the members of society.

Against rational reconstruction and deliberate planification of society, Hayek stresses the importance of rules of conduct and spontaneous orders. A spontaneous order is an order that arises as a result of the fact that its members follow certain rules of conduct. These rules need not be known to the elements of the order, for "it is sufficient," says Hayek, "that the elements actually behave in a manner which can be described by such rules" (1973, 43). The main characteristic of these rules is that they are highly abstract, negative rules that do not prescribe to the agent any one particular action. Rather, within certain classes of situations they constrain the range of accessible courses of action. As noted above with regard to Hobbes's literary rules, they are never the sufficient causes of any actions but act as constraints on actions induced by other causes. Rules of conduct do not exist in an isolated manner; together they form a system of rules. Such a system should be distinguished from the overall order that results when agents abide by the rules, for the same regularity in the behavior of the elements, the same negative rules, may produce a wholly different regularity at the level of the whole when they interact with the environment (1967, 78). What is more, Hayek argues that such rules are "likely to be fairly constant, especially so long as they are not articulated in words and therefore also are not discussed or consciously examined" (1973, 19).[21] There are many reasons for this, but the main one is that rules of conduct are "adaptations to the impossibility of anyone taking conscious account of all the particular facts which enter into the composition of society" (1973, 13). Given this, our rational evaluation of the rule will usually be distorted through lack of relevant information, and the rule will seem completely unjustified. According to Hayek, rules of conduct, although they cannot be rationally grounded, are nonetheless justified by evolutionary success, through a process of natural or cultural selection.

Hobbes's literary rules and Hayek's rules of conduct clearly have a lot in common. They share the crucial characteristic of being highly abstract, negative rules that do not prescribe any particular action. Hobbes's literary rules can also be seen as a response to the poet's and audience's inability to take into account all the particular facts entering into the order of poetry, a point that is, in fact, suggested by the fourth paragraph of the *Virtues*. There, Hobbes says that men who do not know what is best can judge what is good, and he proposes his rules as a means of determining the good: "For he that can judge what is best, must have considered all those things, though they be almost innumerable, that concur to make the reading of an heroic poem pleasant" (1675, iii), clearly an impossible task. Hobbes's rules enjoin the poet to achieve coordination with his public's expectations concerning metrics, diction, choice of metaphors, and the characteristic manners of heroes. Like rules of conduct, they do not spell out the content of these expectations. Rather, with the advantage of hindsight, they claim that this is what successful poetry has always done. The poet's success in this endeavor clearly rests on shared beliefs, but, contrary to Lewisian conventions, it does not rest on common knowledge, as the precise content of the public's expectations is usually unknown to the author. Where Hobbes's literary rules part company with Hayekian rules of conduct is on the issue of rationality. For Hobbes, literary rules are dictates of reason, prudential imperatives designed to promote the goals of epic poetry. Apparently, it is their rational foundation that explains their stability and that allows them to function as explanatory hypotheses with regard to changes in the poet's overt behavior.

Nothing of the sort is found in Hayek. Rational examination endangers the stability of rules of conduct. We have seen one reason why this is so, but there is another closely related reason why rules of conduct are not subject to rational evaluation. According to Hayek, such rules do not serve any purpose, and as a result they fall outside the realm of instrumental rationality. The rules are often unconscious, and the order to which abiding by them gives rise is usually not known to the agents. [22] It is a spontaneous order, a self-organizing social system, that is neither willed nor designed by anyone, and the only "purpose" that rules of conduct serve is to maintain this system (1973, 35–54). They do not serve any particular purpose. They allow us as a group to achieve coordination and cooperation, and hence permit everyone to follow his or her own goals and ends. In that sense, rules of conduct appear as the conditions for the application of instrumental rationality (1988, 21–23).

Yet, at a slightly lower level of abstraction, the same may be said of Hobbes's literary rules. They allow the poet and his public to pursue their own multiple ends in and through poetic communication. They are not designed or instituted by anyone, for they emerge spontaneously. The critic's only role is to identify them as aspects of practices that facilitate the poet's and the poem's success. In that sense, one may also want to say that their entrenchment is the result of a process of cultural selection, though Hobbes, of course, would not put it that way. What Hobbes suggests is that their stability results from their rationality in a game of coordination and cooperation.

This naturally brings us to Lewis's concept of convention, which he construes as a coordination equilibrium in a game of cooperation. The first thing to point out is that Hobbes's literary rules cannot be Lewisian conventions, or at least cannot arise spontaneously through a Lewisian mechanism.[23] On first approximation, a convention for Lewis is a regularity R in the behavior of members of a population P when they are agents in a recurrent situation S, which satisfies the three following conditions: "(1) everyone conforms to R; (2) everyone expects everyone else to conform to R; (3) everyone prefers to conform to R on condition that the others do, since S is a coordination problem and uniform conformity to R is a proper coordination equilibrium in S" (1969, 42). Such a regularity of behavior will arise spontaneously, through a system of concordant mutual expectations based on salient aspects of the situation. It will then become stabilized through repetition because R gains conspicuousness as a previously reached coordination equilibrium in a recurrent situation. The problem is that Hobbes's literary rules and Hayekian rules of conduct are not regularities in the behavior of agents, nor do they describe any conspicuous regular behavior. The rule that says that the limit of poetic liberty is resemblance to nature does not describe the behavior of poets. It does not tell us what they do but refers us to what they do not do. In fact, its only interest is that it allows us to subsume under one explanatory hypothesis what at first appears as vastly dissimilar behavior: invoking or not invoking the Muses. Negative rules do not correspond to any one regularity in the behavior of the agents. On the contrary, a wide range of regular behavior may be seen as conforming to the rule. They thus lack the salient or conspicuous character that allows for the emergence of Lewisian conventions. This is another way of saying that such rules need not be known to the elements of a system; it is sufficient that the agent's behavior can be described as acting in accordance with the rules.[24] Rules of conduct will usually not satisfy the condition of common knowledge and hence will not be Lewisian conventions.

Hobbesian literary conventions are clearly closer to Lewisian conventions. They correspond to regular and recurrent behavior on the part of the poet, which can be seen as a fixed point in a game of coordination. What is more, these conventions retain an arbitrary character, at least from the point of view of the negative rule from which they arise. But there is one major difference between Hobbes's and Lewis's conventions, apart from the fact that Lewis's concept is more precise and articulate. Hobbesian conventions are changing agreements against the background of (presumably) immutable negative rules. Lewis's conventions cannot change; or, to put the matter differently, Lewis's concept of convention does not allow us to understand how conventions can change. The demonstration is straightforward. What makes a convention a convention, according to Lewis, is the way it is maintained through conditional preference for R on the basis of almost everybody's conforming to R. Given that the first condition in the definition of a convention is that almost everybody conforms to R, (1969, 78), nobody has any reason not to conform. It follows that conventions are metastable, and the agents' conditional preferences for R allow us to understand its stability in spite of its arbitrary character. But how do conventions change, for we do know that they change? The only possible answer, from Lewis's point of view, is that conventions change either because the agents are irrational and do not act in accordance with their conditional preferences or because they do not have the stated conditional preferences, in which case R is no longer a convention.

The interest of Hobbes's two-tier system, in spite of its programmatic and in many ways vague character, is that it offers the promise of understanding rationally both the transformation and the stability of conventions, while retaining their arbitrary character. In Hobbes's text this is no more than a promise, but it is one that I consider worthy of pursuing further, particularly in the light of recent concepts of rules and conventions that tend either to sacrifice rationality to an evolutionary explanation of change or change to a rational explanation of the stability of conventions.

CHAPTER SIX

Conventions
and Arbitrariness

ALAIN BOYER

As Eugène Dupréel (1925) has remarked, the notion of convention seems at first glance to be entirely at odds with the most basic thrust of the philosophical project, the search for what is universal, true, and natural: "Ainsi philosopher c'est, semble-t-il, s'éloigner du convenu" (90). The notion of convention points toward the artificial, the irrational, the fictitious, the false, and the contingent. In what follows, I try to establish two points: first, that the theme of convention is philosophically very rich; second, that we should beware of assuming that conventions necessarily entail arbitrariness. Finally, I explore the question of why we convene or agree at all.

The Domain of Convention

"Convention" is used in many different ways, leaving untouched virtually none of what Cornelius Castoriadis (1986) has referred to as the "domaines de l'homme."

FUNDAMENTAL ANTHROPOLOGY

In anthropology or sociology, nearly all "globalizing" theories rely on more or less sharp binary oppositions: community, for example, is opposed to society, and the latter is itself characterized as either archaic or modern, open or closed, cold or hot, holist or individualist, just as solidarity may be either mechanical or organic. Whatever the value of these ideal types may be, they inevitably raise the following question: where, and how, does modernity "begin"? Following Karl Raimund Popper (1944, chaps. 5, 10) and Castoriadis (1986), the principal impulse

Translated from French by Mette Hjort.

may be traced back to the ancient Greek city-states.[1] Thus, Popper argues that the questioning of the relation between *nomos* and *physis* played a crucial role in the thought of Pindar, the tragedians, the pre-Socratics, and, especially, the sophists. Indeed, one might even claim that this opposition is constitutive of sophistry as such.

Nomoï are at once "laws" and "customs." The term refers to all regularities that are human in origin and that can in principle be called into question or even changed. *Physis,* on the other hand, imposes itself from the outside in the form of a necessity stemming from an external source. Each set of *nomoï* defines a community, which does not rule out the emergence of a conflict of norms (*Antigone*) as several distinct layers of *nomoï* come into contact and gradually fuse. The process whereby a given convention is denaturalized is itself accompanied by a problematizing of this very convention, at which point it is possible to raise what is, properly speaking, *the* political question: what is the best form of society? Yet if it could be shown that some of the countless human customs were "closer" to "nature" than others, then, in that case, nature would itself be a norm, and it would thus be appropriate to respect it.

The emphasis on the diversity of conventions may also, however, lead to their global rejection on the grounds that none of them corresponds to nature: they are, after all, only conventions, the one being as arbitrary, and hence as unnatural, as the next. Thus, the "radical" Sophists are able to conclude that *nomos* is but mere appearance having no ontological weight.[2]

In both cases—natural law and anarchistic naturalism—the conventional is dispelled into the shadows of the arbitrary, where all choices are without reason: no nature, no legitimation.

POLITICAL PHILOSOPHY

It is in political philosophy that we encounter the notion of convention *stricto sensu*. In this domain it is a matter of a rule based on an agreement, one brought about by the common will that emerges in the course of a deliberative process, this agreement itself being the means by which the "conveners" commit themselves to observing the rule.[3] It is telling that the Latin *conventio* refers both to the gathering or assembly and to the commitment that is made in its midst. The Greeks knew of no such ambiguity, the element of commitment being evoked by the term *sunthèkè* (meaning originally a peace treaty, particularly between two city-states). How, it was asked, could the problem of violent confrontation be resolved if the third thief can always profit from the conflict between the other two? The Greeks, we know, used *homologia* or *omonia* to refer to the aspect of conventions that created harmony, for in bringing about unity, a given convention was assumed to put an end to dispute. That the very idea of the social contract is of Greek origin should come as a surprise to nobody.[4] For the social contract is but an extrapolation from the idea of a convention or agreement posited at the very origin of culture, of the nomic — in short, of the conventional itself.[5] Yet, as a solution to the "state of nature game," the social contract does not constitute a convention in Lewis's sense, for the latter clearly stipulates that a convention allows for the resolution of *coordination* problems in situations in which the players discern several optimal equilibria, the only problem being that of achieving coordination around one and the same possible point of equilibrium (such as driving either on the left or on the right side of the road — an exclusive disjunction).

As a result, all conventions of the Lewisian type presuppose that the choice involved be *arbitrary*, and that no external instance be necessary to guarantee that the players honor their commitments. In my mind, these requirements suggest that even if Lewis's concept of convention may be held to formalize the idea of "pure" convention, it cannot rightly be considered as a satisfactory *explicans* for everything that we would be inclined to characterize as a convention, particularly contracts.[6] Indeed, in the language of classical political philosophy, the connotations of the term "arbitrary" are as pejorative as those of "convention" are positive. I am thinking, for example, of the "arbitrary discretion of the Sovereign" (*l'arbitraire du Prince*).

LAW

In the French Civil Code, a subtle and perhaps somewhat obsolete distinction is drawn between convention and contract, the latter being but a species of the former (article 1101).[7] In this legal text, all conventions are characterized by the idea of an *intersubjective commitment* (which is not necessarily a mutual commitment, for there exist "unilateral contracts," such as donations). A convention is valid if and only if it upholds the principle of *autonomy* with respect to the persons involved: whence the very complex theory of vitiated consent (*vices de consentement*), which delineates the different ways in which a contract may be deemed juridically nonexistent once one of the contractees no longer can be assumed to have acted freely and in full knowledge of the issue at hand. What is more, the law traces limits to what may constitute the object of a convention, thus restricting conventions to what may be legally exchanged: inasmuch as the body, for example, can be neither bought nor sold, it cannot be the object of a contract, albeit between consenting persons. Not every convention is legal, but one must distinguish between those conventions that exist outside the law (an association of criminals) and those that are simply not inscribed in the law, such as the rules of politesse.

SOCIAL SCIENCE

In any number of social situations, it is not a matter of a zero-sum game, and it thus becomes crucial to discover the stable means by which agents coordinate their actions. A first mistake would be to imagine that every institution is the product of a rational will's explicit project. This is the *constructivist* illusion, as described by Friedrich August von Hayek (1973). More specifically, constructivism wrongly leads us to assume that every convention in Lewis's sense is the result of a shared and explicit process of deliberation, rather than of trial and error or imitation.

Yet the fallacy of *spontaneous generation* is equally deceptive. Indeed, it is what Emile Durkheim (1893, chap. 7) denounces in his critique of the liberal philosopher Herbert Spencer, the former arguing that phenomena such as the modern market cannot be interpreted in complete abstraction from the legal relations that constrain and modify the practices involved.[8] Whence the importance of the notion of *contract,* which implies that the agreement somehow is guaranteed by a third instance. It is in my interest to conform to the rule even if others do not do so, at least as long as the threat of sanctions remains credible. Social scientists should not be satisfied with the concept of convention proposed by Hume and Lewis, and defined as follows in the latter's *Convention: A Philosophical Study* (1969).[9]

A regularity R in the behavior of members of a population P when they are agents in a recurrent situation S is a *convention* if and only if it is true that, and it is common knowledge in P that, in any instance of S among members of P,

(1) everyone conforms to R;

(2) everyone expects everyone else to conform to R;

(3) everyone prefers to conform to R on condition that the others do, since S is a coordination problem and uniform conformity to R is a coordination equilibrium in S. (58)

Andrew Schotter (1981) rightly considers Lewis's definition of a social convention inadequate inasmuch as it fails to accommodate the not negligible case of institutions that are not "self-policing" and that "require some external authority, such as the state, to enforce them" (11). He thus proposes the following definition of a social institution:

A regularity R in the behavior of members of a population P when they are agents in a recurrent situation Γ is an *institution* if and only if it is true that and is common knowledge in P that (1) everyone conforms to R; (2) everyone expects everyone else to conform to R and (3) either everyone prefers to conform to R on the condition that the others do, if Γ is a coordination problem, in which case uniform conformity to R is a coordination equilibrium; or (4) if anyone ever deviates from R it is known that some or all of the others will also deviate and the payoffs associated with the recurrent play of Γ using these deviating strategies are worse for all agents than the payoff associated with R. (11)

AESTHETICS

Aesthetics is as a whole governed by the nature/convention opposition.[10] Yet, according to the proponents of the classical doctrines, certain conventions are held simply to be "natural," and are not, as a result, recognized as conventions. Romantic aesthetics rebels violently against this naturalization of the conventional, denouncing these very conventions as both artificial and arbitrary.[11] But once again this denunciation presupposes that what is not natural must necessarily be arbitrary. "Conventional" evokes the unnatural and unoriginal, the rote and mechanical application of some procedure. In Immanuel Kant's *Kritik der Urteilskraft* (1790) and Victor Hugo's *Cromwell* (1827), convention is diametrically opposed to life, nature, and genius, qualities that are all embodied in the unique individual who breaks the conventional constraints while creating new ones. For it is nature that speaks through the genius, at least until imitation reifies his or her exceptional style into a convention.

Contemporary literary theory, which is globally hostile to the "romantic lie," has tried to do without the idea of nature.[12] The real would be nothing but the result or particular "effect" of one convention among others, and as such it would have no decisive influence on any given work. To construe everything as a function of conventions is, however, to deprive the idea of convention of all substance.[13] It is clear that one cannot describe something independently of certain conventions or principles of selection and organization, but in itself a convention describes nothing: it is a prescription. To overlook the descriptive function of language, in Karl Bühler's sense, is to overlook reference and truth, and, by the same token, the very difference between the descriptive and prescriptive, between the utterance (whether true or false) and the norm (whether applied or not). The very idea of a "true convention" is a grammatical error in the Wittgensteinian sense. All is not conventional.

LANGUAGE

The debate over the arbitrariness of the sign began with the Sophists. Is language (or perception, in the case of Democritus) *nomô* or *kata physin*?[14] Hermogenes did not consider words to be voluntary in origin, for he characterized them, not as *thései*, but as *éthei kaï nomô*. But if the origin of words is a matter of indifference, then all lexical or semantic choices must be arbitrary. Sophism consists of inferring the arbitrariness of all discourse (the compound) from that of the sign (the component part). Whence the position adopted by Cratylus: one must presuppose (in the manner of a transcendental argument) the true (or original) meaning of words. Plato, in *Cratylus* (1961), and particularly Aristotle, in *On Sophistical Refutations* (1955), carefully ensure that truth is independent of the arbitrariness of the sign: if truth does not depend on the speaker (in general), then it is not arbitrary. (Popper [1963, 19] notes that it is our fondness for words that leads us to search for their origins: for the first use is closer to the original meaning; yet in the case of propositions, the relation to the origin is irrelevant, for the first use of a given sentence may very well have been such that the sentence was false.)

Ferdinand de Saussure (1916) and Emile Benveniste (1966), it is true, have developed new approaches to the same problem; but let us no longer extol the "arbitrariness of the sign" as a quintessentially modern and particularly stunning discovery.

The contemporary debate concerning the importance of rules and the conventional nature of language is, on the other hand, very lively. While Noam Chomsky (1975) seems somewhat reluctant on this score, pragmatists such as John Searle (1969) and Lewis (1969) have not hesitated to base their approach to language on an analysis of the conventions that are presupposed within a given community, the observance of these conventions being what makes reciprocal understanding possible.

PHILOSOPHY OF LOGIC

Rudolf Carnap (1935), we know, was a great advocate of pragmatic decisions, for "in logic there are no morals" (52). Unlike Willard Van Orman Quine (1976, chaps. 11, 12), Carnap believed that conventionalist pragmatism would be able to resurrect the analytic/synthetic distinction. There would be analytic truths in a system, given the constitutive rules of the game in question. Ludwig Wittgenstein (1976) was willing to go several steps further, abusing the category of "language games" in his effort to explain the necessity of the nonnecessary. The main difficulty faced by this kind of approach is that radical conventionalism cannot account for the apparent objectivity of logical consequences, which are in no way arbitrary and which do not even seem to allow for choice.[15]

EPISTEMOLOGY OF THE EMPIRICAL SCIENCES

Conventionalism finds its origin in the early works of Pierre Duhem (1892), as well as in those of Edouard Le Roy (1901), and in certain texts by Henri Poincaré (1902). The latter, we recall, was intent on replacing the synthetic a priori, and it is clear that the importance attributed to the theme of conventions in twentieth-century philosophy of science stems from this ambitious promise. Yet, as used in the tradition influenced by Poincaré, the term "convention" carries a far weaker sense than in other contexts. For there is no real talk here of common agreements, of discussion, or of compromise. We all choose the same system because we are subject to the same determinations (imperatives based on convenience). (One wonders whether John Rawls's [1971] idea of a choice under the veil of ignorance — meaning that each individual abstracts from his or her individuating or differentiating features — really evokes a process that would be capable of producing a convention in the strict sense of an agreement of differing minds.)

Poincaré, we know, did not countenance the idealist extremes that Le Roy embraced and that have led many to proclaim everything to be a construction, a slogan that has not failed to *épater les bourgeois*. Poincaré, on the contrary, maintains that there are facts and not only conventions.

Popper (1934, chap. 5) discussed conventionalism at great length. More specifically, he developed a theory of the "empirical basis," which construes the (common) acceptance of observation statements as a decision or convention. One understands why he wished to claim that such statements could not be deduced from anything else: the correct description has to be chosen, and this choice has in principle to be made by all researchers. Yet this "convention" is only a convention in the sense of a common decision, and not in the sense that other solutions are possible, and certainly not in the sense specifying that the choice of solution is arbitrary from a logical point of view.[16] Popper does, however, appear to be justified in speaking of methodological conventions in relation to the rules governing the search for truth.

Conventionalism, then, has a curious dimension, for it turns on a kind of (nonsuperstitious) anthropomorphism with regard to the laws of nature. It is not our conventions that are natural, but the laws of nature that are *nomo*. Yet, in actual fact, the crucial point is that when it comes to choosing one convention over another, nature is silent.

Arbitrariness

If the role of what is arbitrary is underestimated, superstitious rationalism is the result; if, on the other hand, the power of the arbitrary is overestimated, then some form of hypercritical irrationalism emerges.

The term *arbitrary* stems from the Latin *arbitrarius*, which does not seem to have an exact synonym in Greek. That which is *arbitrarius* can be decided by an independent (third) party where litigation is involved. In this sense, the arbitrator becomes the master, for his will is not connected to that of any of the individuals on whose behalf he makes a decision, nor does he have to account for his actions. The only clause is that the parties must agree in their choice of arbitrator: excepting cases of ignorance or deception, such an agreement guarantees that the arbitrator, in being equally distant from the two parties, identifies as much as possible with the interests of both. In principle, the arbitrator's decision is free and rational. In this sense, it is not arbitrary to accept the particular and negative conclusion of a syllogism of the second figure, the major premise of which is universal and affirmative, and the minor premise of which is negative and particular. For it is quite simply true that the Baroco mode of the second figure is valid. Even God, according to Leibniz, cannot be the arbitrator of such matters, since he did not create them. Instead, the absolute arbitrator would be something like Descartes's God, for his divine choice is sovereign, neutral, and actually constitutive of the creation of what is chosen. Divinely speaking, truth is arbitrary. Technically, a neutral choice could take the form of a lottery, for this is in fact the criterion of the purely arbitrary. The arbitrary thus points to the power of arbitration, as well as to the absence of justifications, which in turn gives rise to the idea of a neutral choice that cannot be justified.

The arbitrator is the master if, that is, the parties embroiled in conflict so decide. After all, in one of Jean de La Fontaine's fables (1668), the weasel and the little rabbit address themselves to Raminagrobis in an attempt to resolve their differences: "Un saint homme de chat, bien fourré, gros et gras / Arbitre expert sur tous les cas" (bk. 7, no. 16). But, as we know, "the good apostle," "Mit les plaideurs d'accord en croquant l'un et l'autre." For while the arbitrary is without reason, it is so only in the following relative sense: the decision of the arbitrator is not motivated by an a priori preference for one of the two parties. In the case of the purely arbitrary—that of the Cartesian God—the choice is wholly without reason, inasmuch as it concerns alternatives that are in no way significantly different. At this point it seems somewhat arbitrary to use "arbitrary" to refer to everything that is "neither deducible from nature nor from logic" (Bourdieu and Passeron 1970), although this usage readily permits statements to the effect that schools are but vehicles of cultural arbitrariness or symbolic violence. The aim of sociology is, of course, to reveal what is socially arbitrary. Yet, one might ask whether it really is arbitrary to prefer Mozart to Salieri.

It would appear to be necessary, then, to avoid conflating the genus and the species in a reduction of all conventions to merely arbitrary choices. The main features of conventional phenomena can, in my mind, be summed up as follows:

(1) A convention is an artifact.

The expression "innate convention" is oxymoronic. (Chomsky [1975] criticizes the conventionalist doctrines of Searle and Lewis on the grounds that the linguistic competence known as universal grammar is innate.) It is true that certain biologists, such as John Maynard Smith (1982), do not hesitate to speak of conventional behavior with reference to animal conflict — rituals of seduction, territorial display behavior, and so on. Yet this way of using the term is clearly anthropomorphic: it is *as if* these behaviors were the result of conventions. In the human sphere, conventions institute newness ex nihilo, that is, in a manner that is not deducible from nature alone.

(2) All conventions presuppose a choice between different possibilities.

The notion of a "necessary convention" is oxymoronic; whence perhaps the inability of radical conventionalism to account for logical necessity.

(3) A convention is based on an agreement (whether explicit or tacit) between agents.

The idea of a "convention with oneself" is problematic, a point that Jean-Jacques Rousseau clearly acknowledges in his description of the "first convention" (*Pacte Social*): "chaque individu, contractant, *pour ainsi dire*, avec lui-même, se trouve engagé sous un double rapport" (1762, 53). A contract with oneself is, in fact, mediated through the unanimous agreement of the members of society. It is crucial to distinguish two subjects within one and the same person, the one being part of the sovereign, the other a member of the state.

Similarly, when French legal experts speak of a "convention with oneself" — which should not be confused with a simple promise — it is in fact a matter of two juridical personalities incarnated within the same individual: thus, the legal guardian of someone who is mentally unsound may, as a private individual, wish to buy something belonging to the handicapped person.[17]

(4) Conventional agreements must be freely made.

The idea of "imposing a convention on someone" is absurd; whence the fundamental status accorded within the law to the principle of autonomous parties. The issue involved is a delicate one, for it is a matter of evaluating the nature of the information available to the respective parties and of assessing the extent of their good faith.

(5) A convention does not describe, it prescribes.

Just as nature is to be distinguished from convention, so it is important to grasp the difference separating what are, properly speaking, conventions and what Popper (1944, 67) calls the "natural laws of society" — "laws" of economy, for example — which are *facts* or, more precisely, constraints on the sum totality of *possible* (as opposed to *permissible*) facts. A convention is a norm and cannot be refuted by counterexamples. Indeed, one of the essential features of conventions is the fact that they can be transgressed; whence the necessity of anticipating and preventing such possible violations.

(6) All conventions imply a commitment.

Conventions determine future behavior, placing constraints on it and thereby creating a social bond. Conventions are performatives and are much like mutual promises.

(7) The conditions under which the commitment is undertaken must be public or must, at the very least, be capable of being made public.

This public knowledge must at least be shared by the parties in question, and perhaps even by the arbitrator. Strictly speaking, a convention cannot be the result of a blind process that would collapse if its mechanism were to be revealed. Ideally (and following Rousseau, Kant, and Rawls), conventions are situated in the openness afforded by public space, rather than in the shadows cast by the cunning of reason. Even when they are implicit, as they are in Hume and Lewis, they can be made explicit without loss, for they are always already common knowledge. (It is worth noting that some item of information may be common knowledge without being public, whereas the opposite is not the case.)

In order to obtain a tacit convention in the sense of Hume and Lewis, we need to add the following specifications to our list:

(8) It is in the interest of a given individual to conform to a conventional rule, if and only if this rule is observed by others. I shall speak of this type of compliance as *conditional preference*.

(9) The choice encompasses a fundamental element of arbitrariness.[18]

(10) The agreement is not arrived at by means of a shared deliberative process and does not require explicit promises (matched with sanctions).

Inasmuch as no third party is required, this kind of convention has every chance of being stable. We note that an arbitrary convention in the specified sense does not presuppose an arbitrator in order to function. What is more, we note that inasmuch as choice is necessary, the choice will be contingent. The imperative of action dictates choice, and the skeptical *epochē* is thus out of place here. Yet the choice is contingent, for there exists a set of possibilities that are held to be equally desirable: in other words, the coordination equilibria are multiple. The choice is purely arbitrary if the solution can be established by drawing lots, each solution's probability of success being equal to that of the others: it is a matter here of a purely procedural form of justice, for the result is fair, whatever it may be, if and only if the procedure has in fact been followed. Yet if the choice is arbitrary (driving on the left or right), it is crucial that it be the same for everybody, or at least that the behavior of each agent be coordinated with that of the others by the means of some rule. Every convention, even when it is arbitrary, produces the necessary effects by virtue of having been chosen. *Nomos* engenders *anankē*. Every original choice entails historical effects, and it soon becomes difficult to consider the common rule as one among many equally desirable possibilities. In the case of a choice from a discrete set, even the possibility of a transition is ruled out, as is illustrated by the following joke: in order to accommodate our English friends, a European government decides to institute driving on the left. Yet since this operation is a somewhat delicate one, they decide to proceed by stages, starting with trucks.

With time, norms acquire a certain rigidity. In the *Nicomachean Ethics,* Aristotle defines "legal justice" as "that which is originally indifferent, but when it has been laid down is not indifferent" (V.1134b18). *"Ouden diaphérēi . . . diaphérēi,"* says the text, more precisely, thereby opposing an original indifference to the difference resulting from the simple fact of duration. Thus, difference emerges from indifference. The process whereby the indifferent is differentiated is also one in which the arbitrary is naturalized. Whence the retrospective illusion of the necessity of the original choice, the forgetting of its arbitrary nature.

The greater the number of secondary conventions engendered as a logical consequence of a given convention, the greater is the latter's rigidity. As conventions become more and more systematic, it becomes increasingly difficult to modify them, even if they appear less than optimal when examined individually. (Incidentally, in my opinion the dual insistence on the fact that conventions transcend their origin and have a constraining character is in no way incompatible with methodological individualism when properly understood.)

Why Agents Convene and Agree

Had providence or nature been all-foreseeing, there would have been no need to institute agreements. Convention is rooted in the insufficiency of nature. Let us not go so far as to endorse the Kantian (1803) and Fichtean idea that human beings have no instincts. Instead, let us simply admit that humans are incomplete beings, the behavioral programs guiding them being "open," to adopt Ernst Mayr's (1976, 23) expression. This is basically the position adopted by Protagoras: the insufficiency of *physis* makes necessary the invention of *nomoï*.

According to Arnold Gehlen (1940), humans are by nature cultural beings. Evolution, remarks Konrad Lorenz (1963, chap. 13), has fashioned them in such a way that their nature needs to be filled in by cultural tradition. Convention, then, understood *stricto sensu* as a peace treatise, is a fragile barrier against violence. It takes the place of inadequate and failing systems of innate inhibitions.

More generally, agreements are necessary in order to try to resolve the problems of collective action or cooperation that are engendered by social evolution itself, independently, that is, of the human animal's "nature."[19] On the condition that others do the same, it is in the interest of every agent to deprive him or herself of certain possible actions.

Action presupposes anticipation. It is thus in the interest of a given individual actively to search for the regularities of his or her ecosystem. It is impossible to act in a world that is entirely without order or regularity. In this sense, traditions and institutions have the same function as do natural laws: they make possible anticipations, organizing the horizons of expectation in such a way as to favor mutual trust.[20] In a word, they constitute a cultural cosmos, a familiar world. It is often better to follow a rule that is less than optimal than to search for a better one and thereby provisionally to risk being incapable of foreseeing what Popper (1945, 94) has called the "resistance of the social stuff [to our attempts to mold it]." Thus, conventions, whether tacit or explicit, help to structure the social world and to stabilize behavior. Yet, modernity is defined by a critical unsettling of tradition and of the conventions that have solidified over time. Thus, the political problem is raised whether it is desirable to try to improve a given convention or whether the risk of destabilization is more dangerous than the status quo. The dialectic of legislation favors the resolution of this dilemma: through legislation, Parliament is able to transform certain social relations while at the same time stabilizing the expectations of agents. Modern society both extends the sphere of freedom enjoyed by individuals and provides the state's guarantee that mutual commitments will be respected. Yet, "tout n'est pas contractuel dans le contrat," as Durkheim (1893, 189) rightly points out in his critique of Spencer's economism and of the idea that the emergence of industrial society could be accounted for uniquely in terms of free contracts between individuals. Law, far from being simply a "complément utile des conventions particulières, en est la norme fondamentale" (1893, 189). Yet, the Lewisian notion of convention does not take into consideration contracts that are juridically regulated (1969, 103). The definition, in short, is overly restrictive and incapable of doing full justice to the richness of the notion of convention, capturing instead only one of its aspects.

At this point, the law would appear to assume three crucial functions:

(1) *A protective function:* the state, which promulgates the law, guarantees autonomy of will on the part of the individuals involved. In determining which conventions are licit, the law establishes the autonomy of agents by setting limits to their liberty.

(2) *A stabilizing function:* law reinforces trust. Given that "les conventions tiennent lieu de loi à ceux qui les ont faites" (article 1134), conventions share the rigidity of the law: if somebody else does not respect his or her commitments, I know that I can obtain an indemnity, and this eliminates the uncertainty inherent in the psychological notion that someone may be trusted to keep his or her word. Besides, it is not in the interest of a given individual to betray me, for he or she thereby runs the risk of being legally pursued. Finally, he or she knows that I find myself in a similar situation, and he or she will perhaps be inclined to engage in a contract as a result.

(3) *An ethical function:* while certain conventions may be irreproachable, when examined in terms of the autonomy of the parties involved, they may nonetheless be illicit because they run contrary to basic human rights. Thus, in French law, only that which may legally be

bought or sold can be the object of a convention, a stipulation that excludes the human body from being the object of contracts. (This raises interesting and difficult questions with regard to current practices: should one, for example, consider the contract between a sterile couple and a surrogate mother to be legitimate? Does transsexualism authorize us to modify the idea of the inalienability of the state?

It is true, thank God, that not everything is juridical, and certain conventional rules need neither guarantees nor sanctions to persist: it is precisely those rules that Lewis defines so rigorously. The boundary between the two types of convention (those that are self-regulating and those that are guaranteed by the state) is, in fact, anything but stable. I respect the arbitrary convention following which it is appropriate to drive on the right (or on the left) because:

(1) I am indifferent to the distinction: only a superstitious mentality or a pronounced taste for systematic disagreement could modify this indifference;

(2) given that the convention is common knowledge, I know that it is in my interest to respect it if and only if others do so;

(3) the police either are, or could be, present to call me back to order if I were to transgress the rule, whether as a result of negligence or a desire to be transgressive. The convention dictating that I drive on a specific side of the road is thus at once "self-policed" and "policed by an external authority," to use Schotter's words.

Man is the animal that convenes and agrees. This "(be)coming together" gives rise to an order that seems to transcend all individuals but is in fact only the product — at times the unexpected product — of their ways of convening. Yet, this cultural world is open: in spite of their inertia, or *conatus,* these conventions that attach us to one another can be called into question; as a result, they may even evolve. Naturalism, which deems all conventions to be arbitrary and thus illegitimate, misrepresents both the indeterminacy of nature and man's ability to contain violence by means of the art of common agreement.

CHAPTER SEVEN

Genres, Laws,
Canons, Principles

JOSEPH MARGOLIS

Genres, fitted to artworks and texts, corresponds to *natural kinds,* fitted to physical and biological nature. Equated with *genera* (with which it is etymologically linked) and *species,* the term may be extended to all of nature and human culture and may even refer to one inclusive order of reality, provided, that is, that this order has an invariant structure, either metaphysically or epistemologically. The first option is favored in the classical world, notably by Aristotle, since the powers of human science are characteristically taken there to conform to unchanging reality: necessity *de dicto* conforms to necessity *de re.* The second option is favored in the modern world, at least at its inception, as in the thought of René Descartes, where the priority of changeless reality is still assured, even as our ability to discern its fixed features is placed in doubt — although retrievably so: necessity *de dicto* recovers necessity *de re.* The ramifications of this seemingly bland formulation are remarkable when applied to the various forms of practical life.

I

Aristotle begins his *Poetics* in the most matter-of-fact way: "Our subject being Poetry, I propose to speak not only of the art in general but also of its species and their respective capacities" (1.1447a). Although suitably adjusted to his topic, this formula is essentially the same as the one offered in the *Physics,* the *Metaphysics,* the *De Anima,* the *Parts of Animals,* the *Generation of Animals,* the *Prior* and *Posterior Analytics,* the *Nicomachean Ethics,* and, only a little more loosely, in the *Politics, Rhetoric,* and *Topics.*

It is all quite stunning, provided only that what is real *is* invariant, and that invariant reality *is* sufficiently transparent to human cognition as to yield an accurate and exact body of knowledge. "Every art and every inquiry," says Aristotle at the beginning of the *Nicomachean Ethics,* "and similarly every action and pursuit, is thought to aim at some good; and for this reason the good has rightly been declared to be that at which all things aim" (1094a). Aristotle is speaking of each and every art, inquiry, and action, of everything that is deliberate in human history and culture. But since, on his view, there is a final cause "underlying everything," as he says in many places, and since this affects both the sciences qua sciences as well as what the sciences are about, there are natural norms that apply everywhere. This accounts for the dual emphasis in the *Physics* and *Metaphysics,* and for the assumption that art, inquiry, and action are as much a part of nature as are the processes involving physical and biological entities. Indeed, the same is even true of logical argument. For Aristotle, then, reality (or nature) establishes no essential difference between theory and practice, laws and rules, *physis* and *poiēsis,* or between the natural and the conventional in human affairs. This is the point of the strategy adopted in the *Topics* and the *Rhetoric,* justifying our somewhat tendentious mixing of contemporary distinctions with Aristotle's own, as though he would have approved of our extension.

But the classical world is no more. Even Descartes's world is gone — that is, the modern world extending from Descartes, through the exertions of that last and most radically uncompromising Cartesian, Edmund Husserl, who fused (in a more extreme manner than Immanuel Kant ever did) the conditions of the intelligibility of nature and the reflexive work of thought itself. At the end of the twentieth century we either disbelieve, or are prepared to allow that it may be untrue, that what is real either is or must entail what is invariant and exceptionless, and that what passes for human knowledge and inquiry, anywhere and everywhere, actually does (and must) grasp, by whatever approximation, changeless reality or the changelessly limiting structures of conception that constrain the very intelligibility of reality.[1]

What are the most extreme, contemporary options that follow (almost ineluctably) from the reversed priority of epistemology over metaphysics? In moving from Descartes through Kant, through Husserl and beyond — once reality is denied invariance and transparency, and once cognized world and cognizing humans are inextricably fused and then historicized as such — I am led to theorize that all things posited as stable enough to support some form of inquiry are themselves constructed, artifactual, provisionally and consensually agreed upon within that very symbiotized and horizoned space.

So seen, everything threatens to be "conventional," structured by the tacitly imposed rules of the interested agents we take ourselves to be, without the least assurance of any congruity between our apparent constructions and whatever we suppose (within our ken) to be independent of and unaffected by our investigations. Indeed, even the coherence of that last conjecture (that is, of a discernible, independent world) becomes doubtful. For the symbiosis of world and word is now construed as entailing a world that is partly constructed by cognizing subjects who are themselves constructed by that world, while remaining somewhat blind to it even as they affect it. Practice absorbs theory in the sense (contra Aristotle) that reality is in flux or lacks the changeless structure by reference to which local change and local commitment *could* (as Aristotle claimed) be brought under principles that would hold everywhere and without exception, thus ensuring total intelligibility.

Practice absorbs theory, then, either in the sense that theory must be redefined as functioning in a world that lacks invariant structure, or in the sense that it must be dismissed altogether as answering to nothing in reality. On the first option, theory loses the very privilege by which practice could in principle be linked to the invariant structures that would guarantee it a diminished, yet genuine, cognitive standing— practice, following the ancient account, dealing only with the sensible, the perceptible, the inconstant, the intuited, the context-bound, and the particular, that make action and production effective at all. In just this sense, theorizing *is* or becomes practice, a search for conceptually formulable structures in the real world that would be sufficient only to guide the perceived or apparent success of action and production, without providing any assurance of invariance. On the second option, practice is simply cognitively blind. The first option the ancients dismissed as utterly incoherent; the second cannot even be coherently stated. But the philosophical drift of our own age inexorably commits us to making sense of what Aristotle (who already dared to go beyond what Parmenides and Plato could possibly have allowed) would never have countenanced. It is a fact, we may add, that only a very small number of theorists have ever been able to remain entirely faithful to the constraints of the first option, the vast majority having either fallen back on privilege and invariance or embraced denials that were ruled out by their own say-so.

Aristotle never tires of leading us back to his own master conception of the ordered difference between theory and practice. In the *De Partibus Animalium*, for instance, he introduces the question of the difference between a systematic science addressed to *anything*, and an educated acquaintance with the informally sorted parts of some domain of inquiry: "there must," he says, "be certain canons, by reference to which a hearer shall be able to criticize the method of a professed exposition, quite independently of the question whether the statements made be true or false." He alludes to his doctrine of the four causes (*aitíai*) and emphasizes the priority of the final cause: "that cause is the first which we call the final one. For this is the Reason, and the Reason forms the starting-point, alike in the works of art and in works of nature." He goes on to summarize his entire scheme of things:

in the works of nature the good end and the final cause is still more dominant than in works of art such as these [that is, in the art of the physician and the builder], nor is necessity a factor with the same significance in them all. . . . For there is absolute necessity, manifested in eternal phenomena; and there is hypothetical necessity, manifested in everything that is generated by nature as in everything that is produced by art, be it a house or what it may. (639a–b)

But all this collapses if, first, it is not incoherent to deny that reality is changeless, and, second, if it is not incoherent to affirm that human inquiry and intelligent behavior may still count as, or as entailing, knowledge, the stable structures of nature and art that are thus comprehended being inherently subject to change.

2

My present concern is not to explicate Aristotle but to understand what we today may mean by *genres, canons, rules, laws, principles, norms, natures, species, kinds, conventions,* and the like, particularly as these terms apply to the arts, but also with an eye to the inclusive range of things that Aristotle once embraced with such elegance. A crucial factor is the widespread and dual contemporary assumption that there is no invariance in nature (or in art, action, or inquiry), and that we nonetheless do manage to achieve a working command of the contingent regularities of nature and of the reasonable direction of art and conduct. It is striking to discover how often expositors who apparently are committed to a changing world have recourse to a patch of invariance (to necessities *de re*) in order to ensure some measure of descriptive, interpretive, or normative rigor. It is also impressive to learn that there as yet is no strong, fully ramified account of these distinctions that simply abandons, without disadvantage, the entire Aristotelian or "archic" notion.

The important point to bear in mind is that, although the question of conceptual rigor under radical change may be tellingly pressed within the boundaries of what Aristotle views as "practical" (*praxis* and *poiēsis*) — particularly the arts — its lesson extends, on his argument, to the whole of science (to *epistēmē* and *theoria*) as well. The upshot, then, is that we can expect a fundamental similarity between the fate (the utter failure or transformation) of "laws" (of nature) in the physical sciences, and that of "rules" of conduct (in the moral sphere), and of "genres" and "canons" (in the arts) — if, that is, invariance and transparency are rejected.

To put the entire charge in a word: *principles* of every kind (*aitíai*, in Aristotle's account of science) are radically affected, both formally and substantively, if the findings of theory cannot be disconnected "in principle" from the inherent inconstancies of practice (or of *praxis*, in the deep sense suggested by Karl Marx's account).[2]

When leveled against the sciences (against the unity of science program, for instance), the charge is most strategically expressed in terms of a characterization of the natural sciences as abstractions made within the scope of the human sciences; in the domain of ethics and politics, it leads to the defeat of all forms of moral realism and universalism, as well as to the defense of a social constructionist account of persons; and as far as the arts, criticism, and history are concerned, it replaces the thesis that artworks and texts form natural kinds, allowing us to maintain instead that these are generated only in historically contingent ways that answer to human interests and that remain intelligible in spite of the limits that historicity imposes on description and interpretation.

Under the conditions provided, the analysis of genres bears a conceptual load that is at once heavy and surprising given its habitual academic specificity. The defeat of essentialized genres in the arts, and of universal canons of taste, proves to be equivalent to the denial of the nomic universals of physics and of the valid necessities of logic and mathematics. The conceptual leap I am encouraging here will no doubt be resisted, for the claim is not yet an argument. But what we need to appreciate is the unity and range of the commanding argument intended, once the unity of Aristotle's canon is grasped and its homogeneous vulnerability exposed. For its defense and our attack are merely metonyms for an endless contest between the supposed necessity of an invariant reality (archism) and the denial of that necessity (anarchism). There is no prior or posterior reason why that contest should go one way in one field of honor, and another in another.

There is one immensely important clue that affects the relative strength of the opposing strategies I have sketched. Canonically, there are at least two entirely different views of induction at work in the ancient and modern worlds: one is Aristotle's, more or less; the other, also more or less, links Hume's approach and the sanguine enthusiasm of inductivism (with regard to the discovery of genuine nomic universals). Following the first, the real world is said to harbor substantive necessities — necessities *de re* — that an educated sampling of consensual experience will lead us to grasp in an appropriate cognitive leap. According to the second, we construe the contingent regularities of experience in such a way that the principle of their invariant order may be treated as deducible from posited axioms, thereby casting this order as necessary: initially this principle is formulated *de dicto* and may subsequently, depending on the supposed realism of the exercise involved, be defined as *de re*. (Clearly, Humeans and inductivists need not agree here.)

The first strategy, Aristotle's, may be called *essentialist induction*. The scatter, the contingency, the randomness, the fragmentary nature of experience fall into an order suited to science when, from its disconnected parts, human intelligence grasps the invariant structure of the natural kinds of which those bits harbor the cognitive clue. It is entirely possible that deviant and unnatural phenomena obtain on occasion; but their own deviance is intelligible only by comparison with what is normal. Science proceeds in its fixed way; the four "causes" define, as always, the changeless, natural kinds to which we approximate by stages, as causes are variously matched with experience.

The argument is exactly the same in the *Physics* and the *Poetics*. So Aristotle is able to proceed briskly to the task of sorting the "natural" species (the genres) of poetry. They are said to be concerned with imitating actions. Their essential differences are marked by the treatment of that single generic feature: "the objects the imitator represents are actions, with agents who are necessarily either good men or bad — the diversities of human character being nearly always derivative from this primary distinction, since the line between virtue and vice is one dividing the whole of mankind" (2.1448a). The genres of poetry, then, are natural kinds answering partly to what is normatively natural for the species man, and partly to what is instrumentally preferred in the various arts (in terms of the means and manner of imitation). It is obvious that Sophocles is Aristotle's exemplar, invariantly explicit in all respects regarding the four causes, particularly the final cause. Euripides may still be recovered, however, if one rightly understands what is implied in his having said that "he drew men . . . as they were," rather than "as they ought to be" (25.1460b); although, if even that much cannot be said of a particular dramatist, then the poet may at least, or perhaps even must, present men "in accordance with opinion" (25.1460a). Presumably, on this slim basis, scientific induction may still succeed.

Aristotle's analysis of genres, and of their analogues in other sectors of inquiry, is unique in that he alone articulates a singularly powerful conception of how science actually grasps the structure of reality. What is more, he does so by applying the same method to physical science, ethics, poetry, and argument, and thus the findings accompanying each such partition may be harmonized at once with the results generated by every other. All of nature divides into fixed kinds; the human species is preeminent among these, by virtue of its members' capacity for intelligent action; ethics and politics sort out the natural norms of human existence in a manner that is congruent with the essential structure of the species; the arts imitate the latter's generically defining feature (true action); and argument and persuasion are shown to be maximally effective where they facilitate the perspicuous grasp of *principled* distinctions.

Nevertheless, seen from a perspective that joins the most contemporary and the most ancient philosophical themes, there is a fatal flaw here: Aristotle's conception of science as dealing with necessities *de re* proves not to be necessary, for it is not conceptually unavoidable.[3]

Thus, in the *Metaphysics,* Aristotle introduces what he regards as "the most certain of all principles," one answering to the "science" of the natural philosopher and to the demands of the "one kind of thinker who is above even the natural philosopher (for nature is only one particular genus of being)." The principle in question fixes the form of every inquiry that "is universal and deals with primary substance": "the same attribute cannot at the same time belong and not belong to the same subject and in the same respect" (4.3.1005b). Stated formally, the principle of noncontradiction seems secure enough. But in Aristotle's hands, it is made to entail, as a necessary and direct consequence of its unconditional certainty, that we cannot avoid attributions of essential properties if we admit apparent ones (such as perceptual properties), and that we cannot abandon the principle of excluded middle. The reason is that the principle of noncontradiction depends, when applied in a given inquiry, on the necessary truth that "there is [in all real things] something whose nature is changeless" (1010a, 1007b). Yet, that principle is *not* itself a necessary truth.

As soon as the countermove is conceded, the inherent weakness of Aristotle's master strategy becomes apparent. First, the idea that there are natural norms for art and conduct, and that these somehow can be inferred from the applied *aitíai* that explain all phenomena involving the human species, is one that may be effectively contested;[4] second, we are forced to consider that the cognitive aptitude for discerning true universals, which Aristotle must posit—the capacity for discerning changeless predicables among inductively relevant bits of potential evidence—is never, and cannot really ever be, secured by any known epistemological argument.[5] With the loss of invariant species goes the dream of construing ethical norms (in the sphere of conduct) and genres (in the domain of the arts) as invariant principles (or as findings resulting from the application of such principles to the natural-kind properties of man). By a related argument, the necessity of invariant causal laws (that are not necessarily confined to the "folk" species of our own and of Aristotle's macroscopic world) must also tumble.

3

It is extraordinary how many theories of genres in the arts, and of natural kinds in the sciences and ethics, really devolve from something like

Aristotle's argument. Of course, in the modern world, the Aristotelian thesis is not likely to be offered neat; it is, on the contrary, often melded in one way or another with a strong causal view that invokes the second sort of induction hinted at a while ago, or some equally accessible alternative (communicative intent, for instance). Perhaps Heinrich Schenker's (1935) view of tonal music suggests a conception of genres that combines an Aristotelian-like essentialism with a causal analysis of the significance of musical intervals. Alternatively, and perhaps more sympathetically, Schenker's analysis favors some Goethean-like harmony between the innate sensibilities of man and the invariant, minimal order of tones in nature that the musician can "prolong" as he "unfolds" (*auskomponiert*) these very tones (*Klänge*). Thus, an ideal *Ursatz* is externalized in a manner not altogether dissimilar to Goethe's conception of the *Urpflanze*. In Schenker, music is mimetic, based on innate, invariant, and necessary structures, capable of supporting compositional variety only within a fixed order. In fact, in his early *Harmony* (1906), Schenker seems actually to have in mind a parallel between drama (perhaps tragedy) and "the life of a [musical] motif" (13):

> We should get accustomed to seeing tones as creatures. We should learn to assume in them biological urges as they characterize living beings. . . . Man repeats himself in man; tree in tree. In other words, any creature repeats itself in its own kind, and only in its own kind; and by this repetition the concept "man" or the concept "tree" is formed. Thus a series of tones becomes an individual in the world of music only by repeating itself in its own kind; and, as in nature in general, so music manifests a procreative urge, which imitates this process of repetition. . . . the motif lives through its fate, like a personage in a drama. (6, 13; see also 3–4)[6]

One can also find more than a suggestion of a confluence of the two just noted notions of induction in Northrop Frye's (1957) influential contemporary account of literary genres:

> A theory of criticism whose principles apply to the whole of literature and account for every valid type of critical procedure is what I think Aristotle meant by poetics. Aristotle seems to me to approach poetry as a biologist would approach a system of organisms, picking out its genera and species, formulating the broad laws of literary experience, and in short writing as though he believed that there is a totally intelligible structure of knowledge attainable about poetry which is not

poetry itself, or the experience of it, but poetics. One would imagine that, after two thousand years of post-Aristotelian literary activity, his views on poetics, like his views on the generation of animals, could be re-examined in the light of fresh evidence. Meanwhile, the opening words of the *Poetics* . . . remain as good an introduction to the subject as ever, and describe the kind of approach that I have tried to keep in mind for myself. (14)

Frye actually says that "sciences [including poetics] normally begin in a state of naive induction" and move on to their characteristic "inductive leap":

It occurs to me that literary criticism is now in such a state of naive induction as we find in a primitive science. . . . Criticism seems to be badly in need of a coordinating principle, a central hypothesis which, like the theory of evolution in biology, will see the phenomena it deals with as parts of a whole. The first postulate of this inductive leap is the same as that of any science: the assumption of total coherence. (15–16)

Frye's proposal differs in spirit from Schenker's, at least inasmuch as the latter construes genres as having a normative force that results from their being natural kinds. Schenker thus has a stronger sense of the closure of essential kinds that defines the boundaries within which artistic invention is admissible. In fact, as is well known, Frye urges us to "get rid" of all the "sonorous nonsense" of normative, ethical, ideological, and similar talk as far as poetics and the science of criticism are concerned: "value-judgments are [all] subjective," unsuited to the aspirations of a science. Frye is prepared to leave all such matters to the tradition of Matthew Arnold and T. S. Eliot (18, 20, 24, 26). Yet, in thus insisting on a disjunction between the descriptive and explanatory, on the one hand, and the normative, on the other, Frye cannot really be subscribing (as he believes he is) to Aristotle's model; and if his statement is intended to suggest that it would merely be a matter of approximating the causal covering laws of literature, then it is fair to say that the project specified at the beginning of his account has been abandoned. Still, he does allow for the cultural relativity of prevailing taste, ideology, conviction, and the like; hence, in that distinctly attenuated sense, he allows for something like a transient literary *canon*. But, otherwise, "all efforts of critics to discover rules or laws in the sense of moral mandates telling the artist what he ought to do, or have done, to be an authentic artist, have failed" (26). Science, in Frye's view, is evidently *wertfrei*.

Hayden White (1978), who follows Frye to the extent of privileging the latter's literary genres in a "scientific" analysis of the forms of history, returns to Aristotle's conceptual linkage between science and normative judgments by way of a structuralized, or constructivist, view of social reality. Generalizing over more than history—but at least over history—White declares that "it is not a matter of choosing between objectivity and distortion, but rather between different strategies for constituting 'reality' in thought so as to deal with it in different ways, each of which has its own ethical implications. . . . But the moral implications of the human sciences will never be perceived until the faculty of the will is reinstated in theory" (22–23).[7] In speaking of the human faculties, White construes his own theory as Kantian. What is noteworthy, however, is that his "realism" is marked more by late phenomenology, hermeneutics, structuralism, and poststructuralism than it is by either Aristotle or Frye. And this is why he restores the normative or ethical element to the alternative "constitutings" of social reality with which he is concerned. White is already a "late" theorist of historical genres, for he signals the anomalous possibilities of extending a "realist" account of genres within history and literature, at a time when both the Aristotelian conception of induction and the modern model spanning Hume and the unity of science program are perceived as needing to be superseded. I shall return to this issue.

A more familiar Aristotelian and realist theory of history may be found in Paul Ricoeur's (1983) account of narrative, for this philosopher explicitly builds on Aristotle's *Poetics* and Augustine's *Confessions*. Ricoeur clearly means his account of history to be mimetic, realist, and rationally ordered along the lines of distinct narrative genres. Yet, in a manner suggesting the influence of both phenomenology and hermeneutics, he also believes the realism of the representation of human action to be constructed. He does not, however, assume that no valid representations of reality are possible as a result: "action," he says, "is the 'construct' of that construction that the mimetic activity consists of" (32–37). One begins to see here the possibility of an endless variety of alternative "inductive" strategies, for this approach allows at the very least for what may be called "didactic induction" (in a phenomenological vein), just as, by virtue of its association with the hermeneutic tradition to which Hans-Georg Gadamer belongs, it makes room for "horizonal induction" (in the form of a *Horizontsverschmelzung*). It is helpful to take due note of such possibilities, but I would be led too far afield if I were to pursue them in greater detail. Their distinctive features will become clearer at a later stage in my argument.

In the recent hermeneutic tradition proper, E. D. Hirsch, Jr. (1967), clearly revives the Aristotelian conception of mimetic genres via August Boeckh's notion of "purpose" (*Zweck*), although Hirsch does insist on the purely metaphorical sense in which literary works could possess intrinsic purpose. Hirsch observes that, by *"Zweck,"* Boeckh must mean "something like an Aristotelian final cause," and goes on to add:

> My [own] description [of genres] departs from that of Aristotle and the neo-Aristotelians by its insistence on the entirely metaphorical character of an entelechy when that concept is applied to a form of speech. A verbal genre has no entelechy or will of its own. It is not [one might almost say, against Schenker's view] a living thing with a soul or vital principle. It is mute inert matter that is given "soul" or "will" by speakers and interpreters. In other words, the purpose of a genre is the communicable purpose of a particular speaker, nothing more or less. (101, n. 19)

Since, in Hirsch's view, *"Meaning* is that which is represented by a text; it is what the author meant by his use of a particular sign sequence; it is what signs represent" (8), the problem of objective interpretation of texts is straightforwardly cognitive, nothing more or less than the recovery of the author's intent:

> This book has concerned itself . . . with establishing that interpretation does at least have a determinate object of knowledge—the author's verbal meaning—and it has shown that such knowledge is in principle attainable. Validation is the process which shows that in a particular case such knowledge has probably been achieved. (163)

Hirsch's inductive procedure (the use of the term "probably" is intended in a rigorous way) is ultimately grounded on the dual assumption that authors know what they intend (at least to a first approximation), and that interpreters proceed inductively to discern the constraints under which an inference regarding the meaning of a text can be made objective. The decisive intervening structure to be discerned is, for Hirsch, the "intrinsic genre" of a speaker's text or utterance. Thus far, it is clear that Hirsch proposes a hermeneutic analogue (or even an extension) of Aristotle's notion of genres, the difference being that the reality of the genres in question does not depend on Aristotle's essentialist metaphysics. Or, at least, so it seems. And induction to genres will of course proceed differently from causal induction proper, inasmuch as genres are intentionally complex and not readily treated in a causal way (even if they do entail a causal thesis about external influence). Unless, therefore, we can reduce the human sciences to the physical, we will have to admit a variety of inductive strategies.

Hirsch's notion of "intrinsic genres" requires additional attention. "All understanding of verbal meaning," Hirsch declares, "is necessarily genre-bound" (76). What *is* a genre? we cannot help asking. Hirsch offers what may well be the boldest and most explicit picture of intrinsic genre-invariance that contemporary literary theory can boast:

> The variability of the genre conception is entirely a feature of interpretation, not of speaking. The interpreter has to make a guess about the kind of meaning he confronts, since without this guess he possesses no way of grounding and unifying his transient encounters with details. An individual trait will be rootless and meaningless unless it is perceived as a component in a whole meaning, and this idea of the whole must be a more or less explicit guess about the kind of utterance being interpreted. (78)

The point at stake here is twofold. First, *speaking* (and, by extension, "uttering" written texts) is to be construed in terms of the *actions of speakers*. It is thus intrinsically and constitutively genre-bound. Second, *interpreting* — the heterotelic activity of trying to understand what is said or written — proceeds heuristically. Initially it is a matter of intuitive guesses, but the interpretive process is ultimately guided by the invariant notion that a partial meaning, a part or fragment of a meaning, may be rendered properly meaningful when, and only when, it is incorporated into "a whole meaning," that is, into a meaning that is suited to some "whole" action on the part of a human agent. This seems to be Hirsch's hermeneutic reading of the Aristotelian conception of the imitation of an action (and it amounts, in effect, to a resolution of the benign hermeneutic circle).

Hirsch explicitly repudiates any instrumentalist or pragmatist conception of genres:

> Genre ideas . . . have a necessary heuristic function in interpretation, and it is well known that heuristic instruments are to be thrown away as soon as they have served their purpose. Nevertheless, a generic conception is not simply a tool that can be discarded once understanding is attained, because . . . understanding is itself genre-bound. The generic conception serves both a heuristic and a constitutive function. It is because of this that the genre concept is not hopelessly unstable. For if correct understanding has in fact been achieved, and if understanding is genre-bound, it follows that verbal meaning must be genre-bound as well. A genre conception is constitutive of speaking as well as of interpreting, and it is by virtue of this that the genre concept sheds its arbitrary and variable character. (78)

We see, then, that according to Hirsch, the entire science of interpretation will fail if genres are not themselves invariant and real. Admittedly it might not fail on more current views of the nature of science — even physical science. But Hirsch is either unwilling or unable to give up his hermeneutic reading of Aristotle (and Kant). In fact, understanding an author's meaning presupposes a distinction between "meaning" and "subject matter" (including the actual phenomenon of authorial meaning); for it is on just this basis that Hirsch repudiates Gadamer's radicalized hermeneutics. Hirsch claims that when Gadamer attacks "the premise that textual meaning is the same as the author's meaning," thereby taking issue with both Schleiermacher and Dilthey, while also embracing, at least to some extent, Luther's distinction between *res* and *sensus*, "his exposition appears [wrongly] to imply that textual meaning can somehow exist independently of individual consciousness" (247–48; see also 20, including n. 17).

Hirsch rightly rejects Gadamer's notion that "the text [is] an autonomous piece of language[,] and interpretation an infinite process," an idea that really denies that "the text has *any* determinate meaning, for a determinate entity is what it is and not another thing, but an inexhaustible array of possibilities is an hypostatization that is nothing in particular at all" (249). More precisely, Hirsch is right to reject Gadamer's view and thus to remain consistent with his own conception — particularly if he can show that this conception is both necessary and unavoidable. But, of course, Hirsch's entire argument collapses once the Aristotelian thesis regarding the invariance of reality and the necessity of construing true science as the ability to grasp that invariance (the "archic" notion) is shown to be indemonstrable or false, once the stability of reference and predication is disjoined from a *de re* essentialism. Also, regardless of its fate in other respects, Gadamer's thesis is at least *not* incoherent on this score. For, in Gadamer's view, two radical claims are true. First,

> Language is the fundamental mode of operation of our being-in-the-world and the all-embracing form of the constitution of the world. (1966, 3)

Reality, then, is itself hermeneutic and bounded by historical horizons. Second,

> There is nothing like an "I and thou" at all—there is neither the I nor the thou as isolated, substantial realities. I may say "thou" and I may refer to myself over against a thou, but a common understanding [*Verständigung*] always precedes these situations. (1966, 7)

We, as well as the world, are constituted by "a comprehensive [indissolubly symbiotized] life-phenomenon" (1966, 8) to which we belong through tradition, science, and practical life; and "Prejudices are [the] biases of our openness to the world [itself]. They are simply conditions whereby we experience something—whereby what we encounter says something to us" (1966, 9).

Whether Gadamer remains consistent with this vision is another matter altogether (in fact, he does not); but by rejecting the invariance of reality and embracing (in part at least) a historicized constructionism regarding selves and world, Gadamer can be defended against Hirsch's attack involving the supposed disjunction of "meaning and subject matter." There is no such disjunction in Gadamer. Hirsch cannot see this, because of his strong adherence to the fixity of authorial intent and the invariance of cultural realism that that entails. What is more, Hirsch hedges his own conception of an "intrinsic genre" so that, first, he does not actually have to rely on the direct discernibility of such a genre, and, second, he is able to probabilize (or idealize) its discovery by a hermeneutically adjusted version of Aristotelian induction:

> the essential component of a context is the intrinsic genre of the utterance. Everything else in the context serves merely as a clue to the

intrinsic genre and has in itself no coercive power to codetermine partial meanings. . . . To know the intrinsic genre and the word sequence is to know almost everything. But the intrinsic genre is always construed, that is, guessed, and is never in any important sense given. (87–88)

"Context" signifies a heuristic guess at the "whole meaning" to which a part belongs *and* "those givens in the milieu [of utterance] which will help us to conceive the right notion of the whole" (87). The entire exercise is probabilized by Hirsch, who explicitly extends the notion to history and to the human sciences while making the following decisive concession: "The basic fact about any probability judgment is its uncertainty. It refers to a reality that is partly unknown and which may (as in the case of interpretation) never be known with certainty" (174–75; see also 173–80).[8] But in what sense can we know that the "unknown reality" *is* suitably invariant and discernible?

Hirsch never explains how. In fact, the logical standing of Hirsch's theory of genres is precisely the same, despite radically different conceptions of induction and falsification, as Karl Popper's untenable notion of verisimilitude in the sciences. The one draws on Aristotelian induction; the other, on modern conceptions of frequency and regularity. Yet both require an underlying essentialism.[9] Hirsch's insistence on ideally invariant genres (cast in the same spirit as Popper's progressivism) presupposes a fixed human nature and a fixed world that we cannot ever actually fathom, although we have a rational right to assume that we may know it by approximation. Neither in Hirsch nor in Popper is there the slightest argument to confirm the unavoidability, or even the mere reasonableness, of that conjecture. And much of current philosophy is, of course, inclined to reject such claims altogether.

4

The strategy of induction favored in the modern period is overwhelmingly associated with the discovery of invariant nomic universals. David Lewis (1973) offers an elegant interpretation of F. P. Ramsey's remarks about the laws of nature as "consequences of those propositions which we should take as axioms if we knew everything and organized it as simply as possible in a deductive system" (73–75).[10] As soon as one begins to worry this formulation by way of any of the usual difficulties regarding the artifactual nature of human knowledge — including opacity, historicity, horizonal blindness, practical interest, the cognitive inexhaustibility of the actual world (and of possible worlds), the emergent and diachronically constructed and reconstructed nature of cognizing selves — Lewis's formulation can neither yield valid criteria of nomologicality nor be usable in any teleological or asymptotic account of a realist sort. Induction, here, is entirely heuristic or pragmatic in import. It cannot play a strong realist role or be explicitly linked to nomological invariance. The laws of nature can be nothing more than alternative idealizations aimed at supposed invariance (if they must be invariant). They are selected for explanatory or related purposes; and, inasmuch as they are useful, explanation cannot simply be construed in straightforwardly realist terms.[11]

Yet Lewis's intention is, in fact, a realist one. He thus succeeds in providing nothing more than an ideal account of what it would mean to *believe* that some candidate formulation was definitely of the kind, "law of nature"; he cannot provide anything like a workable criterion for the true laws of nature. Furthermore, if would-be laws cannot, in the full realist sense, be known to be invariant and exceptionless when formulated, then we have good reason to reject Lewis's God's-eye conception.[12] Laws will be hostage, for instance, to intervening models of the world that will relativize them; and these models can never be completely unaffected by the investigator's tacit interests, which are formed within the *praxis* of his own enveloping society. The same is true of the reasons one might have for constructing these models in this way rather than in that, for deeming their fit to be adequate to the observable world, or for construing the observable world as fitting this model better than that one.

Van Fraassen has put the point compellingly, if, that is, one is inclined to accept what I term the "artifactual" nature of human knowledge. Van Fraassen opposes both scientific realism and instrumentalism, advocating his own "constructive empiricism" (or antirealism) on the strength of the point at stake. But we need not follow him in this, for the issue is a purely global one, being indifferent to the *distributed* fortunes of all such competing claims, van Fraassen's included. Such claims may continue their contest, much as before, entirely within the confines of the following consideration:

With the realist I take it [says van Fraassen] that a theory is the sort of thing that can be true or false, that can describe reality correctly or incorrectly, and that we may believe or disbelieve. All that is part of the semantic view of theories. It is needed to maintain the semantic account of implication, inference, and logical structure. There are a number of reasons why I advocate an alternative to scientific realism. One point is that reasons for acceptance include many which, ceteris paribus, detract from the likelihood of truth. In constructing and evaluating theories, we follow our desires for information [shared by our interests] as well as our desire for truth. For belief, however, all but the desire for truth must be "ulterior motives." *Since therefore there are reasons for acceptance which are not reasons for belief, I conclude that acceptance is not belief.* It is to me an elementary logical point that a more informative theory cannot be more likely to be true—and attempts to describe inductive or evidential support through features that require information (such as "Inference to the Best Explanation") must either contradict themselves or equivocate. (1989, 192)

Van Fraassen is right, of course—but for one major difficulty: there is no way to disjoin the desire for "truth" from whatever colors our desire for "information." Hence, not only is Lewis's and Ramsey's option unusable, but there is no way, solely on the strength of van Fraassen's point, to favor scientific realism, instrumentalism, *or* antirealism. Let us grant this much: the invariance of laws can, reliably, be no more than an artifact of our (interested) models of the world, but it can at least be that; nevertheless, there *need* be no laws of nature at all. Causal and modal (necessitarian) discourse would then be best construed as governed and mediated by those models rather than as directly descriptive of an independent world (van Fraassen 1989, 188, 210–14). If, then, we were contingently to introduce invariances (necessities *de re*), we would not need to be skeptical or dismissive of them, but neither could we possibly confirm them inductively or advance asymptotically through them—say, by serial falsification. In fact, to put the matter thus is to make it abundantly clear that, if induction were construed metaphysically, as providing for explanations or natural regularities by capturing laws of nature, then the circularity of the charge that the rejection of laws of nature beyond empirical regularities is itself "eccentric" or "skeptical" would be exposed at once. What is more, this same circularity would establish that induction *cannot* be treated in a purely formal way. Induction, that is, must surely be shaped by the same tacit interests that govern the search for the invariances of nature.[13]

It is here that the parallel with genres lies. For, the essentialist reading of scientific laws is itself cognitively inaccessible to human investigators, *under induction*. The physical sciences are, it is true, not concerned with genres in the sense introduced, but they are concerned with "natural kinds." And, on the Aristotelian view of induction, natural kinds are just those kinds whose proper instances exhibit real essences; and, on the modern view, just those kinds whose proper instances can be explained in terms of real nomic universals. Inductivism, then, is the realist-minded theory that holds that *induction by enumeration, by frequency,* or by any other suitably similar formal procedure may be taken progressively to approach the limit of an actual invariant law. Its rationale is, therefore, identical with those underwriting realist theories of genres, and of norms of conduct, though its specific devices are obviously different. (Let us call the modern version of induction *regularity induction*).

5

We have now seen the essentialism of Aristotle's model of induction bleed into regularity induction. Aristotle's practice fails because it is inescapably arbitrary at the precise point at which cognitive privilege is required. Regularity induction fails because it exceeds its intrinsic resources: there is no formal or epistemically assured basis for moving from empirical regularity to necessary invariance. Once we insist, however, on pragmatist constraints on knowledge or on the symbiotized world we claim to know (that is, once we insist on opacity, preformed interests, historicity, and so on), we move on to a third form of induction that not merely saves the phenomena but also the kind of regularity that Aristotle and canonical modern science pursue. This does, however, presuppose that we deny such regularities their essentialist bite. This is why the genre studies of Aristotle and Hirsch are so instructive. There can be no doubt that Aristotle offers a compelling account of classical tragedy (though only one among many alternatives, if we favor, say, Aeschylus or Euripides over Sophocles) or of tragedy *sans phrase,* if we include Shakespeare or more recent playwrights.

Hirsch is even more instructive than Aristotle, for Hirsch's practice illustrates what we may call *equilibrative induction,* the generic form of reasoning that is aimed at merely salient or consensually stable "invariances" or "universals" of the pragmatist (not essentialist) variety. On the argument intended, our own age cannot escape the pragmatist orientation. (And, of course, Hirsch cannot but misrepresent the metaphysics of the genres he invokes.) In a word, essentialist and regularity inductions are never more than equilibrative, and they simply masquerade as instances of realist invariance. Just as Aristotelianism bleeds into scientific induction, Humean-like regularities aspiring to strict invariance are really equilibrative at bottom. We deform the "world" to ensure uniformity; and we smooth out our observed regularities to fit the world we know.

We may, of course, delude ourselves, for we may imagine, for example, that a given equilibrium in fact is an objective accommodation, and that it is consistent with either of the two practices we have just dismissed. There is no better example of the sort of delusion involved than the one so innocently offered in John Rawls's (1971) well-known conception of "reflective equilibrium." Rawls, it is true, is not concerned with genres, but he is intent on identifying the generic form of human rationality that would yield an objective norm of justice. That Rawls should make the following observation is by no means accidental: "this state of affairs [which] I refer to as reflective equilibrium"—"the process of mutual adjustment of principles and considered judgment[—]is not peculiar to moral philosophy" (20). In this same context, Rawls acknowledges his debt to Nelson Goodman's *Fact, Fiction, and Forecast* (1955), where, he says, one can find "parallel remarks concerning the justification of the principles of deductive and inductive inference" (1971, 20, including n. 7). This is a most convenient conceptual linkage, for it permits me to bring together, in an economic and uniform manner, my analysis of genres (in art), laws (in science), and rules and principles (in morality as well as in argumentative reasoning), and to integrate all these elements into a pragmatist conception of equilibrative induction.

It needs to be said at once that equilibration exhibits a horizontal and a vertical component, each affected by the fortunes of the other. The vertical component is the one that Rawls acknowledges, "the process of mutual adjustment of principles and considered judgment"; the horizontal component concerns the recognition of common predicables (universals). Both are affected by the contingencies of context, tacit interests, and horizonal limitation, on the one hand, and the relative resistance of the brute world, on the other. So, in viewing the adjustment of each and both as subject to constant diachronic restructuring, we need not construe their relative artifactuality as signifying a preference for a strongly idealist theory: pressures issuing from either source need not be denied, though they are ultimately incapable of exerting any privileged weight on distributed findings.

Goodman himself neatly links the two parameters along the lines of what Rawls calls *reflective equilibrium:*

> The task of formulating rules that define the differences between valid and invalid inductive inferences is much like the task of defining any term with an established usage. If we set out to define the term "tree," we try to compose out of already understood words and expressions that will apply to the familiar objects that standard usage calls trees, and that will not apply to objects that standard usage refuses to call trees. A proposal that plainly violates either condition is rejected; while a definition that meets these tests may be adopted and used to decide cases that are not already settled by actual usage. Thus the interplay we observed between rules of induction and particular inductive inferences is simply an instance of this characteristic dual adjustment between definition and usage, whereby the usage informs the definition, which in turn guides extension of the usage. (66)

Goodman's clue is a peculiarly compressed one and does not, in fact, quite anticipate his own more recent line of speculation. But it is followed at once, and is clearly meant to introduce, the "new riddle of induction" that depends in a crucial way on the possibility of distinguishing "lawlike statements" from "merely contingent or accidental generality." For, in Goodman's view, only the first are "capable of receiving [inductive] confirmation from an instance of [such a statement]; accidental statements are not" (73). Goodman draws attention to the *semantic* complexity of lawlike statements — the issue that is brought into focus by the famous "grue"/"bleen" case — which purely *syntactic* studies of induction like Carl G. Hempel's do not touch at all. In his most recent collection, Goodman brings the duality of what I have called the *vertical* and *horizontal* components of the matter directly to bear on his disagreement with the strongly syntactic approach of Willard Van Orman Quine:

Individuation is, as Quine says, determined by "a cluster of related
grammatical particles and constructions: plural endings, pronouns, the
'is' of identity and its adaptations 'same' and 'other.'" He neglects to
mention that the interpretations of these particles and constructions
cannot be settled without considering the sort of thing they are individuating. They need to be interpreted as part of a broader system,
and their interpretation varies as they are incorporated into different
systems. . . . What counts as being the same thing varies from one
sort of object to another. (Goodman and Elgin, 1988, 8–9)[14]

Goodman clearly contests the reliability of methodological and logical
rules cast as strictly formal or syntactic invariances. The truth is that,
given his own argument (the role attributed to so-called analytical
hypotheses and the analytic/synthetic dogma), Quine should have
agreed with Goodman—here at least.[15]

Goodman's clue is a radical one, and it is absolutely decisive for the
standing of both deductive and inductive logic: *all* formal, syntactic,
rulelike, and lawlike structures depend on contextual, semantic, and
"interested" concerns—on *praxis*, in the deepest sense. There is no way
of separating the validity of formal rules and canons from their range
of application; *and* predicable similarities and differences within that
range are a function of what Rawls more pointedly terms "reflective
equilibrium." Goodman's actual analysis of what effects such equilibria, particularly of what he calls *entrenchment*, is, however, noticeably
thin, although his statements do allow him to bridge his disagreement
with Quine, and to do so in a distinctly pragmatist spirit.[16]

The difference between Goodman's use of his own notion of reflective equilibrium and Rawls's application of it to justice and other moral
concepts is enormous—a difference not clearly perceived by Rawls himself. This is perhaps why Rawls fails to understand the sense in which
his own theory yields mere ideology rather than an objective set of principles collected by way of a mental equilibration:

I . . . turn to the notion of reflective equilibrium. The need for the
idea arises as follows. According to the provisional aim of moral philosophy, one might say that justice as fairness is the hypothesis that the
principles which would be chosen in the original position [roughly:
under the condition that all parties in that position are equal, suitably
rational, ignorant of their socially determined contingent differences,
and intent on selecting "the most favored interpretation of justice"

under that condition] are identical with those that match our considered judgments and so these principles describe our sense of justice.
But this interpretation is clearly oversimplified. (Rawls 1971, 48)

Two obvious differences separate Rawls and Goodman: first, Rawls
never introduces the problem of similarity regarding the extension of
relevant terms or predicates, so he apparently does not appreciate the
unmanageably large bias (recall van Fraassen's discussion) that determines what will be perceived as similar and different as far as objectivity goes; second, Rawls insists on complete ignorance about the background conditions for rationally determining the objective principles of
justice, where (on Goodman's argument) such an assumption would, in
context, be utterly pointless. The result is that Rawls actually believes
his proposed universal principles to be objective, just as he assumes
that their invariance may be justified by the scrupulous use of reflective
equilibrium; but, on the argument mounted (Goodman's at least,
though it too is lacking in historical or hermeneutic sensitivity), no
principles can be exceptionless — a fortiori, no moral principles can be
either.

Rawls might have considered the different "natural" species (or
genres) of justice: he is clearly interested in questions of justice between
generations and in international justice, and he explores such matters
elsewhere. But here the equilibrative exercise is obviously undertaken
in an attempt to discern the unique generic concept that could be
deployed objectively, universally, and consistently within its various
"genres." Rawls eschews essentialism, or so, at least, it would appear.
But the equilibrative exercise, which is apparently applied to all contingencies, is nevertheless dependent on what Rawls takes to be an invariant model of rationality. In Goodman's argument, even reflective
equilibrium cannot be based on an invariantly neutral practice. It is, in
fact, the presumption of the normative invariance (or rationality) of
human nature that links such seemingly different enterprises as
Rawls's regarding justice and Hirsch's regarding the interpretation of
texts. It is not that either adopts Aristotle's view outright: it is enough
that they are metaphysically and methodologically optimistic about
linear progress, verisimilitude, and rational consensus, much as is
Jürgen Habermas (1981, chap. 1), who espouses a cognate view. No
grounds are provided anywhere for such confidence. Rawls, of course,

is aware of the impossibility of exhausting "all possible descriptions and
. . . all philosophically relevant arguments" about justice. "The most we
can do," he says, "is to study the conception of justice known to us
through the tradition of moral philosophy and any further ones that
occur to us, and then to consider these." This is how he intends to proceed, and he is confident that his own principles "would be chosen in the
original position in preference to other traditional conceptions of justice,
for example, those of utility and perfection; and that these principles give
a better match with our considered judgments on reflection than those
recognized alternatives. Thus justice as fairness moves us closer to the
philosophical ideal; it does not, of course, achieve it" (49–50).[17]

There can be no doubt that Rawls thinks of reflective equilibrium as
conceptually (and perhaps even metaphysically) neutral and invariant
(chap. 25). In a way, his conception is the moral analogue of Popper's view
of science, except that it is both inductivist and falsificationist. (There is,
of course, a form of progressivism favored in either direction.)[18]

I should add at once that the convergent theme underwriting Goodman's and van Fraassen's refusal to disjoin anything like the abstract
equilibrative principle from a larger sense of social context, tacit interest, *praxis,* and the like (in Goodman: with reference to entrenchment
and lawlikeness; in van Fraassen: regarding the adequacy rather than
the truth of theories) needs to be brought to bear as well on logical and
mathematical rules and canons. Perhaps it will be sufficient to cite the
penetrating observation offered by John Stachel (1983) in his response
to Maria Luisa dalla Chiara's discussion of the question, "Can empirical theories influence or even transform logic?" (1983), the context
being that of so-called quantum logic. Stachel objects to dalla Chiara's
separation of "the formal and the empirical sciences (logic and mathematics being the supposed 'formal sciences')" and to her subsequent
attempt "to establish the proper relationship between the two groups":

> It seems to me that this separation is fundamentally based on the tra-
> ditional approach to the "theory of knowledge," with its radical separa-
> tion of subject and object; the major effort then being expended in
> explaining how the subject is able to arrive at knowledge of the object.
> A more fruitful approach to the sciences, I have argued, is based upon
> regarding each of them as a theoretical practice, working upon and
> transforming even conceptual materials to produce the particular
> object of knowledge characteristic of that science at a certain stage of

its development. The whole hierarchical organization of the sciences into logic, mathematics, the empirical sciences—each earlier term supposedly founded independently of, and serving as part of the foundation for, the later ones—must be rejected as the consequence of an incorrect starting point in the division of formal and empirical sciences. (92)

Stachel's point is entirely in accord with, and even lends support to, what I have been urging here and what van Fraassen (1989, 57–64) specifically recommends.

In short, once we favor the usual pragmatist (or practical) constraints on cognition, an analogous treatment is required of genres, rules, canons, principles, and the like, whether in the arts, the sciences, morality, or formal arguments. This is a remarkably comprehensive finding, one that plainly articulates the converging, yet rarely acknowledged, philosophical consensus of our own world. The essential themes are the ones that are here presupposed and applied to the specialized practices of human life with which I have been concerned. I should perhaps assemble them a little more formally as the pragmatist themes that they in fact are: (i) the denial of a principled disjunction between theory and practice; (ii) the assumption of an indissoluble symbiosis of world and word within which cognizing subjects and cognized objects are provisionally sorted; (iii) the denial of essentialist invariances or necessities *de re;* (iv) the admission that all questions of similarity and difference regarding predicables and identities are context- and interest-bound, inseparably grounded in the *praxis* of a society; (v) the denial of cognitive transparency and privilege; (vi) the acknowledgment of the horizonal, preformed, and historicized nature of human cognition and interest; (vii) the affirmation of the socially constructed and emergent functions of persons or selves; (viii) the recognition of the diachronically equilibrated fit between theory and practice within some encompassing form of life; and, redundantly, (ix) the admission that all closed systems (whether extensional or syntactic), invariances, strict universals, essences, necessities, and the like are no more than artifactual posits internal to the entire space defined by (i)–(viii).

6

It is, of course, entirely possible to apply equilibrative induction in a purely heuristic or arbitrary way—for some transient purpose or other.

But there must be a sense, in the sphere of the practices targeted here, that its use also yields "genres" or "kinds" or "rules" or "principles" that do have a *realist* thrust without by the same token entailing essentialism or necessities *de re*. This comes as a surprise to the advocates of Aristotelian induction and scientific inductivism. It is, however, consistent with acknowledging that the realism ascribed to cultural phenomena depends, in a sense that is never invoked with respect to an "independent" physical world, on its being the case that in the human sciences the cognizing subject and cognized object are one and the same, sharing a common form of life, a *Lebenswelt*, tradition, practice, or history. What is more, this subject and object cannot possibly be globally mistaken about the meaningful structure of their own spontaneous, socially acquired behavior.

Objectivity need not be strictly punctuated in cultural matters in the way usually favored in the physical sciences; it can and needs to accommodate interpretive divergences, historical changes, and accretions; it can admit a realist critique of consensual understanding, but it cannot depart very far from a consensual holism; and it is in general more labile than realism in the physical sciences.[19] Nevertheless, realism is not irrelevant in cultural matters; for, given any viable network of social practices, there is a sense of weighted saliencies of experience, of a somewhat exclusionary horizonal orientation, of limits of consensual tolerance and expectation, and of the resistance of the brute (social) world to which we belong. And this sense affects our critical appraisal of whatever we take the real structure of that world to be. There is also no reason at all why this kind of realism should not extend to norms and values, provided only that they are construed as embedded in given social practices, as open to description, and as not yet legitimated as obligatory, categorically binding, apodictic, or the like. They need only be conformable (thus far) with a given form of life or its *Sitten*.

Here, once again, genre studies are particularly instructive. One literary theorist, Adena Rosmarin, adopts a purely heuristic view of genres (which she characterizes as "pragmatic"). As a result, it is true, she fails to accommodate the relaxed sense (just recommended) of the realism of genres and similar cultural structures, which her own account surely requires. Her practice nonetheless confirms the rigor of equilibrative induction:

Genre is a finite schema capable of potentially infinite suggestion . . . a genre is chosen or defined to fit neither a historical nor a theoretical reality [she means either a restricted *geistlich* or an unrestricted, universally invariant, reality], but to serve a pragmatic end. It is meant to solve a critical problem, a problem that typically involves justifying the literary text's acknowledged but seemingly inexplicable value. The critic accordingly "finds" his genre by correcting a previous genre . . . a genre that is erroneous not because it is inherently wrong but because for certain poems it explains insufficiently well. And the new genre is correct not inherently but pragmatically: because it explains sufficiently well, the power to explain being identical with the power to correct the old genre, to remedy its deficiencies, to make it workable. . . . But unlike the "theoretical" [the essentialist] genre, its choice or definition is not itself constrained by a "deeper" ground, whether it be an entity or a category. It is always constrained pragmatically and rhetorically, by the critic's suasive purpose and audience. (Rosmarin 1985, 44, 50)

Rosmarin convincingly shows that there are, in particular, important differences between such poems as Robert Browning's "My Last Duchess" and "Andrea del Sarto" and T. S. Eliot's "Love Song of J. Alfred Prufrock," which are often indifferently classified together as "dramatic monologues," the assumption being that they provide the warrant for a strong improvisation of a distinctive genre, the "mask lyric" (109–15). (My concern here, of course, is with the strategy of the argument, not with the purely literary question.) If, however, "realism" is construed in the sense I have favored (one that does not require invariant essences independent of the salient interest of a given critical cohort), then the success of Rosmarin's own effort is somewhat misdirected by her own "pragmatism"—her effort to construct a pertinent continuum of poetic instances that could be tested in accord with the sensibilities of trained readers. The practice is clearly equilibrative—in such a way that it is obviously impossible to disjoin the "vertical" parameter involving the reconciliation of theory and practice (the "theoretical" and the "historical," in Rosmarin's words) from the "horizontal" one that reconciles the meaning of general predicates and their capacity to range over particular instances. Yet this is precisely what we should expect from a pragmatist (but realist) view of social existence. The decisive feature of the illustration lies, first, in the gradual invention of a reasonably stable new genre that is fitted (equilibratively) to the saliencies of recently emerged poetic specimens that accord (again, equilibratively) with the still-viable array of older genres; and second, in the impossibility of construing that invention in any strongly essentialist manner; and finally, in the precise similarity between the resolution of the genre question in these cases and the resolution of the larger question of fitting general terms or predicates to all the encountered items of evolving experience.

Rosmarin follows E. H. Gombrich's (1961) example here, which is also notably equilibrative, although Gombrich's notion is hostage to a sort of verisimilitude based on causal discovery (as a result of a privileging of Popper's falsificationism, and as a consequence of his own emphasis on pictorial naturalism): "if 'fit' is acknowledged to be philosophically impossible but pragmatically possible, if our purpose is not finding accurate comparisons [since representational resemblance is ineluctably constrained by variable social conventions: there is no 'innocent eye'] but, in Gombrich's words, 'inventing comparisons which work,' then we are free to define 'work' as we will" (Rosmarin 1985, 45). Not quite: as Gombrich remarks, in effect commenting on the equilibrative use of the vertical and horizontal parameters of genre fit, even in discerning naturalism in seemingly unlikely pictorial conventions,

> there is no doubt . . . that [say] Egyptian art had long been adapted to the functions of portrayal, of presenting visual information and memories of campaigns and ceremonies. . . . It is sometimes thought paradoxical that the Egyptian artists showed themselves such keen observers of animals and foreign races while they were satisfied with the conventional stereotypes of the ordinary human figure. But from the point of view of a diagrammatic art, this habit looks less puzzling. Wherever the difference between species matters, the schema is modified to admit the distinction. (121)

The same equilibrative tendency may be found in Hirsch's analysis, except, of course, that Hirsch never relinquishes the notion of an "intrinsic genre." When, for instance, he remarks that "all understanding of verbal meaning is necessarily genre-bound" (76), he cannot but mean that there are genres that interpretable texts are rightly taken to instantiate. But that would preclude a practice like Rosmarin's, in which a genre is contrived *after the fact* in order to render perspicuous the fine interpretation of a particular text. Hirsch requires, in advance

of interpretation, essential genres that are fixedly real; but his own formulation (as we have seen) actually treats genres only as idealizations
of some sort (possibly in a way not altogether unlike Max Weber's treatment of ideal types).[20] Hirsch does add, finally: "There is this one
immense distinction: the fundamental categories of experience are, no
doubt, immutable, whereas the everyday types by which we constitute
experience are open to revision" (273). But even here he makes it clear
that he means the latter concession only in a verisimilitudinous sense.
Since he cannot actually specify his "immutable" genres, and since he
admits a kind of equilibrative fit in practice, Hirsch cannot really
defend his own strong thesis. This is so because he cannot show it to be
necessary for avoiding incoherence or for ensuring objectivity of the
sort that is suited to cultural realism.

7

Rosmarin's weakness is really the counterpart of Rawls's. Rawls fails to
note that equilibration (in Goodman's model) requires a resolution of
the vexed question of generic similarity as well as of the (pragmatic)
relation between theory and practice; and Rosmarin, even as she
adopts the pragmatist's stance, pretends that the question of discerned
resemblances need not affect the force of her purely heuristic claim.

These lapses are the comfortable result of supposing that there are
reliable normative grounds, however unspecified, for ensuring the viability of certain critical practices, even when real invariances are
denied or discounted. The facilitating assumptions tend to take either
of two distinct forms; they also appear in remarkably parallel ways in
the different substantive inquiries involving genres (in the arts), laws
and explanatory theories (in the sciences), and rules and principles (in
morality and politics). On one assumption, pertinent confidence col-
lects in favor of the view that the salient historical traditions of different
(perhaps all possible) human societies converge, even under the contingencies of history, on determinate norms of truth, validity, rationality,
intelligibility, virtue, reasonableness, and the like that remain effectively
constant as the unaccountable result of the reflexive processes of the
societies involved. But if we were to accept any version of (i)–(ix) of my
earlier tally, such confidence would be utterly unfounded. (I label this
challenged line of thinking *traditionalism:* the assurance that contingent

history somehow approximates the very invariances that a frank essentialism claims rigorously to have discerned.)[21] The pattern is nowhere clearer than in the strongly historicist reading of the "classical," in Gadamer's *Truth and Method* (1960)—which, in effect, transforms what is merely a labile *genre* into a strict or invariant *canon:*

> The classical is fundamentally something quite different from a descriptive concept used by an objectivising historical consciousness. It is a historical reality to which historical consciousness belongs and is subordinate. What we call "classical" is something retrieved from the vicissitudes of changing time and its changing taste. . . . it is a consciousness of something enduring, of significance that cannot be lost and is independent of all the circumstances of time, in which we call something "classical"—a kind of timeless [and normatively pertinent] present that is contemporaneous with every other age. (256)

There could be no more doubtful pronouncement of arbitrary confidence, given Gadamer's own insistence on the universality of the (historicized) hermeneutic problem and the (broadly) constructionist view of selves that he espouses.

A perfect analogue may be found in the moral domain, the second form of arbitrary confidence appearing in Alasdair MacIntyre's *After Virtue* (1981). MacIntyre specifically rejects Aristotle's essentialism in the study of historical societies, but then pretends to discern an invariant structure of legitimating virtues that would be distributively internal to the various forms of life expressed within different well-formed societies. Where Gadamer favors a *convergent traditionalism,* MacIntyre favors a *divergent* (or distributed or relativistic) *traditionalism.* But the argument remains essentially the same and is fatally flawed for the same reason: genres are made (by both strategies) to yield canons, even where realist or essentialist invariances are denied.

MacIntyre's argument is a most instructive one—ingeniously Aristotelian in its form and teleologized spirit but not Aristotelian (so it is claimed) in any essentialist sense. It rests on something very close to the discrimination of genres, namely, the discrimination of the "essential" (historically relativized) virtues internal to the contingent practices of particular societies: "A virtue [MacIntyre says, as a first approximation] is an acquired human quality the possession and exercise of which tends to enable us to achieve those goods which are internal to practices and the lack of which effectively prevents us from achieving any such goods" (191). Viable social practices need not, of course, be such that discernible virtues in MacIntyre's sense may always be abstracted from them; that they should fail, on occasion, to be thus discernible does not mean that it is impossible, implausible, arbitrary, or irrational to impute "virtues" (or moral rules or principles, for that matter) to such practices; nor does it follow that particular practices should be able to support, perhaps equilibratively, only one ideally adequate set of moral norms.

MacIntyre is an Aristotelian who favors Aristotle's model of practical reasoning over his essentialism: he explicitly opposes the reductive view that construes man as a creature "who has nothing but a biological nature" (161); we are apparently formed, however divergently, in cultural history (see chap. 12). Nevertheless, the historicized model of practical reasoning, which locates the teleological import of individual life within a societal context, and which links virtue and practice, remains invariant for MacIntyre, presumably without adversely affecting the "inductive" discovery of virtues suited to this society and that. In fact, in MacIntyre's view, "whenever the virtues begin to lose their central place, Stoic patterns of thought and action at once reappear," that is, "patterns of thought" in which laws and formal principles displace the virtues. This is the basis, of course, for MacIntyre's well-known attack on Kantian and Enlightenment models of morality: the Aristotelian model, he believes, is capable of articulating the structure of "moral life in terms both of the virtues and of law," whereas the assumption of the primacy of law or rules cannot accommodate "the achievement of some good beyond the law" (169–70). This may easily be disputed, of course, if what is "beyond" the law is not to be invariantly fixed; but I am not concerned with that issue here.

All this is very elegantly turned. But there is no place in MacIntyre's account for the conceptual possibility that, just as man has a socially constructed nature (as MacIntyre seems to concede), any legitimated scheme of virtues, laws, or principles will be correspondingly constructed as the plausible, potentially compelling, internal norms of this particular society or that. Such a view would subvert at a stroke what cannot be defended anyway, once essentialism is abandoned: any form of induction except the equilibrative or pragmatist sort. No prioritizing of virtues over rules, or of laws over virtues, would be needed. Also, we would not then disallow the possibility of *equilibratively* matching radically divergent virtues to the same social practices. The picture is peculiarly appropriate to contemporary Western societies. It is even compatible with MacIntyre's formal vision:

> Unless there is a telos which transcends the limited goods of practices by constituting the good of a whole human life, the good of a human life conceived as a unity, it will both be the case that a certain subversive arbitrariness will invade the moral life and that we shall be unable to specify the context of certain virtues adequately. These two considerations are reinforced by a third: that there is at least one virtue recognized by the tradition which cannot be specified at all except with reference to the wholeness of a human life—the virtue of integrity or constancy. (203)

The avoidance of arbitrariness cannot by itself eliminate the deep normative disputes of our age. It can only provide an additional idiom for preserving them.

What MacIntyre does not openly acknowledge, and what the review of the question of genres makes clear, is that the seemingly formal or conceptual insistence on the universal adequacy of Aristotle's model of practical reasoning cannot really be separated from the exemplars of its own best application. This is related to the consequence I earlier drew from Stachel's account of the relation between mathematics and empirical science. We now see its analogue in the peculiar weighting that MacIntyre assigns to the "virtue of integrity or constancy." There can be no doubt that MacIntyre assigns this virtue a substantive and powerful role akin to the one already illustrated by Gadamer's account of the "classical." So it may perhaps not even be possible to avoid the arbitrariness (or authoritarianism) of "divergent traditionalism" if, that is, the latter is completely disconnected from some grander version of "convergent traditionalism."[22]

Several brief supporting considerations permit me to bring my argument to a full close. For one thing, MacIntyre does not adequately acknowledge that a *canon*—a principled way of interpreting the normative import of an array of specimen cases—begins to emerge (cannot avoid being "inductively" discerned) as a result of an agent's having initially and prejudicially favored one set of exemplars rather than another. This is something genre studies have always made clear.

Joseph Kerman (1984), for instance, forcefully demonstrates how the modern musical canon emerged from the contingencies of nineteenth-century practice, particularly from the regularization of musical scores. He agrees, here, with Edward Cone's well-known pronouncement: "An analysis is a direction for a performance" (180–84).[23] ("Direction" is, of course, a normatively intended notion.) He applies the lesson directly to Schenker's rigid insistence on the legitimacy of an exclusive canon. The same point may be made with respect, say, to F. R. Leavis's views of poetry and fiction.[24] There is no discernible reason why MacIntyre's implicit use of a moral canon should not be similarly viewed as a privileged consequence of an essentially equilibrative practice. Having used this moral canon, he effectively discards it since it *cannot* yield any uniquely satisfactory solutions.

Second, it needs to be appreciated that "skepticism" about objective or essential moral, literary, musical, cognitive, and scientific norms is *not* equivalent to skepticism about a plausible recovery of such norms under conditions that are "constructive" or "inventive" in the spirit of equilibrative induction.[25] The pertinent skepticism is second-order, directed at exclusive legitimative arguments, not at the mere viability, or even effectiveness, of actual norms and canons. MacIntyre implicitly entrenches a favored legitimative strategy that he cannot show to be exclusively required.

Third, there is, particularly in the recent poststructuralist literature (despite its penchant for conceptual suicide), a distinctly plausible reading of legitimative arguments that shows them to be ultimately inseparable from the dynamics of exploitative power relations in a society. One sees this already in Cone's more standard view that the analysis of a score (itself normalized by the development of a canon) is a "direction for a performance."

8

There are a number of genuinely radical themes that may be collected from the preceding discussion—or may be strengthened with very little effort. The most important, perhaps, are these: (i) the problem of normative invariance applies in more or less the same way in the description and interpretation of the arts (genres), in moral and political conduct (virtues, rules), in scientific explanation (laws of nature), and

in formal argument (logical rules or laws); (ii) such would-be invariances can be legitimated (if at all), once the transparency and essential
fixity of nature is denied, only by way of equilibrative induction;
(iii) such induction cannot ensure any uniquely best or changeless
norms or any uniquely best or changeless legitimative strategies for
securing such norms in any sector of inquiry.

All this is radical enough, but it may be radicalized further by construing (i)–(iii) in terms of historical *praxis*. On that condition, all cul-
turally emergent "artifacts" — persons, artworks, sciences, codes of conduct and reasoning — not only cannot be made to yield fixed canons or
principles, but whatever canons, principles, or "natures" may be equilibratively produced will be subject to two further constraints: (iv) the
"natures" of things — hence the canons or principles by which they are
taken to be constitutively or regulatively governed — are alterable as a
result of the history of classifying and interpreting such things; and
(v) the legitimation of would-be canons or principles yielding the rules
and laws of particular domains is subject to the historicity of legitimation itself.

Both (iv) and (v) are among the most radical philosophical claims
that can be made: (iv) runs completely contrary to the well-known (but
irrelevant) objection that "intentionality is not a mark that divides phenomena from phenomena"; for how could it be, one demands, that "to
change the description [of an object] is to change the object[?] What
sort of thing is a different thing under different descriptions? Not any
object" (Dennett 1969, 28–29). What makes the objection irrelevant is,
first, that cultural objects, as opposed to what we posit as physical
objects, *do* possess intrinsically intentional properties; second, that
there is no known conceptual strategy by which to eliminate the intentional or to reduce it to a merely heuristic instrument. Artworks and
persons, and therefore also logics and mathematics (if inseparable from
empirical science) are diachronically altered by fixing their historically
shifting range of application, by changing the theories under which
they are specified, and by serially evolving interpretations of their serially interpreted intentional features. Things of this sort have no
(changeless) natures; they do not form "natural kinds" to which invariant canons, principles, essences, rules, and laws could ever plausibly
apply. *They are, or have, only histories.*

Claim (v) is, if anything, even more radical. For (v) isolates the consequences of admitting the practical nature of all forms of generality, including legitimation. We need only bear in mind that the fitting of theories to selected paradigms (in an ocean of possible matchings that remain ignored or undiscovered) and the fitting of general terms to selected exemplars (again, in an ocean of possible matchings, since everything resembles everything else in some respect) depends on deeply entrenched societal interests that preclude others from evolving or from being more than marginally effective. In this sense, a sense that is perhaps ultimately grounded in Nietzschean views and that is favored in various ways (occasionally madly) by such poststructuralists as Michel Foucault, Jean-François Lyotard, Gilles Deleuze, Luce Irigaray, and similar spirits, there is a profoundly political dimension to legitimation which is itself an effect of subterranean processes of power. This hardly means that legitimation is dispensable, or nothing more than the prize of some unequal political struggle: it only means that second-order legitimation cannot conform with any supposedly invariant canon of neutral and objective conceptual necessity. First- and second-order discourse cannot, in this argument, be logically disjoined; and whatever proves, in a historicized sense, to be legitimatively convincing in this society or that will depend on the shifting pragmatic saliencies (as of covering theory and covering classification) perceived to be relatively stable within the society affected—where, of course, such saliencies betray the same sort of political intrusion.

We may perhaps risk a feminist formulation of the attack on first-and second-order neutrality (not, however, intended to lead us to conclude that we could function without either first- or second-order discourse), if we bear in mind that the philosophical charge at stake is by no means simply captured by this or that particular local interest. Here, then, are some well-known remarks by Irigaray (1977):

> *What remains to be done, then, is to work at "destroying"* the discursive mechanism [of the patriarchal regime, e.g., Freud's]. . . . we have had to go back to it [philosophical discourse in general, Freudian and Lacanian psychoanalysis in particular: "patriarchal" or "phallocentric" discourse] in order to try to find out what accounts for the power of its systematicity, the force of its cohesion, the resourcefulness of its strategies, the general applicability of its law and its value. That is, its *position of mastery,* and of potential reappropriation of the various productions of his-

tory. . . . This domination of the philosophic logos stems in large part from its power to *reduce all others to the economy of the Same*. (74, 76)

"The Same" signifies the tacit enforcement, at once conceptual and "economic," of a normalizing regime of particular distinctions. Seen this way, neither first-order nor legitimative discourse can escape the constellations of power that obtain in the society affected.

In *The Differend: Phrases in Dispute* (1983), Lyotard brings the issue to bear directly on the question of genres, the latter being universalized to include all classificatory regulations of discourse:

> As distinguished from a litigation, a differend [*différend*] would be a case of conflict, between (at least) two parties, that cannot be equitably resolved for lack of a rule of judgment applicable to both arguments. One side's legitimacy does not imply the other's lack of legitimacy. However, applying a single rule of judgment to both in order to settle their differend as though it were merely a litigation would wrong (at least) one of them (and both of them if neither side admits this rule). Damages result from an injury which is inflicted upon the rules of a genre of discourse but which is reparable according to those rules. A wrong results from the fact that the rules of the genre of discourse by which one judges are not those of the judged genre or genres of discourse. (xi)[26]

Here, "genre" absorbs every conceptual distinction and is clearly seen by Lyotard to disallow the emergence of alternative "genres" (or, effectively, other "interests") of discourse and activity. The attack of the poststructuralists is an attack on the implied (more than explicit) suppression of the "other" (*l'autre*), that is, on the assumption that we progress toward the inclusiveness and neutrality of a totalized system of distinctions; it is an attack that applies primarily to second-order legitimative discourse, but it is indifferent to the distinction between first- and second-order discourse more than it is opposed to singling out legitimation, since what is suppressed (the "other") is marked by a surd, what is forever not yet discursively classified. Exceptionless principles, therefore, cannot fail to violate the poststructuralist constraint.

Principles and canons are either the visible schemes of regularizing thought and behavior matching the dominant forces within any society (class, race, gender, ethos, caste, or more amorphous constellation) —

the expression of collective interests (beyond which we cannot go, though they themselves are always historically alterable) — or would-be invariant norms somehow vindicated by inspecting the seemingly invariant structure of reality. Since, in this argument, there is no strictly invariant structure, the latter can be nothing more than a variant on the former.[27]

Objectivity, neutrality, nomologicality, universality, rationality, and legitimation are all artifacts of a historicized odyssey of inquiry that, despite its own unperceived bias and horizonal limitation, searches productively for those stable saliencies of first- and second- order discourse that best serve these idealized objectives under whatever dialectical contingencies obtain.

CHAPTER EIGHT

To Follow
a Rule

CHARLES TAYLOR

I

Great puzzlement arises about rules and conventions, once we try to understand their place in human life in the light of modern philosophy. One aspect of the problem was pressed most acutely and famously by Ludwig Wittgenstein (1953) in his *Philosophical Investigations,* and further explored by Saul Kripke (1982) in his book on the subject. It concerns what it means to understand a rule. Understanding seems to imply knowledge or awareness, and yet Wittgenstein shows that the agent not only is not, but *never could* be aware of a whole host of issues that nonetheless have a direct bearing on the correct application of a rule.

Wittgenstein establishes this point by raising the possibility of misunderstanding. Some outsider, unfamiliar with the way we do things, might misunderstand what to us are perfectly clear and simple directions. "You want to go to town? Well, just follow the arrows." Yet what if this stranger felt that the natural way of following the arrow was to go in the direction of the feathers rather than the point?[1] One might imagine, for example, that there are no arrows in his culture, only a kind of ray gun, the discharge of which fans out like the feathers on our arrows.

This kind of example triggers a certain reaction in our intellectualist philosophical culture. What the outsider fails to understand—the fact that one follows arrows toward the point—we must surely understand. We, after all, *know* how to follow arrows. But what, more precisely, does this statement mean? From the intellectualist perspective, it implies that somewhere in our mind, whether consciously or unconsciously, a premise must necessarily have been established about how arrows are to be followed. From another angle, once we perceive the stranger's mistake, we can explain to him what he ought to do. Yet, if we can provide this kind of explanation, then we must already be in possession of the explanation in question. Thus, the thought that one follows arrows in this particular way is assumed to reside somewhere within us.

The same point can be approached in a somewhat different manner. If we do not in fact have the thought in question, we will experience genuine doubt when faced with the issue of whether we really ought to follow arrows toward the point. How, in such a situation, would we know that this way of proceeding is right? And how, more specifically, could we possibly follow the directions? Yet, this kind of response encounters insuperable difficulties, the reason being that the number of such potential misunderstandings is endless. Wittgenstein makes this point over and over again. There exists an indefinite number of instances in which, given a certain explanation of a rule and a certain range of paradigm cases, someone nonetheless could fail to grasp the appropriate meaning, just as our stranger misunderstood the injunction to follow the arrows. For example, I might say that by "Moses" I mean the man who led the Israelites out of Egypt, but then my interlocutor might have trouble with the words "Egypt" and "Israelites" (1.87). "Nor would these questions come to an end when we get down to words like "red," "dark," "sweet" (1.87). Nor would mathematical explanations be invulnerable to this kind of danger. Imagine teaching someone a series by providing him with a sample range, say 0, 2, 4, 6, 8 . . . He might continue successfully till he reaches 1,000, proceeding from then on with 1,004, 1,008, 1,012. When told that he has failed to grasp our intentions, he becomes indignant, having understood our sample range to be an illustration of the rule "Add 2 up to 1,000, 4 up to 2,000, 6 up to 3,000, and so on" (1.185).

If, in order to understand directions or to know how to follow a rule, we have to know that all these deviant readings are deviant, and if this in turn means that we already need to have formulated thoughts to this effect, then our heads must contain an infinite number of thoughts if we are to follow even the simplest of instructions. Yet, this is clearly an insane proposition. The intellectualist is tempted to treat all these potential problems as issues that we need to resolve before we can begin to understand the directions. ("It may easily look as if every doubt merely *revealed* an existing gap in the foundations; so that secure understanding is only possible if we first doubt everything that *can* be doubted, and then remove all these doubts" [1.87]). Inasmuch as any single explanation necessarily leaves some potential issues unresolved, the former stands in need of further explanations to bolster it. Yet, all further explanations will have precisely the same shortcoming, and as a result the task of explaining to somebody how to do something is literally endless. "'But then how does an explanation help me to understand, if after all it is not the final one? In that case the explanation is never completed; so I still don't understand what he means, and never shall!'—As though an explanation as it were hung in the air unless supported by another one" (1.87).

The last remark, not in single quotes, is Wittgenstein's reply to his interlocutor, and it hints at the mind-set of the intellectualist. The latter seeks securely founded knowledge, thereby revealing an obsession that we recognize as a characteristic of the modern intellectual tradition from Descartes onward. The desired certainty is not regarded as problematic by this tradition's thinkers, since they believe that it is possible to discover the requisite, solid foundations—in explanations, for example, that privilege self-explanatory or self-authenticating features. That is why the imagined interlocutor places his hopes in words like "red," "dark," and "sweet," thereby referring to basic empirical experiences on which everything else might be grounded. The force of Wittgenstein's argument lies in its radical undercutting of all such foundationalism.

Why can someone always misunderstand? And why is it that we do not have to resolve all these potential questions before *we* can understand? The answer to these two questions is the same. Understanding always occurs against a background of what is simply relied on and taken for granted. Someone can always come along who lacks this background, and thus the most straightforward matters can be misunderstood, particularly if we let our imagination roam, allowing ourselves to conjure up individuals who have never even heard of arrows. Yet, at the same time, the background—what is just taken for granted—is not itself the locus of resolved questions. If the misunderstanding stems from a difference of background, what needs to be said in order to clear it up has the effect of articulating some aspect of the explainer's background that may never before have been articulated.

Wittgenstein stresses the unarticulated, and on occasion even the unarticulable nature of this kind of understanding. "Obeying a rule," he says, "is a practice" (1.202). What is more, the process of giving reasons for the kind of practice that is involved in following a rule must necessarily come to an end at some point: "My reasons will soon give out. And then I shall act, without reasons" (1.211). Or later: "If I have exhausted my justifications I have reached bedrock, and my spade is turned. Then I am inclined to say: 'This is simply what I do'" (1.217). More laconically: "When I obey a rule, I do not choose. I obey the rule *blindly*" (1.219).

There are two broad schools of interpretation of what Wittgenstein is driving at with such statements, and they essentially correspond to two different ways of understanding the phenomenon of the unarticulated background. The first interprets the claim that I act without reasons as an expression of the view that no reasons can be given here; no demand for reasons can arise. This is so because the connections that make up our background are not susceptible to justification, being merely a series of de facto links. Thus, for instance, they are regarded as simply imposed by our society; we are conditioned to make the connections in question. They become "automatic," and it is for this reason that the question of justification never arises. The view that society imposes these limits provides the core of Kripke's interpretation of Wittgenstein. Alternatively, the links could perhaps be considered as somehow "wired in" — it is a basic fact about the way we are that we react in a particular way in certain circumstances, blinking, for example, when something approaches our eyes. In that case, too, justifications are not in order.

The second interpretation, on the other hand, assumes that the background really does incorporate *understanding*. It embodies our grasp of things, a grasp that, although unarticulated, nonetheless allows us to formulate reasons and explanations when challenged. In this case, the links would not simply be de facto but would make a kind of sense, the latter being precisely what one would try to spell out in the process of articulation.

In the first view, then, the bedrock on which our explicit explanations rest is made up of brute connections; in the second, it is a mode of understanding and thus makes a kind of unarticulated sense of things.

The first interpretation finds a basis in phrases like "I obey the rule blindly," and perhaps even in the image of bedrock itself, the unyielding nature of which perhaps implies that nothing further *can* be said.

The passages that tell against it are those in which Wittgenstein claims, for example, that following a rule is unlike the operations of a machine (1.193–94), or in which he says the following: "To use a word without justification does not mean to use it without right" (1.289) (although I can imagine an interpretation of this that would be compatible with the first view). Above all, I believe that the privileging of brute connections is at odds with Wittgenstein's insistence on the idea that rule-following is a *social* practice. It is true, perhaps, that this emphasis fits with Kripke's version of the first view. At the same time, I think that in reality this connection between background and society reflects an alternative vision that departs radically from the old monological outlook that has been dominant in the epistemological tradition.

Whatever Wittgenstein may ultimately have believed, the second view seems to me to be the correct one. What the first cannot account for is the fact that we *do* give explanations, that we often *can* articulate reasons when challenged.[2] Following arrows toward the point is not just an arbitrarily imposed connection; it makes sense, granted the way that arrows move. What we need to do, then, is follow a hint from Wittgenstein and attempt to give an account of the background as understanding, thereby situating it in social space. This is what I would now like to explore.

2

The following exploration runs against the grain of much modern thought and culture, particularly that of our scientific culture and its related epistemology. Yet it is this very culture that has molded our contemporary sense of self.

Among the practices that have helped to create the modern self are those that seek to discipline our thought by emphasizing the virtues of a disengaged stance with regard to embodied agency and social embedding. Each of us is thus called upon to become a responsible, thinking mind, capable of forming autonomous judgments (this, at least, is the standard notion). Yet this ideal, however admirable in some respects, has tended to blind us to important facets of the human condition. There is a tendency in our intellectual tradition to read it less as an ideal than as something already present in our very constitution. This reification of the disengaged first-person-singular self is already evident in the thought of figures such as Descartes and Locke, both of whom were founders of the modern epistemological tradition.

It means that we easily tend to see the human agent as primarily a subject of representations — first, of representations of the world outside; second, of depictions of ends that are either desired or feared. What emerges is a monologic conception of the subject. S/he is in contact with an "outside" world — including other agents, the objects s/he and they deal with, and his/her own and others' bodies — yet, this contact is through the representations s/he has "within." The subject is first of all an "inner" space, a "mind," to use the old terminology, or a mechanism capable of processing representations, if we follow the more fashionable computer-inspired models of today. The body and other people may form the content of my representations and may even be causally responsible for some of these representations. Yet, what "I" am, as a being capable of having such representations, the inner space itself, is held to be definable independently of either body or other. It is a center of monological consciousness.

It is this stripped-down view of the subject that has made deep inroads into social science, breeding the various forms of methodological individualism, including the most recent and virulent variant, the current vogue for rational choice theory. It stands in the way of a richer and more adequate understanding of what the human sense of self is really like, and hence of a proper understanding and knowledge of human beings and of the genuine variety of human culture. This kind of consciousness leaves out the body and the other that will both have to be brought back into the picture, if we are to grasp the kind of background understanding to which Wittgenstein seems to have been alluding. Indeed, in restoring the first we necessarily retrieve the second. I shall briefly outline what is involved in this close relation between body and other.

A number of philosophical currents in the last two centuries have tried to get out of the cul-de-sac of monological consciousness. Prominent in this century are the works of Martin Heidegger (1926), Maurice Merleau-Ponty (1945), and, of course, Wittgenstein himself. What all these have in common is a perspective in which the agent is *not* primarily the locus of representations, being engaged rather in practices, as a being who acts in and on a world.

Nobody, of course, has failed to notice that human beings act. The crucial difference is that these philosophers situate the primary locus of the agent's understanding in practice. In the mainline epistemological view, what distinguishes the agent from inanimate entities that also are able to affect their surroundings is the former's capacity for inner representations, whether these are placed in the "mind" or in the brain understood as a computer. What we have and what animate beings lack—understanding—is thus identified with representations and the operations we perform on them.

To situate our understanding in practices is to see it as implicit in our activity, and hence as irreducible to representations. It is not a matter of claiming that we do not frame representations, for we do indeed explicitly formulate what our world is like, what we aim at, and what we are doing. At the same time, however, much of our intelligent action in the world, sensitive as it usually is to our situation and goals, is carried on unformulated. It flows from an understanding that is largely inarticulate.

This tacit understanding is more fundamental than the explicit representational variety in two ways: (1) it is always there, whereas we sometimes frame representations and sometimes do not; (2) the representations that we actually do form are only comprehensible against the background provided by this inarticulate understanding. It is thus the very context that allows these representations to make whatever sense they do. As opposed to being the primary locus of understanding, representations prove to be nothing more than islands in the vast sea of our unformulated practical grasp on the world.

To come to see that our understanding resides first of all in our practices is to attribute an inescapable role to the background. This connection between understanding and background figures, albeit in different ways, in virtually all the philosophies of the contemporary countercurrent to epistemology, being a famous feature, for example, of the thought of both Heidegger and Wittgenstein.

As a result of this insight, the role of the body appears in a different light. Our body is not just the medium through which we enact the goals that we frame, nor is it simply the locus of causal factors shaping our representations. Our understanding is itself embodied. That is, our bodily know-how, the way we act and move, embraces aspects of our understanding of self and world. I know my way around in a familiar environment inasmuch as I am able to get from place to place with ease and assurance. I may be at a loss when asked to draw a map, or even give explicit directions to a stranger. I know how to manipulate and use the familiar instruments in my world, usually in the same inarticulate fashion.

Yet it is not only my grasp of the inanimate environment that is thus embodied, for so in large part are my sense of self and of the footing that I am on with others. The deference I owe you is evident in the distance I stand from you, in the way that I fall silent when you begin to speak, in the way that I hold myself in your presence. Alternatively, the sense I have of my own importance may find expression in a brazen swagger. Indeed, some of the most pervasive features of my attitude toward the world and others is encoded in the manner in which I project and carry myself in public space; whether I am macho, or timid, or eager to please, or calm and unflappable.

In all these cases, the person concerned may not even possess the appropriate descriptive term. For instance, when my demeanor is respectful and when I thereby defer to you, I may not have the word "deference" in my vocabulary. Frequently such words are coined by others (who are more sophisticated), in order to describe important features of people's stance in the world. (Needless to say, these others are often social scientists.) This understanding is not at all, or only imperfectly, captured by our representations. It is carried in patterns of appropriate action, that is, in action that conforms to a sense of what is fitting and right. An agent with this kind of understanding recognizes when s/he or others "have gotten off on the wrong foot." Their actions are responsive throughout to this sense of rightness, but the norms may either be wholly unformulated or articulated in only the most fragmentary fashion.

In recent years, Pierre Bourdieu (1980) has coined the term *habitus* to capture this level of social understanding. This is one of the key terms needed in order to provide an account of the background understanding invoked in the previous section. I shall return to this point in a minute. First, I want to establish the connection that exists between reintegrating the body and the other into the philosophical picture.

It is not hard to see why the other must figure in an account of embodied understanding, for some of the practices that encode this tacit understanding are not instantiated in acts performed by some isolated or single agent. The above example of deference is a case in point.

The person who does the deferring and the agent who is deferred to play out their social distance in a conversation, often with heavily ritualized elements. Indeed, conversations generally rely on micro rituals that escape focal awareness.

Perhaps, however, I should first say a word about the distinction that I am drawing between acts of a single agent (monological acts), and those involving more than one agent (dialogical acts).[3] From the standpoint of the old epistemology, all acts are monological, although the agent often coordinates his or her actions with those of others. Yet this notion of coordination fails to capture the way in which some actions require and sustain an integrated agent. Think of two people sawing a log with a two-handed saw, or of a couple dancing. Rhythm or cadence is a very important feature of human action. Every apt and coordinated gesture has a certain flow. When one loses this, as occasionally happens, one falls into confusion and one's actions become inept and uncoordinated. Similarly, the mastery of a new kind of skilled action is accompanied by the ability to give one's gestures the appropriate rhythm.

Now, in cases like the sawing of a log and ballroom dancing, it is crucial to the rhythm that it be shared. Such dialogical acts only succeed when we place ourselves in the common rhythm that subsumes our individual contributions to the shared action. This is a different experience from that of simply coordinating my action with yours, as I do, for instance, when I run to the spot on the field where I know you are going to pass the ball.

Sawing and dancing are paradigm cases of dialogical actions. At the same time, however, there is frequently a dialogical level to actions that are otherwise merely coordinated. A conversation is a good example. Conversations with some degree of ease and intimacy move beyond mere coordination, manifesting something like a common rhythm. The interlocutor not only listens but participates by means of head-nodding, the occasional "uh-huh," and similar expressions. And at a certain point the "semantic turn" passes over to him or her by virtue of a common movement, the appropriate moment being jointly experienced by both partners as a result of the shared rhythm. The bore, the compulsive talker, thin the atmosphere of conviviality because they are impervious to this. There is a continuity between ordinary, convivial conversation and the more ritualized exchanges, such as litanies, or alternate chanting that one finds in many earlier societies.[4]

I have taken actions having a common rhythm to be paradigm cases of the dialogical, whereas they in fact are but one particular type of such actions. An action is dialogical, in the sense specified above, when it is effected by an integrated, nonindividual agent. This means that for those involved in it, its identity as such and such an action essentially depends on the agency being shared. Thus, these actions are constituted by the shared understanding that exists between those who make up the common agent. Integration into a common rhythm is one of the forms that this shared understanding can take. This does not mean, however, that the latter can come about only in situations involving a face-to-face encounter. In a different way it may also be constitutive of a political or religious movement, whose members may be widely scattered, but who are jointly animated by a sense of common purpose. I am thinking, for example, of what linked the students in Tienanmen Square to their colleagues back on the campuses and, indeed, to a large part of the population of Peking. This kind of action exists in a host of different forms involving any number of different levels.

The importance of dialogical action in human life points to the utter inadequacy of the epistemological tradition's view of the subject as a monological vehicle of representations. We cannot understand human life uniquely in terms of individual subjects who react to others as they frame representations about them, for a great deal of human action only takes place inasmuch as the agent understands and constitutes him- or herself as an integral part of some "we."

Much of our understanding of self, society, and world is carried in practices consisting of dialogical actions. In fact, language itself serves to set up spaces of common action on a number of levels, both intimate and public.[5] This means that inasmuch as our identity necessarily situates us in a given social space, it can never simply be defined in terms of our individual properties. We define ourselves partly in terms of what we come to accept as our appropriate place within dialogical actions. In the event that I really identify with my deferential attitude toward wiser people like you, this conversational stance becomes a constitutive dimension of my identity. This kind of social reference figures even more clearly in the identity of the dedicated revolutionary.

3

The background understanding invoked in the first section, which underlies our ability to grasp directions and follow rules, is to a large degree embodied, and this in turn helps to explain the combination of features that it exhibits: it is a form of *understanding*, a making sense of things and actions, yet at the same time it is entirely unarticulated, just as it can provide the basis for new articulations. As long as we think of understanding in the old intellectualist fashion, as residing in thoughts or representations, it is hard to explain how we can know how to follow a rule — or how to behave correctly at all — without having the thoughts that would justify this behavior as right. We are driven to a foundationalist conception, which allows us to presuppose only a finite list of such thoughts justifying an action from scratch, as it were. Failing this, we are forced to conceive of a supporting background in the form of brute, de facto connections. This is so because intellectualism establishes a false choice between an understanding that consists of representations, and no understanding at all. Embodied understanding provides us with the third alternative that we need in order to make sense of ourselves.

What is important about this kind of understanding is its connection to social practice. My embodied understanding exists in me, not only as an individual agent, but as the co-agent of common actions. This, I believe, is how we should understand Wittgenstein's claim that "obeying a rule" is a practice, that is, a social practice (1.202). Earlier, he asks: "what has the expression of a rule — say a sign-post — got to do with my actions? What sort of connection is there?" His answer is: "Well, perhaps this one: I have been trained to react to this sign in a particular way, and now I do so react" (1.198). Initially this kind of statement seems wholly compatible with the first interpretation mentioned above: some kind of training would instill in the agent a brute, de facto tendency to react in a certain way, and thus the connection between the perception of the sign and the subsequent action would be merely causal. Yet Wittgenstein goes on to reject this reading. His imaginary interlocutor says: "But that is only to give a causal connection," and the Wittgenstein voice in the text answers: "On the contrary; I have further indicated that a person goes by a sign-post only in so far as there exists a regular use of sign-posts, a custom" (*einen ständigen Gebrauch, eine Gepflogenheit*).

Standing social usage is what establishes the connection in question here, which cannot, as a result, be understood as a merely causal one. The regular use does not forge what would amount to a brute causal link but actually gives my response its *sense*, a meaning or significance that is embodied, rather than represented. This is why Wittgenstein can ask the following question in the next passage: "Is what is called 'obeying a rule' something it would be possible for only *one* man to do only *once* in his life?" (1.199). This rhetorical question demanding a negative answer is understood by Wittgenstein to point not just to a factual impossibility but to something that simply makes no sense. "This is a note," he adds, "on the grammar of the expression 'to obey a rule.'" Yet if the role of society were simply to set up the causal connections underlying a given agent's reactions, it would perhaps be strange, but not necessarily nonsensical, to assume that those connections hold for that individual alone, on some isolated occasion. In actual fact, however, the social practice imparts to my action the meaning that it has, and this is why there cannot be only one action with this meaning.

4

Just as the wrongheaded intellectualistic epistemology made deep inroads into social science, to ill effect, so it is important that the scientific consequences of embodied understanding be developed. This is what makes Bourdieu's notion of habitus so important and potentially fruitful.

Anthropology, like any other social science, cannot do without some concept of rules. Too much of human social behavior is "regular," in the sense not just of exhibiting patterns of repetition but of responding to demands or norms that have some generalizable form. In certain societies, women defer to men, young to old. There are certain forms of address and marks of respect that are repeatedly required. The failure to conform is seen as wrong, as a breach. And thus we naturally say, for example, that women use these forms of address not just haphazardly, or as a result of some reflex, but "following a rule."

Suppose we are trying to understand this society, that we are anthropologists, for example, who have come here precisely in order to get a picture of what the life of these men and women is like. In that case, we would have to discover and formulate some definition of the rule governing the relation between the sexes. We would begin by identifying certain kinds of predicaments: a woman meeting her husband, a woman meeting a man who is not her husband, in the village, in the fields, in a range of different places. We would then try to define what is required in each of these situations, and having done so, we would perhaps discover that these different situational requirements allow us to infer some more general rule. The point is that, in one form or another, we would be defining a rule through a *representation* of it. To formulate is in this case to create a representation.

I have no quarrel with this way of proceeding. Indeed, this kind of approach would appear to be wholly necessary. Yet, when intellectualism enters the picture, we wrongly begin to see the rule-as-represented as somehow causally operative. Thus, for example, we may attribute to the agents formulations of the rule in the form of thoughts. Inasmuch, however, as this kind of attribution seems most implausible in many cases, we are inclined instead to see the rule-as-represented as defining an underlying structure. We construe the latter as the crucial causal determinant, operative, as it were, behind the backs of the unsophisticated agents.

Such, following Bourdieu, is the error underwriting intellectualism: "L'intellectualisme est inscrit dans le fait d'introduire dans l'objet le rapport à l'objet, de substituer au rapport pratique à la pratique le rapport à l'objet qui est celui de l'observateur."[6] ("Intellectualism is inscribed in the fact of introducing into the object the intellectual relation to the object, of substituting the observer's relation to practice for the practical relation to practice.")[7] Writing in the French context, Bourdieu naturally gives an important place to structuralism, which is his main target here. Structuralism, it is true, bulks less large in the English-speaking world. This does not mean, however, that the reified understanding of rule-as-representation haunts only the school of Lévi-Strauss, for it obtrudes in confused and uncertain forms wherever the issue that Bourdieu wants to raise has yet to be squarely faced: just how do the rules that *we* formulate operate in *their* lives? What is their *"Sitz im Leben"?* As long as these questions remain unanswered, we are in danger of embracing one of the two types of reification that accompany the intellectualist's epistemology:

Passer de la *régularité,* c'est-à-dire de ce qui se produit avec une certaine fréquence statistiquement mesurable et de la formule qui permet d'en

rendre raison, au *règlement* consciemment édité et consciemment re-
specté ou à la *régulation inconsciente* d'une mystérieuse mécanique
cérébrale ou sociale, telles sont les deux manières les plus communes
de glisser du modèle de la réalité à la réalité du modèle. (67)

To slip from *regularity*, i.e. from what recurs with a certain statistically
measurable frequency and from the formula which describes it, to a
consciously laid down and consciously respected *ruling* (*règlement*), or to
unconscious *regulating* by a mysterious cerebral or social mechanism,
are the two commonest ways of sliding from the model of reality to the
reality of the model. (39)

There is clearly a mistake here, but is it an important one? If we have
to represent the rules in order to grasp them, and if we do, in fact, end
up defining them correctly, then what does it matter whether we properly understand the manner in which they operate within the lives of
the agents? Bourdieu argues that an important distortion occurs when
we see the rule-as-represented as the effective factor. His claim, more
specifically, is that this distortion arises when we take a situated, embodied sense or meaning and provide an explicit depiction of it. The
difference in question may be illustrated by the gap separating our inarticulate familiarity with a certain environment (which enables us to
make our way without hesitation) from the map that provides an explicit representation of this terrain. The practical ability exists only in
its exercise, which unfolds in time and space. As you make your way
around a familiar environment, the different locations and their inter-
relations do not all impinge on you simultaneously. Your sense of them
varies in function of where you are and where you are going. What is
more, some relations never impinge on your consciousness at all. The
route, and the relation of the landmarks, look quite different on the
way out from how they appear on the way back; the way stations on the
high road bear no relation to those on the low road. In practice, you
make your way in and through time. The map, on the other hand, lays
out everything simultaneously, relating each and every point, one to
the other, without any discrimination whatsoever (58–59).

Maps or representations, by their very nature, abstract from lived
time and space. To construe this kind of abstraction as the ultimate causal factor is to make the actual practice in time and space merely derivative, a mere application of a disengaged schema. It is the ultimate in

Platonism. Yet it remains a constant temptation, not only because of the intellectualist focus on representations, but because of the prestige enjoyed by the notion of law as used in the natural sciences. An example of such a timeless, aspatial formula is the inverse square law "dictating" the behavior of all bodies everywhere. Should we not, asks the intellectualist, be seeking something similar in human affairs? This invitation to imitate the really successful modern sciences encourages the reification of rules.

Yet, reification distorts in three crucial, related ways: it blocks out certain features that are essential to action; it does not allow for the difference between a formula and its enactment; and it does not take account of the reciprocal relation between rule and action, the fact that the latter does not simply flow from the former but actually transforms it.

Abstracting from lived time and space means abstracting from action, for the time of action is asymmetrical inasmuch as it projects a future that is always to some degree uncertain. A map or a diagram of the process imposes symmetry. Take a society such as those described by Marcel Mauss, or the Kabyle communities studied by Bourdieu, where a reciprocal exchange of gifts plays an important role in defining and confirming relationships. One can make an atemporal schema of these exchanges and of the rules that they obey. One may then be tempted to insist, as Lévi-Strauss does, that it is the formula of exchange "[qui] constitue le phénomène primitif, et non les opérations discrètes en lesquelles la vie sociale les décompose" ("that constitutes the basic phenomenon, and not the discrete operations to which it is reduced by social life").[8]

What is left out of this account is the crucial dimension of action in time. Bourdieu identifies several ways in which this might matter, not all of which directly support his main claim. For instance, he points out that there is a proper time (a kairos) for reciprocating a favor. If one gives something back right away, it stands as a rebuff, as though one did not want to be beholden to the original giver. If one delays too long, it is a sign of neglect. Yet this dimension of time could itself be expressed in some abstract formula. The temporality of action becomes crucial, on the other hand, when we have to act under conditions of uncertainty and when our action will irreversibly affect the situation. In the rule book of exchanges (which would be an anthropologist's artifact), the relations look perfectly reversible. In practice, however, there is always uncertainty, for there are difficult judgment calls. In Kabylia, the gift relation involves a recognition of an approximate equality of honor between the participants. This means that you can make a claim on a higher-ranked person by giving him a gift, although you may expose yourself to the danger of a brutal refusal if you somehow presume too much. If, on the other hand, your gamble pays off, then your prestige will be increased. At the same time, you dishonor yourself in spontaneously offering a gift to someone who is too far below you.

What on paper is a set of dictated exchanges under conditions of certainty is experienced as suspense and uncertainty in practice. This is partly because of the asymmetrical time of action (1), but also because of what is involved in actually acting on a rule (2). The latter does not automatically apply itself; it has to be applied, and this may involve difficult and finely tuned judgments. This was the point made by Aristotle, and it is central to his understanding of the virtue of *phrónēsis*. Human situations display extraordinary variety; as a result, determining what a norm actually amounts to in any given situation requires a great deal of insightful understanding. The ability to formulate rules will not in itself be enough. The person of real practical wisdom is not so much characterized by an ability to formulate rules as s/he is by the knowledge s/he ably demonstrates in determining how to act in each particular situation. There is, as it were, a crucial phronetic gap between the formula and its enactment, and this too is neglected by explanations that give primacy to the rule-as-represented.

Together these two features yield the uncertainty, the suspense, and the possibility of irreversible change that accompanies all significant action, however rule-guided. I give you a gift, in order to raise myself to your level. You pointedly ignore it, and I am crushed. I have irremediably humiliated myself, and my status has declined. My humiliation takes on added importance once we take into consideration point (3), the way, that is, in which rules are transformed through practice. The latter is not the simple putting into effect of unchangeable formulae. The formula as such only exists in the treatise of the anthropologist. In its operation, the rule exists in the practice it guides. Yet, as we have seen, the practice not only fulfills the rule but gives it concrete shape in particular situations. Practice is, in effect, an ongoing interpretation and reinterpretation of what the rule really means. If enough of us give a little "above" ourselves, and if our gesture is reciprocated, we will have altered the generally understood margins of tolerance for this kind of exchange between equals. The relation between rule and practice is like that between *langue* and *parole* for Ferdinand de Saussure: *parole* is only possible because of the preexistence of *langue*, but at the same time the acts of speech actually sustain language. They renew it, and in so doing they alter it, and thus the relation in question is a reciprocal one. *Parole* requires *langue*, yet what language is in the long run is itself determined by the multiplicity of acts of speech.

It is this element of reciprocity that is entirely overlooked by the intellectualist theorists. And what it shows is that the rule essentially resides *in* the practice. The rule is what animates the practice at any given moment and not some formulation behind it, inscribed in our thoughts, brains, genes, or whatever. That is why the rule, at any given instant, is what the practice has made it. Yet, if this is so, then it is clearly scientifically disastrous to conceive of the rule as an underlying formula, for in so doing we miss the entire interplay between action under uncertainty and varying degrees of phronetic insight, on the one hand, and the norms and rules that animate this action, on the other. The map provides only half the story; to make it decisive is to distort the whole process.

How can there possibly be a rule that exists only in the practices it animates and that does not require, and may not have, any explicit formulation? The answer is: as a result of our embodied understanding. This is what Bourdieu is trying to get at with his notion of habitus. The habitus is a "system of durable and transposable dispositions" (88), that is, bodily behavioral dispositions to act, to gesture, or to hold oneself in a certain way. A bodily disposition is a habitus when it encodes a certain cultural understanding. In this sense, the habitus always has an expressive dimension. It gives expression to certain meanings that things and people have for us, thereby making these meanings exist for us.

Children are inducted into a culture, are taught the meanings that constitute it, partly through inculcating the appropriate habitus. To a large extent, we learn how to hold ourselves, how to defer to others, or how to be a presence for others by adopting different styles of bodily comportment. Through these modes of deference and presentation, the subtlest nuances of social position, of the sources of prestige, and hence of what is valuable and good, are encoded:

On pourrait, déformant le mot de Proust, dire que les jambes, les bras sont pleins d'impératifs engourdis. Et l'on n'en finirait pas d'énumérer les valeurs faites corps, par la transsubstantiation qu'opère la persuasion clandestine d'une pédagogie implicite, capable d'inculquer toute une cosmologie, une éthique, une métaphysique, une politique, à travers des injonctions aussi insignifiantes que "tiens-toi droit" ou "ne tiens pas ton couteau de la main gauche" et d'inscire dans les détails en apparence les plus insignifiants de la *tenue,* du *maintien* ou des *manières* corporelles et verbales les principes fondamentaux de l'arbitraire culturel, ainsi placés hors des prises de la conscience et de l'explicitation. (Bourdieu 1980, 117)

Adopting a phrase of Proust's, one might say that arms and legs are full of numb imperatives. One could endlessly enumerate the values given body, *made* body, by the hidden persuasion of an implicit pedagogy which can instill a whole cosmology, through injunctions as insignificant as "sit up straight" or "don't hold your knife in your left hand," and inscribe the most fundamental principles of the arbitrary content of a culture in seemingly innocuous details of bearing or physical and verbal manners, so putting them beyond the reach of consciousness and explicit statement. (Bourdieu 1990, 69)

This is one way in which rules can exist in our lives, as "values made flesh." Of course, it is not the only way. Some rules *are* formulated. But these are closely related to our habitus. The two normally dovetail and complement each other. Bourdieu speaks of habitus and institutions as "deux modes d'objectivation de l'histoire passée" (95–96) ("two modes of objectification of past history" [57]). Institutions are generally the locus of explicit rules or norms. Yet rules, as we have seen, are not self-interpreting; without a sense of what they are about, and an affinity for their spirit, they remain dead letters or become a travesty in practice. This sense and this affinity can only exist where they do, in our unformulated, embodied understanding. They are embedded in the domain of the habitus, which "comme sens pratique opère la *réactivation* du sens objectivé dans les institutions" (96) ("is a practical sense which reactivates the sense objectified in institutions" [57]).

5

I return here to the question that I started with, the place of rules in human life. The puzzle, recall, was as follows: how can an agent understand a rule and be guided by it without having even an inkling of a whole host of issues that must, it would seem, be resolved before the rule can guide him or her properly? The intellectualist bent of our philosophical culture makes this combination of features seem paradoxical. Yet the paradox dissolves once we recognize that our background understanding makes all such issues irrelevant, effectively keeping them off our agenda. Rules operate in our lives as patterns of reasons for action, not just as causal regularities. Explicit reason-giving has a limit and must in the end repose on another kind of understanding.

What is this understanding? I have been arguing that we should see it as embodied. Bourdieu has explored how this kind of understanding can arise and how it can function in our lives, along with the institutions that define our social existence. So he too has recourse to a picture that is very much like the one I would like to attribute to Wittgenstein. Explicit rules can only function in our lives along with an inarticulate sense that is encoded in the body. It is this habitus that "activates" the rules. If Wittgenstein has helped us to break the philosophical thrall of intellectualism, Bourdieu has begun to explore how social science could be remade, once freed from its distorting grip.

CHAPTER NINE

Challenging Conventions
in the Fine Art of Rap

RICHARD SHUSTERMAN

> . . . rapt Poesy,
> And arts, though unimagined, yet to be.
> — Shelley, *Prometheus Unbound*

Rap is today's fastest-growing genre of popular music, but also the most maligned and persecuted. Its claim to artistic status is drowned under a flood of abusive critique, acts of censorship, and commercial cooptation.[1] This should not be surprising. For rap's cultural roots and main following belong to the black underclass of American society, and its militant black pride and thematizing of the ghetto experience represent a threatening siren to that society's complacent status quo. Given this political incentive for undermining rap, one can readily find aesthetic reasons that seem to discredit it as a legitimate art form. Rap songs are not even sung, only spoken or chanted. They typically employ neither live musicians nor original music; the sound track is instead composed from various cuts (or "samples") of records already made and often well known. Finally, the lyrics seem to be crude and simple-minded, the diction substandard, the rhymes raucous, repetitive, and frequently raunchy. Yet, as my title suggests, these same lyrics insistently lay claim to and extol rap's status as poetry and fine art.[2]

I wish to examine more closely the aesthetics of rap, or "hip hop" (as the cognoscenti often call it).[3] Since I enjoy this music, I have a personal stake in defending its aesthetic legitimacy. But the cultural issues and aesthetic stakes are much larger. For rap, I believe, is a postmodern popular art that challenges some of our most deeply entrenched aesthetic conventions, conventions that are common not only to modernism as an artistic style and ideology but to the philosophical doctrine of modernity and its sharp differentiation of cultural spheres. Yet while challenging such conventions, rap still satisfies the most crucial conventional criteria for aesthetic legitimacy that are generally denied to popular art. It thus undermines any rigid distinction between high and popular art made on purely aesthetic grounds, just as it calls into question the very notion of such grounds. To substantiate these claims, I first consider rap in terms of postmodern aesthetics. But since aesthetic legitimacy is best demonstrated by actual critical perception, I devote most of my effort to a close reading of a representative rap, which shows how the genre can answer the major aesthetic indictments against popular art.

Postmodernism is a vexingly complex and contested phenomenon, and its aesthetic thus resists clear and unchallengeable definition. Nonetheless, certain themes and stylistic features are widely recognized as characteristically postmodern, which is not to say that they cannot also be found in some modernist art.[4] These include recycling and appropriation rather than unique and original creation, the eclectic mixing of styles, the enthusiastic embracing of mass-media technology and culture, the challenging of modernist notions of aesthetic autonomy and artistic purity, and an emphasis on the localized and temporal rather than the putatively universal and eternal. Whether or not we call these features postmodern, rap exemplifies and often consciously highlights them, and they are essential to an adequate understanding of rap.

Appropriative Sampling

Artistic appropriation is the historical source of hip-hop music and still remains the core of its technique and a central feature of its aesthetic form and message. The music derives from selecting and combining parts of prerecorded songs to produce a "new" sound track. This sound track, produced by the DJ on a multiple turntable, constitutes the musical background for the rap lyrics. These in turn are frequently devoted both to praising the DJ's inimitable virtuosity in sampling and synthesizing the appropriated music and to boasting of the lyrical and rhyming power of the rapper (called the MC). While the rapper's vaunting self-praise often highlights his sexual desirability, commercial success, and property assets, these signs of status are all presented as secondary to and derived from his verbal power.

Some whites may find it difficult to imagine that verbal virtuosity is greatly appreciated in the black urban ghetto. But sociological study reveals that it is very highly valued there; and anthropological research shows that asserting superior social status through verbal prowess is a deeply entrenched black tradition that goes back to the griots in West Africa and has long been sustained in the New World through such conventionalized verbal contests or games as "signifying" or "the dozens."[5] Failure to recognize the traditional tropes, stylistic conventions, and constraint-produced complexities of African-American English (such as semantic inversion and indirection, feigned simplicity, and covert parody—all originally designed to conceal the real meaning from hostile white listeners)[6] has induced the false belief that all rap lyrics are superficial and monotonous, if not altogether moronic. But an informed and sympathetic close reading will reveal in many rap songs not only the cleverly potent vernacular expression of keen insights but also forms of linguistic subtlety and multiple levels of meaning, whose polysemic complexity, ambiguity, and intertextuality can sometimes rival that of high art's so-called open work.[7]

Like its stylized, aggressively boasting language, rap's other most salient feature—its dominant funky beat—can be traced back to African roots, to jungle rhythms that were taken up by rock and disco and then reappropriated by the rap DJs, musical cannibals of the urban jungle. But for all its African heritage, hip hop was born in the disco era of the mid-seventies in the grim ghettos of New York—first the Bronx, then Harlem and Brooklyn. As it appropriated disco sounds and techniques, it undermined and transformed them, much as jazz (an earlier black art of appropriation) had done with the melodies of popular songs. But in contrast to jazz, hip hop did not take mere melodies or musical phrases, that is, abstract musical patterns exemplifiable in different performances and thus bearing the ontological status of "type entities." Instead, it lifted concrete sound-events, prerecorded token performances of such musical patterns. Thus, unlike jazz, its borrowing and transfiguration did not require creative skill in composition or in playing musical instruments but only in manipulating recording equipment. DJs in ordinary disco clubs had developed the technique of cutting and blending one record into the next, matching tempos to make a smooth transition without violently disrupting the flow of dancing. Dissatisfied with the tame sound of disco and commercial pop, self-styled DJs in the Bronx adopted this technique of cutting in order to concentrate and augment those parts of the records that could provide for better dancing (Toop 1984, 151).

In short, hip hop clearly began as dance music to be appreciated through movement, not mere listening. It was originally designed only for live performance (at dances held in homes, schools, community centers, and parks), where one could admire the dexterity of the DJ and the personality and improvisational skills of the rapper. And even when the groups moved from the street to the studio where they could use live music, the DJ's role of appropriation was not generally abandoned and continued to be thematized in rap lyrics as central to the art.[8]

From the basic technique of cutting between sampled records, hip hop developed three other formal devices that contribute significantly to its sound and aesthetic: "scratch mixing," "punch phrasing," and simple "scratching." The first is simply overlaying or mixing certain sounds from one record with those of another already playing.[9] Punch phrasing is a refinement of such mixing, in which the DJ moves the needle back and forth over a specific phrase of chords or drum slaps of a record so as to add a powerful percussive effect to the sound of the other record playing all the while on the other turntable. The third device is a more wild and rapid back-and-forth scratching of the record, too fast for the recorded music to be recognized but productive of a dramatic scratching sound that has its own intense musical quality and crazed beat.

These devices of cutting, mixing, and scratching provide rap with a variety of forms of appropriation that seem as versatile and imaginative as those of high art — as those, say, exemplified by Marcel Duchamp's mustache on the Mona Lisa, Robert Rauschenberg's erasure of a De Kooning canvas, and Andy Warhol's multiple re-representations of pre-packaged commercial images. Rap also displays a variety of appropriated content. Not only does it sample from a wide range of popular songs, it feeds eclectically on classical music, TV theme songs, advertising jingles, and the electronic music of arcade games. It even appropriates nonmusical content, such as media news reports and fragments of speeches by Malcolm X and Martin Luther King.

Though some DJs took pride in appropriating from very unlikely and arcane sources and sometimes tried to conceal (for fear of competition) the exact records they were sampling, there was never any attempt to conceal the fact that they were working from prerecorded sounds rather than composing their own original music. On the contrary, they openly celebrated their method of sampling. What is the aesthetic significance of this proud art of appropriation?

First, it challenges the traditional ideal of originality and uniqueness that has long enslaved our conception of art. Romanticism and its cult of genius likened the artist to a divine creator; it advocated that his works be altogether new and express his singular personality. Modernism, with its commitment to artistic progress and the avant-garde, reinforced the dogma that radical novelty was the essence of art. Though artists have always borrowed from one another's works, the fact was generally ignored or implicitly denied through the ideology of originality, which posed a sharp distinction between original creation and derivative borrowing. Postmodern art such as rap undermines this dichotomy by creatively deploying and thematizing its appropriation to show that borrowing and creation are not at all incompatible. It further suggests that the apparently original work of art is itself always a product of unacknowledged borrowings, the unique and novel text always a tissue of echoes and fragments of earlier texts.

Originality thus loses its absolute originary status and is reconceived so as to include the transfiguring reappropriation and recycling of the old. In this postmodern picture there are no ultimate, untouchable originals, only appropriations of appropriations and simulacra of simulacra; so creative energy can be liberated to play with familiar creations without fear that it thereby denies itself the opportunity to be truly creative by not producing a totally original work. Rap songs simultaneously celebrate their originality and their borrowing.[10] And as the dichotomy of creation/appropriation is challenged, so is the deep division between creative artist and appropriative audience; transfigurative appreciation can take the form of art.

Cutting and Temporality

Rap's sampling style also challenges the work of art's traditional ideal of unity and integrity. Since Aristotle, aestheticians have often viewed the work as an organic whole so perfectly unified that any tampering with its parts would destroy the whole. Moreover, the ideologies of romanticism and *art for art's sake* have reinforced our habit of treating art works as transcendent and virtually sacred ends in themselves, the integrity of which should be respected and never violated. In contrast to this aesthetic of austere organic unity, rap's cutting and sampling reflects the "schizophrenic fragmentation" and "collage effect" characteristic of the postmodern aesthetic.[11] In contrast to an aesthetic based on devotional worship of a fixed, untouchable work, hip hop offers the pleasures of deconstructive art — the thrilling beauty of dismembering (and rapping over) old works to create new ones, dismantling the prepackaged and wearily familiar into something stimulatingly different.

The DJ's sampling and the MC's rap also highlight the fact that the apparent unity of the original artwork is often an artificially constructed one, at least in contemporary popular music, where the production process is frequently quite fragmented: an instrumental track recorded in Memphis, combined with a back-up vocal from New York and a lead voice from LA. Rap simply continues this process of layered artistic composition by deconstructing and differently reassembling prepackaged musical products and then superimposing the MC's added layer of lyrics so as to produce a new work. But rap does this without the pretense that its own work is inviolable, that the artistic process is ever final, that there is ever a product that should be so fetishized that it could never be submitted to appropriative transfiguration. Instead, rap's sampling implies that an artwork's integrity as object should never outweigh the possibilities for continuing creation through use of that object. Its aesthetic thus suggests the Deweyan message that art is essentially more process than finished product — a welcome message in our culture, where the tendency to reify and commodify all artistic expression is so strong that rap itself is victimized by this tendency while defiantly protesting it.

In defying the fetishized integrity of artworks, rap also challenges traditional notions of their monumentality, universality, and permanence. No longer are admired works conceived in Eliotic fashion as "an ideal order" of "monuments" existing timelessly and yet preserved through time by tradition.[12] In contrast to the standard view that "a poem is forever," rap highlights the artwork's temporality and likely impermanence, not only by appropriative deconstructions, but by explicitly thematizing its own temporality in its lyrics. For example, several songs by BDP include lines like "Fresh for 88, you suckers" or "Fresh for 89, you suckers."[13] Such declarations of date imply a consequent admission of datedness; what is fresh for 88 is apparently stale by 89, and so superseded by a new freshness of 89 vintage. But, by rap's postmodern aesthetic, the ephemeral freshness of artistic creations does not render them aesthetically unworthy, no more than the ephemeral freshness of cream renders its sweet taste unreal. For the view that aesthetic value can only be real if it passes the test of time is simply an entrenched but unjustified presumption, ultimately deriving from the pervasive philosophical bias that equates reality with the permanent and unchanging.

By refusing to treat artworks as eternal monuments for permanent hands-off devotion, by reworking works to make them work better, rap also questions their assumed universality. Although it typically avoids violently excluding white society, hip hop is proudly localized as "ghetto music," thematizing its roots in and commitment to the black urban ghetto and its culture. The lyrics focus on features of ghetto life that whites and middle-class blacks would rather ignore: pimping, prostitution, and drug addiction, as well as rampant venereal disease, street killings, and oppressive harassment by white policemen. Most rappers define their local allegiances in very specific terms, often not simply by city but by neighborhood, such as Compton, Harlem, Brooklyn, or the Bronx.

Eclecticism, History, and Autonomy

If rap's freewheeling eclectic cannibalism violates high modernist conventions of aesthetic purity and integrity, its belligerent insistence on the deeply political dimension of culture challenges one of the most fundamental artistic conventions of modernity: aesthetic autonomy. Modernity, according to Max Weber and others, was bound up with the project of occidental rationalization, secularization, and differentiation, which disenchanted the traditional religious world view and carved up its organic domain into three separate and autonomous spheres of secular culture: science, art, and morality, each governed by its own inner logic of theoretical, aesthetic, or moral-practical judgment.[14] This tripartite division was of course powerfully reflected and reinforced by Immanuel Kant's critical analysis of human thinking in terms of pure reason, practical reason, and aesthetic judgment.

In this division of cultural spheres, art was distinguished from science as not being concerned with the formulation or dissemination of knowledge, since its aesthetic judgment was essentially nonconceptual and subjective. It was also sharply differentiated from the practical activity of the realm of ethics and politics, which involved real interests and appetitive will (as well as conceptual thinking). Instead, art was consigned to a disinterested, imaginative realm, which Friedrich Schiller (1795) later described as the realm of play and semblance. As the aesthetic was distinguished from the more rational realms of knowledge and action, it was also firmly differentiated from the more sensate and appetitive gratifications of embodied human nature — aesthetic pleasure residing rather in a distanced, disinterested contemplation of formal properties.

Hip hop's genre of "knowledge rap" (or "message rap") is dedicated to the defiant violation of this compartmentalized, trivializing, and eviscerating view of art and the aesthetic. Such rappers repeatedly insist that their role as artists and poets is inseparable from their role as insightful inquirers into reality and as teachers of truth, particularly those aspects of reality and truth that get neglected or distorted by establishment history books and contemporary media coverage. KRS-One of BDP claims to be not only "a teacher and artist, startin' new concepts at their hardest," but a philosopher and a scientist.[15] In contrast to the media's political whitewash, stereotypes, and empty escapist entertainment, he proudly claims: "I'm tryin' not to escape, but hit the problem head on / By bringing out the truth in a song. . . . It's simple; BDP will teach reality / No beatin' around the bush, straight up; just like the beat is free / So now you know a poet's job is never done. / But I'm never overworked, cause I'm still number one."[16]

Of course, the realities and truths that hip hop reveals are not the transcendental eternal verities of traditional philosophy, but rather the mutable yet coercive facts and patterns of the material, sociohistorical world. Yet this emphasis on the temporally changing and malleable nature of the real (reflected in rap's frequent time tags and its popular idiom of "knowing what time it is")[17] constitutes a respectable and tenable metaphysical position associated with American pragmatism. Though few may know it, rap philosophers are really "down with" Dewey, not merely in metaphysics but in a noncompartmentalized aesthetics that highlights social function, process, and embodied experience.[18]

"Knowledge rap" not only insists on uniting the aesthetic and the cognitive but equally stresses the idea that practical functionality can be part of artistic meaning and value. Many rap songs are explicitly devoted to raising black political consciousness, pride, and revolutionary impulses; some make the powerful point that aesthetic judgments, and particularly the question of what counts as art, involve political issues of legitimation and social struggle in which rap is engaged as progressive praxis and which it advances by its very self-assertion as art. Other raps function as street-smart moral fables, offering cautionary narratives and practical advice on problems of crime, drugs, and sexual hygiene (e.g., Ice-T's "Drama" and "High Rollers," Kool Moe Dee's "Monster Crack" and "Go See the Doctor," BDP's "Stop the Violence" and "Jimmy"). Finally, rap has been used effectively to teach writing and reading skills and black history in the ghetto classroom.[19]

Rap also challenges another well-entrenched modernist convention of artistic purity: the idea that a proper aesthetic response requires distanced contemplation by a transcendental and temperately disinterested subject. Against this aesthetic of distanced, disengaged, formalist judgment, rap advocates one of deeply embodied participatory involvement, with content as well as form. Rappers want to be appreciated primarily through energetic and impassioned dance, not through immobile contemplation and dispassionate study.[20] Queen Latifah, for example, insistently commands her listeners, "I order you to dance for me." For, as Ice-T explains, the rapper "won't be happy till the dancers are wet" with sweat, "out of control" and wildly "possessed" by the beat, as indeed the captivating rapper should himself be possessed so as to rock his audience with his God-given gift to rhyme.[21]

This aesthetic of divine yet bodily possession is strikingly similar to Plato's account of poetry and its appreciation as a chain of divine madness extending down from the divine Muse through the artists and performers to the audience, a seizure which for all its divinity was criticized as regrettably irrational and inferior to true knowledge.[22] More importantly, the spiritual ecstasy of divine bodily possession should remind us of Vodun and the metaphysics of African religion to which the aesthetics of Afro-American music has indeed been traced.[23]

What could be farther from modernity's project of rationalization and secularization, what more inimical to modernism's rationalized, disembodied, and formalized aesthetic? No wonder the established modernist aesthetic is so hostile to rap and to rock music in general. If there is a viable space between the modernist rationalized aesthetic and an altogether irrational one whose rabid Dionysian excess must vitiate its cognitive, didactic, and political claims, this is the space for a post-modern aesthetic.[24] I think the "fine art" of rap inhabits that space, and I hope it will continue to thrive there.

Thus far I have presented rap as a challenging violator of traditional artistic conventions. Why, then, still call it art? True, its lyrics proudly claim it is art — performative self-assertion being a crucial means of achieving such status. But mere self-assertion is not enough to establish the arthood or aesthetic character of an expressive form; the claim must be convincing. Primarily, of course, conviction must come from experience; we must feel a work's artistry and aesthetic power impress itself on our senses and intelligence. But theoretical justification can also help extend art's limits by assimilating previously unaccepted forms into art's honorific category. One proven strategy for such assimilation is showing that despite obvious deviance from established conventions, an expressive form still meets enough of the more crucial criteria to warrant recognition of its artistic or aesthetic legitimacy. Popular art is often refused such legitimacy because of an alleged failure to meet such criteria, particularly those of complexity and depth, creativity and form, artistic self-respect and self-consciousness.

While rap may be the most denigrated of popular arts, its better works can, I think, satisfy these central artistic criteria. The best way to demonstrate this is not by general polemics and pleading but by looking closely at a concrete specimen of the genre. I therefore turn to a close reading of "Talkin' All That Jazz," by the Brooklyn crew Stetsasonic. It is neither my favorite rap nor the one I think most artistically sophisticated. I choose it for its popularity and representative character, as proven by its selection in a number of rap LP anthologies,[25] and because it highlights some of the central aesthetic issues that rap raises.

Though the aim of my close reading is to show this rap's aesthetic richness, the very method of reading — that is, presenting and analyzing this rap as inscribed text — will involve ignoring some of its most important aesthetic dimensions and its intended mode of aesthetic appropriation. For I shall be abstracting from its crucial dimensions of sound, since the printed page captures neither the music nor the oral phrasing and intonation of the lyrics (a point of pride and style among rappers). Nor can it convey the complex aesthetic effects of the multiple rhythms and tensions between the driving musical beat and the word stress of the rap delivery, which in contrast to popular songs maintains its own speech rhythms.[26] A full appreciation of a rap song's aesthetic dimensions would require not merely hearing it but dancing to it, feeling its rhythms in movement as the genre emphatically means us to. The printed medium of our written culture precludes this, thereby suggesting more generally the inherent difficulties in appreciating and legitimating oral culture by academic means so deeply entrenched and trapped in the written.

Nonetheless, if rap can satisfy aesthetic standards in its impoverished form as written poetry, *a fortiori* it can meet them in its rich and robust actuality as music and rhythmic speech. Recognizing, then, that a rap is aesthetically much more than its text, let us see how the text itself can sustain a claim to aesthetic status in terms of the central criteria I have mentioned.

Talkin' All That Jazz

Well, here's how it started,
Heard you on the radio
Talk about rap,
Sayin' all that crap
About how we sample,
Give an example.
Think we'll let you get away with that.
You criticize our method
Of how we make records
You said it wasn't art,
So now we're gonna rip you apart.
Stop, check it out my man.
This is the music of a hip-hop band.
Jazz, well you can call it that.
But this Jazz retains a new format.
Point, when you misjudged us
Speculated, created a fuss,
You've made the same mistake politicians have,
Talkin' all that Jazz.

. . . [musical break]

Talk, well I heard talk is cheap.
Well, like beauty, talk is just skin deep.
And when you lie and you talk a lot,
People tell you to step off a lot.
You see you misunderstood,
A sample's just a fact,
Like a portion of my method,
A tool. In fact,
It's only of importance when I make it a priority,
And what we sample of is a majority.
But you are a minority, in terms of thought,
Narrow minded and poorly taught
About hip-hop's aims and the silly games
To embrace my music so no one use it.
You step on us and we'll step on you.
You can't have your cake and eat it too.
Talkin' all that Jazz.

. . . [musical break]

Lies, that's when you hide the truth,
It's when you talk more jazz than proof.
And when you lie and address something you don't know,
It's so whacked that it's bound to show.
When you lie about me and the band, we get angry.
We'll bite our pens and start writin' again.
And the things we write are always true,
Sucker, so get a grip now we're talkin' about you.
Seems to me that you have a problem,
So we can see what we can do to solve them.
Think rap is a fad; you must be mad
'Cause we're so bad, we get respect you never had.
Tell the truth, James Brown was old,
Till Eric and Rak' came out with "I got soul."
Rap brings back old R & B
And if we would not
People could have forgot.
We want to make this perfectly clear:
We're talented and strong and have no fear
Of those who choose to judge but lack pizazz,
Talkin' all that jazz.

. . . [musical break]

Now we're not tryin' to be a boss to you.
We just wanna get across to you
That if you're talkin' jazz
The situation is a no win.
You might even get hurt my friend.
Stetsasonic, the hip-hop band,
And like Sly and the Family Stone
We will stand
Up for the music we live and play
And for the song we sing today.
For now, let us set the record straight,
And later on we'll have a forum and
A formal debate.
But it's important you remember though,
What you reap is what you sow.
Talkin' all that jazz.
Talkin' all that jazz.
Talkin' all that jazz.

Complexity

At first glance this song seems simple enough, perhaps too simple to war-rant aesthetic consideration. It lacks the trappings of erudite allusion, opaque elision, and syntactico-semantic obscurity, which constitute the characteristic complexity of modernist poetry. Its straightforward state-ment, paucity of metaphor, and repeated clichés suggest that it is sim-plistically shallow and devoid of any complexity or depth of meaning. But semantic complexity is richly enfolded within its seemingly artless and simple language. The song's multiple levels of meanings are detect-able from the very title, and indeed encapsulated in its key word, "jazz." Jazz has, of course, at least two relevant but radically different and differ-ently valorized meanings in the poem's context. The first concerns jazz as a musical art form originating in Afro-American culture, long opposed and discredited by the cultural establishment, but by now cul-turally legitimated throughout the world. The second sense concerns the most common slang use of jazz as "lying and exaggerated talk; also idle and foolish talk"; or "stuffy foolishness: humbug."[27]

This ambiguity and privileging opposition within the very meaning of jazz — its positively valorized standard usage as a musical art over its slang (hence less "legitimate") usage as lies and pretentious talk — is developed into a central theme of this rap and seems central to rap in general. "Talkin' All That Jazz" simultaneously exploits and questions this privileging opposition, presenting rap as a force involved with legit-imating the illegitimate, exposing the sociopolitical factors involved in such legitimation, and challenging the legitimacy of the powers deny-ing legitimacy to rap. In confronting these issues, the song in turn raises deeply philosophical questions about the nature of truth and art and about their sources of authority. For art, we should remember, though now culturally sacralized, was itself sometimes deligitimated as pretentious lies and idle foolishness.

In order to dismiss this kind of reading from the outset, one might be tempted to argue that the term *jazz* is adequately disambiguated by the context of the title, and certainly by the complete song. For the phrase "talkin' all that jazz" seems to suggest that we are concerned not at all with jazz as positive music but only with negative *talk* and lies, spe-cifically the pretentious, foolish lies that constitute the uninformed crit-icism of hip hop, the personified source of which is the confrontational target or "you" of the poem. "Heard you on the radio / Talk about rap, / Sayin' all that crap." The identification of talkin' jazz with lies and foolish talk is confirmed by linking it with the discourse of politicians ("You've made the same mistake politicians have / Talkin' all that Jazz"), and it certainly seems clinched by the lines "Lies, that's when you hide the truth, / It's when you talk more jazz than proof. / And when you lie and address something you don't know, / It's so whacked that it's bound to show."

But just as it is identified with negative lies, talkin' jazz is also posi-tively identified as musical art by the very topic of the song — rap as an art. For, we must ask, what is rap but talkin' jazz? It is not merely jazz-related instrumental music nor even lyrics sung to jazz rhythms or tunes. The most distinctive feature of rap music is that it is defiantly talk rather than song, the word *rap* being a slang synonym for talk. And the linking of rap music with jazz is confirmed in the first stanza: "This is the music of a hip-hop band. / Jazz, well you can call it that. / But this jazz retains a new format."

These lines embody even more semantic complexities of valoriza-tion. The band accepts its identification with jazz as the most respected black cultural form and tradition to which hip hop is genealogically attached; but the acceptance is somewhat hesitant. For rap does not want to be seen as a mere variety of established jazz, not even of progressive jazz; rather, it insists on its originality. Rap's jazz, unlike standard jazz already appropriated by the establishment, "retains a new format," sustains novelty and freshness by maintaining a closer link to changing popular experience and vernacular expression (to the "majority" of the street). There is the hint that hip hop is thus truer to the original spirit of jazz; and there is also the hint that jazz has somehow been tainted through its past treatment by the cultural establishment and through its accommodating compliance with that treatment.[28] For surely the establishment's initial rejection of jazz as wildly exaggerated and foolish music helped give the term its negative slang meaning of foolish pretension and untruth; and this abiding negative meaning maintains a sense of the original rejection, which seems to introduce a troublingly negative trace in even its standard meaning as music and raises the lingering question of whether this music is truly art in the standard sacralized sense in which classical music obviously is.

These deep ambiguities of jazz are most cleverly manipulated by Stetsasonic to make the case for rap as an art. The meaning of jazz as pretentious lies, based both on its identification with art rather than truth and on its further rejection as serious art, is in turn used to dismiss as pretentious lying the renewed rejection of new jazz in the form of rap. The rappers reject as "talkin' jazz" the allegedly legitimate discourse of those who ignorantly reject rap as degenerate, appropriative talkin' jazz. The band at once employs and reverses the jazz versus serious truth distinction by asserting that their talking jazz is true (and true art), while the supposedly serious discourse of the antirap, antijazz critics is really talkin' jazz in the negative sense; for the latter are altogether misinformed, "narrow minded and poorly taught." Their allegedly true talk about true art is neither truth nor art but ignorant palaver devoid of critical understanding or creative pizazz. In contrast to the weak "whacked" lies of its bigoted critics, rap's lines "are always true." Moreover, they are not mindlessly and carelessly uttered like the "cheap" condemnatory "crap" of radio talk, but instead thoughtfully composed in writing[29] and then performed by artists who are "talented and strong" and committed to original expression in this "new format." Thus, in contrast to its denunciatory criticism, rap is claimed to display both truth and artistry; a claim that this rap artfully demonstrates by its ingeniously double-edged and inversive method of asserting it.

Though complexity of meaning and witty twists of argument are undeniably found here, it may be denied that they are actually intended or that they exist for the real rap audience. Perhaps they are merely the product of our academic habit of reading (indeed, even torturing) texts to find ambiguities. Reading rap in this complex way, one might argue, is unfaithful to the spontaneity and simplicity of the genre and its audience. Moreover, by suggesting that simpler responses are inferior understandings, it serves to expropriate the art from its popular use and from the people who use it. Such a process, where intellectualized modes of appropriation are used to transform popular into elite art, is a virtual commonplace of cultural history.[30]

This line of objection to my interpretive reading is serious enough to demand immediate response. First, there is no compelling reason to limit the rap's meaning to explicit authorial intentions; its meaning is also a function of its language, a social product beyond the determining control of the individual author. The ambiguities of "jazz" and the cultural conflicts and history they embody are already there in the language through which the author must speak, whether he intends them or not. Similarly, since art can be appreciated in many ways and on many levels, new modes of appreciation by new audiences cannot be outlawed as necessarily disenfranchising those of the original audience. This only happens when the new intellectualized forms insist on imposing a privileged or exclusionary status as legitimate. But whatever our view on the intentional fallacy and the primacy of intended audience, I think the ambiguities and inversions are too prominent and pointed here to be unintended. Moreover, the average rap audience is very well equipped to understand them. For precisely this sort of ambiguity and inversion is basic to the black linguistic community.

Afro-American English is saliently ambiguous. For example, while "nigger" in white English is univocally a term of abuse, in black speech it is just as often "a term of affection, admiration, approval" (Holt 1972, 155). The reasons for its greater ambiguity should be obvious. "Negro slaves were compelled to create a semi-clandestine vernacular" to express their desires while disguising them from the hostile scrutiny of their overseers, and they did so by giving ordinary English words specific black meanings along with their standard ones (Brown 1972, 135).

One crucial method of multiplying meanings was by inverting them. Since language both embodies and sustains societal power relations, this method of inversion is particularly significant, both as a source of protest and as a source of extremely subtle linguistic skill.[31] It also, of course, helped make the black community especially adept at and familiar with the encoding and decoding of ambiguous and inverted messages. Rap fans, then, through their ordinary linguistic training, have typically mastered a wittily indirect communicative skill, which one researcher regards as "a form of verbal art,"[32] and which enables them readily to process texts of great semantic complexity if the content is relevant to their experience. Thus, Stetsasonic's ambiguous, inversive play on the notion of "talkin' jazz" is hardly beyond the reach of the rap audience, even if it is far less obvious than the text's most transparent and by now commonplace inversion of "bad" to mean good. ("Think rap is a fad; you must be mad / 'Cause we're so bad, we get respect you never had.")

Philosophical Content

Rap can be intellectually rewarding, not merely because of the stimulation linked to its polysemic complexity, but also because of its philosophical insights. For just as popular art has been condemned as inevitably superficial because of its simplistic, undemanding semantic structures, it is similarly condemned for being devoid of any deep content.

Since popular art's use of clichés is often held to be a prime cause of its bland shallowness, something should be said to vindicate the obvious clichés in "Talkin' All That Jazz." For the song is studded with some of the most trite and most commonplace proverbs: "Talk is cheap"; "Beauty is . . . just skin deep"; "You can't have your cake and eat it too"; "What you reap is what you sow." However, within the particular context of this rap, these proverbs acquire new meanings that not only depart from but challenge the clichés of cultural thought that they normally embody. First and most simply, by their very use in arguments against the cultural cliché that rap is not art, these proverbs lose their bland, commonplace character. Second, their use is aesthetically justified as a reinforcing verbal counterpart to the method of appropriative sampling that forms the major theme of this rap. For just as rap DJs cannibalize familiar prepackaged musical phrases to create an original sound by placing them in new contexts, so the MC can appropriate old proverbs and give them new significance by his recontextualizing application of them in his rap.

Consider the first two clichés about truth and beauty, which together form a couplet: "Talk, well I heard talk is cheap. / Well, like beauty, talk is just skin deep." So conjoined in this rap's specific context, these clichés are anything but simplistic and commonplace in meaning. Instead, they undermine with ambiguity the simple, common truths they standardly express while also suggesting philosophical theses on the nature of language, beauty, and aesthetic judgment which radically diverge from and challenge commonplace dogma on these issues.

Of course, "talk is cheap" can surely be understood here in its standard sense; it costs nothing, requires no effort, knowledge, or talent to blast rap with ignorant criticisms. Such uninformed "talkin' jazz" is worthless, cheap talk. The proverb's standard sense also suggests the commonplace opposition between mere talk (which is easy but effects nothing) and real action or performance, which not only costs effort but actually does something. And Stetsasonic employ this opposition in the contrast they draw between the "narrow-minded" critics who, lacking the pizazz to create art, simply talk about and "judge" it, and, on the other hand, the rap artists who are "talented and strong" and fearless enough to act and create rather than merely "speculate" with "cheap talk."

However, over and against these standard senses, the contextual content of the rap is urging, more strikingly, that so-called cheap talk is not really so cheap at all. It is instead very costly. First, its ignorant maligning of rap deceives the public, insults and persecutes rap artists and their audience, and thereby creates a confusing "fuss" over the nature of hip hop. The clichéd distinction between talk and action is thus challenged by showing that mere talk can constitute an action having costly consequences. This argument is painfully confirmed by the actual facts of rap's condemnation and persecution by people totally unfamiliar with the music who rely on the hearsay of others who are themselves as disinclined to listen to rap as to let it be heard.[33] Moreover, as "Talkin' All That Jazz" also argues, the seemingly cheap condemnatory talk of the critics will end up costing them dearly as well; for "when you lie and you talk a lot, / People tell you to step off a lot." Injured by their "talk about rap / Sayin' all that crap," Stetsasonic violently warn rap's denouncers of the high price of such cheap talk: "You said it wasn't art, / So now we're gonna rip you apart."

If uninformed "cheap" talk can have such powerful effects, what is the source of discourse's power and authority? If "talkin' jazz" can be false criticism or true art, if discourse in general can be taken as lies or truth, what determines discursive truth or aesthetic legitimacy? These heady philosophical issues are ingeniously linked in the same clichéd couplet, where talk (or discourse) is identified with beauty as being "just skin deep." Here again we see how the specific rap context provides a bland old cliché with radically new meaning. Given rap's ghetto roots and its aesthetic rejection and persecution as black music, the complaint that beauty is just skin deep is transformed from the hackneyed critique of beauty's superficiality (its concern with surface appearance) and comes to embody the powerfully provocative charge that beauty is connected with racial bias, with reactions linked to the surface color of skin. In more general terms, aesthetic judgment is not the pure, lofty, and disinterested contemplation of form it is standardly taken to be; instead, it is profoundly conditioned and governed by sociopolitical (including racial) prejudices and interests.

Thus, in contrast to the clichéd view that sees truth and beauty as altogether independent of power relations, this rap emphasizes the different power relations involved in determining truth and aesthetic legitimacy. Two sources of discursive authority are located. The first is sociopolitical power as manifested and exercised, for example, by the control of media and political institutions. Though uninformed and inimically biased, the antirap critics deliver their verdicts through the pervasive, legitimating medium of radio. Their condemnation of rap as devoid of aesthetic merit and unworthy of artistic status can therefore pass for truth, since it is broadcast without challenge by the dominant media and thus receives the aura of expertise and authority typically associated with views propagated through privileged channels of mass communication. Rappers, on the other hand, particularly those with an underground political message, have been denied similar radio access, let alone equal time, to present and defend their art. Truth and artistic status are thus in large part issues of sociopolitical control. The song reinforces this message when it links rap's artistic denunciation and denial by the media with the mistakes of politicians who disvalue and disenfranchise the black community. With an implied pragmatist epistemology that puts no store in social truths no one believes or in artistic status no one recognizes, the song suggests that the truth of rap's artistic status is not something independently there to be discovered but rather something that must be made; and it can be made only by challenging and overcoming the established, establishment truth of rap's artistic illegitimacy. The song urges and itself represents such a challenge. Given the serious sociopolitical interests and stakes involved in the struggle for artistic legitimation, the rappers realize that this struggle is an essentially violent one; and to defend hip hop against its media critics, they are prepared to use violence: "You said it wasn't art, / So now we're gonna rip you apart." The threat of violence is seriously intended, for it is repeated later in the song, warning anyone who sounds off against rap: "You might even get hurt my friend."[34]

Aware of the connection between artistic status and sociopolitical power, the rappers also realize that the establishment's rejection of hip hop can be opposed by attacking the contradictions and weaknesses of its sociopolitical base. While American society claims to be a liberal democracy with free speech and majority rule, this is contradicted by its censorship of rap and, more generally, by its cultural leaders' tendency to identify true art with only high art, even though the majority of Americans find more aesthetic satisfaction in the arts of popular culture. In defending their music against its media critics, Stetsasonic argue that these elitist cultural czars are overstepping the democratic power base that empowers their judgments. In terms of taste they "are a minority"; just as "in terms of thought" they are "narrow-minded and poorly taught / About hip hop's aims" for a more democratic and emancipatory black popular art.[35] In contrast, the rappers defend their art by aligning it with the majority. Their insistence that "what we sample of is a majority" aims to justify not only their method of sampling but their resultant musical creation by suggesting that they reflect popular taste and majority interests.

"Talkin' All That Jazz" not only appeals to rap's majoritarian democratic power base, but, through its own polemic, seeks to mobilize and expand rap's popular support. One of its polemical strategies involves the politics of personal pronouns. The whole song is structured on the opposition between "you" and "us." On the narrowest literal level, the "us" is simply Stetsasonic, the hip hop band that is singing this song.

Ordinarily this could suggest that the listening audience would be part of the "you" to whom the song is addressed; and it is of course addressed to its audience. Since the song is, however, an angry protest, it takes care to address its audience not as a "you" but instead distinguishes them, at the very outset, from the confrontational "you" of its hostile message — the radio's antirap critic. For the vast majority of the song's audience are not radio speakers but only listeners.

The audience is further encouraged to assimilate themselves to the celebrated "we" of the song by their opposition to the confrontational "you" who is aggressively attacked as an ignorant and untalented but powerfully oppressive and hypercritical minority. The "we" thus comes to mean not only Stetsasonic but the whole hip-hop community whose cause they are advocating. And it reaches still farther by appealing to those who are not yet fans of hip hop but can identify with it because of their common opposition to the media and political authorities against which this song and hip hop generally are defiantly struggling. Anyone resentful of the weak, "whacked" babblings of media figures and politicians, anyone angry with our society's authoritative spokesmen and their iniquitous exercise of power, any artist (or athlete or laborer) incensed at being negatively judged by critics lacking the talent, strength, or pizazz to perform what they haughtily criticize; to all such people, and their number is legion, this song should appeal through its impassioned spirit of protest and thus should enlist increasing support for rap, outside its original and core ghetto audience.

This strategy of gaining acceptance for rap by widening the sociocultural base of its support is shrewdly pursued through at least three other rhetorical devices. First, in the third stanza, rap is linked to (and "brings back") the music of rhythm and blues (R & B), arguably the source of all rock music and a genre that achieved great popularity among white audiences not only in America but throughout the world. This implicit appeal to a wider and also white audience is subtly developed in the last stanza's invocation of Sly and the Family Stone, a group that, though led by a black (Sly Stone) and committed to black pride, also expressed a pluralistic spirit of brotherhood (manifest in its composition by blacks and whites, men and women) and was extremely popular with white audiences.[36]

Sandwiched between the invocations of Sly and of R & B, we find a third strategy for making rap more acceptable to the general audience:

a reassurance that rap's claim to artistic legitimacy is not a demand for hegemony. In promising "we're not tryin' to be a boss to you," the "Stets" reassure the unconverted audience of hip hop that their aim is simply to be heard, not to silence others, even if they are prepared to "hurt" those whose "talkin' jazz" seeks to censure and censor rap. In proposing the goal and hope of peaceful pluralistic coexistence (as opposed to the "no-win" situation of violent cultural strife), the rappers are cleverly appealing to one of American society's most widely held and deeply cherished tenets, the freedom of pluralist tolerance. If we are tempted to dismiss this ideal as mere bourgeois liberal ideology, it remains effective as an argument to those pervaded by that ideology, and its scope is actually far wider. For it also reemerges in the utopian visions of Marxists like Theodor Adorno, whose sociopolitical (and aesthetic) ideal is "difference without domination." The advocacy of such ideals, of course, adds yet another aspect to the rich philosophical content of this song.

I conclude my discussion of this content by briefly noting the second source of discursive and aesthetic authority that the song recognizes. This is the charismatic authority of artistic and rhetorical power. If truth and artistic status depend on a sociocultural power structure, this structure is not permanently fixed but is instead a changing field of struggle. And one way a population's beliefs and tastes can be transformed is by the expressive power of the discourse or art presented to them, though of course their appreciation of this power will always rest on some of their antecedent beliefs and tastes that remain in place.[37] Thus, the song suggests, we listeners can come to reject the critics' talkin' jazz as lies and instead recognize rap's talkin' jazz as art, truth, and proof by sensing their relative expressive power. While the critic's discourse is palpably weak ("so whacked that it's bound to show") and lacks "pizazz," rap's discourse proves its truth and artistic status by its punch and power, by being "talented and strong."

Such proof through perceptual persuasion is not a confused aberration but an important form of argument in aesthetics and elsewhere;[38] and this song, a rap manifesto in rap, is clearly meant to represent such a perceptually persuasive proof of rap's artistic status by its own specific artistic power. Stetsasonic do not pretend to provide an exhaustive survey or extended "formal debate"; they claim "to set the record straight" about rap and its record-sampling distortions within the mere space of a record by the convincing and exemplary appeal of "the song [they] sing today:" a self-consciously self-asserting and arguably self-validating declaration of the truth that rap is art.

Artistic Self-consciousness, Creativity, and Form

This self-conscious self-assertion of artistic status is more important than it might seem, for artistic self-consciousness is regarded by many aestheticians as an essential feature of art.[39] Thus, one reason why popular arts have been denied artistic status is that they fail to claim it. They do not, Adorno and Horkheimer argue (1944, 121), even "pretend to be art" but rather accept their status as entertainment industries. They do not, Bourdieu argues, insist on their own aesthetic legitimacy but instead meekly accept the dominant high-art aesthetic that essentially negates them.[40] Lacking the requisite artistic self-consciousness and self-respect to claim artistic status, popular art does not merit or achieve it. However true this may be for other popular arts, it cannot be said for rap. Stetsasonic, like countless other rappers, "stand / Up for the music [they] live and play," aggressively claiming and proudly celebrating rap as an art.

"Talkin' All That Jazz" evinces at least five aspects of this proud artistic self-consciousness, apart from its firm assertion of artistic status. First, since art is something that stands out from ordinary conduct and humdrum experience by its superior skill and quality, this song insists on rap's superior talent, strength, and pizazz vis-à-vis ordinary cheap talk. Second, if art's essentially historical character means that to be a work of art is to belong to an artistic tradition, the song underlines rap's connection to such a tradition. It does this most pointedly by first describing itself as a new kind of jazz, thus aligning itself with the black musical form most widely recognized as legitimate art; and then further connecting itself with "old R & B," the established popularity of which is said to be enhanced or insured through rap's "bring[ing] back" of its rhythms. There are also the more specific and intricate intertextual links to Sly Stone, James Brown, and the rap crew Eric and Rakim, which give a fuller sense of rap's place in and shaping of a continuing artistic tradition — one that involves both the recognition and contestation that any healthy and fruitful tradition must display.[41]

A very important aspect of recent artistic tradition (and one often regarded as essential to the very nature of art) is art's oppositional stance. Many maintain like Adorno that art — to qualify as such, to display its defining originality and distinction from the ordinary — must somehow take a stand against a generally accepted but unacceptable reality or status quo (artistic or societal), even if this opposition be expressed only implicitly by art's fictionality or by the difficulties it poses for ordinary comprehension. Popular arts, they argue, cannot display such opposition because their popularity requires an appeal to the most commonly accepted views and standards and to the most elementary modes of understanding. Thus, these so-called arts must not be granted true artistic status.[42]

Whether or not such an oppositional character is indeed essential to art, it is certainly present in rap, not only explicitly but often self-consciously. Violent protest of the status quo — the establishment culture and media, the politicians and police, and the representations and realities they all seek to impose — is, as we have seen, a central and often thematized feature of many rap lyrics. But "Talkin' All That Jazz" most clearly exemplifies rap's self-consciousness as *artistic* opposition, attacking and defying the cultural czars who deny rap aesthetic legitimacy or artistic status. Moreover, apart from this explicit content, its very form, its dramatic monologue of confrontational discourse, is structured by the oppositional stance.

Two other central features of modern artistic consciousness are frequently taken to be essential for any art worthy of the name and are just as frequently denied to the products of popular culture: concern for creativity and attention to form. Both can be connected to art's allegedly requisite oppositional character. For art's creative injunction to be new implies at least some opposition to the old and familiar, while preoccupation with form rather than content seems to reverse our ordinary cognitive and practical concerns (and thus has come to define for some the specifically aesthetic attitude).[43] Both these creative and formalist concerns are powerfully present in "Talkin' All That Jazz," and their demonstration will conclude my aesthetic account of this rap and of rap in general.

Though its method of appropriative sampling challenges romantic notions of unique novelty and pure originality, rap claims to be creative. It moreover insists that originality can be manifested in the revisionary appropriation of the old, whether this be old records or the old proverbs that "Talkin' All That Jazz" samples but creatively endows with new meanings. Indeed, "Talkin' All That Jazz" is all about rap's acute consciousness of its novelty as an artistic form, a consciousness painfully sharpened by rap's having been persecuted as such. With its talking rather than singing, sampling rather than composing or playing, rap's departure from traditional music provoked the denial of its legitimacy, even as a popular art. But in the economy of two lines, Stetsasonic cleverly establish rap's link to artistic tradition through its connection with jazz, while at the same time reaffirming the genre's creative divergence and importance as a new artistic form. "Jazz, well you can call it that / But this jazz retains a new format." Moreover, the single phrase that rap *retains* a new format" (rather than, say, *inventing* one) ingeniously captures the complex paradox of artistic tradition and innovation that Eliot labored to express: the idea that art can and must be novel to be traditional (and traditional to be novel), that one cannot conform to our artistic tradition by simply conforming to it, since artistic tradition is one of novelty and deviation from conformity.

Rap thus refutes the dogma that concern for form and formal experimentation cannot be found in popular art.[44] It moreover displays the thematized attention to artistic medium and method often regarded as the hallmark of contemporary high art. Sampling is not only rap's most radical formal innovation (since some earlier pop songs experimented with speech rather than song); it is also the most concerned with rap's artistic medium — recorded music. And, not surprisingly, it is extremely contested, in the courts of law as well as the court of culture. The aesthetic defense of sampling constitutes the motivating theme of "Talkin' All That Jazz," which from the outset links the issue of rap's artistic legitimacy with that of its sampling method.

> Well, here's how it started
> Heard you on the radio
> Talk about rap,
> Sayin all that crap
> About how we sample,
> Give an example.
> Think we'll let you get away with that.
> You criticize our method
> Of how we make records

> You said it wasn't art,
> So now we're gonna rip you apart.

In order to defend rap's claim to be creative art, sampling must be defended from the obvious and plausible charge that it is just the stealing or copying of already existing songs. The defense is that rap's sampling is not an end in itself, an attempt to reproduce or imitate already popular records, but rather a formal technique or "method" to make from old fragments new songs with "a new format," by innovative manipulation of the technical media of the recording industry: records, turntables, tapes, etc. As with any artistic method or "tool," sampling's aesthetic significance or value depends on how it is used ("It's only of importance when I make it a priority") and thus ultimately needs to be judged within particular concrete contexts; thus, the maligning critics are enjoined to "give an example" of how sampling vitiates rap's artistry. Stetsasonic moreover assert that sampling is only "a portion" of rap's method and not always its highest priority. This message and their challenge to "give an example" are formalistically reinforced by the fact that the actual use of sampling and scratch mixing in "Talkin' All That Jazz" is relatively negligible.

Aware that rap's innovative technique of sampling might be dismissed as an ephemeral gimmick, Stetsasonic explicitly answer the "mad" critics who "think rap is a fad" devoid of creative potential and staying power, by pointing to the "strong" talent of its artists and the enduring "respect" it has won among its growing audience. And the Stets are not just "talkin' jazz." For while the pop culture pundits thought rap would barely survive a season when it appeared in 1979, it is finally achieving some critical recognition. "Now as the 90's begin," writes *New York Times* critic Jon Pareles, rap "is both the most startlingly original and fastest growing genre in popular music."[45]

But while granting its creative originality, Pareles questions rap's achievement of coherent form. Its techniques of sampling and mixing and its fragmented, mass-media mentality prevent the creation of ordered form and logical structure, resulting in songs fractured by "dislocations and discontinuities" where "rhythm is paramount and non sequiturs are perpetual." The songs "don't develop from a beginning to an end," thus giving the sense that "a song could be cut off at any moment." This is certainly true for some rap, and perhaps for that which most immediately attracts attention and hostility by its deviation from accepted form. But it is at best a very partial and exaggerated account of the genre as a whole. For rap is full of songs firmly structured either on clear narrative development or on coherent logical argument. The narrative form includes the many celebratory ballads of the rapper's exploits and the equally numerous cautionary moral exempla about drugs, venereal disease, and the life of crime. The logical format is exemplified by many of rap's songs of protest and black pride, including its frequent manifestoes of rap's self-pride. "Talkin' All That Jazz" falls into this last category, and its formal and logical coherence is undeniable.

It is composed of four clearly structured stanzas, which, though of slightly unequal length, are equally framed by the same instrumental interlude that at once distinguishes and connects them. These stanzas are further formalistically united by their closing with the same one-line refrain, which is also the song's title. Finally, while this closing line appears once in each of the first three stanzas, in the fourth and final stanza it is given three times, as if to recall, reinforce, and sum up the three preceding stanzas and their arguments.

The song's argument in defense of rap is also very coherently structured. The first stanza begins with the condemnation of rap and sampling followed by the threatening, protesting counterclaim of rap's creative artistic status. The second proceeds to refute rap's condemnation by explaining the role of sampling, stressing rap's popular appeal, and pointing to the elitist narrowness and ignorance of its condemnatory critics while continuing the threat of retaliatory violence ("You step on us and we'll step on you"). Stanza three continues the theme of "angry" retaliation against the maligning lies of rap critics while further justifying rap's legitimacy both in terms of the truth, talent, and strength it displays and because of its connection with and renovating preservation of the artistic tradition of Afro-American music. The final stanza, while reinforcing this traditional link and maintaining the song's proud "stand" of resistance and threat of violence, also extends an invitation of peaceful coexistence to rap's as yet unconverted audience, showing that they need not be afraid of granting rap artistic legitimacy. This closing advocacy of pluralistic tolerance (of "not tryin' to be a boss") does not come from the fear of rap's weakness in the face of critical scrutiny. Rap is ready for "a formal debate," but only when it can have an adequate "forum" (i.e., a public space) within which to express itself, a forum that the media and cultural establishment have so far denied it.

Here again we have the insightful and ingeniously telescoped linking of the aesthetic and the political. The struggle for aesthetic legitimacy (a symptom of more general social struggles) can only achieve the form of refined and carefully reasoned debates about form when one can enjoy the security of being heard. The rappers are still struggling for that hearing, and to get it Stetsasonic must "for now" speak more urgently and violently, so less formally. If the denigration and suppression of rap's voice incites violent protest rather than sweet aesthetic reasonings, the enemies of rap are themselves responsible ("What you reap is what you sow").

This prioritization of getting a hearing before going into a formal debate, of securing expressive legitimacy before concentrating on intricacies of form, can be taken as a critical but defensive self-commentary on this song's own formal status, and it raises a crucial formalist issue that rap must face. For while "Talkin' All That Jazz" achieves formal unity and logical coherence, it remains formalistically more simple and traditional than many other raps, which talk much less about sampling but instead apply it much more extensively, complexly, and emphatically. But while such songs produce a far more radically "new format," it is one far more susceptible to Pareles' charge of formal incoherence.

This suggests a tension between rap's aims of formal innovation and its satisfaction of the formal coherence required of art. For rap's artistic innovation, particularly its technique of sampling, is closely connected with elements of fragmentation and the breaking of forms. This tension between formal innovation and already appreciable formal coherence is the formal debate in which rap is now actively engaged. It is still in the process of testing the limits of its innovative techniques and the formal sensibilities of its audience in order to find the right balance—a form that is both new and yet somehow assimilable to our changing aesthetic tradition and sensibility. Less than fifteen years old, rap is still far from a solution and from artistic maturity. It will attain neither if it is not first accorded the artistic legitimacy necessary to pursue its own development and that of its audience without the oppression and dismissive abuse of the cultural establishment and without the compulsion to sell out to the most immediate and crassest of commercial pressures.

"Talkin' All That Jazz," a song advocating rap's new format while remaining comfortably close to traditional form, is an appeal for such legitimacy, and an appealing one because of the way it meets traditional aesthetic criteria. It thus provides us intellectuals with a more tempting invitation to enter the formal debate about rap, a debate that it defers to the future and that only the future will resolve.

CHAPTER TEN

Conventions and
Literary Systems

SIEGFRIED J. SCHMIDT

From Literary Texts to Literary Systems

In the past, rules and conventions were frequently evoked with regard to literary texts, if only to characterize works of elite literature (*Hochliteratur*) as creative instances of rule breaking or as admirable transgressions of a given set of conventions.

In what follows, I focus on the social, as opposed to symbolic, system of literature. My argument thus starts from a lesson that many literary scholars have learned from experience: it is not enough to study only literary texts. Independently of all schools or isms, the research results of the last few decades show that if one wishes adequately to "interpret" literary texts, then the whole domain of so-called literary life must be studied alongside literary texts, more narrowly speaking.

A closer analysis of the activities that in our society accompany literary phenomena in the broad sense indicates that the former may be classified into four distinct action roles:

Literary production embraces all actions whereby a product is created that is deemed by the producer to be literary on the basis of the aesthetic norms with which he or she is operating.

Literary mediation embraces all actions whereby a literary product is made accessible to other agents, in a form that is appropriate to the medium in question.

Literary reception embraces all actions whereby a product judged to be literary according to certain aesthetic standards is granted certain meanings by the agents who appropriate and receive it.

Literary processing embraces all actions whereby a product that is

Translated from German by Mette Hjort.

deemed to be literary is connected to some other product by means of which it is summarized, retold, paraphrased, evaluated, or subjected to formal analysis.

Inasmuch as each of these action roles can accommodate radically different actions, it is necessary to articulate these definitions in a somewhat dry, yet rigorous manner. The term *literary products* is to be understood in the most general sense, as including not only books but radio plays, films, videoclips, photocopies, fliers, and television images. The formula "judged to be literary according to certain aesthetic standards" gives expression to the by now common belief that we no longer can presuppose the existence of a canon of aesthetic standards that would be binding for all, or even for most, agents. Instead, the literary scholar must now ask questions that are empirical, contextual, and pragmatic in thrust: *"Who* attributes literary value to *which* product, and on *what* grounds?" In so doing, one very quickly discovers that although aesthetic judgments have every appearance of being random, they in fact are anything but arbitrary. When agents actually articulate a judgment, they do so on the basis of what they consider to be thoroughly good reasons. And what justifies a given judgment is itself a function of literary socialization, reading habits and experience, and basic values and attitudes.

Systems

This rather abstract and purely descriptive account can be fleshed out by drawing on some concepts from systems theory.

Most generally, *system* is understood to refer to composite wholes that satisfy specific conditions. Systems are comprised of *components* having qualities that can be described. It is the interaction of these components that brings forth the particular *organization* of the system, the latter being to a certain extent independent of the former. Indeed, the individual components are at least to some extent substitutable and may be replaced without endangering the organization of the system as a whole.

Whether applied to biology or sociology, systems theory relies on a basic distinction between the system and its environment (*Umwelt*). If a set of structured and interrelated elements is to become a system, a boundary must be established that separates it from all other systems, as well as from its environment. The limit in question will be determined by means of some salient *difference* and must be such that it leaves open the possibility of interaction. What constitutes an environment with regard to a given system can only be determined from the perspective of the system itself. Yet this distinction between system and environment can also be reiterated within the system, for in creating partial or internal systems, the system as a whole construes itself as an environment. This process is referred to as *systems-differentiation*. By differentiating itself into partial systems, the global system enhances its complexity, just as it increases its possible modes of functioning.

Social systems emerge when agents, through interaction, develop a common interpretation of reality, and when they act and communicate with reference to it. Societies may be described as networks of social systems. In highly differentiated societies, individuals participate in a variety of social systems; that is, they adopt different social roles and thus develop a repertory of ever-changing models of reality, all of which are constitutive of their social identity. Social systems may be said to interact inasmuch as they reciprocally (particularly through communication) open up possibilities for action that can, but need not, be actualized following the specific conditions governing action within a given system. Social systems are self-organizing, for they establish, govern, and further develop themselves and are relatively autonomous as a result. This does not mean, however, that they are independent of their environment. The environment can "perturb" the system, but only the system can assign a meaning to this perturbation through processes that are system-specific. Autonomy produces and maintains not just the boundaries but the actual identity of the system. Self-organizing social systems are complex and dynamic, and as a result they cannot ever be fully described, which is why prognostics concerning the course of their future development rarely prove to be correct. A self-organizing social system is self-referential in two regards: it deals only with the conditions that it itself creates, and each instance of behavior becomes the basis for further behavior.

Not only do social systems rule out all forms of organization based on *hierarchy*, they also do not allow themselves to be governed from some privileged *center*. Instead, order emerges through a combination of spontaneity and planning. All processes determining the system are interconnected, and if one ceases, then so do the others. The idea that social systems are self-referential and self-organizing is, in my mind, one that becomes all the more plausible when connected to an appropriate conception of the agents who act, perceive, and deliberate within them.

In recent years, the pertinent epistemological foundations have been laid down in the context of a constructivist theory of cognition that has tried to forge meaningful connections between empirical arguments and theoretical models drawn from psychology, sociology, biology, and cybernetics. Given that detailed accounts of this theory already exist (Rusch 1987; Schmidt 1987b), I shall provide only a very general sketch of its main features.

Perception is construed as a sensorimotor and socially guided construction of invariants whereby the system accommodates or assimilates significant input to its existing conceptual structures. This process is circular (but not viciously so) insofar as the perceiver and perceived interact and are reciprocally constitutive of each other. Given the theory-laden nature of perception, it cannot be rigorously distinguished from interpretation. Perception is a subject-dependent, action-related process in which heredity, learning, and memory combine. The processes governing perception and the production of knowledge are socially conditioned. Conventions, the accumulation and transmission of experience, changes in the material world, social models for action, standing possibilities for communication, and semiotic systems all function as intersubjectively available schemata, exercising a crucial influence on the subjective processes of cognition.

Knowledge is defined by the *methods* by which it is produced. We may speak of scientific knowledge if the process of production is oriented by explicit methods, and if the results can be methodically tested. Thus, notions of intersubjectivity and method take the place of objectivity and truth as the criteria of scientificity.

From these assumptions, it follows that the living system *constructs* its environment (which includes both objects and agents). Inasmuch as autopoietic systems are self-referential in character, the constructions in question will be measured against the ontological categories and experiences of the agents, rather than against some external reality or "real world." This process of construction nonetheless presupposes an environment and interacting agents (the specifically "other"), for only then is it possible for us to project our own properties onto them (see von Glasersfeld 1987).

Knowing may thus be construed as the most abstract form of action, conveying self-referential representations of reality to the brain. Knowledge indicates the actions that are possible but does not tell us whether they correspond to reality. On the one hand, reality is experience-specific, for it is constructed in and through action. On the other hand, the biological and psychological features of experiencing and knowing agents only develop in the course of grappling with this "reality" within a given social context. Once this self-referential relation is acknowledged, the traditional subject/object models of perception and knowledge become obsolete.

Thus, socialization, conventions, and institutions essentially ensure that individuals belonging to a given social group *incorporate* a set of normative models of reality. The structures of these models bear the mark of social interests and power, as do the gestures by which they are legitimated and sustained. The consensual principles governing the construction of reality are mediated and internalized primarily through language, which is what linguists and sociologists have been telling us for some time now.

Unlike Niklas Luhmann, Peter M. Hejl (1987b) conceives of *social systems* uniquely in terms of agents (living systems), further stipulating that only certain aspects of agents are relevant:

> A *social system* can be defined as a group of living systems that satisfies two conditions:
>
> 1. Within the cognitive sub-systems of each living system there must develop at least one state (normally a set of states) that is ontologically relevant and comparable to at least one of the states of the cognitive systems of the other members of the group.
> 2. Living systems must interact in function of these parallel states.
>
> In other words, the members of the system must have produced a shared reality—a domain of meaningful action and communication—with reference to which they interact. (Examples are: football teams, families, organizations, or the participants in a law suit). (128)

Like all systems, different *social* systems interact in and through the interactions of their component parts; the agents function as self-referential systems, and it is they who perceive and act, develop responses, and articulate decisions. Agents act as components of the global system, if and only if their actions presuppose a system-specific construction of reality, as well as the category of interactions that it makes possible: "In this sense we may, in abbreviated form, speak of the perceptions, decisions, and actions of the system" (Hejl 1987b, 128). As a "point of intersection" (to use a graph-theoretical term) between social systems, each individual is exposed to the influences of different systems of which he or she is also a component. Change occurs when agents bring novel constructions of reality to the social system's processes of interaction and communication. These new elements are perceived either as "challenges" to or as "interpretations" of the system's salient construction of reality; they have as a result to be "dealt with" by the system. That is, they will be either modified and assimilated or isolated and rendered harmless in function of the system's prevailing conditions. "Inasmuch as a given social system rarely is subjected uniquely to the influence of one other system, a heterarchic process of interaction emerges between systems. During this process local instances of hierarchy develop, just as further differentiation occurs" (Hejl 1987b, 130).

Literary Systems as Social Systems

With these concepts in hand, it is possible to rephrase the above description of "literary life" in a more systematic manner: All actions pertaining to phenomena that agents believe to be literary (literary actions) may be conceptually identified as a social system. That is, literary actions are components making up the social system of literature. This system is self-referential, for literary actions necessarily refer to other literary actions: literary reception refers to literary production, literary processing to literary reception, literary mediation to literary production, and so on. The connections between literary actions will be referred to as *literary processes*. The organization produced by the system is thus a closed one, with specific literary actions and processes emerging from a given state and essentially participating in the production of the next state. In this sense, the social system of literature may be construed as both self-referential and self-organizing.

The literary system's structure is determined by the action roles identified above. As stable institutions, these roles specify and order all isolated literary actions.

The literary system's boundaries are produced and maintained because agents develop differentiating criteria allowing them to distinguish between what, for them, is literary and nonliterary. Empirical and historical studies suggest that the boundaries of the literary system in Germany today are established by two basic conventions (Meutsch and Schmidt 1985, 1988; Schmidt 1982, 1989).[1] These macroconventions will be referred to as the *aesthetic convention* and the *polyvalence convention*. These macroconventions are only operative within the literary system and not in other social systems (such as politics, religion, education, the economy, and so on).

The aesthetic convention specifies that utterances figuring in literary texts need not, as would normally be the case, be evaluated primarily in terms of the model of reality that is binding within a given society. They are not, in other words, to be judged in terms of what is true or false following a referential semantics. What is more, the value of literary actions is not to be determined first and foremost by their practical utility. Instead, the aesthetic convention has the effect of orienting literary actions and communication toward values, norms, and meaning rules that are considered by the agents in question to be constitutive of literature, given their particular aesthetic.

The second convention, the so-called polyvalence convention, accords an exceptional degree of freedom to agents operating within the literary system. In dealing with literary phenomena, these agents expect, and are indeed allowed, to pursue what they believe to be the optimal realization of their own subjective capacities for expression and response.

Together the two conventions accomplish the following task: all possible actions in the literary system are *exempted* from the requirement that they be based on socially accepted models of reality; this in turn opens up a vast sphere of freedom in which subjective action and experience, fantasy, creativity, imagination, and fiction may be explored. In this view, it is clear that the literary system is not primarily determined by the set of literary works. What circumscribes it, rather, is the *organizational form* governing actions and instances of communication that are carved out of the totality of social activities following the literary/nonliterary distinction, and that together constitute the social system of literature, as these activities interrelate in a self-referential and self-organizational manner. The distinction in question is socially maintained by the two conventions, just as it is stabilized as a result of the literary socialization of agents within families, schools, social groups, and so on. As long as an agent abides by these conventions, he or she acts within the bounds of the literary system; more precisely, the agent adopts one of the action roles available within this system.

The social system of literature is thus neither an "entity" nor a "place." This system, rather, emerges as an organizational form for literary actions, creating its own order through the production of partial systems and maintaining a dynamic equilibrium.

The Aesthetic versus the Polyvalence Convention

In the course of a wide-ranging inquiry into public opinion concerning the concept of literature in West Germany (carried out in collaboration with the polling institute EMNID in Bielefeld), my colleagues and I obtained the following results with regard to the validity of the theoretically postulated aesthetic convention.[2] As far as a representative cross-section of the 1980 West German population was concerned, the concept of literature is largely *independent of the referential truth* of the utterances figuring in texts, just as it excludes the idea that literary texts might be without fictional elements. The concept of literature is, on the contrary, intimately connected with good style, comprehensibility, and deep or significant issues; literature is assumed to generate a high level of emotional involvement and pleasure and to have entertainment value. These results become all the clearer when they are correlated with the education of those interviewed. The higher the level of education, the more fully the concept of literature is connected with stylistic and aesthetic criteria, the truth of the literary utterances (following a referential semantics) being considered secondary. For these individuals, literature is clearly belles-lettres; its form must be unique or special, and it must realize properly aesthetic values.

This finding is surprising, given our consumer- and profit-oriented society. Even a society as materialistic as our own allows itself a sphere where there is no effective notion of true information and no emphasis on its dissemination through instruction. The value of this sphere for the individual and for society at large is time and again the subject of fierce debate—I have in mind, for example, the endless disputes from 1968 onward over the social function of literature, the complete abolition of literature having been advocated to no effect.

Redundantly, the inquiry also proves that aesthetic phenomena are valued more highly than are social, economic, and religious phenomena, and that literature (belles-lettres) is deemed to be especially ethical, useful, and vital to the emotions. Individuals with advanced degrees were especially likely to judge literature to be "very valuable, useful, and interesting."

Although we on several occasions obtained consistent results concerning the social validity of the aesthetic convention, we did encounter certain obstacles in our attempt to subject the polyvalence convention to empirical study. These difficulties may be accounted for as follows. Polyvalence, as Meutsch and Schmidt (1985, 1988) have shown, involves three distinct and basic aspects:

Semantic polyvalence: the attributions of meaning to literary texts proved to be exceptionally diverse when compared with attributions effected within other social systems.

Functional polyvalence: those interviewed assumed that the function of literary reception involves three dimensions: a cognitive or reflective, a moral or social, and a subjective or hedonistic dimension.

Social polyvalence: agents demonstrated an unusually high level of tolerance with regard to what others might choose to make of a given literary text.

All three aspects were operative simultaneously, as agents grappled with the interpretive problems presented by complex literary texts.

The difficulties involved in an empirical study of literary understanding, as created and regulated by the polyvalence convention, stem from the necessity of artificially interrupting what would otherwise be a hermeneutic process involving no guiding or overarching conscious intent. Inasmuch as agents were asked to assess the problems of interpretation that they encountered, it is hardly surprising that complications related to introspection, self-reflection, and articulation should have arisen.

Given the present state of empirical literary research, here is what can be said about the relation between the two conventions: the aesthetic convention clearly establishes the general framework within which the polyvalence convention then can define the specifics of the hermeneutic process (in a manner that is independent of the receiving agents' context of reception and psychosocial dispositions). In short, the aesthetic convention initiates and legitimates the cognitive contributions of the polyvalence convention that itself specifies the cognitive process called *Verstehen*. The polyvalence convention can only be evoked by those who already have access to the aesthetic convention; and both conventions are a matter of literary socialization.

On The Origin of the Macroconventions in the Literary System of Eighteenth-Century Germany

Since these two conventions have been empirically shown to exist in the literary systems of contemporary democratic societies,[3] the question arises of how they began. When I turn to this issue in the second half of my discussion, I focus on certain historical developments within the German context, some of which are extraliterary.[4] In a discussion of conventions, such historical digressions are inevitable: the claim that the boundaries of the literary system are constituted by macroconventions requires a historical explanation of *how*, and more importantly, of *why* literary communication developed into a *self-organizing social system*, erecting boundaries so as to create an identity that subsequently had to be stabilized in order to ensure the system's continued existence. What is more, once it has been established that conventions did in fact serve the function of defining the literary system's limits, thereby rendering it autonomous, it then becomes crucial to explain *why* this role was assumed by conventions. If all this is to seem even somewhat plausible, I must engage in a particularist, historical discourse.

In the vast sociological and historical literature dealing with the eighteenth century, the far-reaching changes characterizing this period are construed in terms of a transition from a feudal society, organized in function of the estates, to a *functionally differentiated society*. The stratified society based on the estates had become overly complex on account of population growth, communication problems, the increase and expansion of world trade, scientific and technical discoveries, colonialism, the dissolution of religious ties, and so on. From this overly complex society there gradually emerged a set of differentiated social tasks that became the basis for a number of autonomous social systems. This development was not governed by some global social scheme, by the intentions of some one individual, or by the plans of a given social group. Instead, this social transformation followed its own particular laws, giving rise to the modern period somewhere around the end of the eighteenth century.

The old order was supported first and foremost by church and state and was based on forms of life that were rich in tradition. During the process of transformation, this order was severed from the new areas of efficacy and communication that were to gain ever greater degrees of autonomy, while at the same time becoming more and more fully integrated into the social fabric as a whole. The decisive features of this transformational process were (1) increased rationality (the Enlightenment), (2) greater emphasis on organization (bureaucratization), and (3) the scientization of all social life. I shall explore some of these changes in an attempt to clarify the social context out of which the modern literary system in Germany developed.

THE POLITICAL SYSTEM

In the eighteenth century, the decisive sociopolitical development was the separation of state and society. This transition was favored by the powers of absolutism, which construed rulership as a form of political expression, free of moral constraints. The relative political stability of the seventeenth and eighteenth centuries provided the framework within which bourgeois conceptions of morality could be explored, and this stability was itself made possible as a result of the severing of politics from morality. Although the eighteenth-century bourgeoisie remained politically impotent, it did create for itself a whole range of social institutions (stock markets, academies, coffee houses, libraries, newspapers, and secret societies such as the Freemasons' lodges). These institutions, which were ultimately to become the bourgeois public sphere, provided a site where a moral critique of the state could be articulated.

By the end of the eighteenth century, the separation of state and society was fully under way. The state gradually assumed three responsibilities: safeguarding its own existence, upholding the legal order, and ensuring civil liberty. The most important tasks, relinquished by the state and assigned to society instead, were those of explaining away thwarted social expectations and articulating interpretations through which life and world were imbued with meaning. For centuries, the church and the state had enjoyed a monopoly on the production of models of reality and systems of value, a monopoly which was now broken: the "ontological" question (What is real and relevant with regard to the state, society, and the individual?) became the prerogative of society and was further differentiated within the emerging social systems. In this respect, the literary system played a crucial role.

THE ECONOMIC SYSTEM

The separation of the function of rulership from the creation of meaning would have entailed a complete collapse of society, had it not been for the emergence of a new, stabilizing factor: the economy was seen as a means of resolving enduring social questions, particularly through the mechanism of money.

A philosophically grounded rationalization of all forms of social life could gradually be developed on the religious basis provided by changed attitudes toward work (the Protestant work ethic) and money, which was no longer to be wasted in lavish displays of splendor but hoarded for the purpose of investment. The demand for economic freedom was connected with the demand for political freedom and for a citizen's right to own property.

The emergence of speculative capitalism in the modern sense was yoked to subjectivist individualism and to an insistence on democracy. As capitalism gained ground through increased levels of industrialization, labor was transformed into a commodity that could be exchanged on the market. Industry relied on technology, the division of labor, and specialization. Yet, as a result, working individuals became cogs in a machine that they could no longer fathom.

It is true that in Germany the state retained political leadership long into the nineteenth century; its economic dependence on citizens who owned capital did, however, increase. Being based on money—the standard by which all goods and all forms of labor can be converted and exchanged—the economy thus emerged as the overarching system of modern society.

THE LEGAL SYSTEM

A self-organizing process of economic development was possible only on the basis of a legal system that was reliable and binding for all. The legal transformations effected during the eighteenth century can be appropriately described by the following slogan: "From Natural to Positive Law." The legal sphere first detached itself from that of theology (divine law and confession), then from anthropology (that had sought the foundations of the law in the very nature of mankind), and, finally, from ethics and morality. During this process, law was increasingly defined as state legality. The state claimed legislative authority, thereby bringing to a close the theoretical process involving the transition from natural to positive law. Limits were indeed placed on the state's legislative authority and political praxis, by a proclamation of basic human rights that were assumed to be justified by common interests and a collective will. The constitutional state institutionalized conflict between citizens, as well as between citizens and the state. Corporate power relations flowing from a system of estates and their related life forms were replaced by the principle of the equality of all before the law. While the state was committed to safeguarding the rights of the individual and to opening up nonpolitical spheres of action for its citizens, the real consequence of the legal emancipation of the individual was that the latter's energies were free to be harnessed to the process of economic production.

The law, in its positive form, was codified in the national language (in the *Preußisches Allgemeines Landrecht* in 1794, and in the *Allgemeines Gesetzbuch für die Erbländer der Österreichischen Monarchie* in 1811); in principle it ruled out the imposition of religious or political doctrines by means of violence. The differentiated legal system construed freedom as a right and thereby allowed for a high degree of individualization at the level of decisions and belief, ranging from the choice of profession to that of spouse. The functional domains of religion, economics, politics, science, and the family were sharply separated as a result. The private was valorized as public and private spheres were disjoined, and this in turn enhanced the process whereby citizens, construed as equal before the law, were individualized.

THE EDUCATIONAL SYSTEM

Changes in the educational domain had a crucial influence on the development of literature. An independent educational system emerged in Germany during the process of functional differentiation in the eighteenth century. This system became entirely separate from the church, and its relation to the state was specified by legal means. Education was deprivatized. Instead of being educated by members of the family or the church, children were now required by law to attend public schools, and for the first time this regulation included the female sex. The schools were differentiated according to types or kinds, each with its own particular trajectory, curriculum, and tests or examinations. The profession of teaching was institutionalized, just as the training of teachers was professionalized. The educational system assumed the professional training of civil servants and soldiers, of experts in the domains of business and commerce, agriculture, science, literature, and art. It created a reading public and firmly linked literary socialization to schools and universities.

RELIGION

In the course of the separation of church and state, religion forfeited its former function of assigning each and every individual to a divinely ordained position within the social totality. Up until the middle of the eighteenth century, daily existence was entirely monopolized by religion; from that point on, however, the everyday life of the bourgeoisie was drastically secularized, particularly spiritual life. Gradually, philosophy, science, education, and literature all severed their former connections to religion. Religious questions, of course, were not suddenly rendered obsolete, nor did the church entirely cease to exercise influence on the state, philosophy, education, and literature. Rather, what characterized the new situation was the fact that the Christian religion no longer could be considered self-evident. Instead, religion became one particular arrangement among others, individuals being, in principle, free either to embrace or to reject it.

THE SCIENCES

Along with economics, the natural and human sciences played a crucial role in the process of social differentiation in the eighteenth century. The development of these sciences was characterized by the growth of experimental methods that were perfected and applied to ever larger domains of scientific research, as well as by the rise of the human sciences as historical disciplines in which evolutionary thought prevailed. All-encompassing cosmological ideas were replaced by empirical models of reality that in turn gave rise to a temporalized conception of knowledge. The result was twofold: the idea that there is progress

in science was affirmed, as was the insight that all knowledge is historically determined.

The rapid differentiation of knowledge found expression in the creation of more and more subdisciplines and in the invention of specialized technical languages. Scientific communication was thus unhinged
from ordinary or everyday communication, as well as from that of all
other social systems. As science laid more and more emphasis on the
empirical and rational production of truth, the human subject and life
world were progressively excluded from the picture. The more rationalized and specialized scientific knowledge became, the greater was the
individual's need for guidance concerning life choices, personal relationships, basic values, and the interpretation of the world. This need
was aggravated by the autonomy that individuals exercised in these
domains once the religious world-view lost its hold. And, as we shall
see, it is literature that filled the void left by religion.

THE FAMILY

In the social domain, changes at the level of the family stand out as particularly important. Levin Ludwig Schücking (1964) claims that one of
the greatest accomplishments of the bourgeoisie in the eighteenth century was the transformation of the family into a "real community"
(170). Thus, the hostility toward feeling, characteristic of the Calvinistic
or Lutheran family, would finally have been overcome. In this view, the
generation born between 1725 and 1749 enjoyed a warmer and more
open relation to their parents, just as the upper middle class is said to
have appropriated a great many aristocratic customs, integrating them
into a bourgeois conception of education and morality.

The bourgeois model of the family, based on privacy and intimacy, had
to defend itself on two fronts: against aristocratic conceptions and practices, such as that of the extended family; and against attempts on the
part of individual family members to affirm their individuality. The
demands and burdens of the bourgeois family were clearly perceived as
extremely important issues, and it was within the literary system that
they were dealt with at great length. Thus, literature provided propa-
ganda for the bourgeois family, as well as representations of its successes
and failures, with particular emphasis on the latter. Never before had so
much been written about family relations, in such psychological and soci-

ological detail. These new themes gave rise to major genres: the bourgeois tragedy (Gotthold Ephraim Lessing) and the bourgeois family romance and sentimental novel (Christian Fürchtegott Gellert).

Before going on to discuss the emergence of the literary system in the eighteenth century, I need to clear up a possible misunderstanding. What is at issue here is the origin of the *social system* of literature, *not* of the *symbolic literary system*. Authors, texts, audiences, and readers had, of course, existed for centuries. What was radically new, however, was the historical process of functional differentiation whereby literary activities were drawn together in a web of actions and institutions, that is, a self-organizing social system of literature. What is more, in the course of this process, all activities related to literature underwent fundamental changes: they were professionalized, institutionalized, and differentiated, and the relations between them became self-referential. In what follows I outline these developments.

The Changing Role of the Author

Unlike the literary critic (and other agents involved in what I have called "literary processing"), the *literary author* was a familiar figure in eighteenth-century literary life. Yet, for the first time the notion of authorship now became associated with a particular action role. The external form of this role, the way it was understood, and its relation to other social roles all changed so fundamentally that the activity engaged in by authors in earlier centuries can only be described as utterly different from the action role of literary producers within the social system of literature. Here are some of the signs marking this transformation:

1. the beginnings of a professionalization of writing ("independent writer");
2. a significant numerical increase in authors in Germany;
3. changes in the author's social role (rootless intellectual);
4. the clarification of the writer's legal status (by means of notions like "intellectual property");
5. the emergence of a book market organized along capitalist lines, based on increased and more differentiated production;

6. changes in the self-image of the literary producer (the idea of genius);

7. changes in authors' relations to instances of literary mediation (capitalist book market), literary reception (anonymous mass public), and literary processing (literary criticism and literary research).

In what follows I summarize the results of some relevant and detailed research and interpret them in the light of my theoretical framework.

THE EMERGENCE OF THE INDEPENDENT AUTHOR

The emergence of the independent author has to be seen in connection with the genesis of a bourgeois intelligentsia. As far as the latter's social origins are concerned, the role played by Protestant parsonages is frequently cited as crucial, although individuals were also recruited from other levels of society, including that of the lesser aristocracy.

The social situation of writers in the early eighteenth century varied as a function of a number of factors. Casual producers of literary texts tended, on the whole, to have full-time careers as civil servants, priests, professors, or officers (Johann Christoph Gottsched and Gellert are typical of this group). These individuals were firmly tied to their respective institutions and whatever system of rank they imposed. A second group comprised bourgeois authors who achieved economic independence through pensions, interest, or accumulated capital. Yet another group was composed of court poets, political secretaries working for aristocratic corporations, princes, diplomats, generals, librarians, and overseers of manor houses. From these different types of authors, each possessing its own particular tradition, the figure of the independent writer gradually emerged around midcentury. Friedrich Gottlieb Klopstock (1724–1803), Lessing (1729–81), and Christoph Martin Wieland (1733–1813) were pioneers in this regard. The problems encountered by these independent writers can be briefly characterized as follows:

1. The aristocracy, and some of the members of the upper middle class living in cities, continued to have an unambiguous preference for French literature and culture well into the second half of the century.

2. Inasmuch as the princes patronized the arts at all, most of

them privileged architecture, opera, theater, and the plastic arts over literature.

3. Around midcentury, the selling of books did not yet involve the kind of royalties that would support an existence as an independent writer.

4. The plans that Wieland, Klopstock, Johann Gottfried Herder, and others had developed for a state or imperial academy, designed to provide material support for deserving authors, came to nothing.

5. In Germany, a deep-seated prejudice had it that literary production might be legitimately pursued when young but was inappropriate behavior on the part of full-grown middle-class males, unless, that is, they wrote on only the rarest of occasions (see Lessing 1767–69, sec. 96; Goethe 1811, bk. 10).

From the middle of the century onwards the public's taste turned away from the kinds of literature favored by the various courts. The emphasis in sentimental bourgeois drama was on the representation of the middle class and its life-world, and on the dissemination of its moral codes. Certain large cities like Leipzig, Berlin, and Zürich emerged as cultural centers, developing alongside and in competition with the courts. As far as the university towns were concerned, Göttingen stands out as having been of particular literary importance. According to Johann Goldfriedrich (1909), 79 of the 8,000 individuals living in Göttingen around 1790 were writers. With 29,000 inhabitants around the same time, Leipzig is said to have had 170 writers; Berlin boasted a population of 150,000, with 222 writers. Conditions until the end of the century were such that one could survive as an independent writer, but only tenuously so. The broadened base of the reading public and increases in the number of newspapers, magazines, and weeklies publishing literature were responsible for making it possible to do so at all. Even so, writers needed to feel comfortable with a wide range of literary and journalistic tasks — those of editor, reviewer, translator, playwright, novelist, and poet (on this score, too, Wieland and Lessing are exemplary).

The theater did not provide a particularly favorable framework for plays that were aesthetically demanding and that explored modern themes. The transformation of certain court theaters into national theaters following the example of Hamburg (in Vienna, Mannheim, and Berlin) did little for figures such as Lessing, Goethe, or Friedrich Schiller, although it did afford popular writers such as August Wilhelm Iffland, August von Kotzebue, and Christian Felix Weiße the possibility of earning an adequate income.

CHANGING CONCEPTIONS OF LITERARY PRODUCTION

Given the socially and financially unappealing nature of the conditions in question, the decision to become an independent writer presupposed an entirely new conception of literary production and value. For the independent writer, the commitment to literary production was an existential one, fusing vocation and avocation. Economic security and a respectable bourgeois career had to be sacrificed. Yet, only in forfeiting such goods could writers gain spiritual independence and critical freedom, promote love of humanity, and fully develop their own inner resources.

A professional ethos was thus conceived, and it construed literary production as the only existential content of the independent writer's life. The genesis of this ethos corresponded to the transition from a poetics inspired by rhetoric and based on rules to a concept of literary production as guided by values such as originality, spontaneity, feeling, genius, and the absence of rules. It is noteworthy that, unlike the new aesthetics, the older poetics allowed for an artisanal and rational approach to literary production and literary evaluation. Given that literary works stood as testimonies to a self-realizing humanity and provided exemplary interpretations of life, they clearly demanded more than an occasional effort. The creations of some free moment were no longer considered credible as literary works.

THE INDEPENDENT WRITER AND MARKET CONDITIONS

The radical demands for freedom articulated by the independent writer stand in stark contrast to market conditions from the middle of the century onward: although the dependence of the writer was displaced, it was by no means abolished. The varying degrees of economic dependence ranged from that experienced by the independent writer producing goods for the literary market to that of the salaried writer under contract with a press. Royalties, it is true, were steadily increased during the second half of the century, pirate printing became less common, and the legal issues surrounding intellectual property were settled. Yet, at the same time there was an increase in the number of writers: there were between 2,000 and 3,000 writers around 1766, over 6,000 by the end of the eighties, and about 10,650 by 1800. As the ranks of those writing for a living or as a sideline swelled, so did the quantity of literary products published yearly. Here, for example, are the figures that are generally cited with regard to the novel: At the Easter Fair of 1740, novels made up about 2.7 percent (20 items) of the entire book market; by 1770, they accounted for 4 percent (46 items); by 1800, for 11.7 percent (300 items). In 1740, literature cornered 6 percent of the entire book market; in 1770, the figure rose to 16 percent; by 1800, it was at 22 percent.

The production figure cited for books between 1736 and 1816 is around 22,500 volumes. Between 1745 and 1750, the yearly average came to 1,348 titles; and by 1775, it had risen to more than 2,000 titles. By 1783, the average was 3,000 titles, and by 1801 it was at least 4,000.

According to Goldfriedrich, about 3.9 percent of all book production around 1740 was devoted to poetry; by 1750, this figure had changed to 8.7 percent; by 1775, to 14.3 percent; and by 1800, to 27.3 percent. Contemporaries perceived the literary scene as providing work for an entire army of writers. This army was recruited primarily from among the many candidates hoping for scarce positions within the theological, pedagogical, and legal domains; it also attracted a number of poorly paid civil servants who were looking for a way to make some money on the side.

In three articles entitled "The Reasons why there is so much Writing in Germany Today," published in the *Journal von und für Deutschland* (1789 and 1790), the debate centered on three main reasons: the book dealer's desire to expand his business, the public's voracious appetite for reading, and the literati's desire for fame. There were other aspects of the issue: in promoting the mother tongue, writing allowed individuals with no advanced education, including women, to express themselves in a literary and scientific manner; most governments were averse to giving political posts to men who were active in some literary capacity; civil servants were poorly remunerated; and "freedom of the press" was an important principle. Moreover, the profession of the independent writer was seen as an "inner calling" and was assumed, unlike painting, to require no prior or systematic training. Somewhere, then, between the functional poles of entertainment and education there existed a domain of relatively free self-expression; yet, at the same time, the very definition of the writer's position and function within society became an enduring theme of debate.

LEGAL STATUS

The legal definition of the author's status was to play a crucial role. Until well into the eighteenth century, the idea that an author might have property rights over his or her intellectual products was absolutely unthinkable in Germany. (In England, on the other hand, copyright laws had already been introduced in 1710.) Even Lessing, around mid-century, supported the view that an author's writings were *publici juris* once they had been published, and that publishers had every right to reprint these texts and even somewhat alter them. That the censors should have taken such liberties is hardly surprising. In publishing manuscripts or second editions, publishers behaved in the most autocratic manner. Authorization to print was only requested in those cases in which the interests of author and publisher happened to coincide.

In the last three decades of the eighteenth century, the opinion that literary works were the intellectual property of those who created them, and that authors therefore should benefit from the profits resulting from the publication of their manuscripts, finally prevailed. The legal resolution of issues concerning intellectual property could not but affect the question of royalties. Following the lead of Gellert, who received only the equivalent of about 60 marks (20 *Taler* and 16 *Groschen*) in royalties for his stories (although they earned his publisher a fortune), independent writers (particularly the poor ones) began, in the second half of the century, to protest against the wealth of certain publishers. Speaking for all writers concerned, Lessing (in 1772) and Wieland (in 1791) demanded royalties that would take into consideration not only the market value of the product but the labor and time involved in creating it, as well as the acquired skills that were needed in order to produce it.

SELF-AWARENESS

The change in the self-understanding of literary producers as independent writers was crucial, and in this regard the conflict between aristocracy and bourgeoisie played a decisive role. Essentially, this conflict was characterized by three features: a bourgeois critique of feudal social structures based on the concept of estates; a critique of the linguistic and cultural alienation of the francophilic aristocracy and upper middle class; and a critique of the condescending attitudes expressed (and legitimated by state and church) toward reason on the basis of tradition and received Christian representations of salvation. The bourgeoisie saw itself as proposing an alternative based on the concepts of reason and morality. A terrain was thus staked out in which the mission of the bourgeois, literary intelligentsia could be defined as that of providing a public and comprehensive critique of society, a critique that would simultaneously educate it as a whole. Together bourgeois writers were to be the nation's conscience and educator.

This kind of Enlightenment mentality was subject, from the seventies onward, to decisive changes resulting from the emergence of an aesthetics based on the concept of genius (the so-called *Sturm und Drang* period). Two factors in particular unleashed the changes in question: first, the allegedly enlightening critique of the bourgeoisie had produced no political results worth mentioning; second, their program was fraught with contradictions stemming from a one-sided emphasis on reason, from an overly optimistic investment in progress, and from untenable claims concerning the enlightened bourgeoisie's monopoly on morality. The literary self-understanding of the bourgeoisie thus took a characteristic turn away from its former public mission, and a program of self-realization was foregrounded instead. The latter would be morally justified by the bourgeois writers' claim to stand in for all mankind: through their own realization as human beings, the potential of humanity as a whole would be realized. In their writings they felt called "over and again to articulate what the greatest part of humanity feels or thinks, without knowing it," to use Georg Christoph Lichtenberg's representative phrase.[5]

The issue of self-realization embraced the following:

1. freeing of emotion ("right of the heart");
2. primacy of subjectivity;
3. complete spiritual freedom;
4. originality and the exemption from rules and laws as characteristics of genius;
5. emphasis on subjective artistic truth (as beauty) over and against learned poetic truth (as reason).

In theory, these high ideals could be realized by everyone. Yet, the literati soon had to admit that, at best, they could be achieved only by an elite, the literati themselves. For Schiller, the rift between artist and nonartist was already too great to be bridged, the rift between the public and the literary elite being a necessary consequence of modern bourgeois society.

The general public was excluded from the elite group of independent writers on two grounds: members had to demonstrate the kind of perfected subjectivity that was characteristic of the genius, and they were supposed to be inspired by missionary zeal. Poets especially claimed to replace church and state in their earlier role of producing meaning and binding interpretations of the world. For Schiller, the poet was at once sage and guide pointing the way through bourgeois existence. The separation of the independent writers from bourgeois society at large was now complete. Toward the end of the century, bourgeois writers no longer saw themselves as vehicles of bourgeois ideas.

The ensuing conflict between art and morality, art and society, and art and the general public was definitively resolved by Weimar classicism in favor of art, for art could allegedly accommodate religion, ethics, and philosophy. Artistic production became the model for individual self-realization. In the philosophies of art proposed by Immanuel Kant, Johann Gottlieb Fichte, Schiller, and Friedrich Wilhelm Schelling, art promised to overcome the dualisms of subject and object, reason and matter, form and content, and accident and necessity, but not without exacting a price: alienation from the unmediated practices of everyday life.

We get a very different picture when we turn to the entertainment literature that developed in the second half of the century. In this area, literary production faithfully respected the tastes and desires for entertainment of the real, rather than idealized, reading public. As a result, its success at the level of sales and general distribution far surpassed that of elite literature, as is amply evidenced by the catalogues and records of both lending and nonlending libraries. In both theory and praxis, elite and trivial literature grew farther and farther apart. This tendency was exacerbated by the fact that literary critics refused to pay any serious attention to popular literature; at most, the latter occupied an entirely negligible position within literary discussions.

Capitalism and the Eighteenth-Century Book Market

The emergence of the literary system as a social system in the eighteenth century was influenced to a great extent by the development of a book market organized along capitalist lines, by growth in the domain of newspapers and magazines, and by technical innovations in the area of paper production and print. The book market became a capitalist enterprise and essentially assumed the function of middleman. Barter was rendered obsolete by the entrepreneurs who chose to market books as products. In order successfully to do so, they mobilized new media and techniques and effectively exploited the recent phenomenon of literary criticism as an advertisement tool. For reasons having to do with the marketability of its products, the book market favored the development of literary forms and materials, the consistent privileging of high German, and the improvement of facilities serving the literary institution, both in the cities and in the countryside. The royalties that were conceded (although unwillingly so) by this class of entrepreneurs finally made it possible to earn a living as an independent writer.

The publisher Georg Joachim Goeschen (1802) summarized the debate over the literary mediator's status within the literary system as a whole in a single laconic formula: "Whether the book was written by Goethe, or whether it required exceptional intellectual effort, are issues that I, as a merchant, cannot take into consideration; a shopkeeper cannot be a patron."[6]

Peter Schmidt (1980) estimates that about 5,000 titles were available on the market around 1790, the number of total issues amounting to about five million. He assumes that book production in Germany doubled between 1770 and 1780 and that the number of bookstores tripled (78ff.).

The Growth of the Reading Public

QUANTITATIVE GROWTH

According to contemporary estimates and well-known statistics, it is possible to consider about 15 percent of the population above the age of six as potential readers around 1770. By 1800, this same group accounted for 25 percent of the population. These figures are low because reading was almost never a real option for the farmers and peasants who made up the vast majority of the German population (with approximately 90 percent living in the country around 1800). This was so because of poor educational conditions, on the one hand, and the price of books, on the other. Further obstacles were created by the lack of interest on the part of many a German government (though some of them were allegedly concerned with enlightening the people) in widespread reading at the lower levels of the population.

Although we cannot speak of a mass public in the modern sense of the word, it is nonetheless clear that there was a relatively strong increase in the reading public for printed matter of all kinds, particularly in the second half of the century, when many women became readers. In estimating the figures pertaining to book purchases and their correlation with actual readers, we should be working with a factor of at least ten readers per book (the common practice of reading aloud would also tend to make a difference). On the other hand, many books may have been purchased without ever having been read. Book collecting was considered a sign of culture by parts of the bourgeoisie as well as by many aristocrats, and many a drawing room was decorated with books rather than paintings.

Just as women became part of the potential reading public, so did children, young adults, and domestic servants recruited from the lower social classes, all of whom had the time and occasion for a good deal of reading. (Such servants made up 10–20 percent of the population of any given city.)

As mentioned in the above discussion of literary production and mediation, the quantitative expansion of the reading public did not primarily benefit so-called high literature, promoting instead the nonfictional and informative types of literature, such as entertainment, or trivial literature.

The available facts about book production, reading societies, newspapers, and magazines show that literary reception in the eighteenth century underwent a significant numerical increase when compared with earlier centuries. This remains the case even if it clearly is impossible to speak of a complete elimination of analphabetism and of the socioeconomic obstacles to reading, even if the ability to read and a passion for books had yet to penetrate to all social levels.

The growth of the reading public was actively supported by related activities on the part of booksellers and publishers, who increasingly transformed the literary work into a product, and who thus were interested in every possible expansion of the book market. First, reading became easier from a purely physiological point of view: the quality of the paper was improved, becoming whiter, while the print itself was darkened; the actual perception of the text was facilitated by this heightened contrast. Second, a lively discussion erupted over whether Gothic script should be replaced by Roman lettering, or whether reading would be sufficiently facilitated by a simplification of the former. Third, bookstores promoted the rapid dissemination of recent releases, producing pocket books and almanacs in manageable formats in order to facilitate the process. Book formats underwent modernization, with book illustrations becoming a bourgeois art form intended to provide visual support for the text (I am thinking here of Daniel Chodowiecki). Such developments were applauded by the reading societies, concerned primarily with the acquisition and reading of recent publications.

QUALITATIVE CHANGES IN THE READING PUBLIC

The purely quantitative growth of the reading public has to be seen in connection with a number of qualitative changes in the modes of reception and their relation to other social developments in the eighteenth century. One important aspect of this constellation of changes has been characterized by Rolf Engelsing (1970, 959ff.) in terms of a transition from intensive to extensive reading. Rather than reading one book (preferably the Bible) or a few books (mostly edifying ones) over and over again, it gradually became more common for books to be read only once, or only in part.

The most important aspects of the altered attitudes toward reception can be summarized as follows:

1. Collective reading (reading aloud on Sundays and after work was a well-regarded bourgeois practice), followed by literary discussion, was replaced by private and extensive reading (be it in a personal library, in the garden, or in open nature, which is perhaps where an Anton Reiser would have liked to read). Reading became first and foremost a private pleasure.
2. The mode of reception became subjectivist, unreflective, passive, and mimetic or empathetic.
3. Reading no longer served to develop critical opinion within a group. Instead, it allowed solitary individuals to satisfy the

emotional needs that were spurned as sentimental by late Enlightenment criticism. Already in the eighteenth century, connections were drawn between such needs and the alienation of citizens as a result of work, the domination of means-end rationality at the expense of emotional needs, competition, the isolation and struggle for victory characteristic of the economic sphere, and a generalized egotism (evidence to this effect may be found in many articles in Wieland's *Neuer Teutscher Merkur*).

4. Reception was dispersed, partly because of the fashion for almanacs and calendars providing literary excerpts in attractive formats, much in the manner of the *Reader's Digest*.

5. Together the qualitative and quantitative changes in the reading public in Germany had a splintering effect, making its isolated elements anonymous. As far as authors were concerned, readers were a distant and unpredictable group, from which little or no response could be expected. At the outset of the eighteenth century, the public was still defined by the estates and could, as a result, be identified and even directly invoked. Yet, this public went on to become highly enigmatic as a result of the collapse of denominational boundaries, the ascendancy of bourgeois values and practices, and the participation of even the lowest levels of society. In spite of the numerical increase in readers, the advocates of so-called high literature had only a moderate appeal.

6. Given the ever more dispersed nature of the public, reading interests may be assumed to have been quite diverse. What is more, these interests were increasingly governed by fashion ("Werther fever," for example).

The unity of the literary public, one vigorously promoted by the proponents of the Enlightenment, was up until the end of the century repeatedly called into question by the capitalist expansion of the publishing business and book trade. Paradoxically, this form of development was supported by those dedicated to the Enlightenment program, for they regarded books and reading as the most important instruments of spiritual and political reform. The trade possibilities flowing from the Enlightenment model of the public were simply used by the market according to its own laws of increased profits and the creation and satisfaction of needs. Only very rarely were these practices subsequently subjected to public scrutiny and discussion for the purposes of critical justification. Market production was aimed at real buyers. And by the end of the eighteenth century, the latter were by no stretch of the imagination the discriminating and highly conscious readers that the advocates of the Enlightenment had hoped to produce. Instead, particularly from the eighties onward, they were consumers of so-called entertainment, or popular literature, the production of which increased steadily after 1770. The market played the sales-oriented card of "newness," rather than that of moral enlightenment; fashion, in other words, was played off against morality.

Such developments created new trade possibilities for all agents involved in the literary process: as independent writers, literary producers were forced to act in terms of the exchange rather than the use value of their products. That is, they became dependent on the market success of their texts. Literary receivers were faced with an overwhelming range of choices, choosing titles that would be consumed in moments of solitary reading but that would no longer be subjected to critical reflection.

The Changing Nature of Literary Criticism

In the eighteenth century, literary criticism, as construed today, was clearly the most important form of literary processing, having emerged around midcentury. In this context, Gottsched is typically singled out as a particularly important figure. Criticism is the child of the age of critique and clearly shares the claim to power that is also characteristic of public critique. It is for this reason that literary criticism, in Germany, implicitly continues to be understood as a form of political critique. The genesis of literary criticism in Germany can be briefly described as follows: as rhetorical criticism—understood as a testing of literary texts against a stable canon of poetic rules and norms that were in some sense based on the concept of estates—was surpassed, room was created for the development of a different kind of literary processing involving description, analysis, and evaluation. Depending on the theoretical orientation in question, this new kind of criticism took the form of aesthetic judgment, critical reasoning and polemic, sensitive interpretation, or aesthetic reflection.

The attitude toward literary producers thus changed in such a way as to allow the literary critic to fashion an identity as a congenial expert and member of an elite literary group, in whose aesthetic understanding the work of art finally achieved perfection. This particular identity replaced the early Enlightenment view of the literary critic as judge or as knowledgeable friend, servant, or admirer. The critic's relation to the receiver can also be described with relative clarity: at first, readers are pupils; then they are critical middle-class citizens; finally, they become members of an incompetent mass public to which the critic speaks from on high, hoping, at least in theory, to elevate it to a higher plane of existence.

The growth of the book market and increases in literary as well as in newspaper and magazine production served to enhance the need for literary critics as well as their impact: the action role of the literary processor was thus established and professionalized. The literary critic as expert became a mediating instance between other action roles proper to the literary system, their practical and theoretical form developing into an internally systematic process of self-organization. Literary criticism was subject to a process of internal differentiation, involving the following criteria:

1. stylistic (ranging from mere book reviews to philosophical essays);
2. thematic (critics specialized in literary works as opposed to generalists);
3. economic (independent critics as opposed to critics employed by publishers or paid by authors);
4. social (professional critics as opposed to occasional critics; literary producers as critics versus nonliterary producers as critics).

From the outset, the genesis and institution of the new action role was guided by a discourse of legitimation, the latter ultimately giving rise to a particular philosophical discipline, that of aesthetics.

The Emergence of an Autonomous Social System of Literature

From a systems-theoretical point of view, the analysis of the data and tendencies described above can be summed up in a single claim concerning the genesis of the literary system: in the second half of the eighteenth century, there emerged in Germany a self-organizing literary system that essentially followed in the wake of the gradual transformation of what was once a highly stratified society into a network of functionally differentiated societies or social systems.

In referring to the autonomization of the literary system, I certainly do not wish to suggest that the latter somehow was isolated or expelled from society at large. Rather, the literary system became autonomous in and through its interaction with all other functional social systems and thereby developed into a system having its own specific function *within* society.

The autonomization of the literary system in the eighteenth century started from a conscious change in the conception of literature's task or function: over and against the aristocratic view that the primary function of art and literature was one of either entertainment or representation, bourgeois literature was to give voice to a critique directed at the feudal system. As a result, literary communication shifts from a rhetorical to a moral context, where it takes its position alongside science, theology, and philosophy.

As the instrument of advanced Enlightenment, literature in the second half of the century was assigned the additional tasks of contributing to the humanization of individuals and of mediating between theory and praxis. Literature emerged as a kind of "holistic anthropology."

By 1760, the four action roles had stabilized and thereby had created the very structure of the literary social system. And at that point the process of autonomization took a turn in a different direction. Whereas, in the first phase, priority had been given to rejecting all forms of theological and political tutelage, figures such as Karl Philipp Moritz, Schiller, Goethe, and Fichte now helped to articulate the idea of an autonomous work of art, one having inner perfection and purposiveness. Following Moritz, the goal of the work of art is already achieved by the time of its completion. The value of the work of art resides within it, in its originality and authenticity, rather than in some mimetic quality. Representation (*Darstellung*) is no longer construed as imitation, but as realization. The autonomous work of art is no longer required to contribute to the moral development of society, but to the process of humanization whereby individuals achieve self-realization. The work of art is supposed to overcome the divisions caused by social development: the rifts between nature and culture, individual and society, reason and emotion. In introducing the first issue of his newspaper, *Horen* (1794), Schiller proclaimed his intention to reunite the politically divided world under the banner of truth and beauty. Art should, as it were, heal the wounds of social differentiation that were increasingly experienced as a form of alienation.

For Goethe and Schiller, Kant's transcendental grounding of aesthetic judgment in the subject, as well as his doctrine of beauty as a "symbol of morality," were absolutely fundamental. Beauty and morality were thus marked by the same principle of self-determination, a point that was further developed in Schiller's theory of beauty and freedom. In so doing, Schiller drew on Fichte's philosophy of mind, which he brought to bear on the relation between reason and the senses: in its formal structure, beauty symbolizes freedom. Beauty is simply the self-determination of a harmonious instance of subjectivity (perceptible morality); and the experience of beauty mediates between the sensuous drive (*Stofftrieb*) and the rational will (*Formtrieb*). As a result of aesthetic education and play, "the refinement of character" would become a necessary condition for all "political improvement."

That the classical and romantic aesthetics of autonomy should have prevailed over competing conceptions may, from a systems-theoretical point of view, be explained by the fact that they accorded literary communication the very function that has proved to be crucial, even to this day (independently of changing literary-theoretical opinions): the task of repairing the damages inflicted on agents and society as a result of functional differentiation. Examples would be subjectivism, the division of labor, the distortion and fragmentation of communication, specialization, the loss of a stable order and system of values, a problematic relation between reason and desire, and distress related to affective relationships. A possible objection would be that the privileged position enjoyed by entertainment literature and related modes of reception within the market economy of the late eighteenth century points to escapism rather than to the idea that action within the literary system functioned as a means of self-realization for agents.

In brief, my counterargument is as follows: if the "minority voice" of the classical and romantic literary theorists, and related instances of literary production, have managed to prevail to this day, it is, in my mind, because they articulated the strongest argument for what had already, in fact, been completed — the autonomization of the *social system* of literature. At least at the level of argument, these theorists thus aligned the social constitution of literature with the self-understandings motivating literary communication. Furthermore, as applied to literary works and experience, the doctrine of aesthetic autonomy recast the widely experienced practical inefficacy of literature in the most protective of formulae, shielding literary action (particularly production and reception) from all external influences and giving it a certain inviolable dignity. Once again, numbers were hardly decisive, for the classical and romantic doctrines prevailed on very different grounds (and on this score, nothing much has changed).

The category of fiction played a central role in the autonomization of literature. As mentioned above, a society based on the estates was ideologically characterized by the monopoly of state and church on the institution and regulation of models of reality that could, if necessary, involve social sanctions. In other words, the ontological question, the central issue of power and knowledge, was to be answered only by a spiritual and political elite, for only then could the aristocracy (and its representatives) produce the highly consensual model of reality that it required.

As a result of the functional differentiation of society, church and state lost their monopoly on the ontological question: on the whole, the church lost to philosophy and science, and the state to economics, the latter determining what was real (pragmatically speaking) by means of a quantitative approach to money and achievement. Thus, a politically crucial problem area was left to society, as were the mechanisms of social and cognitive self-reference and self-organization.

The protracted literary-theoretical debate (spanning the first half of the eighteenth century) over truth and probability as poetic norms proves just how difficult it was to loosen the grip that certain representations of reality clearly had on the literary system. It shows that only with the greatest difficulty did bourgeois thinking accustom itself to the self-referential option proffered by competing models of reality. By the end of the century, a process had come to a close that I want to call the *fictionalization of literary discourse* within the literary system. Fictionalization, as a property of discourse, can only emerge when a functionally differentiated society is in the position to permit even the ontological question to undergo differentiation. In other words, the fact of tolerating a variety of models of reality should not automatically call into question the status of the (at this point, predominantly economic and technological) model that is binding at the level of society as a whole. In this sense, modern speculative capitalism played an essential role in the fictionalization of literary communication in the eighteenth century.

With the fictionalization of all communication related to literature, the idea that self-organization is a feature of the production of meaning gained historical acceptance within the partial social systems in question. Whereas bourgeois philosophy from Kant to Fichte was plagued by fundamental doubts about knowledge that ultimately rendered the ontological question notorious, the decisive measure of reality within the economic process was money. The theme of truth was taken up by the bourgeois subject and interpreted within the literary system as creative freedom; as the freedom, but also the obligation, to articulate subjective interpretations of the world and to engage in psychological and confessional explorations of the inner self. The interpretation of life and world became a standard practice within the literary system. Poets competed over the correct interpretation, as they promoted what they felt to be their capacities as sages and existential guides. The senses and feelings were recognized as being as important as reason in the discovery of truth. As an interpreter of the world, the poet embodied, as it were, the very displacement of the ontological question to the literary system. There was, however, a price to be paid: that of the individualization, relativization, and fictionalization of all pronouncements concerning truth. For the literary system stabilized its borders by means of an opposition between the literary and the nonliterary, and this difference was governed, not by notions of truth and falsehood, but by aesthetic values. By the end of the eighteenth century, the social convention referred to above as the aesthetic convention was firmly in place and has continued to be operative to this very day.

The so-called polyvalence convention also developed during this period and is equally valid within today's literary system. The literary system of the late eighteenth century invested so heavily in the human subject that it was impossible not to acknowledge the subjective nature of the actions carried out within it. Thus, literary action essentially became a matter of individual taste or inclination. In dealing with literary phenomena, the agent sought the immediacy of experience that was first articulated at the outset of the century in the pietists' conception of their relation to God. Over and against the collective appropriation of literature that had been the aristocratic norm, the bourgeois subject insisted on reading alone. He or she read for the sake of reading itself, that is, for the purpose of optimizing certain processes of the self (self-certainty, self-knowledge, self-realization). Religious and ethical scruples were easily swept aside, for the perfected self was taken to express the gradual realization of humanity, the idea of perfecting one's subjectivity being justified as a form of progressive humanism.

From the end of the eighteenth century onward, literature occupied the space abandoned by the exact sciences, one where knowledge is pursued in a manner that is subjective and unconstrained by method. Literature came to multiply the models of reality at the level of the imagination, anticipating through utopian critique certain possibilities for action and experience and thereby promising the continuity of everyday existence and culture. It took on the moral problem of the alienated and endangered individual, and did so publicly. At the same time, literary action came to promise an experience of art that is subjectively rewarding. This continues to be true today.

Boundaries and Effects

What, if any, are the implications of the above systems-theoretical reflections for the debate over literary effects (*Wirkungsdebatte*)? If one is warranted in assuming that cognitive (conscious) systems and social (communicative) systems are self-organizing and self-referential, then these systems have to demonstrate a certain degree of autonomy. What is ruled out, then, is the idea that one system might directly influence another. Yet, within a differentiated society, a change within one system is at the same time an occasion for other social systems to respond, for all social systems are interconnected. Just as one cannot *not* communicate, so it is impossible *not* to react within functionally differentiated societies. Each and every change in a system alters the environment of other systems. Changes in communication modify the environment within which consciousness is operative, and these modifications in turn have an effect on communication.

In order to have an impact, literary agents must give rise to literary communication, which is why the media play such a decisive role. Only by modifying literary communication do literary actions produce changes in the environment of other systems, changes that can then be transformed into meaning in ways that are system-specific. This means that if the literary system is to be effective, it must preserve *alterity*, that is, maintain its macroconventions and the very boundaries they create. Literature, in other words, must remain itself; it cannot become a form of politics or science. Literature can be of importance to "life," politics, or belief only insofar as it *is* literature. Interaction between the literary system and other modern social systems is productive, not as a result of an effacement of difference or elimination of alterity, but by virtue of a capacity to make this difference a source of meaning, in and through individuals acting according to certain roles, within any number of social systems. Because it is *other*, literature makes evident the improbable nature of different types of order, values, and entrenched meanings, contradicting the wishful bourgeois representations of autonomous work and of the stability and self-evidence of all meaning. In the free space that is thus carved out, literature explores some of the possible actions that might allow the modern dream of the unalienated subject to be realized.

The literary system was not intentionally created, but emerged in the course of the eighteenth century. Nor can its destruction or elimination be intentionally willed, not as long as we continue to live in a functionally differentiated society. In the future it will be a matter of using all available means to make its potential functions accessible to as many of society's members as possible.

CHAPTER ELEVEN

Linguistic and Literary Conventions

PETER J. McCORMICK

Much recent work in contemporary philosophy of language centers on arguments about the role of conventions in communication. Perhaps the crucial dispute arises between those like Michael Dummett who claim that conventions are necessarily involved in linguistic communication and those like Donald Davidson who grant that conventions are present in such communication but deny that they must be.

In examining this issue, I follow Davidson's suggestive examples from drama (Richard Sheridan) and poetry (William Shakespeare's sonnets) and look closely at several key instances of dramatic speech conventions. The point is to bring out important differences that hold, I think, between linguistic conventions and literary ones. I argue that current debates in contemporary philosophy of language between Davidson and Dummett about linguistic conventions sharpen our understanding of the vague notion of literary convention. Conversely, the particular uses of some literary conventions in dramatic contexts raise important questions about the satisfactoriness of the overly general understanding of linguistic convention in ongoing philosophical discussions.

I

Recall one of the many celebrated passages in Shakespeare's dramatic works where drama and poetry intertwine.

> *Romeo* [*to Juliet*]. If I profane with my unworthiest hand
> This holy shrine, the gentle sin is this,
> My lips, two blushing pilgrims, ready stand
> To smooth that rough touch with a tender kiss.
> *Juliet.* Good pilgrim, you do wrong your hand too much
> Which mannerly devotion shows in this,

95

For saints have hands that pilgrims' hands do touch,
And palm to palm is holy palmers' kiss.
Romeo. Have not saints lips, and holy palmers too?   100
Juliet. Ay, pilgrim, lips that they must use in prayer.
Romeo. O then, dear saint, let lips do what hands do:
They pray, grant thou, lest faith turn to despair.
Juliet. Saints do not move, though grant for prayers' sake.
Romeo. Then move not while my prayer's effect I take.   105
Thus from my lips, by thine, my sin is purg'd.
[*Kissing her.*]
Juliet. Then have my lips the sin that they have took.
Romeo. Sin from my lips? O trespass sweetly urged!
Give me my sin again.
[*Kissing her again.*]
Juliet. You kiss by th'book.

(1.5.92–109)

When read attentively, this passage may solicit almost as many different responses as readers. For readers from various languages, cultures,
backgrounds, and contexts, as the success of this play around the world
shows, find enough suggestions in the many echoes and complexities
here to engage at least some of their central interests. The dramatic sonnet exhibits an evocative linguistic richness of sound and sense, with its
multiple phonetic, syntactic, semantic, and even pragmatic aspects, so
that most attentive readers discover themselves caught up almost unwit-
tingly in the work of interpretation.

Some general sense of the passage can be gleaned from the summary
comments of recent editions. Thus, in the Arden Shakespeare edition
of *Romeo and Juliet* (1980), Brian Gibbons says that "the motifs of hands
and pilgrimage are intertwined by the lovers in a series of conceits that
advance courtship while exalting, purifying and intensifying feeling;
the lovers are separated from the rest of the company [at the Capulets'
masked ball] in a special and quite new tone" (118). And, in the New
Cambridge Shakespeare Edition (1984), G. Blakemore Evans writes:
"This first exchange between Romeo and Juliet, with its formal patterning and gentle expression of human love through religious metaphor,
conveys an antiphonal ritual effect that balances the lovers' delicate
sparring with a nice blend of male ardour and seeming maidenly reserve" (85). Note that each of these overviews also includes some ref-

erence to the linguistic complexity of the passage with talk about motifs, conceits, and tone, in the one case and, in the other, about formal patterning, metaphor, and ritual effect.

Closer inspection of the passage reinforces the general impression of linguistic complexity. Thus, in line 93, as the editors indicate, "holy shrine" is a metaphor for Juliet's hand, which itself is an instance of taking the part, Juliet's hand, for the whole or Juliet herself (synecdoche). In line 94, Romeo metaphorically calls his lips two "pilgrims" because he imagines them worshiping at the shrine of Juliet, and "blushing" pilgrims because of course he fancies his lips colored red. In line 97, "mannerly" is a quibble meaning mainly "decent" or "modest" but in its French etymology ("la main") suggesting as well "belonging to the hand." In line 99, another quibble is on exhibit in the expression "palm to palm" in the play between a "palm" as both "hand" and "pilgrim" ("palmer," or one who having been to the Holy Land has returned with a palm branch). In line 102, "let lips do what hands do," the conceit — that is, the figure of speech that sets up an elaborate and striking parallel between two dissimilar things — is that lips are to be allowed the same privilege (kissing) as hands (pressing together). In line 105, Romeo's reversal of Juliet's "not move" as "move not" brings out an ambiguity between not moving physically (Romeo had implied that Juliet was a statue) and not taking the initiative. And finally, Romeo succeeds in kissing Juliet while claiming "my sin is purg'd." In response to her logical complaint, he goes on to kiss her a second time after expostulating, "give me my sin again." Even Romeo's name shows complexity, as Juliet will later emphasize in her balcony speech "what's in a name?" (2.2). "Romeo may choose the pilgrimage motif," Gibbons writes, "in self-conscious play upon the meaning of *romeo* in Italian, which Florio records as *roamer, wanderer,* or *palmer. . . .* there is a private meaning for him in the conceit, since he feels himself, unlike his companions, dedicated to love and its service" (118). With such linguistic complexities (a profusion of "deviant expressions"?), interpretation seems a necessity.

That work itself is various. But at least two initial concerns are at the center of interpretive understanding: first, questions about meaning and sense — what does the poem say? (for example, the line "Thus from my lips, by thine, my sin is purg'd") — and second, questions about truth and significance — is what the poem says right? (for example, "Then have my lips the sin that they have took"). We may, of course, prefer to put these concerns in other terms, and many other questions arise as well. Moreover, depending on the individual reader's interests and cultural contexts, these other questions may quickly become the crucial ones for that individual. But, in general, without some sense of the poem's meaning and putative truth, no matter how we finally parse these problematic terms, such crucial questions can hardly be explored intelligently.

Like so many other central texts in Western cultural history, Shakespeare's dramatic sonnet immediately challenges its readers to articulate a response to these issues, however provisional such an interpretation must remain in the ceaseless succession of creative and interpretive generations. Yet, we do not ourselves need to attempt a full critical reading here to recognize this challenge. For whatever the many questions the poem's complex representations and rhythms raise throughout, the poem concludes strikingly with an enigmatic exchange that immediately invites reflection:

> *Romeo*. Thus from my lips, by thine, my sin is purg'd.
> [*Kissing her.*]
> *Juliet*. Then have my lips the sin that they have took.

Part of what makes this exchange enigmatic is the elusiveness of just what the spectator or reader is to understand by the particular conjunction of romantic and religious imagery. Here, and generally in literature, we find frequent difficulties with the relations between normal and deviant expressions, literal and nonliteral meaning, and more generally between meaning and truth. In such cases, many interested readers turn quickly to literary critics for help. Northrop Frye (1986), to take one widely read example only, has called attention to just how crucial this passage is in marking the sudden maturing of both Romeo and Juliet. Before this scene each uses language in a strongly restricted way, whereas after such a meeting "their command of language" changes substantially (24–25).

More particularly, Frye thinks that we are not able to appreciate the ways in which this passage marks such a change without understanding the conventions that are at work.

"Love" in *Romeo and Juliet* covers three different forms of a convention. First, the orthodox Petrarchan convention in Romeo's professed love for Rosaline at the beginning of the play. Second, the less sublimated

love for which the only honourable resolution was marriage, represented by the main theme of the play. Third, the more cynical and
ribald perspective that we get in Mercutio's comments, and perhaps
those of the Nurse as well. (20–21)

Finally, this second form sometimes includes a further convention, as
here — the convention of courtly love, where the language of religion is
used. "The mistress was a 'saint'; the 'god' supplicated with so many
prayers and tears was Eros or Cupid, the God of Love; 'atheists' were
people who didn't believe in the convention; and 'heretics' were those
who didn't keep to the rules" (21–22).

Yet this talk of convention, however promising, seems obscure, its
pertinence to a satisfactory understanding of this cardinal passage controversial, and the nature itself of convention elusive. Are the four conventions mentioned here all equally important for our understanding
and appreciation of this passage? If the courtly love convention of the
religion of love is the most important among them, then exactly how
does our understanding and appreciation of the text depend on our
understanding of this convention? And if an understanding of this convention is a necessary condition for understanding and appreciating
the text, just how are we to construe the nature of such a convention?

Some of these questions dissipate if we rearticulate Frye's important
but overly general talk of conventions in sharper ways. Thus, with
Meyer Howard Abrams, we may distinguish among three senses of literary convention. First, the audience attending a production of *Romeo
and Juliet* accepts the assumption that a three-walled stage or a theater
in the round represents a four-walled banquet room at the Capulet
palace. In this broad sense, a convention is a device "accepted by a kind
of implicit contract between author and audience, for solving the problems imposed by a particular artistic medium in representing reality"
(Abrams 1957, 33). Second, Romeo deploys a certain linguistic strategy
in extravagantly addressing Juliet. In this narrower sense, a convention
is a set of conspicuous stylistic features such as recurring "kinds of diction and style," including the stock metaphors, synecdoches, puns,
quibbles, and conceits of Romeo's speech. Third, understanding Romeo
and Juliet's peculiarly patterned use of metaphor involves understanding how their use of figurative language draws on the intertwining of
religion and love. In this sense, as R. S. Crane proposed, a convention
is "any characteristic of the matter or technique of a poem the reason

for the presence of which in the poem cannot be inferred from the necessities of the form envisaged but must be sought in the historical circumstances of its composition" (1953, 198, n. 62).

But, while helpful, these clarifications still leave open several key questions. For example, how are we to understand the distinction between the literal and the figurative that seems to underlie the appeal to convention in the attempt to understand conspicuous stylistic features? Moreover, what is the nature of the "implicit contract" between author and audience or reader that allows an understanding of convention in the broad sense? And finally, how are we to construe the narrow notion of convention as nonperceptual and noninferential background information that allows some linguistic exchanges to bring about effective communication?

Without trying to answer all of these questions, I would like to turn to some recent philosophical discussions of my initial concerns with meaning and truth in the hope, if not of answering all such questions, at least of reformulating several of the more important issues about the nature of linguistic and literary conventions.

2

If we are to have a more nuanced grasp of the complex relations between meaning and truth in our understanding especially of linguistic and literary conventions in literary works of art, we need to look in some detail at representative contemporary philosophical approaches to such issues.

Donald Davidson has not paid the kind of sustained attention to works of art that some other contemporary philosophers have. But he has been very busy with questions of sense and significance. His interests have centered more on linguistics and logic than on aesthetics. More recently, however, in several essays about metaphor, communication, and "the limits of the literal," Davidson has looked closely at some of the metaphorical and stylistic peculiarities that occur widely in different uses of language, especially in literature. Behind these essays are to be found the more general questions that have engaged Davidson for many years in his attempts to build on and finally move beyond the seminal work of his teacher, Willard Van Orman Quine.

Perhaps the center of Davidson's interests may still be taken to constitute his twofold answer to the question "what is it for words to mean what they do?" For Davidson, understanding what it is for words to mean what they say is captured in describing what someone who understands those words implicitly knows—for example, describing what Juliet knows. This requires a theory that would recognize "the holistic nature of linguistic understanding" in providing an "interpretation of all utterances, actual and potential, of a speaker or group of speakers." And it also requires a theory that "would be verifiable without knowledge of the detailed propositional attitudes of the speaker," that is, a theory that would not turn on the very concepts it is designed to explain (1984, xiii).

In such a theory, the primitive notion is taken to be truth; and from an account based on the idea of truth conditions, we are to arrive at an understanding of meaning. The model for the structure of truth when truth is taken as a primitive would include, among other elements, a critical appropriation of salient features in Alfred Tarski's formal semantics, the relation of satisfaction between entities and expressions, "disquotational" features of truth predicates, "the pattern of assents to sentences," a maximization of the "right sort" of agreement among competing theories of interpretation (a principle of charity), and an antiempiricist refutation of scheme-content dualisms.[1] Although much of this continuing work remains quite technical and specialized, some of the more recent essays examine certain peculiarities of poetic uses of language in straightforward terms. A very important case in point is the 1985 essay, "A Nice Derangement of Epitaphs," whose title alludes to Sheridan's character Mrs. Malaprop and her striking utterances in *The Rivals*. Davidson insists here on distinguishing between the literal or "first meaning" of expressions and any nonliteral or "second meaning" (whether we construe this second meaning as "speaker's meaning" or otherwise). Note, however, that literal and nonliteral are not to be understood strictly as two species of meaning, since nonliteral meaning is for Davidson an aspect of use. The point of calling literal meaning first meaning can be seen, Davidson thinks, if we reflect on what we need to know in order to explain images in poetry—for example, the controlling image in these lines from Shakespeare's Sonnet 53:

> Speak of the spring and foison of the year,
> The one doth shadow of your beauty show,
> The other as your bounty doth appear . . .
>
> (159)

Now, however nonliteral the meaning of these lines may be, Davidson holds that this nonliteral meaning cannot be grasped unless the reader "first" understands the dictionary meaning, "based on actual usage" in Shakespeare's time, of the word *foison*. (Imagine a parallel claim for understanding the nonliteral meaning of Romeo's "my sin is purg'd.")

Although this clarifies Davidson's talk of first meaning, the example does not suffice to characterize first meaning fully enough. For, as Davidson himself points out, readers often determine first meaning without initially moving to the dictionary. Sometimes they just pick out "what the speaker was getting at" and then determine the literal meaning; other times, they "guess at the image and so puzzle out the first meaning" (159). After exploring other keys to first meaning such as speaker's intentions and hearer's ability to understand those intentions, Davidson goes on to specify three principles that may characterize in particular the linguistic meaning as opposed to the meaning of nonlinguistic signs or signals (161). First meaning thus is taken to be systematic ("there must be systematic relations between the meanings of utterances"), shared (a method of interpreting such relations needs to be shared by a speaker and a hearer or what he calls loosely "an interpreter"), and prepared (i.e., the speaker's and hearer's knowledge of these relations "is learned in advance of occasions of interpretation and is conventional in character"). As we shall shortly note, however, these principles are not without difficulties, as Davidson's elliptical reference to "conventional" knowledge already suggests.

After setting in place this attempt to articulate a satisfactory account of the differences between literal and nonliteral meaning, Davidson describes a second and related distinction between the two kinds of theory that he believes both speakers and interpreters require for effective communication, a prior and a passing theory. Davidson's "simplified and idealized proposal" (167) (recall the complexities of the communication between Romeo and Juliet) about what goes on in linguistic communication goes as follows. From one side, "an interpreter has, at any moment of a speech transaction," a theory, and the interpreter changes that theory as his or her interlocutor speaks, "entering hypotheses about new names, altering the interpretation of familiar predicates, and revising past interpretations of particular utterances in the light of new evidence." From the other side, "the speaker's view of the interpreter's prior theory . . . is an important part of what he has to go on if he wants to be understood." Thus, "for the hearer, the prior theory expresses how he is prepared in advance to interpret an utterance of the speaker, while the passing theory is how he *does* interpret the utterance. For the speaker, the prior theory is what he *believes* the interpreter's prior theory to be, while his passing theory is the theory he *intends* the interpreter to use" (168).

The key point is that the passing theory needs to be shared because, without such a sharing, understanding cannot be complete. Although the shared passing theory is not to be identified with, say, linguistic competence in any general way, nevertheless it does describe the understanding of a speaker's words (on this occasion) because it includes a variety of particular items that are the result of a particular occasion only. Nor is the passing theory a theory of "an actual natural language" like the English of Shakespeare's play or the Italian that we are to imagine Romeo and Juliet to be speaking, for knowing how to interpret on a particular occasion is no guarantee that one would know how to interpret on another. Rather, the passing theory is where understanding and agreement strive to coincide in a grasp of meanings. And the understanding of these meanings is where Davidson brings together his double discussion of literal meaning and passing theory. "Every deviation from ordinary usage," he writes, "as long as it is agreed on for the moment (knowingly deviant, or not, on one, or both sides), is in the passing theory as a feature of what the words mean on that occasion. Such meanings, transient though they may be, are literal; they are what I have called the first meanings" (169).

When we turn our attention to such deviant uses of language as malapropisms in, say, Sheridan's *The Rivals,* we immediately see problems with this characterization of first meaning. For deviant utterances generally, and malapropisms in particular, "introduce expressions not covered by prior learning, or familiar expressions which cannot be interpreted by any of the abilities so far discussed" (162). The problem is not so much with the systematic and shared aspects of literal meaning as with their conjunction with the prepared nature of that meaning. Accordingly, Davidson attempts to modify his three principles of literal meaning so that in some more perspicuous formulation they can finally accommodate malapropisms and similar phenomena, such as some of the expressions in the Romeo and Juliet exchange. The key, he believes, is to invoke something along the lines of a Tarski "truth definition" as a way of accounting for just how an interpreter (as Davidson prefers to call the hearer or reader) can be said to have a system for interpreting potentially unlimited utterances of novel sentences. And what does such a definition do? The Tarski truth definition, Davidson believes, "provides a recursive characterization of the truth conditions of all possible utterances of the speaker, and it does this through an analysis of utterances in terms of sentences made up from the finite vocabulary and the finite stock of modes of composition" (163).

But Davidson's conclusion, once all the various ramifications of the difficulties with handling malapropisms and other deviant expressions have been explored, turns out to be very surprising. The first two principles for understanding literal meaning, and by extension Davidson's general problem ("I want to know how people who already have a language . . . manage to apply their skill or knowledge to actual cases of interpretation. . . . My problem is to describe what is involved in the idea of "having a language" [167]), are salvageable only in "rather unusual ways" (174). The third principle cannot be salvaged at all. Consequently, the third principle must be abandoned. This entails the abandonment as well of the theory of literal meaning as first meaning. The conclusion, then, is that "in linguistic communication nothing corresponds to a linguistic competence" as Davidson and so many other analytic philosophers and linguists have described it.

With this unexpected negative conclusion before us, what then in retrospect and summary are the major points that call for second thoughts? This account, we recall, arises out of a very general interest in articulating how competent speakers of a language succeed in interpreting one another. And the particular problem here is that of providing a satisfactory account of what it is "for words to mean what they do," an account comprehensive enough to comprise the understanding of deviant expressions. The answer to this question is supposed to assume the form of a theory. The theory provides sufficient resources to account for understanding heretofore unheard utterances of "the same language." Just why such a theory is required and in what sense is not spelled out, despite the discussion of the characteristics of Tarski's definition of truth. Further, the theory must avoid begging questions and must recognize "the holistic nature of linguistic understanding."

The key element in such a theory is the double primacy of truth over meaning and literal over nonliteral meaning. Davidson says little here about truth, a topic he discusses extensively elsewhere. He proposes instead to characterize literal meaning in detail. Literal meaning is more properly to be understood as first meaning in the sense that the understanding of literal meaning is one prerequisite for understanding nonliteral meaning; the others are what turn out to be the three faulty principles. Deviations from ordinary instances of literal meaning are subsumed, thanks to the further distinction between prior and passing theory, beneath literal meanings in the passing theory. But even the attempt to explicate the systematicity and sharedness of first meanings by appeal to Tarski's recursive description of truth conditions finally is unsuccessful. The result is an intriguing notion of the primacy of literal meaning, a notion, however, that has yet to be satisfactorily described.

Roughly speaking, then, these initial analytic distinctions of meaning and truth might be formulated along some such lines as these:

1. Understanding what it is for words to mean what they do requires constructing a nonquestion-begging theory of the holistic nature of linguistic understanding, a theory, moreover, that is comprehensive enough to explain deviant as well as normal expressions.

2. In such a theory, "truth" is to be taken as a primitive term in the light of which meaning is to be explained, and literal meaning is to be explained as epistemically prior to nonliteral meaning, if there is any such thing.

3. Further, ordinary literal meanings are to be understood in terms of the prior and passing "theories" of both speaker and interpreter, while apparently deviant meanings are to be construed in terms of literal meanings in the interpreter's passing theory.

In short, whatever it may be both for the words in the exchange between Romeo and Juliet ("Thus from my lips, by thine, my sin is purged." / "Then have my lips the sin that they have took") "to mean what they do," and for competent readers to succeed in "interpreting" the difficult relations here between literal and nonliteral meaning in a holistic, nonquestion-begging way while awarding the notion of truth a primacy over that of meaning, is not evident, because, at least according to Davidson, there is no such thing to be done.

Before trying to draw out the major implications for sharpening our understanding of my two initial questions about sense and significance in connection with literary conventions, consider a second, closely related representative account in contemporary Anglo-American philosophy of similar matters.

3

In an important paper entitled "A Nice Derangement of Epitaphs: Some Comments on Davidson and Hacking," Dummett (1986) has offered a series of comments on Davidson's views. These comments allow us both to clarify our understanding of what Davidson's views are and to win some critical distance from them. Moreover, they focus on Davidson's radical and yet deeply puzzling claim that follows from his inability to explain linguistic communication with the help of a set of principles flexible enough to accommodate the literal or first meanings of the kinds of deviant expressions that frequently occur in poetic and dramatic uses of language. That claim runs: "There is therefore no such thing as a language, not if a language is anything like what many philosophers and linguists have supposed it to be" (Davidson 1985, 174).

Dummett offers a summary of Davidson's argument for this claim, a summary that includes several clarifications that we can usefully adopt.

> The apparatus of prior and passing theories, or, as I have called them, long-range and short-range theories, is required to explain the phenomena of malapropisms and of deviant and unfamiliar uses. . . . It is also sufficient to explain linguistic communication in general. But neither the short-range nor the long-range theory has the right form to be described as a theory of a language. Hence the notion of a language is not needed for the philosophy of language, but only that of language. (466)

Before examining the details of this argument, however, I need to fill in some of the background of these formulations while keeping in mind the particular details of my lead example, the exchanges between Romeo and Juliet.

Earlier in his comments, Dummett calls attention to a pervasive ambiguity in Davidson's talk of a "prior" theory. "Prior" can mean either the antecedent theory that participants bring along to a conversation or reading and that subsequently modifies their "linguistic propensities," or the already modified theory in each stage of the conversation or reading that continues to undergo revision. To simplify, a prior theory in the first sense is brought to the conversation, whereas in the second sense a prior theory is already included in the conversation. The second sense is for Dummett the operative one for Davidson. (Throughout, where Davidson and Dummett speak of a conversation we have to keep in mind for our purposes a reading as well.)

This first clarification of prior theory gives rise to a further clarification of the operative sense of a "passing" theory. A prior theory needs to be taken, as for example in the case of the hearer (not the "interpreter," an expression Davidson uses too broadly),[2] as the hearer's "theory about how, in general, to understand S [the speaker] when S addresses H [the hearer]; and this theory may obviously change in response to what S says in the course of the particular conversation" (459–60). Thus, the hearer's passing theory needs to be construed as "a theory about how to understand specific utterances of S made during that conversation" (460). A passing theory may incorporate surmises concerning our understanding of particular nonstandard utterances that the speaker may make during the conversation, surmises that are not included in the evolving prior theory. This is the case because, no matter how the prior theory itself evolves, it remains a theory about how to understand the speaker in general and not in particular.

As a result, Dummett thinks this distinction can be sharpened by substituting, as he does in his summary of Davidson's argument, talk of long-range and short-range theories for prior and passing ones so long as we can succeed in making the new distinction more precise. Thus, if we turn to the speaker (think of Romeo), a long-range theory is not to be taken as comprising what the speaker believes makes up the prior theory of the hearer. Rather, the speaker's "initial long-range theory comprises his expectations concerning how, in general [think of Juliet], H is disposed to understand S when S addresses H" (460). These expectations are to be taken as "certain suppositions about what, at that moment, are H's long-term dispositions to understand in particular ways what S says to him" (460). And the speaker's short-range theory is better described not as the passing theory that the speaker intends the hearer to use but as relating to "how he intends, and expects, H to understand particular utterances he makes during the conversation, when he does not intend, or expect, H to incorporate his interpretations of those utterances into his long-range theory" (460). Thus, part of what the revised distinction brings out clearly is Davidson's own persistent concern not so much for articulating shallow differences between what a speaker means and what his words mean but deeper differences "between what a speaker, on occasion, means, and what his words mean" (Davidson 1985, 158).

With this background in view we can now better appreciate the general concern that provokes Davidson's reflections on malapropisms. As Dummett sees the matter,

> Davidson is concerned with . . . a hearer's understanding of a word or phrase in a sense unfamiliar to him. A speaker cannot attach a meaning to an expression, Davidson says, unless he intends his hearer to understand him as doing so, and he cannot intend him to understand him thus unless he has a reasonable expectation that he will. The phenomenon occurs in three kinds of cases: that in which, unknown to the speaker, the hearer is unfamiliar with the expression; that in which the speaker inadvertently makes a deviant use of a word (the malapropism); and that in which his deviant use is deliberate [the Romeo case]. In the third case, he will drop clues prompting the hearer either to modify his long-range theory, or to adopt the correct short-range theory, as the case requires, and may therefore well succeed in conveying his meaning. In the first two cases, he has a false long-range theory concerning the hearer, that is, a false idea of the hearer's long-range theory, but the hearer may still succeed in understanding him as he intended. (461–62)

It is this general concern, as Ian Hacking (1986) has pointed out, that enables one to understand how Davidson has confounded the notion of a language such as English or Italian with a particular speaker's use of a language at a particular time and place, with a particular use of an idiolect. For Davidson, an idiolect (a speaker's individual speech habits) is more fundamental than language in the sense that a common language is to be understood "as a range of overlapping idiolects." Even more precisely, as Dummett writes, "We must take a language in the fundamental sense to consist, not of the general speech habits of an individual at a particular time, but, rather, his habits of speech when addressing a particular hearer at that time" (469) — Romeo's habits of speech (may we say conventions?) when addressing Juliet at the Capulet ball.

Moreover, Davidson not only favors the notion of an idiolect over that of a common language but, despite his attention to communication between speakers and hearers, his concern is curiously noninteractional. Communication, in his view, is more an exchange of monologues than dialogue. As Dummett writes, "In his picture, there is no interaction, no exchange of the roles of speaker and hearer: the hearer remains mute throughout the conversation, or, rather, monologue. The hearer can therefore seek from the speaker no elucidation of what he has said" (462). Dummett rightly opposes this view.

A further distinction is now called for in the case of linguistic communication, since, as we have seen, more than one theory is at issue. When Davidson uses the term *theory,* as for example when he speaks about "an interpreter" or hearer having a theory at any particular moment in a linguistic interaction, he does so "only because a description of the interpreter's competence requires a recursive account" (Davidson 1985, 167). But this talk of "recursive" is misleading, as both Hacking and Dummett point out in different ways. "Recursive" can be construed as "effectively decidable" or as "specified inductively." The latter sense is what Dummett takes to be the operative one.

If the theories are such in the sense of being inductively specifiable accounts, the further question arises as to whether the long-range and short-range theories are both supposed to be theories of the utterances of a speaker (Dummett, 466). Now, any theory that is about another theory we may label *second-order,* as opposed to *first-order.* Thus, Davidson's theories about both the speaker's and the hearer's long-range and short-range theories are second-order. Of course, Davidson may rejoin that these agents do not have *theories* about these, merely expectations. But Dummett argues that Davidson, in order to avoid an infinite regress, needs to provide a first-order theory and has not done so (see esp. 467–70). This missing first-order theory, Dummett holds, cannot be one of meaning.

To isolate the point at issue, Dummett distinguishes between "a language, a theory of meaning for that language, and a second-order theory" (467). He writes:

> A language is an existing pattern of communicative speech: it is not a theory, but a phenomenon. A theory of meaning for that language, as conceived by Davidson, is a theory of the content of expressions belonging to it — what that content is and how it is determined by the

composition of the expressions. It does not itself employ the notion of meaning, but can be recognized as an adequate representation of the meanings of words and expressions of the language. It serves to explain how the language functions, that is, to explain the phenomenon of speech in that language; but it does so only indirectly. This is so because the theory itself contains no reference to speakers or to their beliefs, intentions or behaviour, linguistic or non-linguistic. Instead it uses theoretical terms such as "true" applying to certain expressions of the language. In order, therefore, to assess a theory of meaning for a language as correct or incorrect, we must have some principles, implicit or explicit, that make the connection between the theoretical notions and what the speakers of the language say and do. These principles are not regarded by Davidson as part of the theory of meaning itself: they are presumably constant over all theories of meaning and all languages. We may call them the linking principles. Save in their presence, it will make no sense to speak of believing or disbelieving a theory of meaning, since they alone provide a criterion for its being correct.

A second-order theory is of a quite different character. If it is a long-range theory, it consists of a set of beliefs about what expressions of some language mean, or about what certain individuals intend or take them to mean; if it is a short-range theory, then about what certain specific utterances were intended or taken to mean. (467)

This comment is helpful, but several questions remain. One is whether the linking principles referred to here "connect the theory of meaning to the linguistic practice by imputing theories to the speakers" (467). Following Dummett, as opposed to Davidson, we need to distinguish between interpretation in this strict sense — what Wittgenstein calls a *Deutung* and what Davidson propounds when he explains that Mrs. Malaprop means "a nice arrangement of epithets" — and interpretation in the broad sense as a way of understanding or *Auffassung* of what Mrs. Malaprop herself may understand by "a nice derangement of epitaphs." We also need to distinguish between second-order theories about what the long- and short-range theories of both speakers and hearers comprise and theories of meaning — does Mrs. Malaprop have a second-order theory about some belief, or does she hold some theory of meaning?

Sorting through such issues requires explicating the linking principles. Dummett continues:

Only the linking principles, when made explicit, will reveal whether a theory of meaning for a language is genuinely an object of knowledge, in some mode of knowledge, on the part of everyone who knows that language. Independently of whether it is or not, however, someone's knowledge of the language may be schematically represented by attributing such a theory to him. In knowing the language, he thereby attaches to expressions belonging to it the meanings they have in that language. The theory of meaning purports to provide the only possible analysis of what it is for those expressions to have those meanings. The speaker himself may be ignorant of that analysis: but, by attributing to him the corresponding theory of meaning, we simultaneously represent him as attaching those meanings to the expressions and supply an analysis of their having those meanings. In the same way, a second-order theory is not literally to the effect that such-and-such a theory of meaning is correct, or is the theory held by a certain individual. Its literal content is that certain expressions have certain meanings, or that some individual intends them to have or takes them as having those meanings. Since a theory of meaning makes explicit what it is or would be for them to have those meanings, however, the second-order theory can be represented as a theory about that theory of meaning. (468)

Again, we may find this helpful, but at least one further question also needs answering. Exactly what is to count as the language at issue if we identify, as Dummett wants us to do, *pace* Davidson, the first-order theory with a theory of meaning? Here Dummett urges us to take the relevant sense of "language," what he calls elsewhere "a pattern of communicative speech," as referring to a common language such as French or English or a dialect rather than construing a language as Davidson arguably does in terms of different overlapping idiolects. Such a choice still means, of course, that a theory of meaning would have to deal with deviant expressions, because no speaker of a common language or a dialect has perfect mastery. Here the task of a theory of meaning will be to "give the meanings that its words and expressions in fact have" (468) in the speaker's use of a common language or a dialect while treating the speaker's idiolect as a second-order theory. In short, in Dummett's view, "common language is related to an idiolect essentially as the rules of a game are related to a player's beliefs about what they are" (469).

Part of the disagreement here focuses on which aspects of language are taken as primary, roughly its communicative role or its cognitive role. Dummett puts the matter this way:

> Language is both an instrument of communication and a vehicle of thought; it is an important question of orientation in the philosophy of language which role we take as primary. I welcome Davidson's attention to the communicative function of language, since I am disposed to take that as its primary role: language is a vehicle of thought because it is an instrument of communication, and not conversely. And yet it is an error to concentrate too exclusively on communication. Wittgenstein is well known to have taken language primarily as a social activity; and yet his challenge to say one thing and mean something else thereby has to do with language in its role as a vehicle of thought. (470–71)

Behind this cautionary reminder lies Dummett's concern that Davidson has constructed a theory of linguistic communication by focusing his attention mainly on the admittedly numerous but nonetheless exceptional cases instead of on the usual ones. The result is the relative neglect of the primacy of theories of linguistic meaning, which give way to a fascination for second-order theories of speakers' and hearers' meanings.

What, then, are the major insights and disagreements encountered when we take into consideration additional representative work in contemporary Anglo-American philosophy of language? The substitution of talk about long-range and short-range theories for talk of prior and passing ones brings to the fore the dramatic poet's general expectations about the reader's perduring disposition to understand expressions in particular ways. Attention is also called to the poet's particular expectations and intentions with regard to a specific text, the idea being that the reader will understand specific expressions without having to modify his or her long-term dispositions. The stress falls on distinguishing between what the expressions mean and not just what the poet means but what the poet means in using these expressions on this occasion. Moreover, when the poet uses deviant expressions, the assumption should be that the poet writes neither inadvertently nor ignorantly but deliberately, perhaps even leaving clues for the reader's interpretation. Further, the criticism of the monologic character of Davidson's account of spoken linguistic communication actually brings out one of the crucial asymmetries between spoken and written communication; the latter, unlike the former, almost never allows for interaction.

As for the hearer or reader, the task is to interpret (in the strict sense of providing an account of an expression's meaning instead of resting content with its loose apprehension) the poet's language where "language" is to be construed as the poet's specific patterns of speech addressed to an implicit reader of a particular poem, rather than the poet's speech habits. The reader's strict interpretive account is to be a theory of the poet's specific language patterns in the poem in the sense that each salient element in the reader's account is inductively specifiable. Finally, we need to take note of a major disagreement in these closely related accounts: are we to understand the meaning of the central expressions that interest us as a function of the primacy we choose to award to some account of truth, or is the truth of those central expressions to be understood by proceeding from a theory of meaning? To return to my example, when Shakespeare has Romeo say, "Thus from my lips, by thine, my sin is purg'd," and has Juliet respond after Romeo's kiss, "Then have my lips the sin that they have took," can competent readers be properly said to succeed in their interpretations when, to simplify, they provide inductively specifiable accounts of how it is such expressions as "my sin is purg'd" mean what the poet with his readers in mind expects and intends the words to mean on this occasion while construing meaning after truth, or, conversely, truth after meaning?

In short, we might articulate informally in this second representative analytic discussion of meaning and truth several further elements as follows:

4. Instead of a prior theory, the speaker's or writer's long-range theory may be taken to include general expectations about and intentions with regard to a hearer's or reader's interpretive dispositions to construe both normal and deviant expressions the speaker or writer addresses to her in particular ways. And the speaker's or writer's short-range theory is similar except that in this case, but not in the previous one, the speaker or writer neither intends nor expects the hearer or reader to modify her own long-range dispositions.

5. The hearer's or reader's long-range theory may be taken as comprising general strategies as to how a hearer or reader is to

understand an individual speaker or writer, and her short-range theory as comprising particular strategies as to how a hearer or reader is to understand a specific utterance or text of the speaker or writer.

6. An interpretation is an inductively specifiable account of specific patterns of expression in a specific text where the account itself, deriving from a first-order theory where "meaning" is primitive, includes discussion of the putative truth of such expressions.

4

Without trying to construct a composite account that would merely paper over the genuine disagreements in these two closely related but different analytic views, we may ask nevertheless just how satisfactory these views of meaning and truth really are when confronted with conventions in literary texts. Consider briefly a section from another central text in Western cultural contexts, this one not from the Elizabethan but from the modernist period.

"My nerves are bad to-night. Yes, bad. Stay with me.
"Speak to me. Why do you never speak. Speak
   "What are you thinking of? What thinking? What?
"I never know what you are thinking. Think."

I think we are in rats' alley
Where the dead men lost their bones.

"What is that noise?"
          The wind under the door.
"What is that noise now? What is the wind doing?"
          Nothing again nothing.
                                        "Do
"You know nothing? Do you see nothing? Do you remember
"Nothing?"

     I remember
Those are pearls that were his eyes.
"Are you alive, or not? Is there nothing in your head?"

Interpreting the sense and significance of, for example, talk of "nothing" in this citation from T. S. Eliot's "The Waste Land" (1922, 33–34) seems more complicated than interpreting "my sin is purg'd" in Shakespeare's *Romeo and Juliet*. For in this case the expressions at issue are part of a represented dialogue, one of four sections not in a play but in an extended poem, itself comprising five major divisions, whose title is followed by a citation in Latin and Greek and a dedication in English and Italian and whose final lines in Sanskrit are followed by the notoriously ambiguous "Notes on the Waste Land."

Before turning to my philosophical account, I need to note several initial elements in this text. There seems to be a representation of a dialogue. Yet no quotation marks enclose one of the two interlocutors' words. The expression "nothing" sometimes occurs within a citation and sometimes not. Further, the expression here echoes an important line from section 1 of the poem, "The Burial of the Dead":

> "You gave me hyacinths first a year ago;
> "They called me the hyacinth girl."
> —Yet when we came back, late, from the hyacinth garden,
> Your arms full, and your hair wet, I could not
> Speak, and my eyes failed, I was neither
> Living nor dead, and I knew nothing,
> Looking into the heart of light, the silence.
> *Oed' und leer das Meer.*
>
> (30)

And the expression here also anticipates a passage in section 3, "The Fire Sermon":

> "On Margate Sands.
> I can connect
> Nothing with nothing.
> The broken fingernails of dirty hands.
> My people humble people who expect
> Nothing."
>
> (41)

Another initial point is that readers today, by contrast with both the poem's first reader, Ezra Pound, who debated various drafts with Eliot, and contemporary silent readers, have on hand a wealth of often painful biographical information about, for example, Eliot's first marriage, as well as an enormous secondary literature. Finally, readers today also have access to recordings of Eliot reading the entire "Waste Land" and hence can attend in particular to his curious reading of those lines without of course being able to talk with him as in a genuine conversational exchange.

When taken together, the analytic accounts do provide us with some helpful considerations in trying to elucidate apparently deviant expressions in such important literary texts. Three points stand out in particular. The notion of an "interpretation" centered on specific patterns of expression in a literary text while also trying to accommodate the writer's and the reader's intentions strikes a helpful balance between formalist and pragmatic considerations. That an interpretation must be articulated in such a way as to be inductively verifiable is also a necessary precaution against many impressionistic or intuitive readings of literary texts. Moreover, the distinction between long-range and short-range intentions and expectations on the side of both writers and readers clearly underlines the need to direct an interpretation to very specific aspects of an extremely complex phenomenon. Finally, the insistence in these accounts on explicating the presuppositions of an interpretation with respect to the priority of either questions about meaning or questions about truth is a sober reminder that, however specific an interpretation's ends may be, the expressions used to formulate the interpretation require critical attention in their own right.

Yet, these positive reminders arise against a background that itself requires critical scrutiny. Recall that the question to which these accounts are addressed as answers—what is it for words to mean what they do?—is quite general, whereas the questions to which the interpretation of a literary text is addressed are much more specific. This difference suggests that some of the elements in the analytic views here are not so pertinent to the understanding of texts such as Eliot's "The Waste Land" as they may at first appear. Three points in particular seem troublesome when we confront this account with extended examples from "The Waste Land" and *Romeo and Juliet* and not just with the occasional citation from a Sheridan play.

The key notion of theory seems equivocal, for it is applied to very diverse matters. We are urged to develop a "theory" of linguistic communication, a "theory" of long-range and short-range expectations and intentions, a "theory" of literal versus nonliteral meaning, a "theory" of interpretation, a first-order and a second-order "theory," even a "theory" of meaning and a "theory" of truth. But this is too much theory. Even if we favor Dummett's construal of a recursive theory as an inductively specifiable account, we are still not sure just what this theoretical account is to focus on in the first instance. Is such a theory in, say, the domain of literary texts the same sort of account that we may find in the domain of the social sciences or in that of the natural sciences? Finally, in literary studies, can we talk of "theory" in anything other than a systematically misleading way? One serious difficulty, then, is our inability as yet to characterize the appropriate sense in which an account of meaning and truth with regard to the conventions of poetic expression is theoretical.

A second problem arises with regard to the important distinctions between literal versus nonliteral meanings and normal versus deviant expressions. Just how these distinctions relate is not evident, although the assumption is most likely that some normal and deviant uses of language can be taken to exhibit both literal and nonliteral meaning. But in the domain of modernist poetry, talk of normal and deviant uses of language seems moot. And trying to elaborate an understanding of meaning on the basis of a problematic notion of the literal that leaves no room for the symbolic seems foolhardy. However useful these distinctions can be made, they surely cannot stand alone without further discussion and supplementation.

Finally, the central disagreement about the respective primacy of either a theory of truth or a theory of meaning needs to be resolved if we are to provide literary conventions with coherent and consistent conceptual underpinnings. Are we "first" to settle the meaning of Eliot's talk of "nothing" in "The Waste Land" before we raise the question of its truth? Or rather must we "first" settle on what "truth" amounts to in texts like these before we can address questions of meaning? Part of the difficulty here, just as in the previous cases of theory and different uses of language, lies in paying sufficient attention to the specificity of the domain of discourse that is at issue. Questions of meaning and truth, and disagreements about their respective priority, may accommodate more than one kind of reasonable discussion, depending on whether the pertinent domain is logical, mathematical, scientific, humanistic, and so on. Or are we to take the analytic disagreement here as pertaining to all domains of discourse in exactly the same respect? This seems unlikely. The crucial remaining problem, then, is one of specifying just how these matters are to be understood in the domain of literary and not just linguistic conventions.

CHAPTER TWELVE

The Temporality
of Convention:
Convention Theory
and Romanticism

CLAUDIA BRODSKY LACOUR

At a symposium on analytic philosophy held in Royaumont, France, in 1958, Peter F. Strawson responded to the objections of a nonanalytic philosopher as follows:

> I believe . . . that for you the object of philosophy is not to understand conceptual reality through language, as the latter is perceived through the observable facts of languages, but, rather, to understand the world. . . . [Y]et if what we are attempting is, precisely, to elucidate the conceptual structure which orders our customary ways of thinking the world, such as these ways reveal themselves in everyday language, then our essential if not unique point of contact is in the language in which our concepts take on articulate form. I don't believe this point admits of any argument.[1]

The purpose of the Royaumont Colloquium was to identify avenues of *rapprochement* between Continental and Anglo-Saxon philosophers: to undo, that is, rather than mend fences between them. The participants at the colloquium, including, in addition to Strawson, Gilbert Ryle, Willard Van Orman Quine, John Austin, A. J. Ayer, J. O. Urmson, Maurice Merleau-Ponty, Jean Wahl, and Lucien Goldman, identified themselves as practitioners of some form of either linguistic or metaphysical philosophy. Apart from that classification it would hardly be exaggerated to state that the only perception generally shared by both philosophical schools was some version of Strawson's intransigence. The proceedings of the symposium record its failure to achieve its aim: that of arriving, through discussion and debate, at a historic reconciliation of an earlier conceptual bifurcation, a split in the notion of the linguistic status of philosophical investigation.

That split has persevered, widened by theoretical and methodological developments often advancing in opposite directions, with the result that distinct ideas about what doing philosophy entails have probably, at least in postclassical philosophy, never been more different. Rather than jump into the breach or pretend to bridge it, in the present discussion I aim at the more limited purpose of description, focusing not on an eventual meeting of analytic and speculative objectives but on a specific point of departure between them, a common origin that is also a forking path. That origin is the issue and origin of conventions, for the investigation in modern linguistic philosophy of the institution and purposes of conventions recalls in many respects eighteenth-century speculative investigations into the origin of language as a whole. At stake in both cases is the nature and scope of the relationship between language and reason, with modern linguistic philosophers seeking to redescribe language as the neutral repository of truth, whether by constructing an artificial "ideal" language or submitting "ordinary" natural language to new analytic rigors.

One of the results of the analytic identification of the workings of language with those of logic — a result legible not only in the Royaumont proceedings but in almost any Anglo-Saxon university course catalogue — is the relegation of nonanalytic philosophy to an antediluvian state of metaphysical inquiry, usually called "the history of philosophy," and, along with metaphysics, all those questions of meaning irreducible to purely logical terms. Two major fields of study have paralleled this eclipse of metaphysical, or conceptual, investigation: the development of systems of substitutive notation aligning philosophy more closely with mathematics, and the elaboration of theories of "possible" or "alternative" worlds aimed at increasing the logical scope of language beyond the referential limits of its normal use.

By contrast, eighteenth-century and romantic theorists analyzed language, not primarily as a logical corpus whose rules automatically reflected permanent patterns of thought, but as a diachronic invention whose history of institution paralleled the history of human societies. Following in the wake of Port Royal grammarians, eighteenth-century philosophers of language regarded linguistic structures as the natural repositories of human reason; but they also credited those structures, their formation and development, with the creation and possibility of social formations. Not only logical but also ethical, legal, political, and aesthetic conventions were viewed as intimately tied to the conventions determining language use (and abuse) over time, and the propriety of governing norms and conventions was treated in eighteenth-century investigations as an explicitly historical issue.[2] This was and remains especially true of discussions of *literary* conventions, for the representation in literature of social conventions by way of linguistic ones provides a unique—if fictive—occasion for reflecting on the ways in which different historical norms intersect.[3]

Recent literary criticism that has sought to underscore this intersection of society and language in literature testifies to the acumen of eighteenth-century insights into the historical nature of linguistic conventions. Yet, for the most part, literary-critical approaches to "cultural history" have tended to sacrifice theoretical reflections on social and linguistic conventions to the gathering of literal data from archival sources. The attempt to understand the structure and motivation of conventions has characteristically been set aside for the elaboration of details reproduced through direct citation, as if recorded facts, once unearthed and repeated, needed only to speak for themselves. At the same time, the modern analytic interest in the theoretical status of conventions has developed in breathtaking independence from the consideration of actual and historical life among language users, the kind of linguistic experience addressed by literary and social critics and historians.[4]

Convention theory in contemporary linguistic philosophy bypasses the problem of the social and historical nature of linguistic conventions by equating convention with language and language with the vehicle of analytic truth *tout court*. The conclusion of David Lewis's *Convention: A Philosophical Study* states the premises of the analytic interest in conventions directly and succinctly: "Analyticity is truth in all possible worlds. What is analytic for someone depends jointly on the facts about the possible worlds and on the language he is using. The language he is using depends on the conventions he is party to. And these conventions are regularities in behavior, sustained by an interest in coordination and an expectation that others will do their part" (208).

Two apparently extralinguistic, or empirical, considerations figure in Lewis's summation of the role of conventions in the analytic approach to "truth." One is his reference to the analytic philosopher's dependence upon "facts about the possible worlds and the language he is using." Simply put, those "facts" are any hypotheses one can think of as alternatives to the operations of language and of experience possible in this world. The only limit to these hypotheses is the law of contradiction, the irreducible syntactical unit of logical analysis that must also hold true of all "worlds" and be translatable throughout the terms of any language, if theories of "possible worlds" are to be of any "use" to analytic philosophy at all (I return to this quality of usefulness later). Lewis states the limit of contradiction, using that oddly favored analytic example of unreconstructable nonsense, "the married bachelor," as follows: "Say, if you like, that it is by convention that there are no *rightly so-called* married bachelors. But do not say that it is by convention that there are no married bachelors, in this world or any other. There couldn't be" (1969, 207).[5] The "facts" that rule "possible worlds" are not temporal and historical but logical and hypothetical, modeled on their resemblance, as Lewis has argued elsewhere (1986, 20–69), to discrete facts we identify and beliefs we hold concerning the world we consider our own.

The second seeming constraint upon Lewis's description of pervasive conventionality is the "interest in coordination" that must be maintained by all involved, coupled with or reflected by "an expectation that others will do their part." This is the less obvious condition, the most pernicious with regard to any historical consideration of conventions and, for Lewis's theory, the most centrally necessary. Its circularity, rather than disguised, is restated throughout Lewis's exposition of how conventions work. The mental Moebius strip of mirrored "interest" and "expectation" that constitutes conventional behavior for Lewis is at once the thread that holds his theory together and the brackets that theory places around all nonconventional behavior, including the institution of previously nonexistent conventions. The paradigm remains a rationalist one, based on a common desire among agents for "coordination." Lewis states: "The outcomes the agents want to produce or prevent are determined jointly by the actions of all agents. So the outcome of any action an agent might choose depends on the actions of other agents. That is why . . . each must choose what to do according to his expectations about what others will do" (1969, 8).

"Expectations," Lewis goes on to explain, engage in a seamless interplay with acts of "replication," which he defines as "second-order expectations," or expectations about expectations. Combining at a virtual third order with their own expectation — that is, the expectation about an expectation — acts of replication effectively restrict the realm of action to the inevitable fulfillment of projected expectations, thereby keeping the path of coordination ever straight, its constitutive acts interchangeable: "Whenever I replicate a piece of your practical reasoning, my second-order expectations about matters of fact, together with my first-order expectations about your preferences and your rationality, justify me in forming a first-order expectation about your action" (1969, 28). Furthermore, acts of replication in no way allow for the possibility of a differential or dialogical slant on given "expectations." Lewis cautions:

> Note that replication is *not* an interaction back and forth between people. It is a process in which *one* person works out the consequences of his beliefs about the world — a world he believes to include other people who are working out the consequences of their beliefs, including their belief in other people who . . . By our interaction in the world we acquire various high-order expectations that can serve us as premises. In our subsequent reasoning we are windowless monads doing our best to mirror each other, mirror each other mirroring each other, and so on. (1969, 32)

A theory of convention that positions Leibniz's image of incommunicable entities developing individually according to divine design within the secular context of a funhouse hall of mirrors yields a description of experience that only the theorist (somehow removed from the infinite regress of conventional "reasoning")[6] can see, a description in which any moment of experience only enforces its identity to the next. The very notion of development, let alone origination or change, is replaced by a view according to which the purely formal content of every moment of action is synonymous with that of every other moment *and* at the same time insures that the future will bring more of the same. A final passage from Lewis — whose descriptions of convention, reflecting his theory of conventions, both replicate and amplify each other — makes his fully intentional occlusion of the temporal problems of the instantiation and development of conventional behavior clear:

> Each new action in conformity to the regularity adds to our experience of general conformity. Our experience of general conformity in

the past leads us, by force of precedent, to expect a like conformity in the future. And our expectation of future conformity is a reason to go on conforming, since to conform if others do is to achieve a coordination equilibrium and to satisfy one's own preferences. And so it goes — we're here because we're here because we're here because we're here. Once the process gets started, we have a metastable self-perpetuating system of preferences, expectations, and actions capable of persisting indefinitely. . . . [C]onforming action produces expectation of conforming action and expectation of conforming action produces conforming action.

This is the phenomenon I call convention. (1969, 41–42)

While as a description of the vacuity of conventional behavior this account seems irrefutable, it also signals a theoretical vacuum that no number of mutually enforcing expectations and replications can fill up. "Once the process gets started" remains Lewis's point of departure; and, even if, for the sake of argument, one accepted the view that rational agents desired, and desired equally, equilibrium and coordination, *how* the process gets started remains beyond the scope of the argument. With the exception of the appeal to "precedent" (1969, 36–41), a begging of the question of origins, all we know about how the process begins — how the norm becomes the norm, or, for that matter, alters — is that it does.

That Lewis's omission of the origin of conventions entails logical difficulties of its own appears most evident in his discussion of an example of convention in action, which (fittingly enough) he reproduces from another source, David Hume's *Treatise of Human Nature* (1740) (Lewis also cites Hume's thesis that regulative behavior is grounded in "a general sense of common interest" (3.2.2) as tantamount to his own): "Suppose you and I are rowing a boat together," the example begins, concluding, expectably, that the boat will advance "smoothly" only if "we row in rhythm" (1969, 3–4). Emphasizing the vacuity of conventional behavior, Lewis's point is that "it matters little to either of us at what rate we row" as long as synchrony is achieved through expectation: "each is constantly adjusting his rate to match the rate he expects the other to maintain" (1969, 5–6).

Now, we may grant that, as rational agents, both rowers are apprised of and are agreed upon where their boat is to go. Still, without precedent, without previous agreement, and without any explicit agreement reached midstream, there is absolutely nothing to prevent each rower from mistaking the expectations of the other, to prevent each adjustment from being a misadjustment and the boat from turning endlessly in the physical equivalent of Lewis's theoretical premise, the circular and, in this case, mutually frustrating recognition that "we're here because we're here . . ."

Lewis takes up Hume's example again when arguing that "knowledge of our conventions" "may be irremediably nonverbal knowledge" (1969, 63). Once more sidestepping the issue of how conventions are formed in the first place by asserting that "a tacit and temporary convention" may provide the "evidence" needed for knowledge of a "convention" proper, he concludes: "Like it or not, we have plenty of knowledge we cannot put into words. And plenty of our knowledge, in words or not, is based on evidence we cannot hope to report" (1969, 64). This is no doubt true, but such unarticulated knowledge can never be taken as conventional, whether in a fuzzily "tacit," "temporary," or more conventionally normative sense. The only way to stop a boat from turning in a circle, perhaps a whirlpool, of false expectations is to institute, by fiat or by agreement, a rule of thumb from that moment on, and knowledge of such a rule can only be "ha[d]" in a language whose conventions both parties already agree upon (a language that indeed may be "nonverbal" in the literal sense, but that must employ established signs, gestures, substitutive tokens of some kind).

If barred from the use of a conventional language, as Lewis's use of Hume's example would have it, one of the two rowers rowing—call him Eddy—had better instead be a *non*rational agent, in Lewis's words, "a child or an idiot," if the boat is to go straight. For only a subject who replicates *without* expectation, who "may conform without reason" (1969, 51), may also escape the whirlpool effect of rational anticipation, and it is just this kind of agent whom Lewis explicitly excludes from his description of conventional behavior: "When children and the feeble-minded conform to our conventions, they may not take part in them *as conventions*" (1969, 75; emphasis in original).[7] The *non*rational agents Lewis necessarily and categorically excludes from his conception of convention, those who mirror others as mirrors rather than as rational agents, who "conform to our conventions" without taking part "in them *as* conventions"— those, in short, who do not "reflect" in the figurative sense and so give the lie to the notion of "truth" founded in convention—are also the only agents who may be free from the domino effect of false expectations. The "we" who are "here because we are here" and not because we have so convened would be less likely to be here if we *were* rational agents, interested in and capable of attempting to second-guess one another; that is, capable of the very activity Lewis accords to "philosophers" alone: the activity of "thinking twice."[8] The agents of convention, as Lewis describes them, must be nonrational to the extent that they must lack the capacity to reflect upon actions in terms of the presence or absence of cause and effect. They must, in short, be idiots when it comes to thinking about things twice, or thinking about things differently, which is to say, not circularly but temporally and historically. This is not to say, however, that most of the time we are not idiots, carrying on conventional behavior in precisely this sense.

In describing how conventions operate once in force, Lewis is not concerned with the circularity, or resultant illogic, of a theory of conventions that does not account for their origin. Quine, in his foreword to *Convention*, is concerned with just that. Like Rousseau in the *Second Discourse* (1755), Quine recognizes that language would already be required for the establishment of linguistic conventions, that "an original founding of language by overt convention is not merely unhistorical but unthinkable" (1969, xi).[9] Nor do covert, "tacit," or "temporary" conventions qualify as historical origins before the fact. A convention that is and is not one—just the kind of logical contradiction that Lewis excludes from the purview of possible worlds—contradicts the logical definition of convention itself. For, "what," Quine asks, "is convention when there can be no thought of convening?" (1969, xi).

The "vicious regress" involved in "appealing to convention where there can have been no thought of convening" extends, according to Quine, across the entire analytic method it underpins (1969, xi). Just as it occludes the "thought of convening," philosophy that takes linguistic conventions as the vehicle of logical truth cannot account for how conventions themselves acquire logical usefulness. Much as the conventions described in modern linguistic philosophy seem to precede their own formation, so logic seems to inform philosophers' use of conventions as the medium of logical analysis. For if we were to "count logical truth analytic," that is, as delimited solely by adopted conventions, then, Quine explains, "a circularity would arise if we were to take the conventions explicitly. The predicament is that in order to apply any explicit conventions that were general enough to afford all logical truth, we would already have to use logic in reasoning from the general conventions to the individual applications" (1969, xi–xii).

Quine had already noted the logical circularity of the analytic use of conventions in "Truth by Convention": "In a word, the difficulty is that if logic is to proceed mediately from conventions, logic is needed for inferring logic from the conventions" (1936, 104).[10] Quine concedes that "we can adopt conventions through behavior, without first announcing them in words," but cautions that "it is not clear wherein an adoption of the conventions, antecedently to their formulation, consists; such behavior is difficult to distinguish from that in which conventions are disregarded" (1936, 105–6). Lewis's "rejoinder" to Quine, that not "language or any other conventional activity" but merely "manifestations of a propensity to conform to a regularity" are needed to "create a convention" (1969, 87–88) only underscores the limited notion of language, and the resulting blind spot of his method, since to be effective such "manifestations" would first have to be understood and agreed upon, and so would constitute linguistic conventions of the very sort they are meant to found.

In contrast to Lewis, Quine offers a noncircular account of the origin of conventions, which has both historical and literary implications. In "Carnap and Logical Truth," Quine criticizes "the linguistic doctrine of logical truth" that analyzes sentences by substituting one conventional expression for another. Arguing against the notion of "truth by language," which holds that linguistic terms that are not already "logical particles" ("or," "and," etc.) can be fully transcribed into synonymous descriptions, Quine describes a nonanalytic activity that is "something very like convention in an ordinary non-metaphorical sense of the word. We find ourselves making deliberate choices and setting them forth unaccompanied by any attempt at justification other than in terms of elegance and convenience. These adoptions, called postulates, and their logical consequences (via elementary logic), are true until further notice" (1954, 117).

By Quine's account, there are two kinds of acts of postulation. "Discursive postulation" selects from previously adopted truths, while "legislative postulation" sets forth such unjustified adoptions: it "institutes truth by convention," posits a convention instead of translating between conventions. Each positing in turn constitutes the origin of a history of philosophical procedure (1954, 118). In this view, conventions are not the medium of nontemporal logical truth but artificial instantiations of temporary truths, and conventionality is not the condition of truth but the adoption of a truth "until further notice." The postulation and adoption of a truth does not insure its own historical validity; on the contrary, it insures the possibility of historical change. In opposition to the circular and tautological view by which language, conventionality, and logical truth are at all times co-extensive,[11] Quine defines "conventionality" as "a passing trait . . . a trait of events and not of sentences," adding incisively that to speak of "a sentence as forever true by convention if its first adoption as true was a convention . . . involves us in the most unrewarding historical conjecture" (1954, 119).

At the same time as it rejects the circularity of analytic accounts of what makes conventions true, Quine's notion of "truth by convention" may appear to smack of relativism, to demote the claims of logical coherence to fiction. By pointing out that all inferences from conventions to logic must already be logically motivated, and by refusing to attribute the origin of conventions to already conventional activity, Quine does imply that the legislative postulation of conventions has instead a certain ungrounded or fictional aspect. Neither logical nor conventional in motivation, the unjustified "event" of setting forth a convention for the sake of "elegance and convenience" introduces a nonanalytic element into philosophical discourse, one that could not be considered "true by synonymy and logic"[12] and that Quine defines instead as inalterably "artificial": "Legislative postulation contributes truths which become integral to the corpus of truths; the artificiality of their origin does not linger as a localized quality, but suffuses the corpus" (1954, 119–20). The artifice or fiction at the "origin" of the "truths" postulated by convention makes the notions of absolute truths and of the integrity of an enduring "corpus of truths" at the very least questionable.

Still, the unsettling of absolutism in Quine's refutation of the analytic appeal to conventions does not result in the Humean relativism proposed, for example, by Nelson Goodman, who argues that the elusive difference between facts and conventions depends solely on one's point of view, or "stance," and that stances are either a consequence of "habit," or, less frequently, of reasonable "choice" (1989, 84). Neither of these accounts of conventions taken for truths resembles Quine's insistence that the artificial origin of conventions involves both a break with the past and a necessary, rather than freely chosen, change in the corpus of truths transmitted across history. Nor does Quine's view of the artificiality of truths adopted by convention resemble Lewis's view of what he calls "truth in fiction." For Lewis, the category of "fiction" (limited by his own example to detective stories) functions analytically like a counterfactual or possible world situation (1978, 269–70). Conforming to the analytic model and "use" value of counterfactual or alternative worlds, what is "true" in "the worlds" of fictional stories "is what would be true if those stories were told as known fact rather than fiction" (1978, 279). And, as in the case of counterfactual or possible world situations, what we take in fiction as something that would have been "true" in fact and in our world depends on two considerations: its resemblance to our world and consonance with our beliefs about our world (1978, 270–72). Lewis judges "truth in fiction" by the same notions of verisimilitude and doxa by which he judges possible worlds,[13] and while these notions may uphold the analytic premise of synonymity, they are rudimentary if not flatly reductive bases for understanding how we locate truth in discursive fiction.

Quine's notion of "truth by convention" as temporally instituted artifice is closer to literary theory than Goodman's relativism or Lewis's circular theory of convention and related theory of fictional worlds because it implies, precisely, the fictional or literary dimension of discourse in this world, including discourse that attempts to analyze the world and discourse itself. For, finally, how many worlds must we make use of, how many circumstantial situations must we make up, to make up for the limits prescribed by the analytic equation of language with logic; limits that exclude such notions as temporality and fiction from our understanding of language and the actual world (and that divide the world, as it happens rather too neatly, among philosophers, conventionalists, and idiots)? How many alternative conventions must, after all, be hypothesized to compensate for the absence of an account of the origin of any convention, including those conventions most useful to analytic philosophy, such as the very notion of possible worlds? Usefulness as its own reward — the tautology at work in Lewis's analyticity — seems more a criterion of language logicians than of language users, who experience linguistic conventions, as they do this world, in ways that change, rather than render synonyms for, the object they use.[14]

Another analysis of conventions, which, like Quine's, describes a dimension of conventionality unavailable to traditional analytic methods, is proposed by Saul Kripke (1972). Kripke views one kind of convention, names or "rigid designators," as *non*synonymous with analytic descriptions. Naming in Kripke is not unlike Quine's act of legislative postulation; it functions to "fix a reference," but, Kripke argues, "It is in general not the case that the reference of a name is determined by some uniquely identifying marks, some unique properties satisfied by the referent and known or believed to be true of that referent by the speaker" (106). Contrary to the view of Gottlob Frege and Bertrand Russell, a name is *not* "simply . . . a definite description abbreviated or disguised" (27). In analyzing names as linguistic conventions that cannot be translated logically by other conventions, Kripke points to a kind of conventional usage that, ungrounded in the rules of conventionality, contradicts one of the central premises of modern linguistic philosophy:

> According to Frege, there is some sort of looseness or weakness in our language. Some people may give one sense to the name "Aristotle," others may give another. But of course it is not only that; even a single speaker when asked, "What description are you willing to substitute for the name?" may be quite at a loss. In fact, he may know many things about him; but any particular thing that he knows he may feel clearly expresses a contingent property of the object. (30)

Names, then, are linguistic conventions that cannot be sufficiently defined, referents irreplaceable by adequate descriptions, conceptual wholes always larger than what we can know and state of their parts. As a result, like Quine's conventions, Kripke's "names" (by which, at first, Kripke says he means "proper nouns" (24), while suggesting later, however, that his theory extends to most nouns and even to adjectives),[15] are not available to logical analysis: "If . . . 'Moses' is not synonymous with any description, then even if its reference is in some sense determined by a description, statements containing the name cannot in general be *analyzed* by replacing the name by a description, though they may be materially equivalent to statements containing a description" (33; emphasis in original).

According to Kripke's argument, the relationship between names and descriptions is irreversible: one does not begin with a qualitative description and generate a name, a fact he takes to be best demonstrated by the use of names in "transworld identification." Without the working premise of referential constancy unconstrained by contingent definitions, Kripke reasons, the identification of a reference in alternative world or counterfactual situations could not obtain. In short, in order to describe an identity across possible worlds, one must first be able to refer to it: "it is *because* we can refer (rigidly) to Nixon, and stipulate that we are speaking of what might have happened to *him* (under certain circumstances), that 'transworld identifications' are unproblematic in such cases" (49; emphasis in original).[16]

Names are required for logical analysis but do not admit of such analysis; knowledge of their identity is "necessary" but not necessarily *"a priori."*[17] That is to say, because the referential character of a name does not depend on specific characteristics thought to be described by the referent — because the meaning of a name cannot be subsumed by an analytic statement, indeed, because such meaning cannot be accurately stated — the knowledge of identity, which names are used to indicate, cannot be *a priori* knowledge. It is, instead, in Kripke's terms, historical. Arguing that in attempting to construct a "description picture" of reference, "one might never reach a set of necessary and sufficient conditions," Kripke concludes: "In general our reference depends not just on what we think ourselves, but on other people in the community, the history of how the name reached one, and things like that. It is following such a history that one gets to the reference" (94–95). Kripke gives the following account of how names, when used over time and in the absence of any knowledge of their reference, may take on a historical life of their own:

A teacher tells his class that Newton was famous for being the first man to think there's a force pulling things to the earth; . . . we may suppose that just being told that this was the sole content of Newton's discovery gives the students a false belief *about Newton,* even though they have never heard of him before. If, on the other hand, the teacher uses the name "George Smith" — a man by that name is actually his next door neighbor — and says that George Smith first squared the circle, does it follow from this that the students have a false belief about the teacher's neighbor? The teacher doesn't tell them that Smith is his neighbor, nor does he believe Smith first squared the circle. He isn't particularly trying to get any belief *about the neighbor* into the students' heads. He tries to inculcate the belief that there was a man who squared the circle, but not a belief about any particular man — he just

pulls out the first name that occurs to him — as it happens, he uses his
neighbor's name. It doesn't seem clear in that case that the students have
a false belief about the neighbor, even though there is a causal chain
going back to the neighbor. I am not sure about this. At any rate more
refinements need to be added to make this even begin to be a set of necessary and sufficient conditions. (95–96; emphasis in original)

The "causal chain going back to the neighbor" does not properly
identify referent here with reference, "George Smith" with "'George
Smith.'" For no logical reason, at a historical moment, a name was
used to mean something that even its user knew it didn't mean. By the
same token, we can take that causal chain forward and imagine the historical moment when, by chance, the teacher's students run into the
referent, "George Smith." They might believe themselves in the presence of the genuine article, or they might come to the conclusion that
there must be at least two such referents, or even realize, on the basis
of intervening discoveries, that for no good reason their teacher was
putting them on. Whatever the appellation "'George Smith'" then
comes to mean to them by convention, wherever the causal chain leads
them, will remain a matter of experience over time. The point is that
even as a conventional term remains stable, its referential meaning
may itself become a subject of conflict, changing, rather than mirroring itself, as one follows out its history. Kripke describes this historical
predicament with regard to a commonplace version of the "'George
Smith'" problem, nonproper nouns, which necessarily have multiple
references (his example is "the term 'tiger'"): "If there are two kinds of
tigers that have something to do with each other but not as much as we
thought, then maybe they form a larger biological family. If they have
absolutely nothing to do with each other, then there are really two kinds
of tigers. This all depends on the history and on what we actually find
out" (121).

But perhaps what we find out about tigers we find out from another
referentially irresponsible teacher; perhaps "what we actually find out"
is really about leopards who change their spots and gain the characteristics of tigers in another Just-So story on the order of the accomplishments of "'George Smith.'" Since this is what can happen to names in
history, it is difficult to imagine a way in which history and "a set of necessary and sufficient conditions" could ever overlap. What this implies,

in turn, is that names are both "necessary"—as Kripke argues—and temporal conventions or fictions: not that "George Smith" and the name "'George Smith'" don't exist or could not have existed, but that the connection between them may be replaced by another, entirely different convention, and that it may only be a question of time, of the accidents and vicissitudes of history, before that change in meaning occurs.[18]

It is as a safeguard against just such historical occurrences that Kripke formulates a kind of rule for the temporal transmission of names:

> When the name is "passed from link to link," the receiver of the name must, I think, intend when he learns it to use it with the same reference as the man from whom he heard it. If I hear the name "Napoleon" and decide it would be a nice name for my pet aardvark, I do not satisfy this condition.*
>
> [*I can transmit the name of the aardvark to other people. For each of these people, as for me, there will be a certain sort of causal or historical connection between my use of the name and the Emperor of the French, but not one of the required type.] (96, n. 43)

While there is no logical or describable reason to name an aardvark for "the Emperor of the French"—and that is Kripke's point in proposing this example—there is also no reason to turn to aardvarks in order to demonstrate the fragility of transmitted linguistic conventions. To know how to fail to "satisfy [the] condition" of intentional referential conformity even as one creates a new "causal and historical connection"—a connection of "a certain sort but not . . . of the required type"—we need only consider the many connections created by the regular historical use of the name here abused. Few names in modern history have been charged with more—and more multifarious—causal connections than "Napoleon," perhaps because the referent of that reference was interested in changing precisely those connections; in destroying, revivifying, and creating conventions; in "changing history" or doing whatever we mean at different times by those terms. By chance connection, my final argument for considering the question of the temporality of conventions comes from a literary author who both experienced firsthand the historical upheavals associated with the conventional use of the reference "Napoleon" and also reflected on the erratic rule of all conventions formed and transmitted through history. In *Racine et*

Shakespeare (1823), the name Stendhal gives to the historical change of conventions is "romanticism."

Connected by a causal chain that led as far as Moscow, Stendhal's own history, including his introduction to the theory of romanticism, followed the course of changing events and meanings associated with the rigid designator "Napoleon."[19] Returning in exile to Italy in 1814, Stendhal remained in Milan during the Hundred Days, learning of the emperor's transmutation from phoenix to Icarus from afar. But Stendhal's personal allegiance with the losing side at Waterloo had an inverse effect on his literary affiliations. Inspired by manifestoes for "romanticism" published in *Il Conciliatore*,[20] Stendhal took the part of Shakespeare in the debate on literary conventions, a debate that, back in Paris, had spread from the academy to the streets; in July 1822, an English theatrical troupe was chased from a Paris stage by adherents of the classical tradition. Such dramatic turns of events in the history of drama are rare, and the historical underpinnings of this one were unusually clear. For, at the time, the difference between the referents of "Shakespeare" and "Wellington" may well have seemed merely a matter of convention, as both were English and threatened to eclipse France, the contest for the rules of dramatic unity taking up where imperial rule left off. In defending Shakespeare, Stendhal apparently linked his fervor for Napoleon with the Bard, a political and cultural association under the aegis of "romanticism" that quickly became conventional in Italy and throughout Europe.[21] But Stendhal implies that even this historically motivated convention will change with the passage of time. The summary third chapter of *Racine et Shakespeare*, entitled "What Romanticism Is" ("Ce que c'est que le romanticisme"), begins with a delineation of "romantic" and "classic" that is not so much contained *by*, as it is coextensive *with*, history:

> *Romanticism* is the art of presenting to peoples those literary works which, in the actual state of their customs and beliefs, are susceptible to giving them the most pleasure possible.
>
> *Classicism*, on the other hand, presents to them the literature which gave the most pleasure to their great-grandfathers.
>
> Sophocles and Euripides were eminently romantic . . .
>
> To imitate Sophocles and Euripides today, and maintain that these imitations will not make the Frenchman of the nineteenth century yawn, is classicism. (1823, 71)

When Stendhal goes on to state, "I do not hesitate to assert that Racine was romantic" (*a été romantique*) (71), it is evident that there is more (or less) to the conventional opposition between "romanticism" and "classicism" than meets the eye. If nothing defines "romanticism" but its actuality, is there nothing in literary works that makes actuality, as it "was" experienced, survive? Stendhal's answer appears to be an emphatic no. "Romanticism" is a conventional term for literary works that please at the present moment; it does not entail regular — conforming and self-mirroring — conventions of its own. To imitate "romanticism" is, precisely, to yield "classicism," no matter what instance of "romanticism" one imitates, no matter the rules one invokes. Or, as Stendhal writes in the *Racine et Shakespeare* of 1825, his response to the public counterattack against the first *Racine et Shakespeare* conducted by M. Auger, then director of the *Académie française:* "Correctly stated, ALL GREAT WRITERS WERE ROMANTIC IN THEIR TIME. It is the people who, a century after their death, copy them instead of opening their eyes and imitating nature, who are classic" (106).

If the attempt to be "romantic" by way of imitating past "romantics" defines one instead as "classic," there is no way to be "romantic" by general accord or convention. Like eighteenth-century theories of the origin of language, as well as modern analytic theory of convention, theory of "romanticism" faces a structural quandary. In Kripke's terms, it names a referent it can never describe, for as soon as a literary work conforms to recognized characteristics of "romanticism," it no longer is "romantic." "Romanticism," then, is the literary-historical version of a convention that is and is not one. Stendhal's modern reader may be reminded here of Russell's famous paradox, that of the barber who could only shave himself and could not ever shave himself because he shaved all and only those who didn't shave themselves.[22] Like Russell's logically non-self-containing class, Stendhal's "romanticism" cannot contain itself, for as soon as it does it is what it is not, "classicism." Nor does "classicism," defined oppositely as the convention of literary conventionality, escape the difficulty here described. For by imitating "romanticism" at a temporal remove, "classicism" does not — as its proponents conventionally assert — imitate life. According to Stendhal, it is "romanticism" that, "imitating nature," affords "the most pleasure possible" at any historical moment, but the imitation of that imitation resembles a fiction, which is to say, not nature. In brief, "classicism" does not conform to the conventional characteristics of "classicism" because it is *modeled* on (past) "romanticism." Both terms signify literary works that afford pleasure through imitation; what distinguishes them is what they imitate — roughly, prior imitations of nature or nature as perceived according to contemporary "customs and beliefs" — which in turn can only be defined in terms of temporal conventions.

But at any moment, lacking the knowledge of celebrity afforded by an intervening "century," how can we tell an imitation of "romanticism" (that is, "classicism") from a pleasing imitation of life (that is, actually unrecognizable "romanticism")? Again, there may be more (or less) to the conventional opposition between the terms than meets the eye. As quoted above, Stendhal stated that "all great writers," the "romantics" of their time, "open eyes and imitate nature." Yet, the "pleasure" they effect, he argues, is tied to the experience of "illusion," eyes opened upon a "fictive time," which is *not* actually transpiring, and closed to the "*material* time," which is (55; emphasis in original). Stendhal's "Romantic" attempts to describe this experience to an "Academic":

> Deign to observe with attention what is happening in your head. Try to remove for a moment the veil thrown by custom over actions which take place so quickly that you have almost lost the ability to follow them with your eye and see them *transpire*. Let's agree about this word *illusion*. When one says that the imagination of the spectator figures to itself that the necessary time for the events represented on stage transpires, one does not understand that the illusion of the spectator proceeds to the point of believing all this time has really elapsed. The fact is that the spectator, carried along by the action, is not shocked by anything; he gives no thought at all to the time that has elapsed. . . . The spectator, when he is not a pedant, is entirely occupied with the actions and the developments of passions which one places before his eyes. (57; emphasis in original)

The first thing, then, one must "agree" or convene on in distinguishing "classicism" from "romanticism" is the term "illusion." Once clear on the meaning of "illusion," one should have a convention for identifying "romanticism"; and "illusion," Stendhal states conventionally, "means the action of a man who believes in something which is not. . . . Theatrical illusion would be the action of a man who believes the things which transpire on stage truly exist" (58). We may all, indeed, agree on this description; but Stendhal's account of "illusion" proceeds one step further. For illusionary belief, Stendhal explains, is not *continuously* entertained by the spectator. Rather than replicating and reinforcing itself, "illusion" is experienced only at "moments." "All the pleasure" afforded by "romanticism" occurs at "moments of *perfect illusion*" (58, 59, 60; emphasis in original); "but these moments," Stendhal goes on to state, "last an infinitely short time, a half-second or quarter-second, for example" (59). And this is where the temporal bases of the paradox of convention theory are most plain. For if "romanticism" consists of moments when one's eyes open upon a "perfect illusion" — an imitation created "so that the veil of custom can be torn away" (61) — then conventional imitation, "the veil of custom" itself, can also only be recognized by way of such moments: when, by way of artifice, one "sees" fictive actions "transpire." "Romanticism," in other words, is a temporal phenomenon that occurs at unidentifiable intervals within "classicism." It tears the veil of conventional imitation, but only temporarily; it allows us to see nature, but only by way of a momentary "illusion." "Romanticism" does this, but when we stipulate that this is what it does, rather than actually "see" this action "transpire," we are describing an imitative model of "romanticism" — "classicism." Just as we become conscious of time after having lost track of it, if only for a moment, conventional activity, according to Stendhal, is constantly interrupted by "romantic" or nonconventional experience, whether at intervals of a half-second or a half-century. But there can be no convention for describing this kind of change.

There is, however, an impure, or only partially conventional, activity that marks the return to normative beliefs. The name Stendhal gives to this action is "laughter." Specifying "two conditions" of "the comic" — "clarity and the unexpected" — Stendhal describes the experience of laughter as the inverse of "perfect illusion," as the moment the veil of custom falls back into place: "There can be no more *laughter* if the disadvantage of the man at whose expense we are supposed to laugh makes us think, from the first moment, that we, too, can run into this misfortune" (64). While chapter 1 of *Racine et Shakespeare* discusses "romanticism" and "classicism" within the context of tragedy — poking fun at the notion that one could please through rationally willed acts of replication (the view then represented by a rule-bound academy), the chapter is entitled, with considerable humor, "In Order to Create Tragedies That Could Interest the Public in 1823, Must One Follow the Errant

Ways of Racine or Those of Shakespeare?" Chapter 2, entitled simply, "Laughter," implies that the temporal alternation between romantic "illusion" and classical "custom" is as involuntary as it is comic, which is how Stendhal treats the very notion that one or the other could emerge victorious from this literary-historical debate. If the difference between the two is purely temporal, if classical conventions imitate prior instances of "romanticism," and if "romanticism" consists of instances of "perfect illusion," absolute fictions whose actual effect depends on their momentary break with conventions, then convention theory must be unable to define such change. Adequate to that inability, the following definition of romanticism may be offered:

> Romanticism is nothing at all like a system of literary composition; or rather, romanticism does not exist, it does not have a real life. It is a phantom which evaporates the moment that one approaches it and tries to touch it.[23]

These words were stated by Auger — historically, Stendhal's adversary — and the irony, of course, is that they say nothing with which Stendhal could not agree. At the heart of a historic argument regarding the continuity of literary conventions, there seems to be an unwitting convention that the break with conventionalism cannot be grasped. Stendhal might also add to Auger, as Quine adds to Lewis, and Kripke to Russell and Frege, that whenever one tries to touch the nonsystematic origins of convention, they turn into conventions; that, just as romanticism becomes classicism, convention theory evaporates at our approach. What is interesting is that while Stendhal the romanticist, Auger the classicist, and philosophers from Rousseau to Quine and Kripke could be in accord on this — could take it, in Quine's terms, as a truth by convention — the temporality of conventions insures that theory of convention will continue its historical approach.

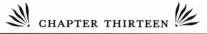
Conventions and Rationality

GÖRAN HERMERÉN

Introduction

In this contribution I discuss traditions and conventions (without assuming that there is a sharp boundary between them) in art and in the art world.[1] I focus on the extent to which familiarity with such traditions and conventions is necessary or sufficient for understanding art, and on the possibility of rationality in the interpretation and explanation of artworks, particularly when such works are explored by critics and scholars from different intellectual and aesthetic traditions.

"Traditions" and "conventions," as I use these words, cover a variety of phenomena, ranging from regularities of which artists and critics may, but need not, be aware to more or less arbitrary stipulations of which the people involved are fully aware, as well as from regularities exemplified by nearly all artists, critics, and researchers to those exemplified by small avant-garde groups.

These regularities, varying in scope, also vary in other dimensions. They are not just regularities in artistic behavior and in the behavior of artists (which are not necessarily synonymous), as well as in the behavior of other stakeholders in the art world; they are also regularities in the expectations and preferences regarding such behavior, and in the expectations regarding these expectations and preferences, and so forth.[2]

Instead of repeating the clumsy expression "traditions and/or conventions," I simply use "conventions" with the understanding that it is used in a fairly wide sense. When I explicitly want to make clear that I am talking about rules and regularities in a narrow and well-defined sense, I use the word "codes." However, when I wish to make clear that I am referring to rules and regularities with a more diffuse beginning and circulation in time and space, I use the word "traditions."

The Elusive Shadow

Although I draw primarily on examples from the history of painting, a literary example may also be useful: Hans Christian Andersen's elusive story "Skyggen" ("The Shadow").

Very briefly, this story is about a learned man — who writes about the true, the good, and the beautiful in this world — and his shadow. They part company for some time (the shadow leaves the man for a beautiful young girl), but they meet again later. Toward the end of the story, the shadow demands that his former master be his shadow. When the learned man refuses, he is declared insane and sentenced to death. The former shadow then marries the daughter of a king.

Literary critics and scholars have interpreted this story in a bewildering variety of ways, and their efforts represent many literary and intellectual traditions. In fact, more than eighteen different interpretations have been proposed of this story.[3]

The first interpretations were more or less biographical, for they were based on the assumption that it contained references to Hans Christian Andersen himself and to people that he had met, like the famous scientist H. C. Ørsted and the poet Edvard Collin, though opinions differed as to who was who. Some scholars identified the learned man with Ørsted or with Andersen himself, whereas the shadow was identified variously with Collin, a caricature of the author, the critic Johan Ludvig Heiberg, or the poet H. P. Holst.

Later the story was interpreted as being about the antagonism between a great thinker and those who use and exploit his thoughts by popularizing them. Sadly enough, according to this interpretation of the story, those who exploit the works of original thinkers turn out to be victorious.

Scholars with rather more psychological than biographical interests suggested that the story was not about two different people; the man and his shadow represented different sides of the same person. Psychoanalytic approaches have also been tried. For example, Eigil Nyborg has interpreted the tale in the light of C. G. Jung's theories and has construed the shadow as an archetypical figure, as our "alter ego." Arne Duve has proposed a straightforward and simple psychoanalytic interpretation of the story, in which the shadow becomes Andersen's false consciousness.

Sven Möller Kristensen has suggested that the learned man never even comes close to reality, and that he only in his dreams surmises what is important in life. According to Kristensen, the shadow has the power in this world, and the ideals of the learned man have a corresponding lack of power. According to Niels Kofoed, however, the man and his shadow are two potential sides of the same personality. The story preaches the world-view of the Nietzschean superman and the gospel of nihilism.

There are also several Marxist interpretations. Harald Rue sees the story as a conflict between creative spirits and those who administer them to death, and as an attack on the Danish bureaucratic system. A more consistent Marxist approach has been suggested by Peer Sören-sen, who has denied that the shadow is a study in individual psychology. In his interpretation, the tale is an individualized conception of a social state of crisis. In this view, life in a capitalist society appears the way the shadow has portrayed it.

Two Problems

The two main problems presented in this chapter can be stated as follows:

(P1) What role (or roles), if any, does knowledge of various kinds of tra-ditions and conventions play in the understanding of works of art?

(P2) If there are no tradition-independent criteria of rationality, in what sense can there be rational comparisons between interpreta-tions proposed in different traditions?

The connection between the two problems may not seem obvious. But one of the aims of criticism of the arts and of research on art, literature, and music is to help us understand and appreciate works of art. With this in mind, (P1) leads to questions about the extent to which our under-standing of works of art is tradition-dependent.

The thesis that there are no tradition-independent criteria of ration-ality has been vigorously put forward and supported by, for example, Alasdair MacIntyre (1988, 351).[4] Another well-known critic of the idea of tradition-independent standards of rationality is Joseph Margolis. As an alternative to naive realism and self-defeating relativism, Margolis (1976) has proposed what he calls a "robust relativism."[5] Having dis-cussed Margolis's views elsewhere, I shall comment briefly on some of MacIntyre's views at the end of this essay. Should these views be mistaken, then obviously the problems of commensurability and rationality in the explanation and interpretation of works of art would be much easier to come to terms with.

SOME ASSUMPTIONS

To simplify the discussion of these problems, I shall put forth three assumptions. I have argued for the first assumption at some length elsewhere,[6] and I shall not repeat the arguments and qualifications given there but simply state the assumption as briefly as possible:

(A1) Art is not primarily a form of communication.

If art were primarily or merely a form of communication, then familiarity with certain types of codes and conventions would obviously be necessary—and perhaps also sufficient—for understanding both what the works mean and what the artist meant. But it is more difficult and hence more interesting to discuss the problems just stated on the assumption above.

Already in 1975 I advocated what I then called "the action-focused conception of art."[7] The progress made since then in the philosophical theory of action has made this proposal appear more fruitful today than it perhaps was then. Thus, the second assumption can be stated as follows:

(A2) To create a work of art is to perform an action, or a series of actions.

This assumption, if taken seriously, encourages critics and theorists to explore the possibilities of applying the conceptual framework used in the analysis of actions to, for example, descriptions, explanations, and interpretations of artworks, as well as to the emergence of new traditions and movements within the various art forms. One thing that can be gained by the action-focused approach is, I think, a clearer picture of the relations between different modes of understanding works of art, particularly between interpretations and explanations.

To what extent are rules and conventions embedded in the actual actions and practices of artists and critics? Under what conditions can they be abstracted from these practices in a nonarbitrary way by scholars and critics? These questions are central both to our understanding of art and to the idea that criticism and scholarship is a form of rational inquiry.

The third assumption is this:

(A3) Traditions and conventions can in a nonarbitrary way be abstracted from the practices of artists and scholars.

Obviously, conventions and traditions do not exist in a pure or raw form; they are embedded in the practices of artists and other agents participating in the art world, and they have to be described and interpreted. Like everything else, these practices can be described and interpreted in many ways.

The major sources of our information about traditions and conventions are:

words	actions	attitudes
of/by the artist		
of/by others		

I shall assume that it is possible to abstract traditions and conventions in a nonarbitrary way by combining information of these various kinds and by correcting one kind of information in the light of other kinds in an attempt to achieve coherence and simplicity. This, of course, raises a number of questions about the possibility of knowledge in the humanities and the social sciences. But to explore these problems here would carry us too far afield at the present time; I shall simply assume that such knowledge is possible and, in particular, shall proceed on the assumption that (A3) is reasonable.

The Role of Conventions

Returning for a moment to Andersen's "Skyggen," it is clear that there are various sorts of genre expectations and conventions involved both in the production and in the reading of this story. Is it a fairy tale, a fable, a myth, or a disguised memoir? What genre it is supposed to belong to is obviously important for how it is understood.

In distinguishing among conventions of different types and exploring their roles, I draw both on recent analytic philosophy of language and on the concept of "habitus" developed by the French sociologist Pierre Bourdieu. What role does knowledge of these conventions play in the understanding of cultural change? How are they related to different types of interpretation?

The first general thesis to be discussed here can be stated in the following way:

> (T1) Familiarity with some conventions is necessary but not sufficient for understanding artworks and the interactions between artists and beholders.

A weaker thesis is, of course, that knowledge of conventions is useful, though neither necessary nor sufficient, for understanding works of art. However, I shall stick my neck out and argue for the stronger thesis that such knowledge is indeed necessary—with qualifications to be made explicit below.

Thesis (T1) is hardly trivial. Many scholars seem to think that the importance of conventions for creating, understanding, and evaluating works of art has been exaggerated by George Dickie, Jonathan Culler, Umberto Eco, Ernst Gombrich, Nelson Goodman, and others, who in different ways have stressed the crucial role of conventions in the arts. Brian Baxter (1983), for example, has tried to show that knowledge of conventions in works of art is either irrelevant or otiose:

> What I have argued so far, then, is that knowledge of conventions where they occur in art works is irrelevant to our understanding of art works unless they furnish descriptions appropriate to imaginative perception of the works, but that when they do this they are otiose, for the features so described can be grasped under alternative descriptions which do not involve reference to conventions, and in the case of some important classes of works, this has to occur. (330)

> To put the point in a nutshell—we fully understand a work of art if we are alive to whatever poignancy it possesses, and a work does not possess poignancy by convention, even if there are conventional ways of achieving poignancy. (332)

Here Baxter seems to suggest that knowledge of conventions is not sufficient for understanding artworks, a very different claim from the one I am making. Even so, I have not been convinced by his arguments that (T1) is untenable. For one thing, his arguments presuppose a certain view of the nature of art and of the function of art in our lives. Yet these views are not made explicit in his paper.

Of course, the word "poignancy" does suggest the general direction of his thinking. But it is not clear to me why the perception of a work's poignancy cannot be facilitated by information about traditions and conventions. Personally, I experience Nicolas Poussin's *Et in Arcadia Ego* as more poignant after having read Erwin Panofsky's interpretation of it than I did before;[8] vision can be armed by knowledge. At any rate, it may be worth making a case for (T1). But first, a few words of clarification.

Admittedly, this thesis is obscure in some important ways. To make clear which thesis I am arguing for, I shall comment on some of these obscurities in the hope of being able to eliminate or somewhat clarify them. To begin with, it should be noted that the expression "understanding art works" is elliptical. What, more precisely, is it that should be understood? Understanding how they were technically executed? What the structure of artworks is? The meaning of artworks? What they express? What the artist meant? Or perhaps something else?

Second, works of art, like anything else, can be understood more or less well. We must therefore also distinguish among *degrees* of understanding. The prima facie plausibility of thesis (T1) varies with the degrees of desired understanding. The lower the degree is, the more implausible, in my view, is the thesis. In other words, it is easier to argue for (T1) if full understanding is what is at stake, though it should be noted that this is precisely what Baxter seems to deny, since he writes, "we *fully* understand a work of art if we are alive to whatever poignancy it possesses" (332, my italics).

To understand something fully, we must, it seems, know everything there is to know about it. In that case, it is in my view fairly clear that knowledge of several of the kinds of conventions mentioned below is both useful and necessary. But in order not to make things too easy for myself, I shall suppose that "understanding" in (T1) can be replaced not only by "full or complete understanding" but also with "adequate or good understanding." Since, however, there is a gradual and not a sharp distinction between "full" and "adequate," I shall resist the temptation of trying to spell out the criteria for these varying degrees of understanding.

By supplementing the thesis in these and similar ways, the general thesis (T1) can be replaced by a number of more precise and specific theses. Moreover, the thesis does not say that it is necessary to be familiar with *all* conventions, only with some, to understand works of art. Obviously, then, we have to specify which ones. To be able to do this, we need to distinguish among conventions of different kinds: some of them may be necessary, others not, for understanding works of art in one sense or another.

Different Kinds of Traditions and Conventions

LIFE-STYLE TRADITIONS (HABITUS)

Here the natural point of departure is the work of the French sociologist Pierre Bourdieu (1979). Like Bourdieu, I want to distinguish between the objective or material conditions of individuals and their habitus; the habitus is conditioned by objectively classifiable conditions of existence as well as by the position occupied within the structure of these conditions (437).

The habitus, in Bourdieu's sense, is not a mental state of a certain person or class of persons. He makes explicit that this concept should be understood in a dispositional sense: "The habitus is necessity internalized and converted into a disposition that generates meaningful practices and meaning-giving perceptions; it is a general transposable disposition which carries out a systematic, universal application — beyond the limits of what has been directly learnt — of the necessity inherent in the learning conditions" (170). Bourdieu also makes clear that the person or group in question need not be aware of these dispositions.[9]

The concept of a habitus could be a useful conceptual tool in the attempts to study the changing social functions of art and the social history of artists, critics, and writers. One of the interesting features of Bourdieu's analysis is the explicit connection made between this concept and the concept of taste: "Taste, the propensity and capacity to appropriate (materially or symbolically) a given class of classified, classifying objects or practices, is the generative formula of life-style, a unitary set of distinctive preferences which express the same expressive intention in the specific logic of each of the symbolic sub-spaces, furniture, clothing, language or body hexis" (173).[10]

The idea of the habitus as both a "structuring structure, which organizes practices and the perception of practices" and a "structured structure" (170) can be applied to the situation of artists as well as any other group in the art world: critics, gallery owners, museum curators, collectors, and so forth. The explicit connection between "habitus" and "taste" makes such applications very natural.

CONVENTIONS OF THE CRAFT

Conventions of the craft vary across the different art forms. A description that would try to cover at least all the major art forms would be both complex and space-consuming. To simplify, I therefore concentrate on painting. Here, too, there are traditions and conventions of many different kinds. For example, there are traditions and conventions concerning the choice of canvas, the way the canvas should be prepared (white color, glue, grisaille . . .), the kinds of colors to be used, how they are to be mixed, how these colors are applied to the canvas, what sort of brushes are to be employed, whether the entire canvas should be covered with color or parts of it left uncolored, how much turpentine, oil, or wax is to be used in the preparation of a given color, how thick or thin the color in question should be, the extent to which varnish is applied in between different layers of color or once the painting is finished, and so forth.

Some of these conventions are of obvious aesthetic importance. For example, variations in the preparation of the canvas will give varying tones to the painting, as does varnish. The aesthetic importance is perhaps even more obvious when we consider the effects produced by the brushwork, the thickness of the colors (one thin layer as opposed to several thick layers on top of one another), and by the way in which the colors are mixed (which can be demonstrated by comparing the works of, say, Vincent van Gogh and Paul Gauguin).

AESTHETIC/ARTISTIC CONVENTIONS

The distinction between conventions belonging to this group and to the previous one cannot always be sharply maintained. For example, conventions concerning how the colors are to be applied to the canvas pertain both to the craft and to aesthetics. In this respect, it may be instructive to compare, for instance, the pointillistic technique of Georges Seurat or Alfred Sisley with the technique of the expressionists Emil Nolde or Edvard Munch, or those of Fernand Léger and Bengt Lindström.

David Novitz (1976) has called attention to the important distinction between what he calls "umbrella conventions" and "schemata." The former are exemplified by general methods of representing things, like stick-figure drawings, whereas the latter are rules for representing objects of a particular kind, like an ear, a face, a foot. In his now classical book *Art and Illusion*, Ernst H. Gombrich has given us many examples of such schemata and has called attention to their importance in pictorial representation.[11]

Other kinds of conventions also belong to this group. For example, it goes without saying that this category includes traditions concerning modulation and modeling, as well as ways of achieving rhythm, movement, and depth in pictures (by perspective, overlapping, colors, and so on). The same holds for the convention of furnishing titles of different kinds (and with different functions), like *Distressed Woman* or *Opus I*.

Genre conventions of various kinds can also be characterized as aesthetic/artistic: for example, they define the border separating landscape paintings, still lifes, and collages. In literature, there are conventions characterizing sonnets, novels, short stories, and other literary forms of expression, which provide the writer with a challenge that he or she can meet in a variety of ways.

SEMANTIC (SYMBOLIC) CONVENTIONS IN A NARROW SENSE

To this group belong codes and conventions that may or may not be recorded in books like those by Andrea Alciati and Cesare Ripa, which served as dictionaries for painters, particularly from the fifteenth century to the seventeenth century. But both before and after this period, painters have used motifs with a recognized and well-established symbolic significance, such as a skull (to stand for death), a mirror (to represent vanity), a lion (to stand for strength, among other things), a halo with a cross (to identify God or Jesus), or a palm leaf (to identify pilgrims), to mention only a few obvious examples.

The underlying conventions that are the basis of the symbolism may be more or less widely accepted, temporally and geographically. Their roots may vary, and they may dissolve for different reasons. Many of these symbols are ambiguous and can have multiple meanings. But since I have discussed symbols of this kind extensively elsewhere,[12] I have chosen to be brief here.

SPEECH-ACT CONVENTIONS

To create a work of art is to perform a certain kind of act, as suggested in (A2), above. To understand what the artist wanted to say, it is necessary to know what he wants those who look at (read, listen to . . .) the work to think of, that he wants them to recognize that this is what he intended, and that he wants this recognition to be achieved by means of their familiarity with the features of the work and with the tradition and genre to which it belongs, and so forth.

Speech-act conventions have to do with the communicative aspects or functions of works of art. They are not exclusive to or uniquely characteristic of works of art. On the contrary, they abound in the sort of communication that takes place in ordinary language.[13] Hence, to call attention to conventions of this kind is not to abandon assumption (A1), above. It is to point out that the creation of certain works of art may share a number of features with other human activities or productions: gestures, advertisements, blueprints, and commercials, for example.

Thus, if these conventions are relevant to the understanding of a particular work of art X, they are in my view not relevant to X qua work of art. I realize that this is controversial and goes against the views expressed by scholars like David Carrier (1983), Sören Kjörup (1978), David Novitz (1977), and Mark Roskill (1983). But once again I refer the reader who is interested in a fuller discussion of the view suggested here to some of my other writings.[14]

CONVENTIONS OF VIEWING

Conventions of viewing include those concerning when, where, how, and by whom works of art should be contemplated. For what sort of audience is the work intended? How long, under what conditions, in what setting, and in what light should the work be presented and viewed? Should the viewer let him- or herself be absorbed by the interplay of colors, forms, and shapes, look for provocations, or use the work politically? What sort of comments are appropriate? How are different motifs perceived? What conceptions of, and attitudes toward, men and women and their relations to each other are revealed by the ways in which more or less naked men and women have been depicted in different cultures?[15]

Similar questions could be asked about literature. Social changes and technological innovations have had an impact on the relations between authors and readers in several ways.[16] The rise and decline of literary salons, the emergence of public libraries, urbanization and the increasing need to commute daily on trains and subways between home and work, and the rapid development of the press and television are all indications of changes that are likely to affect many of the conventions of when, where, how, and by whom books are to be read (and written).

The possibility of reproducing works of art may ultimately change both the concept of art and the relations of large groups to works of art, including their preferences and expectations.

The relations between these different kinds of conventions would be worth exploring in some detail. For example, it should be noted that Bourdieu stresses that habitus "generates meaningful practices and meaning-giving perceptions" (170). But I shall have to leave this for another occasion. In order to explore these relations, it would be necessary to distinguish further among, for one thing, various senses of "meaning."

Thesis (T1) Revisited

Let us now return to (T1) and determine the relevance of the distinctions suggested in the previous section. I argue that we need to make these distinctions in order to give a correct and balanced picture of the role of conventions in understanding art.

Familiarity with an artist's habitus in the sense indicated above may be necessary for certain explanations of his work, that is, for successful attempts to answer questions like, Why did he make it? Of what objective class conditions, conflicts of interests, and perceptions of such conditions and conflicts is the work symptomatic? But such knowledge is necessary neither for descriptions nor for certain symbolic interpretations of artworks. Whether it is necessary for other types of interpretations depends on the nature of the interpretive goal that is taken for granted.

Familiarity with conventions of the craft of the kinds mentioned above is, however, obviously necessary for certain descriptions of the artist's work, that is, for successful attempts to answer questions like, How did he make it? If certain assumptions about human actions are made (for example, that action, in contrast to behavior, is intentional), knowledge of this kind may also be necessary for certain kinds of explanations of art works.

Moreover, knowledge of aesthetic and artistic traditions of the kind described above is clearly necessary for some common types of descriptions and interpretations of works of art, that is, for successful attempts to answer questions like, What does this express? Why did the artist do this? This latter question is here to be understood as intentionalistic in an innocent sense. To say that he did something in order to achieve depth or movement or tension in a picture presupposes that there is depth, movement, or tension in that picture. But such knowledge is obviously not necessary for understanding the symbolic significance of the work.

Familiarity with semantic codes and conventions in the narrow sense mentioned above is clearly necessary for certain symbolic interpretations of the agent's work, that is, for successful attempts to answer questions like, Are there any symbols or allegories in this work? What is the symbolic meaning of this or that motif? What does this allegory mean? Whether they are also necessary for other kinds of interpretations depends on the interpretive goal that is taken for granted.

Furthermore, knowledge of the conventions that, for want of a better name, I called "speech-act conventions" is not necessary in order to describe a work of art. They *may* be necessary to explain why the work has some of the features it has, given certain assumptions about rationality and human agency. But such familiarity is certainly necessary in order to understand what the artist meant or wanted to say.

Finally, familiarity with conventions of viewing is not necessary for understanding artworks themselves, but it is necessary for understanding variations in the reception of artworks at different times and places, including changes in the history of literary and critical practices, institutions, and so on.

The Possibility of Anachronisms

So far, I have not said anything about the geographical or temporal localization of the conventions distinguished earlier. Nevertheless, it is essential for any theory concerning the understanding of art that this lacuna be filled. For what purpose do we want to understand works of art? The answer to this question is obviously related to deeper questions regarding the nature of art, the role of criticism, and the function of art in our society.

The purposes are numerous, but for the sake of simplicity I shall here distinguish very crudely among only three main kinds, which I call *historical, social,* and *aesthetic* understanding. Schematically, they can be described as follows, in terms of clusters of subgoals:

Historical understanding: the goals are to place the work of art in its historical context: to see it as its contemporaries saw it; to find out what the artist meant, or could have meant; to try to find out how it was understood by contemporary readers, viewers, and listeners.
Social understanding: the goals are to discern what the work has to say or suggest about contemporary psychological, moral, and social problems and to study it in the light of these contemporary problems; to use it to shed light on contemporary living conditions and social interactions; and to let experiences of these conditions and interactions enhance the interest of the work.
Aesthetic understanding: the goals are to exercise and liberate one's imagination; to enjoy the interplay of combinations of colors, shapes, and forms; to get as much enjoyment and gratification as possible out of the work; to make it as aesthetically interesting and rewarding as possible.

Needless to say, both the goals and the methods of arriving at these various types of understanding deserve a much fuller account than I can give here. But for the time being I shall only stress that they need not necessarily exclude one another. Perhaps an exclusive concentration on historical understanding will deprive us of some aesthetic delight and enjoyment. Analogously, perhaps an exclusive concentration on the ability of the work to provide aesthetic enjoyment will impoverish our historical understanding of that work. Whether this is so or not is, in my view, an open and empirical question, which cannot be decided a priori.

Let me illustrate the distinction between historical and aesthetic understanding by drawing on an example discussed by Monroe C. Beardsley (1970, 19). Suppose the phrase "plastic arm" is found in a poem. Suppose also that this expression should not be understood as "an arm made of plastic." Why not?

Is it because such a reading is anachronistic, since the poem was written in 1744, when plastic had not yet been invented? In that case, a historical understanding is sought. The conventions supporting the interpretation have to have been familiar to the artist and his circle, or at least contemporary with him, so that he could have known them. Even if lack of evidence seldom makes it possible to arrive at any definite conclusions, it is at least in principle possible that there could be correct, final, or definite interpretations of this kind. ("Definite" or "final" does not, of course, mean "unequivocal." A final interpretation could very well be that the work is deliberately ambiguous.)

Or is the interpretation mistaken because such a reading does not fit the context, being incompatible with many other features of the text? Because there are alternative and better interpretations, which make the study of the text more rewarding and increase its aesthetic value? In that case, what is wanted is an aesthetic understanding in which the various elements of the poem fit together. The conventions supporting the interpretations need not be known by or contemporary with the artist. To critics embarking on this enterprise, the idea of a "correct" or "final" or "definite" interpretation is a chimera.

How does the earlier distinction between *degrees* of understanding connect with this distinction between *kinds* of understanding? It is not easy to state this relation simply. Perhaps we should begin by distinguishing between degrees of understanding within each of the three kinds. We may then go on to note that a full understanding of a given issue or object can be achieved only if more than one kind of understanding is involved. If understanding presupposes application, as is stressed by Hans-Georg Gadamer and his followers in the hermeneutic tradition, then aesthetic or historical understanding is not enough; full understanding certainly also presupposes what above was called "social understanding."

What about the methods (deductive, inductive; analytical, synthetical; atomistic, holistic) of understanding? Without going into the explanation/understanding controversy,[17] I shall simply assume that understanding is a pragmatic notion in the sense that it must be related to a previous puzzle or to someone's state of ignorance; hence, what may help a person or group A to understand something may not help B understand this, and one of the key methods to be used may involve constructing meaningful patterns or wholes (i) that make sense and (ii) in which the relation between parts and whole is made clear.

The importance of the conventions discussed earlier varies with the kind of understanding that is sought. If, for example, what Gombrich is interested in is historical rather than aesthetic or social understanding, then his emphasis on the importance of conventions is easy to accept. If, however, Baxter wants to achieve aesthetic understanding and nothing else, then his thesis that knowledge of conventions is either irrelevant or otiose becomes more understandable, particularly if this is combined with a certain view of the nature of art and of the role of criticism.

Hopefully this is enough to provide a background for a concluding discussion of the possibility of rationality in the interpretation and explanation of the arts, particularly when works of art are discussed by critics and scholars from different intellectual and aesthetic traditions. Are such interpretations at all commensurable?

A General Thesis about Commensurability

There is an important distinction between interpretations that are different but supplement each other and interpretations that are different and in conflict with each other. The latter ones are perhaps not as common as one might think, but both groups can be found in the interpretations of Andersen's "Skyggen."

A biographical interpretation does not, it seems, necessarily exclude a Marxist or a psychoanalytic interpretation. But it is more difficult to maintain that this story is at the same time both about two persons and about two different dimensions of the same person. Some scholars, like Peer Sörensen, also explicitly reject the interpretations of several of their predecessors.

The problem now is if and to what extent interpretations stated in the conceptual framework of different intellectual traditions, like Marxism, psychoanalysis, or New Criticism, are commensurable; and, if they are, in what sense. If such interpretations are *not* commensurable, then they cannot come into conflict with each other, and it becomes hard to understand in what sense there could be a rational dialogue between critics from these and other different intellectual traditions.

The second main thesis to be discussed can be stated as follows:

(T2) Interpretations proposed in different intellectual traditions (and stated in the conceptual framework of these traditions) are commensurable, especially if the traditions are close to each other.

This thesis is, however, also badly in need of clarification in some important respects. To forestall misunderstandings and to make clear which thesis I am arguing for, I shall now comment on some of these ambiguities in an attempt to resolve or at least somewhat attenuate them.

First, the expression "close to each other" is obviously vague. What I wish to say is merely that the difficulties involved in comparing different interpretations increase if the latter belong to traditions with very different conceptions of art, the role of critics, and the aims of interpretation; with conflicting metaphysical and rhetorical assumptions.

Even if there is a gulf between, say, Marxist and psychoanalytic criticism, both of them originated in roughly the same German-speaking culture in Europe and at about the same time. It should therefore be easier to compare them with each other than with an interpretation stated in the normative and theoretical framework of an alien culture that is far more distant in time and place, particularly if the concept of art in that culture differed sharply from our present-day concept of art, and if art in that culture mainly had ritual, magical, or religious functions.

Secondly, much in this thesis hangs on the expression "different traditions." "Tradition" is a vague notion in several respects. Accordingly, the next important question that arises is, What are the criteria of the identity of traditions? Under what conditions do two artists or artworks belong to the same or different traditions?

For example, we may want to say that two artists (or, *mutatis mutandis,* two artworks) belong to the same tradition, if and only if

a. they have been inspired by the same master or key group of artists (thinkers, writers, prophets), or
b. one of them has been influenced directly or indirectly by the other, or
c. they have solved certain problems in similar ways, or exemplify similar approaches in the way they have solved certain problems, or
d. they share certain fundamental theoretical and normative assumptions, or
e. their thinking and practice have gone through similar epistemological crises, and have been revised in the same way, or
f. they use the same standards of rationality.

A difficulty with suggestion (b) is that there are cases in which one may be tempted to say that one artist was influenced by another, and yet they do not belong to the same tradition. For example, Picasso's early works were clearly influenced by Toulouse-Lautrec's works, and yet there is a sense in which these painters belong to different traditions. If, however, (b) is to appear plausible, it is necessary to be specific about the claims of influence; Picasso's early works can very well have been influenced by some of Toulouse-Lautrec's, although — considering the total oeuvre of these painters — a case can be made for saying that they belong to different traditions.

Anyway, MacIntyre seems to have a different concept of tradition than any of the three first criteria of identity would indicate. As I read him, the last two criteria would fit in better with his description of three characteristic phases or traditions: a first, in which the relevant beliefs, texts, and authorities have not yet been put in question; a second, in which inadequacies of various types have been identified, but not yet remedied; and a third, in which a response to those inadequacies has resulted in a set of reformulations and reevaluations.[18] This account may appear to be more readily applicable to traditions like the Judaic one, where commentaries on and interpretations of the Torah and other religious documents play a crucial role. But I think that it can also be applied to the sorts of conventions that are relevant in the context of art, *mutatis mutandis*.

The third point in (T2) that obviously requires comment concerns the criteria of commensurability. Under what conditions shall we say that two interpretations are — or are not — commensurable? Here are a few proposals, the first of which is inspired by some of Sir Karl Popper's ideas:[19]

(C1) Interpretation A in tradition T is commensurable with interpretation B in T' if what would falsify one of these interpretations is a proper subset of what would falsify the other.

The problem with this criterion is that the idea of true and false interpretations has a very limited range of application in the criticism of art and literature, with the exception perhaps of certain specific kinds of philological and historical interpretations. When the aim of interpretation is to achieve aesthetic or social understanding, in the sense indicated earlier, we need a criterion of a different type.

The criterion above should not be conflated with the stronger one, which Thomas Kuhn (1962) and his followers seem to be flirting with:[20]

(C2) Interpretation A in T is commensurable with interpretation B in T' if T and T' share the same theoretical and in particular ontological, methodological, and normative presuppositions.

A corollary of this criterion seems to be that A in this case cannot be translated into the language of T', and likewise B cannot be translated into the language of T (which is another possible requirement of commensurability).

But even if one of these interpretations cannot be translated into the language of other traditions, they may perhaps be compared by checking, not their connotations and their intensions, but rather their extensions, and by checking the extent to which the proposed interpretations solve common problems (e.g., achieve historical, social, or aesthetic understanding of the works discussed).

The literature on Kuhn's incommensurability thesis is enormous. Fortunately, it is hardly necessary for my limited purposes here to probe into the many exegetical and philosophical problems raised in the wake of the controversies between Popper, Kuhn, and Paul Feyerabend.

In any event, the Kuhnian criterion (C2) seems to me to be too strong in the present context; I therefore opt for the following one:

(C3) Interpretation A in tradition T is commensurable with interpretation B in tradition T' if T and T' share the same standards of rationality.

This seems to be the criterion adopted by MacIntyre. A complication is that the standards of rationality can be divided into several subgroups (logical, etc.), and there may be a partial overlapping between the standards of rationality in different traditions. It need not be a matter of either total agreement or total disagreement. Even so, the criterion has certain advantages over the previous ones. For one thing, it does not on logical grounds preclude the possibility of comparing interpretations in different intellectual traditions of one particular work.

Comments on Some Arguments for and against (T2)

Is (T2) tenable, given the criterion of commensurability (C3) and any of the criteria of identity of traditions mentioned above? This is not obvious. If we begin with the criteria of identity of traditions, there seems to be no problem with the first four, but the remaining ones create difficulties—though I believe they may be overcome.

There does seem to be a workable strategy of comparing different interpretations of the same work in a rational way, which is to check whether they account for all the features of the work under consideration. For example, consider again some of the interpretations of Andersen's story "Skyggen." Does a Marxist or a psychoanalytic interpretation account for all the features of the story? If this question is meaningful and can be answered positively, there does seem to be a way of comparing such very different kinds of interpretation.

The obvious problem with this strategy is that the features of a work of art X are relative to the description of X, and any X can be described in different ways in different traditions. There is no "neutral," tradition-independent way of describing X. To be sure, there are many common features in the various descriptions of "Skyggen," but each focuses on slightly different aspects of the story and describes the relations among the elements somewhat differently.

Two descriptions may have different meanings, and if they are formulated within different theoretical and ontological frameworks, they may well be incommensurable, at least according to (C2). But perhaps it would help to concentrate on an extensional analysis and comparison of these descriptions. There *are* certain basic features of artworks to be accounted for, though I do not want to identify these "basic features" in a positivistic manner with "hard facts" or "raw data."

Moreover, suppose that the goal of a particular interpretation, formulated in a certain tradition T, is to achieve social or aesthetic understanding of the sort indicated earlier. Can we exclude the fact that those critics belonging to T think that this goal has been achieved but that those belonging to different traditions disagree? I admit that this is a genuine difficulty. But how often does it arise? In order that we might answer this question, it would be necessary to analyze the critical disagreements empirically.

What is relevant here is not the possibility that there may be many true but incomplete descriptions of an action or work of art; the point of departure must be all true statements about the work X that would make a difference to the desired historical, social, or aesthetic understanding of a given work. Even if this were not so, to admit the existence of the problem is not to say or suggest that we are caught in a vicious circle or an infinite regress.

It may also be argued against this thesis that when the followers of Jacques Derrida and the followers of the New Critics or Marxists quarrel about how a work of art should be understood, there seems to be no way of finding a common ground. Derrida may be criticized sharply and devastatingly, as he has been by John Ellis (1989), but this apparently has made no impression on his followers: they probably consider such objections to be based on assumptions that they—and Derrida—do not share; hence, they think they can disregard them.

Here it is obviously important to distinguish between saying (i) that it is in principle impossible for any two critics A and B to enter into a rational dialogue with each other if they belong to different traditions; and (ii) that this is in practice very difficult because they have different conceptual frameworks, were brought up in different rhetorical and metaphysical traditions, have different standards of excellence, and so forth; and (iii) that this is difficult because of their personal limitations (their sense of prestige, their lack of imagination or knowledge of each other's traditions, etc.). I would be inclined to accept both (ii) and (iii) but to be skeptical of (i).

In my view, MacIntyre has successfully undermined simple relativistic and perspectivistic arguments against theses like (T2). The relativist and the perspectivist have both failed to see the different ways in which traditions can be rationally criticized.[21] He has also given an interesting and plausible account of how it may be possible to criticize a tradition externally:

> They may find themselves compelled to recognize . . . a cogent and illuminating explanation [within the alien theory]—cogent and illuminating, that is, by their own standards—of why their own intellectual tradition had been unable to solve its problems or restore its coherence. The standards by which they judge this explanation to be cogent and illuminating will be the very same standards by which they have found their own tradition wanting in the face of epistemological crises. (364)

Though the traditions he discusses (Islam, Judaism, Augustinian Catholicism, etc.) differ in important ways from the kinds of traditions I am concerned with here, I think that what he says could also be applied to the problems dealt with in this chapter.

Conclusion

I have tried to show that familiarity with several types of conventions is necessary to understand art, and I have also argued for the possibility of rationality in the interpretation and explanation of works of art, even when these artworks are discussed by critics and scholars from different intellectual and aesthetic traditions. Many questions, however, which I have been able to discuss only briefly, remain to be explored in depth.

Moreover, this set of conventions defines a horizon of expectations, and cultural change and innovation involve challenging this horizon. The artist follows some of these traditions; otherwise, the spectator would not know what sort of object has been created. But certain other conventions are challenged or broken; otherwise, the artist would not have done anything new or original. If this challenge is accepted by others, we have the beginning of a cultural change.[22]

Notes

Chapter One: Again, Theory

1. The article "Against Theory" was originally published in *Critical Inquiry* 8 (1982). It was later reprinted, with critical responses and replies by the authors, in *Against Theory: Literary Studies and the New Pragmatism,* edited by W. J. T. Mitchell (1985). All citations are to the reprinted version.

2. The formulation of these theses is my own. On the one hand, I have attempted to be more explicit than Knapp and Michaels about the kinds of conceptual connections that are supposedly involved in each of the two cases. On the other hand, these formulations are purposely guarded and vague in certain important respects in order that the resulting statements will be at least plausible. For example, I have tried to bypass questions like the following. The particular token of the first sentence of my copy of *The Last Days of Pompeii* was produced by a printing press. I assume that this printed inscription is both meaningful and an instance of an English sentence despite the fact that it, i.e., this very sentence-token, was not produced by an agent intending to mean something by the inscription. I take it that Knapp and Michaels would agree that the inscription is meaningful and is an instance of a sentence in virtue of its bearing the right relation to some earlier inscription by Bulwer-Lytton. Thus, my formulations of the theses attempt to accommodate this. In fact, it is hard to come up with clear, *detailed* formulations that are correct, but I am less interested in the correctness of versions of these theses than in the role of the theses in the larger argument of "Against Theory."

3. The relevant essays, along with others, are collected in Grice 1989. See especially essays 1–7, 14, and 18.

4. The literature generated by Grice's work is enormous. Three important books are those of Stephen Schiffer (1972), Jonathan Bennett (1976), and Brian Loar (1981).

5. See, for example, Schiffer's (1972, 130) well-known account of the "timeless" meaning of a whole utterance (in a linguistic community).

6. Unfortunately, there is no standard terminology for the concept adopted in the literature. My choice of "context-loaded" was suggested by the use of "value-loaded" in Barwise and Perry 1983.

7. If the utterance involves a non-defective use of a declarative sentence, then the context-loaded linguistic meaning is a *proposition* that can be assessed for truth or falsity. Sentences in other moods, e.g., imperative and interrogative, demand distinct but analogous conceptions.

8. The first four characterizations are drawn from Fish 1980, 291, 312, 280, 277 respectively. The last is from Fish 1989, 4. The list could be considerably enlarged.

9. See also the incredible list of sixteen theses, which Fish thinks that a belief in linguistic meaning either presupposes or entails. For example, number 14 is "that the

mark of a civilized (lawful) community is the acknowledgment of that standard [an abstract, 'context-free' standard of rationality] as a referee or judge" (6). The sheer exuberance of Fish's conception here might be refreshing to philosophers of language who are more usually accused of working on narrow, technical, and socially irrelevant topics. However, it also makes it impossible to be sure what Fish thinks he is talking about.

10. Although similar claims can be found elsewhere in Fish's writings, these remarks are especially pertinent, since they appear in the essay "Consequences" (1985), Fish's commentary on "Against Theory."

11. For example, we get an uncharacteristically blunt statement in the remark "any meaning a sentence might be seen to have . . . would not be constrained by any meanings the words themselves (*now a nonsense phrase* [my italics]) contain" (1989, 8). Or, he seems to deny that words have meaning in "a normative linguistic system" (1980, 318).

12. Here, and in much of his writing, Fish is concerned to repudiate the idea that it is a constraint on the correct interpretation of a literary work that it be consistent with facts about the linguistic meanings of the expressions that constitute it. Because he rejects the concept of linguistic meaning, Fish thinks that any such constraint is nonsense. But it is hard to grasp what all the fuss over some putative abstract constraint is about. If, in reading a literary work, I want to know what the author meant to express by using the words he/she did, and, if I believe that he/she did use them to express one or more of the meanings they have in the author's language, then, I *am* constrained to respect the relevant linguistic meanings. But, of course, what thus constrains me are my own beliefs and intentions in reading—not some general, abstract, metaliterary principle. Of course, it is very often the case that competent readers have, quite reasonably, such intentions and beliefs.

13. Later in this article, Fish argues that it is not a part of the linguistic meaning of sentences of the form "Let's do so-and-so" that any meaningful utterance of such-and-such a sentence constitutes a *proposal* to do so-and-so. I believe he is right about this. More generally, I believe that it is false that, in virtue of its linguistic meaning, an utterance in a fixed grammatical mood M thereby constitutes the performance of an illocutionary act of some associated type M^*. However, it clearly does not follow that *no* account can be given of the linguistic meaning of the various grammatical moods. The topic is subtle and difficult. For Fish's discussion of the point first mentioned, see 1980, 285–91.

14. For an extended presentation of his "skeptical" views, see Quine 1960.

15. I will not attempt to comment on a further thesis that Knapp and Michaels put forward—their conception of what they call, using Hirsch's phrase, "the practical nullity of the idea of intention" (101). On this score, they say, "But this [their positive view] doesn't mean the intentionalists win, since what intentionalists want is a guide to valid interpretation; what they get, however, is simply a description of what everyone always does" (18). Part of what seems to be involved in this is the observation that the (purported) fact that the meaning of a work is what its author intended does not provide the interpreter with a methodology for coming to know what the work means. This is no doubt true. We do not, in general, have a methodology for decid-

ing what intentions people have in acting. At the same time, we do have a somewhat amorphous range of beliefs about what does and does not count as evidence that an agent has acted on such-and-such intentions. If "the meaning of a text" is given by the author's intentions, then we are entitled to draw upon this framework in making and supporting our judgments about what the author intended. Certainly the framework is rich enough to guide us in assessing the plausibility of various relevant interpretive claims. But, again, the whole matter deserves extended discussion.

16. Although the authors give roughly equivalent formulations throughout the text, none of them are fully developed enough to resolve several important ambiguities. One problem of this sort is discussed in the following pages.

17. I have taken the term "verbal meaning" from Hirsch and have assumed, with some doubts, that he uses the term as I have explained it in the text. I might note that Hirsch contrasts "verbal meaning" with what he calls "significance" and treats these as if they exhaust the kinds of meaningfulness a work can have. Significance is verbal meaning as it relates "to a larger context, i.e., another mind, another era, a wider subject matter, an alien system of values, and so on" (Hirsch 1976, 2–3). But, if "the verbal meaning of a text" is appropriately construed in the limited way I have indicated, then a great deal of what we seek to interpret in a work will fall in neither of Hirsch's categories. Why this is so should become clear from the ensuing discussion. For reasons I give, even the fact that it is fictional in *David Copperfield* that Dora dies goes beyond verbal meaning and precedes "significance" as Hirsch uses the term. See also Hirsch 1967. For an excellent consideration of crucial aspects of the work of an interpreter, see the section "The Mechanics of Generation" in Walton 1990, 138–87.

18. I should note, however, that Wimsatt and Beardsley say a bit later, "The use of biographical evidence need not involve intentionalism, because while it may be evidence of what the author intended, it may also be evidence of the meaning of his words and the dramatic character of his utterance" (11). This seems to suggest a contrast between what the author intended (in using the words?) and what the words, as he used them there, meant. If this is the suggestion, it is plainly mistaken. No doubt there is a fair amount of confusion in many of the discussions of this topic. Certainly, the passages quoted here and in the text are, when taken together, quite confusing.

19. Noting his own strong agreement with standard readings of the novel, Mizener says, "The only recourse for criticism confronted by disagreement so radical as this is to such evidence of the author's intention as can be discovered outside the novel" (258). But, he fails to explain why he thinks that facts about what Ford Madox Ford might have intended will convince someone who thinks that the novel cannot be convincingly read in the intended mode.

Chapter Two: Conventions, Creativity, Originality

1. See Elster 1989, chap. 3.

2. From an excerpt of his diary, serialized in the *Sunday Times*.

3. See Elster 1986.

4. I leave unresolved the question of the nature of aesthetic value, except for the

following comment. Aesthetic value is ultimately emotional. One value of a work of art is that it helps us focus and understand emotions that we experience in our lives, outside the artistic experience. Another is that it provides a source of the specifically aesthetic emotions created by contrasts, symmetries, echoes, the resolutions of tensions, and the like. In the best works of art, these two effects reinforce each other. As if by magic, the pleasure of a rhyme that falls into place adds to the poignancy of the emotion that is evoked.

5. There may be a trade-off between the level of the maximum and the extent to which it is approached. The idea of a "minor classic" suggests a high degree of approximation to a low-level local maximum. Conversely, the idea of a "flawed masterpiece" suggests a low degree of approximation to a high-level local maximum.

6. Poincaré 1908a, 49–50.

7. Poincaré 1908b, 51–52.

8. For explorations of this idea see Elster 1979, chap. 2, and Schelling 1984, chaps. 3, 4.

9. For explorations of this idea, see Schelling 1960, chap. 5.

10. For this "deadline effect," see Roth 1987, 36ff.

11. In chapter 2, section 10 of *Sour Grapes,* I cite Michel Foucault and Pierre Bourdieu as examples of this tendency. More generally, functional explanation and psychoanalytic theory embody the tendency to find meaning everywhere.

12. Many examples may be found in Thomas 1971.

13. As Joseph Levenson suggested, "An art-form is 'exhausted' when its practitioners think it is" (1966, 41).

14. I set out this theory more fully in chapter 5 of *Making Sense of Marx.*

Chapter Three: Literary Conventions

1. Thus, Siegfried J. Schmidt (1980, 1984) combines an empiricist and scientist literary theory with a radical conventionalism.

2. Saussure has always been an elusive figure. Early Swiss and French disciples (Charles Bally, Antoine Meillet) developed the sociological and stylistic aspects of his teaching. Phonologists of the Prague school and American distributionalists paid tribute to his notion of linguistic system. Louis Hjelmslev, and later Roland Barthes, saw in Saussure the father of semiology. Jacques Derrida, Jacques Lacan, and the American poststructuralists attribute to him an anti-Aristotelian metaphysics of difference. For a balanced account of Saussure's ideas, see Jonathan Culler 1976. Marc Angenot (1984) offers a vivacious criticism of the use that various theories have made of Saussure's name and ideas during the late sixties and early seventies. Umberto Eco's semiotics (1984) proves the possibility of constructing a synthesis between the Saussurean approach and the tradition of philosophy of language, analytical or not.

3. Although Hjelmslev's major linguistic contribution (1943) has been translated into English, his direct impact on American linguistics and semiotics remains minimal. Quite early, Noam Chomsky's virulent criticism of structuralist models (1957) rendered obsolete the few attempts to study Hjelmslev's thought. It is only through

French semiotics and structuralism that his name started to be mentioned again in the late sixties. A critical study of his contributions and influence is still much needed.

4. See Barthes 1968, Hamon 1973, and Brooke-Rose 1981. Pavel (1985) criticizes the conventionalist theory of realism. Menahem Brinker's important paper (1983) strongly argues against radical conventionalism. See, in the same vein, E. D. Hirsch, Jr.'s attack on conventionalism (1983).

5. Notably in Chomsky 1975. Massimo Piatelli-Palmarini (1979) provides the best collection of papers on the debate between constructivist and innatist theories of language learning. For a devastating criticism of radical innatist arguments, see Putnam 1980.

6. A history of the notion between 1500 and 1750 is provided in Manley 1980. See also Reeves 1982.

7. Hume 1739, 490. Cited in Lewis 1969.

8. Herrnstein Smith 1978, 24–40. An important study of conventions of reading, containing a theoretical introduction and precious bibliographical indications, is Steven Mailloux's *Interpretive Conventions* (1982).

9. To simplify the example, I use the two-level accent system, although representations can be devised to include several types of stress. The distinction between meter and rhythm employed here derives from Jakobson's theory (1960), which defines rhythmic pleasure as consisting in frustrated metric expectations. In the light of a Lewisian analysis, I would add *expected* frustrated expectations, since the metrical scheme provides a framework within which the coordination equilibrium is defined.

10. A subtle discussion of genres as reading strategies can be found in Rabinowitz 1985. The interpretive conventions in Stanley Fish's sense (1980) are the object of Steven Mailloux's study (1982); he distinguishes among traditional, regulative, and constitutive conventions. An earlier paper by Rabinowitz (1980) describes the various kinds of audience posited by texts of fiction; his suggestive classification can be read as a typology of the coordination games between writer and public.

11. Should one include thematic studies here? Martha Nussbaum's paper on Plato's and Marcel Proust's fictional thematization of the soul (1983) suggests that fictional hypotheses can be more than mere preconventional games.

Chapter Four: Convention and Literary Explanations

1. This point is ably documented in Reeves 1986b.

2. Lewis relies heavily on Schelling 1960; two other important early sources of game theory are von Neumann and Morgenstern 1944 and Luce and Raiffa 1957.

3. See, e.g., Elster 1986, 29; and Walliser 1989.

4. An example is Lanham 1973.

5. On this point, see Hjort, *The Strategy of Letters* (forthcoming 1993).

6. For clear expositions, see Lewis 1975, Pavel 1986, and Shusterman 1986.

7. I discuss a range of assumptions and issues surrounding concepts of rationality in *Literature and Rationality* (1991).

8. This point is not sufficiently emphasized by Reeves in his otherwise interesting essay devoted to exploring the differences between Lewisian and literary understandings of convention. Reeves states that "the lesson Lewis offers is that conventions must be sought in the relations between texts, not in individual texts" (1986a, 804).

9. This point is stressed in Reeves 1986a.

10. At this point, one might also bring into play Davidson's cogent arguments against any emphasis on conventions in linguistic communication. See, for example, his 1986 essay.

11. See Bennett 1976 (chap. 7) and Lewis 1975. Unfortunately, many of the literary scholars who have discussed Lewis's work have not paid any attention to these developments.

12. See Grice 1989; Grandy and Warner 1986.

13. Lönnroth provides a useful commentary on his approach in his 1980 response to Peter Foote's criticisms; see in particular his schematic contrast between his own model and traditional philological assumptions.

14. It is thus especially significant that in a note, he refers to another critic's interpretive oversight as having derived from a tendency to "see the sagas as expressions of individual authors rather than as attempts to accommodate a specific audience" (1976, 184).

15. I engage in such a reading in *Models of Desire* (1992).

Chapter Five: Hobbes on Literary Rules and Conventions

1. This must have been a rather indirect influence in view of Hobbes's tempestuous relations with the society. See Riek 1977; Shapin and Schaffer 1985.

2. Henceforth referred to as Hobbes's *Answer*. I am using David F. Gladish's modern edition of Davenant's *Gondibert*, which includes Hobbes's *Answer* (45–55).

3. Hobbes once wrote that "there was never anything so deerly bought, as these Western parts have bought the learning of the Greek and Latine tongues" (1651, 268).

4. The criticism is somewhat muted in Lewis, who argues mainly that Hobbes's social contract is not a convention. But the two issues are closely related, since, according to Lewis, it is not explicit agreement that makes a convention a convention.

5. This is different from saying that a convention is an agreement between rational agents. This more modern locution embeds the rationality of the agreement in the structure of the agents, whose rationality is postulated by the theory.

6. It should be noted that this requirement is maintained in a modern concept of convention like Lewis's (1969) but that it is embedded in the definition of the agents as rational and of the situation as a game of coordination.

7. Watkins (1976), of course, is well aware of these examples, especially the second one, since his essay deals with Hobbes's conception of language, and I would not want to misrepresent his position. He argues that Hobbes's approach to language is too individualistic. According to Watkins, Hobbes understands the evolution of language as resulting solely from individual initiatives that somehow get accepted. This, says Watkins, is surely impossible. Be that as it may, a few comments are in order. First, given that Hobbes's account of language comprises two steps, one in

which each individual invents a private language to mark his or her thoughts, and a second in which a language becomes instituted within the community through common consent, presumably no situation ever arises resembling the one described by Watkins (698–99). The difficulty is not for Alpha to teach Beta the meaning of the copula. Hobbes would agree that she has already invented it herself. The problem is that of achieving coordination in relation to certain sounds so as to communicate already known meanings, and this is an entirely different issue. Second, it should be noted that Hobbes tells us very little about the way in which agreement is reached concerning the meaning of words, so that any reconstruction of a Hobbesian argument on this score will involve a great deal of speculation. Lastly, in view of the preceding remark, what we should do, I believe, if our goal is to criticize individualistic accounts more generally (which is apparently what Watkins wants to do), is to give Hobbes the benefit of any modern approach consistent with his individualistic and conventional point of view. I am thinking here of the arguments of Lewis (1969) or of Jonathan Bennett (1976). It is only by challenging head-on such powerful and sophisticated individualistic accounts that Watkins's argument can gain any clout.

8. This is a thorny issue that demands some clarification. According to Hobbes, it is only in an indirect and derivative way that men are governed by laws to which they have agreed; otherwise, there would be no need for a coercive power.

9. Lewis (1969) does exactly the opposite and radically dissociates a convention from its origin. What makes a convention a convention according to him is the means through which it is maintained: essentially, the conditional preference to conform to a regularity of behavior R on condition that most members of the relevant population conform to R. Consequently, Lewis argues, a convention is totally independent of its origin. It does not matter how R appeared within the population, whether it was the result of chance or of an explicit agreement, for it is the conditional preference for R that makes it a convention (1969, 83–88).

10. This device should be seen as closely related to what Robert Nozick has defined as a "potential fundamental explanation" and as giving rise to "hypothetical histories" (1974, 6–9, 292–94).

11. Especially in "The Ideological Context of Hobbes's Political Thought" (1966) and "Conquest and Consent" (1972a), Skinner argues, and carefully documents, that Hobbes was an extremely popular author, not only on the Continent, but also in England, his work being favorably received by large segments of the political class, and even by the clergy, a situation which is at odds with the impression created by such classic studies as John Bowle (1951) and Samuel Mintz (1962).

12. There is no doubt that he did. See Hobbes 1662 and Skinner 1972b, 97.

13. See also Dumouchel (forthcoming).

14. Apart from various remarks scattered in some of his other works, two other indirectly related texts should be taken into account in order to complete the corpus of Hobbes's "literary criticism": his abridged translation of Aristotle's rhetoric, *Briefe of the Art of Rhetoric* (1637), and his introduction to his translation of Thucydides's *Peloponnesian War* (1629).

15. "Nature (the Art whereby God hath made and governes the World) is by the *Art* of man, as in many other things, so in this also imitated, that it can make an

Artificial Animal" (1651a, 81). Clearly, "art" in this sense embraces all human, scientific, and technological activities. Given that Hobbes assumes that we know what we make, and that the goal of science is power — the production of certain effects — science is an imitation of nature, "the Art whereby God hath made and governes the world" (1656, 7–9).

16. This is a thorny issue, and I will only say a few words about it here. In spite of the many essays, mentioned in the first paragraph of this text, that see Hobbes as the father of psychological criticism, I find Talmor's (1984) demonstration persuasive. There is very little in the *Answer* or the *Virtues* which indicates that Hobbes was interested in the creative process going on in the poet's mind. Yet, I think we should distinguish Hobbes's poetics as such from his influence on Cowley or Dryden, which may have traveled through a different channel than either the *Answer* or the *Virtues*. This is something that Talmor does not do. In fact there is clear evidence that Dryden was well aware of and influenced by Hobbes's psychology of imagination (Watson 1955; Forest 1962; Selden 1973, 1974), and we know that he was unhappy with the *Virtues* (Dryden 1700). So, this whole debate is probably misconstrued, as both theses can be true at the same time. The fact that Hobbes's criticism as such is not directed at the psychology of the creative process does not preclude his philosophical psychology from having influenced Dryden and others.

17. We know from *Leviathan* that the religion of the gentiles, according to Hobbes, was a form of politics, and that the separation of religion and politics results from a long historical process (1651a, chaps. 12, 47; Dumouchel forthcoming). Hobbes seems to have thought that the same was true of the separation of poetry from religion.

18. These rules against the two forms of indecencies correspond, respectively, to the fourth and first virtues of epic poems in Hobbes 1675.

19. The *Virtues* opens with the following paragraph: "The virtues required in an heroic poem, and indeed in all writings published, are comprehended all in this one word — *discretion*" (1675, iii).

20. This intellectual error results from a moral fault, hubris, an excessive confidence in the creative powers of human reason.

21. Hayek (1988, 20) somewhat qualifies this statement.

22. It is unfortunate that Hayek is not more specific on this issue. What does it mean to say that the agents do not know the order that results from obeying rules of conduct? Does it mean that they do not know what this order is, as implied in Hayek 1967 (70), or does it mean that they do not know that the order results from their abiding by such rules, as suggested throughout Hayek 1973? Yet, clearly the agents know that they partake of an ordered social system.

23. This is a tricky issue, since Lewis (1969, 83–88) radically dissociates all conventions from their origins. According to Lewis, what makes a convention a convention is the way in which it is maintained, through a system of conditional preferences, independently of the way it was first instituted (by an explicit agreement, through coercion, or whatnot). What makes this issue difficult is that Lewis originally set out to prove that some conventions, at least, could arise spontaneously through a mechanism of expectations without explicit agreement between agents. The fact that he later dissociates conventions from their origins means that we are left with no gen-

eral criteria to distinguish those conventions that may arise spontaneously from those that cannot. This is something that I find discouraging in view of Lewis's own program. In this text, my goal is to show that Hobbes's literary rules, and Hayekian rules of conduct, which share the same logical form, cannot arise through a Lewisian mechanism.

24. Hayek, unfortunately, is not clear about the epistemological and ontological status of rules of conduct. He often acts as if the rules were somehow out there in the world as dispositions to act (or not to act) in a certain way. Hobbes draws our attention to the fact that such rules may be seen as explanatory hypotheses that allow us to understand a wide range of behavior but that do not necessarily correspond to any object in the world.

Chapter Six: Conventions and Arbitrariness

1. See also Guthrie 1971, chap. 4.

2. See, for example, Antiphon, B44, A.

3. The term "covenant" used by Thomas Hobbes as a synonym for "contract" or "pact" is derived from the old French term *covenant*, which is itself derived from the Latin *convenire*. See Hobbes 1651a, 193.

4. David Hume noted that "this fiction of a state of Nature, was not first imagined by Mr. Hobbes, as is commonly imagined" (1777, 189). Yet, as Popper (1944, 114) has pointed out, the notion of contract may be found already, if not in Protagoras, then in Lycophron.

5. See the chapter in Rousseau 1762 entitled "Qu'il faut toujours remonter à une première convention" (49–50).

6. Only the choice of the Sovereign can be arbitrary in this sense, at least according to Hobbes, who thus partly escapes the well-known Popperian critique of theories of sovereignty. See Popper 1945 and Dumouchel's (1986) remarks on this topic.

7. For commentaries, see Weill and Terré 1983, 26, and Carbonnier 1969, 35 ff.

8. See also Orléan 1985, 1989.

9. Lewis explicitly draws on Hume's (1740) remarks on conventions, which are not promises, particularly on the famous example (also cited by Dupréel) of the "two men, who pull the oars of a boat, . . . by an agreement or convention, tho' they have never given promises to each other" (490).

10. See Ferry 1990, chap. 2.

11. See the preface to Victor Hugo's *Cromwell* (1827).

12. See Girard 1961.

13. See Pavel 1988, 170, where he refers to the Humean and Lewisian concept of convention.

14. See Plato's *Cratylus* (1961).

15. See Bouveresse 1987, chap. 4, and Engel 1989, chap. 12.

16. See, for example, the following statements from Popper 1944: "Nearly all misunderstandings can be traced back to one fundamental misapprehension, namely, to the belief that 'convention' implies 'arbitrariness'; that if we are free to choose any system of norms we like, then one system is just as good as any other. It must, of course,

be admitted that the view that norms are conventional or artificial indicates that there will be a certain element of arbitrariness involved, i.e., that there may be different systems of norms between which there is not much to choose (a fact that has been duly emphasized by Protagoras). But artificiality by no means implies full arbitrariness. Mathematical calculi, for instance, or symphonies, or plays, are highly artificial, yet it does not follow that one calculus or symphony or play is just as good as any other" (64-65).

17. See Weill and Terré 1983, 89-94. For an introduction to English contract law, see Duncanson 1979.

18. Most of the examples cited by Lewis (1969) lead him to conclude that the choice of solution is a matter of indifference. Yet, example 8, which is that of the stag hunt as discussed by Rousseau (1755, pt. 2) hardly seems to lend itself to this kind of analysis. On this point, see Boudon and Bourricaud 1982.

19. See Olson 1965 and Boudon 1977 for a discussion of the problem of free riders in the context of public goods.

20. See Popper 1963, chap. 4.

Chapter Seven: Genres, Laws, Canons, Principles

1. I have explored the theme, featuring Aristotle and Protagoras, in "Métaphysique radicale" (1991).

2. See Margolis 1989.

3. This is the thesis of "Métaphysique radicale" (1991).

4. See Margolis, "Moral Realism and the Meaning of Life" (1990).

5. I have explored the issue in two as yet unpublished papers, "Praxis and Invariance," and "Praxis and Universals."

6. For an unconvinced but respectful account of Schenker's developed theory, see Narmour 1977. Narmour chiefly attacks the metaphysical and axiomatic features of Schenker's approach. More recent Schenkerians tend to minimize these aspects, though they may also be persuaded, as Allen Forte (1977) remarks with cautious enthusiasm: "Although Schenker came very close to constructing a complete system, further refinement and amplification are required if it is to fulfill its promise" (20).

7. See also White 1987, chap. 1.

8. I have found the discussion in Rosmarin 1985 helpful, although Rosmarin does not, in her own pragmatist conviction, afford a sufficiently compelling account of the conceptual difficulties confronting all theories (see chap. 1).

9. Popper, of course, is an implacable opponent of inductivism and essentialism (and Aristotle). But it took him a very long time to grasp that his own doctrine of verisimilitude was itself an implicit form of essentialism. He eventually abandoned it but realized that he could not sustain his own falsificationism without it. See Popper 1972; 1983, xxv-xxxvii, 56-62.

10. Ramsey's discussion hardly seems as trim as Lewis's, though it could certainly support it. See Ramsey 1960, e.g., 198. I have benefited here from van Fraassen 1989, chap. 3.

11. See, for instance, van Fraassen 1980 and Cartwright 1983.

12. See, further, van Fraassen 1989, chap. 3.

13. See Armstrong 1983, 5.

14. See Quine 1969.

15. See Quine 1960, 68-79; and 1953, 20-46.

16. See Quine 1953, 9-19, particularly 15.

17. The principles are as follows: (1) the equality of basic rights and duties and (2) the justification of inequalities of wealth and authority only if this results in compensating benefits for all, particularly the least advantaged; and their serial or "lexical" order.

18. I have heard Dagfinn Føllesdal lecture on at least three different occasions in favor of a use of Goodman's equilibrative strategy in the context of (phenomenological) conceptual variation leading in the direction of an ideally invariant finding. I have never seen a published paper of his on this topic; but, on the argument being advanced, Goodman's model would be fatal for any characteristically Husserlian confidence in the asymptotic progress of such an exercise.

19. Habermas (1970) makes the point as follows: "Since Dilthey, we have been accustomed to thinking of the distinguishing feature of the *Geisteswissenschaften* as the relationship within them of the epistemological to an object domain that itself shares the structures of subjectivity. In the idealist [Hegelian] tradition, this particular position of subject and object can be interpreted as spirit encountering itself in its objectivations" (90).

20. Hirsch himself remarks, "Those who have most deeply considered the methodological function of types (I am thinking particularly of Dilthey, Weber, Stern, and Kretschmer) are in accord on one point: type concepts are indispensable in all attempts to understand an individual entity in its particularity" (271). He adds that "types have not only an indispensable heuristic function but also an inescapable constitutive function" (272), though he does not quite see that this has to do with the logic of individuation and not with essentialism.

21. See Margolis 1986, chap. 2.

22. This appears to be the upshot of MacIntyre 1988, particularly chaps. 1 and 19.

23. See also Cone 1960.

24. See Kenner 1984.

25. Without necessarily agreeing with his own arguments and conclusions, this is the general drift of J. L. Mackie's incisive analysis (1977, 48-49).

26. Lyotard's formulation leads directly to the conceptual disaster of his *Just Gaming* (1979), coauthored with Jean-Loup Thébaud. But that is his, not our, concern. The extravagances of the poststructuralists should not obscure the ineluctable extension of the import of genre studies and its equally unavoidable bearing on the advocacy of principles and canons and the strategies of legitimation by which they are entrenched.

27. See Foucault 1971. A particularly egregious example of a proprietary principle bearing on political, legal, and economic matters is unintentionally afforded by Robert Nozick (1974). Nozick introduces (very usefully indeed) the notion of a "patterned principle": "Let us call a principle of distribution [as of goods] *patterned* if it specifies that a distribution is to vary along with some natural dimension, weighted sum

of natural dimensions, or lexicographic ordering of natural dimensions. And let us say a distribution is patterned if it accords with some patterned principle" (156). He himself favors what he calls an "entitlement" principle, which he takes to be *not* patterned: "The entitlement theory of justice in distribution is *historical*: whether a distribution is just depends upon how it came about" (253). One might be led to suppose that patterned principles correspond to "genres" of justice and injustice, and entitlement principles do not. But that would be a mistake. For one thing, entitlement principles (of Nozick's sort) depend on "the *original acquisition of holdings,* the appropriation of unheld things" (150) — which are never really recoverable. And, for another, "historical" means "suitably linked to original acquisition" — which is also not recoverable. Hence, although Nozick's principle may not be "patterned," it is, like patterned principles, premised on an invariant, neutral, normatively discernible rule or principle that, in our argument, must be linked to alterable exploitative constellations.

Chapter Eight: To Follow a Rule

1. Wittgenstein 1953, pt. 1, par. 85; henceforth abbreviated to 1.85.
2. The issue of how to understand Wittgenstein's argument is discussed at greater length in Fultner 1989.
3. See also Taylor 1990.
4. See Urban 1986.
5. See Taylor 1985.
6. Bourdieu 1980, p. 58.
7. Bourdieu 1990, p. 34.
8. Cited in Bourdieu 1980, 167. The quotation is from Lévi-Strauss 1950, xxxviii, and the translation is mine.

Chapter Nine: Challenging Conventions in the Fine Art of Rap

1. Rap's censorship became national news when 2 Live Crew were banned and arrested in Florida in the summer of 1990, but it was prevalent long before then. Of course, more recently, rap has proven too popular not to be coopted and absorbed (in its milder forms) by the established media. Its rhythms and style have been adopted by mainstream mass-media advertising, and one mild-mannered rapper (Fresh Prince) was given his own prime-time major network show. For more details on rap's censorship and rap's complex relation to mass-media culture and technology, see the chapter on rap in *Pragmatist Aesthetics: Living Beauty, Rethinking Art,* in which I develop many of this chapter's points.
2. See, for example, Ice-T's "Hit the Deck," which aims to "demonstrate rappin' as a fine art." There are countless other raps that emphatically declare rap's poetic and artistic status; among the more forceful are Stetsasonic's "Talkin' All That Jazz"; BDP's "I'm Still #1," "Ya Slippin'," "Ghetto Music," and "Hip Hop Rules"; and Kool Moe Dee's "The Best."
3. Hip hop actually designates an organic cultural complex wider than rap. It includes breakdancing and graffiti, and also a stylized but casual style of dress,

where hightop sneakers became high fashion. Rap music supplied the beat for the breakdancers; some rappers testify to having practiced graffiti; and hip-hop fashion is celebrated in many raps, one example being Run-DMC's "My Adidas."

4. For a more detailed account of the aesthetic dimension of postmodernism, see Shusterman 1989.

5. See, for example, Abrahams 1964; this study of a Philadelphia ghetto revealed that speaking skills "confer high social status," and that even among young males, "ability with words is as highly valued as physical strength" (31, 59). Studies of Washington and Chicago ghettos have confirmed this. See Hannerz 1969, which shows that verbal skill is "widely appreciated among ghetto men" not only for competitive practical purposes but for "entertainment value" (84–85); see also Kochman 1972. Along with its narrower use to designate the traditional and stylized practice of verbal insult, black signifying has a more general sense of encoded or indirect communication, which relies heavily on the special background knowledge and particular context of the communicants. For an impressively complex and theoretically sophisticated analysis of signifying as such a generic trope and its use "in black texts as explicit theme, implicit rhetorical strategy, and as a principle of literary history," see Gates 1988, 89.

6. Such linguistic strategies of evasion and indirection (which include inversion, shucking, tomming, marking, and loud-talking, as well as the more generic notion of signifying, are discussed at length in Kochman 1972, Holt 1972, and Mitchell-Kernan 1972.

7. I later try to demonstrate some of this rich complexity by a close reading of Stetsasonic's "Talkin' All That Jazz."

8. See, for example, Ice-T's "Rhyme Pays," Public Enemy's "Bring the Noise," Run-DMC's "Jam-master Jammin'," and BDP's "Ya Slippin'."

9. It is called scratch mixing not only because the manual placement of the needle on particular tracks scratches the records but because the DJ hears the scratch in his ear when he cues the needle on the track to be sampled before actually adding it to the sound of the other record already being sent out on the sound system.

10. See, for example, Public Enemy's "Caught, Can We Get a Witness," Stetsasonic's "Talkin' All That Jazz," and BDP's "I'm Still #1," "Ya Slippin'," and "The Blueprint." The motivating image of this last rap highlights the simulacral notion of hip-hop originality. In privileging their underground style as original and superior to "the soft commercial sound" of other rap, they connect its greater originality with its greater closeness to rap's ghetto origins: "You got a copy, I read from the blueprint." But a blueprint is itself a copy, not an original; indeed, it is a simulacrum or representation of a designed object that typically does not yet (if it will ever) exist as a concrete original object.

11. See Jameson 1984, 73–75. This is not to deny that rap ever achieves any unity or formal coherence of its own; I argue below that it does in "Talkin' All That Jazz."

12. For a critique of this early view of Eliot's and for an explanation of the reasons why Eliot himself abandoned it in formulating his later theory of tradition, see Shusterman 1988, 156–67.

13. See, respectively, "My Philosophy" and "Ghetto Music." The lyrics of "Ya Slip-

pin'" and "Hip Hop Rules" respectively date themselves as 1987 and 1989. Public Enemy's "Don't Believe the Hype" has a 1988 time tag, and similar time tags can be found in raps by Ice-T, Kool Moe Dee, and many others.

14. See, for example, Habermas 1985, 1–22.

15. See BDP's "My Philosophy" and "Gimme Dat, (Woy)." The lyrics of their knowledge rap "Who Protects Us from You?" describe it as "a public service announcement brought to you by the scientists of Boogie Down Productions." In the jacket notes to their albums *Ghetto Music* and *Edutainment,* KRS-One describes himself as "Metaphysician."

16. See "I'm Still #1." For BDP's attack on establishment history and media and its stereotypes, see especially "My Philosophy," "You Must Learn," and "Why Is That."

17. This phrase and notion, for example, provide the central theme of Kool Moe Dee's "Do You Know What Time It Is?"

18. For an account of Dewey's aesthetics and its contemporary relevance, see Shusterman 1992, chap. 1.

19. The best example of this is Gary Byrd, a New York radio DJ who developed a literacy program based on rap. For more details, see Toop 1984, 45–46.

20. Grandmaster Flash complained that, because of the novelty and virtuosity of his cutting, "the crowd would stop dancing and just gather round like a seminar. This is what I didn't want. This wasn't school, it was time to shake your ass." Quoted from Toop 1984, 72.

21. See Queen Latifah's "Dance for Me" and Ice-T's "Hit the Deck." For a similar emphasis on the mesmerizing possession and physically and spiritually moving power of rap in both performer and audience, see Kool Moe Dee's "Rock Steady" and "The Best."

22. The point is made most explicitly in Plato's *Ion.* The direction and valorization of this chain of divine madness is wittily reversed in a song by Kool Moe Dee ("Get the Picture"), where his hypnotic rapping is identified with "knowledge" and "telling you the truth," which brings the rapper's possessed audience up to the level of the gods, challenging their supremacy and captivating them as well: "I start to float / On the rhymes I wrote / Ascending to a level with the gods and I tote / Loads and mounds of people / As they reach new heights / A half a mile from heaven is the party site / And I'm the attraction. / The gods will be packed in / Coming out of their pockets for me to rock it / And Acting / Like they've never ever been entertained / They try to act godly but they can't maintain / . . . And Venus would peak on every word I speak / Zeus would get loose / Fully induced. / I'll make Apollo's rhymes sound like / Mother Goose. / By night's end Mercury is so hyped / He'd spread the word / That there's a god of the mic / Captivating all the other gods / By the masses / Described as a dark-skinned brother in glasses."

23. See, for example, Ventura 1986 and Thompson 1984.

24. For more discussion of these two notions of aesthetics, see Shusterman 1989.

25. It is, for example, the only song to appear on both the popular *Yo, MTV Raps* and *Monster TV Rap Hits* albums.

26. Nor does my printed transcription of the lyrics convey that they are delivered in an antiphonic style by three voices that alternate irregularly between lines and

sometimes within the very same line, adding to the rap's jumpy syncopated style and formal complexity.

27. I take these definitions from Funk and Wagnall's Standard Desk Dictionary and Webster's Collegiate Dictionary. The Random House Dictionary conveys essentially the same meaning of "insincere, exaggerated, or pretentious talk."

28. Rap is far more outspoken in its black pride and challenge of white cultural and political domination than jazz, which is not surprising, since the latter evolved in a black experience much closer to slavery.

29. This emphasis on rap as deliberately composed writing rather than mere talk highlights rap's claim to literacy as well as artistry. The poem does not, however, draw a firm dichotomy between talking as lies and writing as truth; for in presenting the truth to their hostile critics, the rappers are not only writing but "talkin' about you."

30. See, for example, Levin's (1988) excellent study of America's transfiguration of Shakespeare and opera from popular to elite art.

31. As Holt (1972) explains: "Blacks clearly recognized that to master the language of whites was in effect to consent to be mastered by it through the white definitions of caste built into the semantic/social system. Inversion therefore becomes the defensive mechanism which enables blacks to fight linguistic, and thereby psychological entrapment. . . . Words and phrases were given reverse meanings and functions changed. Whites, denied access to the semantic extensions of duality, connotations, and denotations that developed within black usage, could only interpret the same material according to its original singular meaning . . . , enabling blacks to deceive and manipulate whites without penalty. This protective process, understood and shared by blacks became a contest of matching wits . . . [and a] form of linguistic guerilla warfare [that] protected the subordinated, permitted the masking and disguising of true feelings, allowed the subtle assertion of self, and promoted group solidarity" (155).

32. See Mitchell-Kernan 1972, 326–27. This form of verbal art is one that in fine Deweyan fashion is extremely continuous with and enhancive of ordinary life. We should not forget that rapping was a linguistic style before it went musical, and this sense of rapping, of course, remains.

33. An FBI director, for example, issued an official warning regarding a rap by N.W.A. (Niggers With Attitude), without ever hearing the song; a survey of the protest mail received by the group revealed that none of these antirap critics had in fact heard the song in question or were at all familiar with other rap music. Such hearsay-based animosity has resulted in cancellations of rap concerts and the censoring and confiscation of rap records. For more details on these matters, see Marsh and Pollack 1989.

34. The violence of this struggle often exceeds the domain of mere symbolic violence. Beyond critique and counter-critique, the establishment exercises the actual violence of censorship and police coercion, while the rap forces employ the retaliatory violence of rap's blasting noise (which is thematized in many rap songs) and the threat of physical violence born of extended frustration and oppression. These two forms of retaliatory violence are emphasized and cleverly linked in Spike Lee's *Do the*

Right Thing, in which the violent silencing of loud rap leads to a neighborhood riot.

35. The contradictions of the democratic establishment's censoring repudiation of rap is pointedly expressed in the title song of Ice-T's album *Freedom of Speech. . . Just Watch What You Say,* and in the very name of the crew Public Enemy, which mischievously plays on the two different meanings of "public" here in sharp contradiction: the institutionally official versus truly representative of the people.

36. See Marcus 1975, 82. The book contains an excellent chapter devoted to Sly Stone's career (55–111).

37. Hence, the song's appeal to the antecedent beliefs of democratic majoritarianism and pluralistic tolerance, and to the antecedent tastes for R & B and Sly and the Family Stone.

38. I discuss this form of argument in considerable detail in Shusterman 1978, 1981, 1986, and 1988.

39. Wollheim (1968), for example, speaks of "the perennial and ineradicable self-consciousness of art" (16). Indeed, twentieth-century art has been so preoccupied with the concept of art that Danto (1986) can speak of art as having turned into its own philosophy.

40. See Bourdieu 1979, 41, 48, 395), where he is led to suggest that popular culture's implicit acceptance of its denied artistic status means that in a sense "there is no popular art."

41. For an elaboration of this point, see Shusterman 1988, 157–64, 170-90.

42. See Adorno and Horkheimer 1944; Adorno 1970, 320-23, 340-41; van den Haag 1957, 504-36, esp. 514-18; and Broudy 1972, 110-12.

43. See Bourdieu 1979, 3, 30-35.

44. See, for example, Bourdieu 1979, 32-33, and Kaplan 1967, 53.

45. Pareles 1990, 1, 28. Many rap songs, particularly those that trace and celebrate the history of hip hop, explicitly flaunt rap's stunning success at outlasting the critics' constant predictions of its early demise and thereby argue for its value and rich creative potential in terms of its staying power. See, for example, BDP's "Hip Hop Rules."

Chapter Ten: Conventions and Literary Systems

1. The concept of convention used here is that of Lewis (1969) and Schiffer (1972, 154).

2. See Hintzenberg, Schmidt, and Zobel 1980 for the statistical data.

3. Ohtaki (1989) has shown that these conventions are also valid within the literary system of Japan.

4. For a more detailed discussion of these issues, see Schmidt 1989.

5. Cited in Haferkorn 1974, 132.

6. Cited in Zimmermann 1988, 537.

Chapter Eleven: Linguistic and Literary Conventions

1. See especially Davidson's three Dewey lectures, published as "The Structure and Content of Truth" (1990).

2. Cf. Wittgenstein 1953, § 201.

Chapter Twelve: The Temporality of Convention

1. See *La philosophie analytique* (1962, 128). All translations in this essay are my own.

2. Among the most prominent eighteenth-century treatises that deal with the origin and social development of linguistic conventions are Vico 1725, rev. 1744; Condillac 1746; Diderot 1751; Rousseau 174?, 175?, and 1755; Süßmilch 1741; and Herder 1770. In the early nineteenth century, Shelley (1821) made the strongest case for the ligature between linguistic and social change, recasting eighteenth-century theories into a direct appeal to the moral and political effects of poetic language.

3. From the secular *philosophes* on, it is hard to think of an important literary figure, in France and Germany especially, who did not also reflect on extant and possible social relations. The final focus of this chapter is on the relation between literary and social conventions described by an author who conveyed the speculative procedures of the *philosophes* into nineteenth-century fiction, Stendhal.

4. Among ordinary language philosophers, the outstanding exception to this trend, has been, of course, Austin (1962).

5. While there is something about the traditional analytic example of "the married bachelor" that gives pause, Lewis's particular use of it here is especially bizarre, since not only the words "married" and "bachelor" but the facts or existential states "so-called" are themselves already purely conventional, being defined solely by legal, cultural, and psychological mores. By contrast, to paraphrase Lewis, *there could be* unicorns (an equally common *point de repère* in possible world theory). On this point, however, Kripke (1972, 24, 127) differs.

6. Cf. Lewis's claim to possess a nonreplicative conception of convention itself: "It may not be obvious that our regularities of dress should not be called conventions if there are many people who want to see them violated. . . . If the reader disagrees, I can only remind him that I did not undertake to analyze anyone's concept of convention but mine" (1969, 46).

7. Recalling the clearsighted boxing bear of Heinrich von Kleist's (1811) "Über das Marionettentheater," who never mistakes the actual intention of his human adversary's feints and thrusts, we might want to add animals to Lewis's list of nonrational agents who, I would argue, are in fact best suited to enact his conception of convention.

8. Lewis 1969, 1: "It is the profession of philosophers to question platitudes that others accept without thinking twice. . . . [W]hen a good philosopher challenges a platitude, it usually turns out that the platitude was essentially right; but the philosopher has noticed trouble that one who did not think twice could not have met. In the end the challenge is answered and the platitude survives, more often than not. But the philosopher has done the adherents of the platitude a service: he has made them think twice." Thinking twice (and thrice, etc.) before convening is what every rational agent, or rower, I argue, must do, with the effect of delaying convention indefinitely until an explicit institution of convention takes the place of thought. Cf. Lewis's description of agents who also "cannot safely be treated as rational" if, while presenting a "facade of hostility" to others, they both "agree in secret" *and* maintain a "facade" of disagreement "primarily *to themselves*" (1969, 87). Lewis dismisses such

complex activity as self-deception; but the internal mirroring of rationalized external behavior which he describes seems instead a natural and potentially incorrigible
consequence of the very ability to think twice.

9. Rousseau's *Discours sur l'origine et les fondements de l'inégalité parmi les hommes* opens by
distinguishing two kinds of inequality: "natural or physical" inequalities owing to
material differences between individuals, and "moral or political inequality" deriving from "a kind of convention" formed among men. Language, the convention most
apt to promote social inequality because it promotes thought — and with thought,
industry and the accumulation of wealth and power — is also, Rousseau reasons, the
"most difficult to conceive in itself," for, "if men needed language in order to learn
to think, they needed even more to know how to think in order to find the art of
words." Arguing further that a common language could only be formed "by way of
common consent," Rousseau concludes that "words seem to have been absolutely
necessary in establishing the use of words" (157, 189–91).

10. Cf. Quine 1936, 88: "[I]f we are to construe logic also as true by convention,
we must rest logic ultimately upon some manner of convention other than definition:
for it was noted earlier that definitions are available only for transforming truths, not
for founding them."

11. In implicit agreement with Quine's critique, Habermas (1983, 302), following
Hans Albert, has described this analytic position as "the 'Münchhausen trilemma'—
logical circularity, infinite regress, and recourse to absolute certitude."

12. Quine 1954, 129: "'Analytic' means true by synonymy and logic."

13. For "similarity" and "verisimilitude," see Lewis 1986, 2–26; on "*doxastically accessible* worlds" — simply, those that support "one's system of belief about the worlds" —
see 27–40. The thornier issue of "*epistemically accessible* worlds," i.e., those that support
not what we believe but what we know about our world, is elided by Lewis in another
gesture of explicit omission: "Let me concentrate simply on belief, passing over the
added complications that arise when we distinguish someone's knowledge from the
rest of his system of belief" (28).

14. Cf. Quine's classic summation of the hybrid historical status of "truth by convention": "The lore of our fathers is a fabric of sentences. In our hands it develops
and changes, through more or less arbitrary and deliberate revisions and additions
of our own, more or less directly occasioned by the continuing stimulation of our
sense organs. It is a pale gray lore, black with fact and white with convention. But
I have found no substantial reasons for concluding that there are any quite black
threads in it, or any white ones" (1954, 132).

15. Here the problem of sufficiently defining names seems to spill over to the very
definition of "name." See Kripke, 134: "My argument implicitly concludes that certain general terms, those for natural kinds, have a greater kinship with proper names
than is generally realized. This conclusion holds for certain for various species
names, whether they are count nouns, such as 'cat,' 'tiger,' 'chunk of gold,' or mass
terms such as 'gold,' 'water,' 'iron pyrites.' It also applies to certain terms for natural
phenomena, such as 'heat,' 'light,' 'sound,' 'lightning,' and, presumably, suitably
elaborated, to corresponding adjectives—'hot,' 'loud,' 'red.'" It is significant that in
this movement from proper noun to noun to adjective, Kripke directly reverses the

course of linguistic development described in Diderot's *Lettre sur les sourds et muets*. In the *Lettre*, Diderot speculates that at the origin of language, "the adjective is everything," and that nouns are later abstracted from adjectival qualities (1751, 135). Since the historical trajectory Diderot traces ends where Kripke's theory begins — with the "scientific" model of language as an analytic medium coextensive with logic (the Port Royal position) — it is entirely fitting that their reflections on language should cross in this fashion.

16. According to Kripke, theories of transworld identification that do not depart from a notion of rigid designations "have precisely reversed the cart and the horse," since it is the constant designated by a name that makes identifications across hypothetical worlds possible. Kripke criticizes Lewis's theory of "counterparts," or counterfactual situations based on similarity of reference rather than on referential identity, as being, on the one hand, "strictly speaking . . . not a view of 'transworld identification,'" and, on the other, "even more bizarre than the usual notions of transworld identification that it replaces" (45). Still, both Lewis's and more normative possible world theories share the analytic premise that "qualitative resemblance," and not a necessary but nonqualitative convention of reference, constitutes the basis for identity or counterpart relations, and this is exactly what Kripke's theory of names disputes (45).

17. Kripke's discussion of the distinction between the terms "necessary" and *'a priori'* is an important and complicated one, reversing yet another analytic premise, that of the synonymy of the two terms within the scope of linguistic analysis. See Kripke 36–38, 138–40: "The terms 'necessary' and *'a priori,'* then, as applied to statements, are *not* obvious synonyms" (38); "such theoretical identifications as 'heat is molecular motion' are *necessary,* though not *a priori* . . . . The philosophical notion of attribute, on the other hand, seems to demand *a priori* (and analytic) coextensiveness as well as necessary coextensiveness" (138); "Theoretical identities, according to the conception I advocate, are generally identities involving two rigid designators and therefore are examples of the necessary *a posteriori*" (140).

18. A speculative version of this process by which conventional meanings undergo historical change is Rousseau's account of how the referent of "Giant" came to be referred to instead as "man." (See *Essai sur l'origine des langues,* chap. 3, p. 47; cf. de Man, 123–36.) A modern literary history of the "George Smith" type is Balzac's *Colonel Chabert* — in which the titular character lives to see his name rescinded from its referent, his own person — while the earliest literary figures to have felt the sting of the necessity and transferability of names are probably Odysseus and Polyphemus, respectively.

19. On Stendhal's intellectual as well as professional attachment to the revolutionary-become-Emperor, see May 1977.

20. These included the "Dialogue on the Unities" (1819) by Ermès Visconti, which Stendhal would later integrate into the first of the two articles, written for the *Paris Monthly Review of British and Continental Literature* (1822, 1823), that formed chapters 1 and 2 of *Racine et Shakespeare.*

21. It is worth recalling that Stendhal's most famous and most conventionally "romantic" fictional character, Julien Sorel, is a creature of conventions learned prin-

cipally from the writings of Napoleon (and Rousseau). Julien has the rules of romanticism memorized, but throughout *Le rouge et le noir* (1827) he misapplies them; times, the narrative implies, have changed. Julien, then, may seem a romantic because he misjudges other people's expectations, carries out to the letter conventions that are no longer appropriate (including, finally, that of his own beheading), and so appears to be making history when he is in fact going in circles, a rower making a lot of motion and going nowhere. (Not to be too critical of a fictional character, the same also might be said of Julien's historical idol, although the emperor went back and forth from Elba in an admittedly less conventional manner.) It is this experience of conventions out of sync that defines Stendhal's theory of literary-historical conventions in *Racine et Shakespeare*.

22. Cf. Quine 1961, 7-12. The structure of Russell's paradox, which I take to be the structure of the paradox of originary conventions generally—in Stendhal's literary terms, the paradox of "romanticism"—is that of saying what you are is not what you are; in short, "I am lying." Quine calls this form of paradox a "genuine antinomy," on the model of "'not true of self,' being true of itself" (7). True to his thoroughly historical view of conventions, Quine suggests that even such logical antinomies are not fixed but are "part and parcel of the conceptual scheme" of their time: "One man's antinomy is another man's falsidical paradox, give or take a couple of thousand years" (9). The same historical progression (from "genuine antinomy" to "falsidical paradox") cannot be attributed, however, to the imitative cognitive sequence romanticism-classicism. Or, as Stendhal might say, one man's "conceptual scheme" of "romanticism" *is* necessarily his "classicism."

23. "Le Manifeste d'Auger contre le romantisme," in Stendhal [1823] 1970, 247.

Chapter Thirteen: Conventions and Rationality

1. The expression "the art world," as used here, was introduced by Arthur Danto (1964).

2. Cf. the point made by Lewis (1969, 107).

3. In what follows I draw on Elias Bredsdorff's survey in "Fortolkninger av H. C. Andersen's Eventyr *Skyggen*" (1982).

4. MacIntyre 1988, 351: "there is no set of independent standards of rational justification by appeal to which the issues between contending traditions can be decided" (cf. also 8-9).

5. See also Margolis's later *Pragmatism without Foundations* (1986).

6. For example, in "Musik som Språk" (1986), "Representation, Truth, and the Languages of the Arts" (1987), and in my contribution to J. Emt and Göran Hermerén's *Understanding the Arts* (1991).

7. In Hermerén 1975, 22-24, 26-28, and in later writings.

8. Panofsky's interpretation is reprinted in his *Meaning in the Visual Arts* (1955, chap. 7).

9. "The schemes of the habitus, the primary forms of classification, owe their specific efficacy to the fact that they function below the level of consciousness and language, beyond the reach of introspective scrutiny or control by the will" (466).

10. Cf.: "Taste is a practical mastery of distributions which makes it possible to

sense or intuit what is likely (or unlikely) to befall and therefore to befit an individual occupying a given position in social space. It functions as a sort of social orientation, 'a sense of one's place'" (466).

11. See Gombrich, *Art and Illusion* (1960), 30, 87–90, 116, 108–9, 121, 126, 142–48, et passim.

12. See Hermerén, *Representation and Meaning in the Visual Arts* and *Aspects of Aesthetics*, chap. 3.

13. See Austin 1962 and Searle 1969.

14. See the works referred to in n. 6.

15. On different attitudes toward the nude in the history of art, see, e.g., Berger et al. 1972, particularly chaps. 2–4.

16. See Benjamin 1972.

17. For a good survey and discussion, see von Wright 1971.

18. See MacIntyre 1988, 355.

19. See in particular Popper 1959 and 1963.

20. See also the discussion in Lakatos and Musgrave 1970 and Kuhn's replies to some of his critics in that book.

21. MacIntyre 1988, 354, 366.

22. For an elaboration of this point of view, see Hermerén, *Art, Reason, and Tradition: On the Role of Rationality in Interpretation and Explanation of Works of Art* (1991).

Bibliography

Abrahams, Roger. [1964] 1970. *Deep Down in the Jungle: Negro Narrative Folklore from the Streets of Philadelphia.* Chicago: Aldine Press.

Abrams, Meyer Howard. 1957. *A Glossary of Literary Terms.* New York: Holt, Rinehart & Winston.

Adorno, Theodor Wiesengrund. [1970] 1984. *Aesthetic Theory.* Translated by C. Lenhardt. London: Routledge & Kegan Paul.

Adorno, Theodor Wiesengrund, and Max Horkheimer. [1944] 1986. *Dialectic of Enlightenment.* Translated by John Cumming. New York: Continuum.

Ainslie, George. 1986. "Beyond Microeconomics: Conflict among Interests in a Multiple Self as a Determinant of Value." In *The Multiple Self,* edited by Jon Elster, 133–76. Cambridge: Cambridge University Press.

Andersen, Hans Christian. 1982. "Skyggen." In *Samlede Eventyr og Historier,* edited by Svend Larsen, 294–302. Odense: Skandinavisk Bogforlag.

Angenot, Marc. 1984. "Structuralism as Syncretism: Institutional Distortions of Saussure." In *The Structural Allegory: Reconstructive Encounters with the New French Thought,* edited by John Fekete, 150–63. Minneapolis: University of Minnesota Press.

Antiphon. 1954. *Papyrus Oxyrhynus.* In *Discours, suivis des fragments d'Antiphon le sophiste,* edited and translated by Louis Gernet. Parallel text in Greek and French. Paris: Société d'édition "Les belles lettres."

Aristotle. *De Partibus Animalium.* Translated by William Ogle. In McKeon 1941, 643–61.

———. *Metaphysics.* Translated by W. D. Ross. In McKeon 1941, 689–926.

———. *The Nicomachean Ethics.* Translated by W. D. Ross. In McKeon 1941, 935–1112.

———. 1955. *On Sophistical Refutations.* Translated by E. S. Forster. Cambridge, Mass.: Harvard University Press.

———. *Poetics.* Translated by Ingram Bywater. In McKeon 1941, 1455–87.

Armstrong, D. M. 1983. *What Is a Law of Nature?* Cambridge: Cambridge University Press.

Ashcraft, Richard. 1978. "Ideology and Class in Hobbes' Political Theory." *Political Theory* 6: 27–62.

Austin, John L. 1962. *How to Do Things with Words.* Cambridge, Mass.: Harvard University Press.

Axelrod, Robert M. 1984. *The Evolution of Cooperation.* New York: Basic Books.

Barthes, Roland. [1968] 1977. "The Death of the Author." In *Image, Music, Text,* translated by Stephen Heath, 142–48. New York: Hill & Wang.

Barthes, Roland, et al. 1980. *Littérature et réalité.* Paris: Editions du Seuil.

Barwise, Jon, and John Perry. 1983. *Situations and Attitudes.* Cambridge, Mass.: MIT Press.

Baxter, Brian. 1983. "Conventions and Art." *British Journal of Aesthetics* 23: 319–32.

Beardsley, Monroe C. 1970. *The Possibility of Criticism.* Detroit: Wayne State University Press.

Beardsley, Monroe C., and William Kurtz Wimsatt, Jr. [1946] 1954. "The Intentional Fallacy." In *The Verbal Icon: Studies in the Meaning of Poetry,* 3–18. Lexington: University Press of Kentucky.

Benjamin, Walter. 1972. "Das Kunstwerk im Zeitalter seiner technischen Reproduzierbarkeit." In *Gesammelte Schriften,* vol. 1, pt. 2, edited by Rolf Tiedemann and Hermann Schweppenhäuser, 431–508. Frankfurt am Main: Suhrkamp Verlag.

Bennett, Jonathan. 1976. *Linguistic Behaviour.* London: Cambridge University Press.

Benveniste, Emile. 1966. *Problèmes de linguistique générale.* Paris: Gallimard.

Berger, John, et al. 1972. *Ways of Seeing.* Harmondsworth: Penguin Books.

Bond, Donald F. 1937. "The Neo-Classical Psychology of the Imagination." *English Literary History* 4: 245–64.

Boudon, Raymond. 1977. *Effets pervers et ordre social.* Paris: Presses universitaires de France.

Boudon, Raymond, and François Bourricaud. 1982. "Rousseau." In *Dictionnaire critique de la sociologie,* 476–82. Paris: Presses universitaires de France.

Bourdieu, Pierre. [1979] 1984. *Distinction: A Social Critique of the Judgment of Taste.* Translated by Richard Nice. Cambridge, Mass.: Harvard University Press.

———. 1990. *The Logic of Practice.* Translated by Richard Nice. Oxford: Polity Press.

———. 1980. *Le Sens pratique.* Paris: Editions du Minuit.

Bourdieu, Pierre, and Jean-Claude Passeron. 1970. *La reproduction: Eléments pour une théorie du système d'enseignement.* Paris: Editions du Minuit.

Bouveresse, Jacques. 1987. *La force de la règle.* Paris: Editions du Minuit.

Bowle, John. 1951. *Hobbes and His Critics: A Study in Seventeenth-Century Constitutionalism.* London: Jonathan Cape.

Bredsdorff, Elias. 1982. "Fortolkninger av H. C. Andersen's Eventyr *Skyggen.*" In *Tolkning och Tolkningsteorier,* 97–111. Stockholm: Almqvist & Wiksell.

Bremond, Claude. 1973. *Logique du récit.* Paris: Editions du Seuil.

Brinker, Menahem. 1983. "Verisimilitude, Conventions, and Belief." *New Literary History* 14: 253–67.

Brooke-Rose, Christine. 1981. *A Rhetoric of the Unreal: Studies in Narrative and Structure, Especially of the Fantastic.* Cambridge: Cambridge University Press.

Brooks, Cleanth. [1947] 1975. "The Heresy of Paraphrase." In *The Well-*

wrought Urn: Studies in the Structure of Poetry. New York: Harcourt Brace Jovanovich.

Broudy, Harry. 1972. *Enlightened Cherishing: An Essay on Aesthetic Education.* Urbana: University of Illinois Press.

Brown, Claude. "The Language of the Soul." In Kochman 1972, 134–39.

Carbonnier, Jean C. 1969. *Droit Civil: Les obligations.* Paris: Presses universitaires de France.

Carnap, Rudolf. [1935] 1937. *The Logical Syntax of Language.* New York: Harcourt, Brace.

Carrier, David, and Mark W. Roskill. 1983. *Truth and Falsehood in Visual Images.* Amherst: University of Massachusetts Press.

Cartwright, Nancy. 1983. *How the Laws of Physics Lie.* Oxford: Clarendon Press.

Castoriadis, Cornelius. 1986. *Domaines de l'homme.* Paris: Editions du Seuil.

Chiara, Maria Luisa dalla. "Some Logical Problems Suggested by Empirical Theories." In Cohen and Wartofsky 1983, 75–90.

Chomsky, Noam. 1975. *Reflections on Language.* New York: Pantheon Books.

———. 1957. *Syntactic Theory.* The Hague: Mouton.

Cohen, Robert S., and Marx W. Wartofsky, eds. 1983. *Language, Logic, and Method.* Dordrecht: D. Reidel.

Condillac, Etienne Bonnot de. [1746] 1947–51. *Essai sur l'origine des connoissances humaines.* In *Oeuvres Philosophiques,* 3 vols., edited by Georges Le Roy. Paris: Presses universitaires de France.

Cone, Edward T. 1960. "Analysis Today." In *Problems of Modern Music,* edited by Paul Henry Lang, 34–50. New York: Norton.

"Convention." 1970. In *Webster's New World Dictionary.*

Crane, R. S. 1953. *The Languages of Criticism and the Structure of Poetry.* Toronto: University of Toronto Press.

Culler, Jonathan. 1976. *Ferdinand de Saussure.* London: Fontana.

Curtius, Ernst Robert. [1948] 1953. *European Literature and the Latin Middle Ages.* Translated by Willard R. Trask. Princeton: Princeton University Press.

Danto, Arthur. 1964. "The Artworld." *Journal of Philosophy* 61: 571–84.

———. 1986. *The Philosophical Disenfranchisement of Art.* New York: Columbia University Press.

Davenant, William. [1650] 1971. *The Preface to Gondibert, an Heroick Poem Written by Sir William Davenant: With an Answer to the Preface by Mr. Hobbes.* Paris: Matthieu Guillemot. Reprinted in *Sir William Davenant's Gondibert,* edited by David F. Gladish, 3–44; 45–55. Oxford: Clarendon Press.

Davidson, Donald. 1984. *Inquiries into Truth and Interpretation.* Oxford: Clarendon Press.

———. "A Nice Derangement of Epitaphs." In Grandy and Warner 1986, 157–74.

——. 1990. "The Structure and Content of Truth." *Journal of Philosophy* 87: 279–328.

De Man, Paul. 1971. "The Rhetoric of Blindness: Jacques Derrida's Reading of Rousseau." In *Blindness and Insight*, 102–42. New York: Oxford University Press.

Dennett, Daniel C. 1969. *Content and Consciousness.* London: Routledge & Kegan Paul.

Derrida, Jacques. [1967] 1973. *Speech and Phenomena, and Other Essays on Husserl's Theory of Signs.* Translated by David B. Allison. Evanston: Northwestern University Press.

Diderot, Denis. [1751] 1978. *Lettre sur les sourds et les muets à l'usage de ceux qui entendent.* In *Oeuvres complètes*, vol. 4, edited by Jean Varloot and Jacques Chouillet, 129–233. Paris: Hermann.

Dryden, John. [1700] 1926. Preface to the *Fables.* In *Essays of John Dryden*, edited by William Paton Ker. Oxford: Clarendon Press.

Duhem, Pierre. 1892. "Quelques réflexions au sujet des théories physiques." *Revue des questions scientifiques* 31: 134–77.

Dummett, Michael. "'A Nice Derangement of Epitaphs': Some Comments on Davidson and Hacking." In LePore 1986, 459–76.

Dumouchel, Paul. 1986. "Hobbes: La course à la souveraineté." *Stanford French Review* 10: 153–76.

——. Forthcoming. "The Political Problem of Religion: Hobbes's Reading of the Bible." *Oxford Studies in the History of Philosophy.*

Duncanson, Ian. 1979. *Contract.* London: Sweet & Maxwell.

Dupréel, Eugène. [1925] 1990. "Convention et raison." In *L'homme et la rhétorique*, 84–115. Paris: Méridiens Klincksieck.

Durkheim, Emile. [1893] 1978. *De la division du travail social.* Paris: Presses universitaires de France.

Eco, Umberto. 1984. *Semiotics and the Philosophy of Language.* Bloomington: Indiana University Press.

Eliot, T. S. 1957. *On Poetry and Poets.* London: Faber.

——. [1922] 1962. *The Waste Land and Other Poems.* New York: Harcourt, Brace & World.

Ellis, John M. 1989. *Against Deconstruction.* Princeton: Princeton University Press.

Elster, Jon. 1989. *The Cement of Society: A Study of Social Order.* Cambridge: Cambridge University Press.

——. 1986. *An Introduction to Karl Marx.* Cambridge: Cambridge University Press.

——. 1985. *Making Sense of Marx.* Cambridge: Cambridge University Press.

——. 1986. "Self-realization in Work and Politics." *Social Philosophy and Policy* 3: 97–126.

——. 1983. *Sour Grapes: Studies in the Subversion of Rationality.* Cambridge: Cambridge University Press.

———. [1979] 1984. *Ulysses and the Sirens.* Rev. ed. Cambridge: Cambridge University Press.

Engel, Pascal. 1989. *La norme du vrai.* Paris: Gallimard.

Engelsing, Rolf. 1970. "Die Perioden der Lesergeschichte in der Neuzeit." In *Archiv für Geschichte des Buches,* vol. 10, 945–1002. Frankfurt am Main: Spalten.

Ferry, Luc. 1990. *Homo Aestheticus.* Paris: Grasset.

Fish, Stanley. "Consequences." In Mitchell 1985, 106–31.

———. 1989. *Doing What Comes Naturally: Change, Rhetoric, and the Practice of Theory in Literary and Legal Studies.* Durham, N.C.: Duke University Press.

———. 1980. *Is There a Text in This Class? The Authority of Interpretive Communities.* Cambridge, Mass.: Harvard University Press.

———. [1978]. "Normal Circumstances, Literal Language, Direct Speech Acts, the Ordinary, the Everyday, the Obvious, What Goes without Saying, and Other Special Cases." In Fish 1980, 268–92.

Foote, Peter. 1979. "New Dimensions in *Njáls Saga.*" *Scandinavica* 18: 49–58.

Ford, Ford Madox. [1915] 1955. *The Good Soldier.* New York: Random House.

Forest, J. E. 1962. "Dryden, Hobbes, Thomas Goodwin, and the Nimble Spaniel." *N & Q,* n.s. 9: 381–82.

Forte, Allen. 1977. "Schenker's Conception of Musical Structure." In *Readings in Schenker Analysis and Other Approaches,* edited by Maury Yeston, 3–37. New Haven: Yale University Press.

Foucault, Michel. [1971] 1977. "Nietzsche, Genealogy, History." In *Language, Counter-memory, Practice: Selected Essays and Interviews,* edited by Donald F. Bouchard and translated by Bouchard and Sherry Simon, 139–64. Ithaca: Cornell University Press.

Fraassen, Bas C. van. 1989. *Laws and Symmetry.* Oxford: Clarendon Press.

———. 1980. *The Scientific Image.* Oxford: Clarendon Press.

Frye, Northrop. 1957. *The Anatomy of Criticism: Four Essays.* Princeton: Princeton University Press.

———. 1986. *Northrop Frye on Shakespeare.* Edited by Robert Sandler. New Haven: Yale University Press.

Fultner, Barbara. 1989. "Rules in Context: A Critique of Kripke's Interpretation of Wittgenstein." M.A. thesis, McGill University.

Gadamer, Hans-Georg. [1960; 1965] 1975. *Truth and Method.* Translated from 2d ed. by Garrett Barden and John Cumming. New York: Continuum Press.

———. [1966] 1976. "The Universality of the Hermeneutical Problem." In *Philosophical Hermeneutics,* translated and edited by David Linge, 3–17. Berkeley: University of California Press.

Gang, Theodor M. 1956. "Hobbes and the Metaphysical Conceit—A Reply." *Journal of the History of Ideas* 17: 418–21.

Gates, Henry Louis, Jr. 1988. *The Signifying Monkey: A Theory of Afro-American Literary Criticism.* New York: Oxford University Press.

Gehlen, Arnold. 1940. *Der Mensch: seine Natur und seine Stellung in der Welt.* Berlin: Jünker & Dünnhaupt.

Girard, René. 1961. *Mensonge romantique et vérité romanesque.* Paris: Grasset.

Glasersfeld, Ernst von. "Siegener Gespräch über radikalen Konstruktivismus." In Schmidt 1987b, 401–40.

Goethe, Johann Wolfgang. [1811] 1976. *Dichtung und Wahrheit.* In *Poetische Werke,* vol. 13. Berlin: Aufbau Verlag.

Goldfriedrich, Johann. [1909] 1970. *Geschichte des deutschen Buchhandels von Beginn der klassischen Literaturperiode bis zum Beginn der Fremdherrschaft (1740–1804).* Leipzig: Aalen.

Gombrich, E. H. [1960] 1961. *Art and Illusion: A Study in the Psychology of Pictorial Representation.* London: Pantheon Books.

Goodman, Nelson. [1955] 1965. *Fact, Fiction, and Forecast.* Indianapolis: Bobbs-Merrill.

———. 1989. "'Just the Facts, Ma'am!'" In *Relativism: Interpretation and Confrontation,* edited by Michael Krausz, 80–85. Notre Dame, Ind.: University of Notre Dame Press.

Goodman, Nelson, and Catherine Z. Elgin. 1988. *Reconceptions in Philosophy and Other Arts and Sciences.* Indianapolis: Hackett.

Grandy, Richard E., and Richard Warner., eds. 1986. *Philosophical Grounds of Rationality: Intentions, Categories, Ends.* Oxford: Clarendon Press.

Grice, Paul. 1989. *Studies in the Way of Words.* Cambridge, Mass.: Harvard University Press.

Guthrie, William Keith Chambers. 1971. *The Sophists.* Cambridge: Cambridge University Press.

Habermas, Jürgen. [1970] 1988. *On the Logic of the Social Sciences.* Translated by Shierry Weber Nicholsen and Jerry A. Stark. Cambridge, Mass.: MIT Press.

———. [1985] 1987. *The Philosophical Discourse of Modernity.* Translated by Frederick Lawrence. Cambridge, Mass.: MIT Press.

———. [1983] 1987. "Philosophy as Stand-in and Interpreter." Translated by Christian Lenhardt. In *After Philosophy: End or Transformation?* edited by Kenneth Baynes, James Bohman and Thomas McCarthy, 296–315. Cambridge, Mass.: MIT Press.

———. [1981] 1984. *The Theory of Communicative Action: Reason and the Rationalization of Society.* Translated by Thomas McCarthy. Boston: Beacon Press.

Hacking, Ian. "The Parody of Conversation." In LePore 1986, 447–58.

Hadamard, Jacques. 1949. *An Essay on the Psychology of Invention in the Mathematical Field.* Princeton: Princeton University Press.

Haferkorn, Hans J. 1974. "Zur Entstehung der bürgerlich-literarischen Intelligenz und des Schriftstellers in Deutschland zwischen 1750 und

1800." In *Deutsches Bürgertum und literarische Intelligenz, 1750–1800*, edited by B. Lutz, 113–275. Stuttgart: Metzler.

Hallberg, Robert von. 1984. *Canons*. Chicago: University of Chicago Press.

Hamon, Philippe. 1973. "Un Discours contraint." In Barthes et al. 1980, 119–81.

Hannerz, Ulf. 1969. *Soulside: Inquiries into Ghetto Culture and Community*. New York: Columbia University Press.

Harsanyi, John C., and Reinhard Selten. 1988. *A General Theory of Equilibrium Selection in Games*. Cambridge, Mass.: MIT Press.

Hayek, Friedrich August von. 1988. *The Fatal Conceit: The Errors of Socialism*. Chicago: University of Chicago Press.

———. 1973. *Law, Legislation, and Liberty: Rules and Order*. Chicago: University of Chicago Press.

———. 1967. *Studies in Philosophy, Politics, and Economics*. Chicago: University of Chicago Press.

Heidegger, Martin. 1926. *Sein und Zeit*. Tübingen: Niemeyer.

Hejl, Peter M. "Konstruktion der sozialen Konstruktion: Grundlinien einer konstruktivistischen Sozialtheorie." In Schmidt 1987b, 303–39.

———. 1987a. "Zum Begriff des Individuums: Bemerkungen zum ungeklärten Verhältnis von Psychologie und Soziologie." In *Systeme erkennen Systeme: Individuelle, soziale, und methodische Bedingungen systemischer Diagnostik*, edited by Günther Schiepeck, 115–54. München: Weinheim.

Herder, Johann Gottfried von. [1770] 1978. *Abhandlung über den Ursprung der Sprache*. Edited by Wolfgang Pross. München: Hanser.

Hermerén, Göran. 1991. *Art, Reason, and Tradition: On the Role of Rationality in Interpretation and Explanation of Works of Art*. Stockholm: Almqvist & Wiksell International.

———. 1983. *Aspects of Aesthetics*. Lund: Gleerup.

———. 1975. *Influence in Art and Literature*. Princeton: Princeton University Press.

———. 1986. "Musik som Språk." *Svensk Tidskrift för Musik*, 7–16.

———. 1969. *Representation and Meaning in the Visual Arts*. Lund: Läromedelsförlaget (Scandinavian University Books).

———. 1987. "Representation, Truth, and the Languages of the Arts." In *Essays on the Philosophy of Music*, edited by Veikko Rantala, Lewis Rowell, and Eero Tarasti, 179–209. Helsinki: Acta Philosophica Fennica.

Hermerén, Göran, and J. Emt, eds. 1991. *Understanding the Arts*. Lund: Lund University Press.

Herrnstein Smith, Barbara. 1978. *On the Margins of Discourse*. Chicago: University of Chicago Press.

Hirsch, E. D., Jr. "Against Theory?" In Mitchell 1985, 48–52.

———. 1976. *The Aims of Interpretation*. Chicago: University of Chicago Press.

———. 1983. "Beyond Convention." *New Literary History* 14: 389–97.

———. 1967. *Validity in Interpretation*. New Haven: Yale University Press.

Hintzenberg, Dagmar, Siegfried J. Schmidt, and Reinhold Zobel. 1980.

Zum Literaturbegriff in der Bundesrepublik Deutschland. Braunschweig-Wiesbaden: Vieweg.

Hjelmslev, Louis. [1943] 1963. *Prolegomena to a Theory of Language.* Translated by Francis J. Whitfield. Madison: University of Wisconsin Press.

Hjort, Mette. 1993. *The Strategy of Letters.* Cambridge, Mass.: Harvard University Press. Forthcoming.

Hobbes, Thomas. [1650]. *The Answer of Mr. Hobbes to Sir Will. D'Avenant's Preface before Gondibert.* In Davenant 1650. Reprinted in *Sir William Davenant's Gondibert,* ed. Gladish, 45–55.

———. [1637] 1986. *A Briefe of the Art of Rhetorique.* Reprinted in *The Rhetorics of Thomas Hobbes and Bernard Lamy,* edited by John T. Harwood, 24–128. Carbondale: Southern Illinois University Press.

———. [1662] 1840. *Considerations upon the Reputation, Loyalty, Manners, and Religion of Thomas Hobbes.* In *The English Works of Thomas Hobbes of Malmesbury,* vol. 4, 409–40.

———. [1681] 1966. *A Dialogue between a Philosopher and a Student of the Common Laws of England,* edited by T. Ascarelli. Paris: Dalloz.

———. [1656] 1839. *Elements of Philosophy, The First Section, Concerning Body.* In *The English Works of Thomas Hobbes of Malmesbury,* vol. 1.

———. 1839–44. *The English Works of Thomas Hobbes of Malmesbury.* Vols. 1, 2, 4, 10. Edited by Sir William Molesworth. London: John Bohn.

———. [1651a] 1980. *Leviathan.* Edited by Crawford Brough Macpherson. Harmondsworth: Penguin Books.

———. [1651b] 1841. *Philosophical Rudiments concerning Government and Society.* In *The English Works of Thomas Hobbes of Malmesbury,* vol. 2.

———. [1629] 1989. *Thucydides: The Peloponnesian War.* Modern reprint, *The Peloponnesian War: Thucydides: The Complete Hobbes Translation.* Edited by D. Grene. Chicago: University of Chicago Press.

———. [1675] 1844. *To the Reader, Concerning the Virtues of an Heroic Poem.* In *The English Works of Thomas Hobbes of Malmesbury,* vol. 10, iii–x.

Holt, Grace Sims. "'Inversion' in Black Communication." In Kochman 1972, 152–59.

Hugo, Victor. [1827] 1968. *Cromwell.* Paris: Garnier-Flammarion.

Hume, David. [1777] 1975. *An Enquiry Concerning the Principles of Morals.* Edited and Introduced by L. A. Selby-Bigge. Oxford: Clarendon Press.

———. [1739] 1980. *A Treatise of Human Nature.* Edited by L. A. Selby-Bigge. Oxford: Clarendon Press.

Irigaray, Luce. [1977] 1985. *This Sex Which Is Not One.* Translated by Catherine Porter, with Carolyn Burke. Ithaca: Cornell University Press.

Jakobson, Roman. 1960. "Linguistics and Poetics." In *Style in Language,* edited by Thomas A. Sebeok, 350–77. Cambridge, Mass.: MIT Press.

Jameson, Frederic. 1984. "Postmodernism, or the Cultural Logic of Late Capitalism." *New Left Review* 146: 53–92.

Johnston, David. 1986. *The Rhetoric of Leviathan: Thomas Hobbes and the Politics of Cultural Transformation.* Princeton: Princeton University Press.

Juhl, Peter D. 1980. *Interpretation: An Essay in the Philosophy of Literary Criticism.* Princeton: Princeton University Press.

Kant, Immanuel. 1803. *Immanuel Kant über Pädagogik.* Edited by Friedrich Theodor Rink. Königsberg: F. Nicolovius.

———. [1790] 1974. *Kritik der Urteilskraft.* Hamburg: Felix Meiner Verlag.

Kaplan, Abraham. [1967] 1972. "The Aesthetics of the Popular Arts." In *Modern Culture and the Arts,* edited by James B. Hall and Barry Ulanov, 62–78. New York: McGraw-Hill.

Kenner, Hugh. 1964. "The Making of the Modernist Canon." In Hallberg 1984, 363–75.

Kerman, Joseph. 1983. "A Few Canonic Variations." In Hallberg 1984, 177–95.

Kjörup, Sören. 1978. "Pictorial Speech Acts." *Erkenntnis* 12: 55–71.

Kleist, Heinrich von. [1811] 1971. *Über das Marionettentheater.* Zürich: Flamberg.

Knapp, Steven, and Walter Benn Michaels. 1982. "Against Theory." In Mitchell 1985, 11–30.

———. "A Reply to Our Critics." In Mitchell 1985, 95–105.

———. "A Reply to Richard Rorty: What Is Pragmatism?" In Mitchell 1985, 139–46.

Kochman, Thomas. "Toward an Ethnography of Black American Speech Behavior." In Kochman 1972, 241–64.

———, ed. 1972. *Rappin' and Stylin' Out: Communication in Urban Black America.* Urbana: University of Illinois Press.

Kripke, Saul A. 1972. *Naming and Necessity.* Cambridge, Mass.: Harvard University Press.

———. 1982. *Wittgenstein on Rules and Private Language.* Cambridge, Mass.: Harvard University Press.

Kuhn, Thomas S. [1962] 1970. *The Structure of Scientific Revolutions.* Chicago: University of Chicago Press.

La Fontaine, Jean de. [1668] 1954. *Fables.* In *Oeuvres complètes,* edited by René Groos and Jacques Schiffrin, 1–340. Paris: Gallimard.

Lakatos, Imre, and Alan Musgrave, eds. 1970. *Criticism and the Growth of Knowledge.* Cambridge: Cambridge University Press.

Lanham, Richard A. 1973. *"Tristam Shandy" and the Games of Pleasure.* Berkeley: University of California Press.

LePore, Ernest, ed. 1986. *Truth and Interpretation: Perspectives on the Philosophy of Donald Davidson.* New York: Basil Blackwell.

Le Roy, Edouard. 1901. "Un positivisme nouveau." *Revue de métaphysique et de morale* 9: 138–53.

Lessing, Alfred. 1983. "What Is Wrong with a Forgery?" In *The Forger's Art:*

Forgery and the Philosophy of Art, edited by Denis Dutton, 58–76. Berkeley: University of California Press.

Lessing, Gotthold Ephraim. [1767–69] 1972. *Die Hamburgische Dramaturgie.* Leipzig: Reclam.

Levenson, Joseph Richmond. 1966. *Confucian China and Its Modern Fate: The Problem of Intellectual Continuity.* Berkeley: University of California Press.

Lévi-Strauss, Claude. 1950. "Introduction à l'oeuvre de Marcel Mauss." In Marcel Mauss, *Sociologie et Anthropologie,* ix–lii. Paris: Presses universitaires de France.

Levin, Lawrence. 1988. *Highbrow/Lowbrow: The Emergence of Cultural Hierarchy in America.* Cambridge, Mass.: Harvard University Press.

Lewis, David K. [1969] 1986. *Convention: A Philosophical Study.* Cambridge, Mass.: Harvard University Press.

———. 1973. *Counterfactuals.* Cambridge, Mass.: Harvard University Press.

———. 1975. "Languages and Language." In *Language, Mind, and Knowledge,* edited by Keith Gunderson, 3–35. Minneapolis: University of Minnesota Press.

———. 1986. *On the Plurality of Worlds.* Oxford: Basil Blackwell.

———. [1978] 1983. "Truth in Fiction." In *Philosophical Papers,* vol. 1, 261–80. New York: Oxford University Press.

Livingston, Paisley. 1988. *Literary Knowledge: Humanistic Inquiry and the Philosophy of Science.* Ithaca: Cornell University Press.

———. 1991. *Literature and Rationality: Ideas of Agency in Theory and Fiction.* Cambridge: Cambridge University Press.

———. 1992. *Models of Desire: René Girard and the Psychology of Mimesis.* Baltimore: Johns Hopkins University Press.

Loar, Brian. 1981. *Mind and Meaning.* Cambridge: Cambridge University Press.

Lönnroth, Lars. 1980. "New Dimensions and Old Directions in Saga Research." *Scandinavica* 19: 57–61.

———. 1976. *Njáls Saga: A Critical Introduction.* Berkeley: University of California Press.

Lorenz, Konrad. 1963. *Das sogenannte Böse: zur Naturgeschichte der Aggression.* Bonn: G. Borotha-Schoeler.

Luce, R. Duncan, and Howard Raiffa. 1957. *Games and Decisions.* New York: Wiley.

Lyotard, Jean-François. [1983] 1988. *The Differend: Phrases in Dispute.* Translated by Georges Van Den Abbeele. Minneapolis: University of Minnesota Press.

Lyotard, Jean-François, and Jean-Loup Thébaud. [1979] 1985. *Just Gaming.* Translated by Wlad Godzich and Brian Massumi. Minneapolis: University of Minnesota Press.

McCormick, Peter. 1988. *Fictions, Philosophies, and the Problems of Poetics.* Ithaca: Cornell University Press.

——. 1976. *Heidegger and the Language of the World*. Ottawa: University of Ottawa Press.

——. 1990. *Modernity, Aesthetics, and the Bounds of Art*. Ithaca: Cornell University Press.

MacIntyre, Alasdair C. [1981] 1984. *After Virtue*. Notre Dame, Ind.: University of Notre Dame Press.

——. 1988. *Whose Justice? Which Rationality?* Notre Dame, Ind.: University of Notre Dame Press.

McKeon, Robert, ed. 1941. *The Basic Works of Aristotle*. New York: Random House.

Mackie, J. L. 1977. *Ethics: Inventing Right and Wrong*. Harmondsworth: Penguin Books.

Macmillan, Harold. 1989. *The Sunday Times*, June 11.

Macpherson, C. B. 1962. *The Political Theory of Possessive Individualism: Hobbes to Locke*. Oxford: Clarendon Press.

Mailloux, Steven. 1982. *Interpretive Conventions: The Reader in the Study of American Fiction*. Ithaca: Cornell University Press.

Manley, Lawrence. 1980. *Convention: 1500–1750*. Cambridge, Mass.: Harvard University Press.

Marcus, Greil. [1975] 1982. *Mystery Train: Images of America in Rock 'n Roll Music*. New York: Dalton.

Margolis, Joseph. 1991. "Métaphysique radicale." *Archives de philosophie* 44: 379–406.

——. 1990. "Moral Realism and the Meaning of Life." *Philosophical Forum* 22: 1–30.

——. 1989. "The Novelty of Marx's Theory of *Praxis*." *Journal for the Theory of Social Behaviour* 19: 367–88.

——. 1986. *Pragmatism without Foundations: Reconciling Realism and Relativism*. Oxford: Basil Blackwell.

——. Forthcoming. *"Praxis* and Invariance."

——. Forthcoming. *"Praxis* and Universals."

——. "Robust Relativism." 1976. *Journal of Aesthetics and Art Criticism* 35: 37–46.

Marsh, Dave, and Phyllis Pollack. 1989. "Wanted for Attitude." *Village Voice*, October 10, 33–37.

Mauss, Marcel. 1968. *Essais de sociologie*. Paris: Editions du Minuit.

May, Gita. 1977. *Stendhal and the Age of Napoleon*. New York: Columbia University Press.

Mayr, Ernst. 1976. *Evolution and the Diversity of Life: Selected Essays*. Cambridge, Mass.: Harvard University Press, Belknap Press.

Melville, Herman. [1924] 1959. *Billy Budd, Foretopman*. In *Four Short Novels*. New York: Liveright.

Merleau-Ponty, Maurice. 1945. *La phénoménologie de la perception*. Paris: Gallimard.

Meutsch, Dietrich, and Siegfried J. Schmidt. 1985. "On the Role of Conventions in Understanding Literary Texts." *Poetics* 14: 551-74.
——. 1988. *Abschlußbericht zum Projekt "Literarisches Textverstehen als konventionsgesteuerter Prozeß."* Manuscript. University of Siegen.
Mintz, Samuel I. 1962. *The Hunting of Leviathan: Seventeenth-Century Reactions to the Materialism and Moral Philosophy of Thomas Hobbes.* Cambridge: Cambridge University Press.
Mitchell, W. J. T., ed. 1985. *Against Theory: Literary Studies and the New Pragmatism.* Chicago: University of Chicago Press.
Mitchell-Kernan, Claudia. "Signifying, Loud-Talking, and Marking." In Kochman 1972, 315-35.
Mizener, Arthur. 1971. *The Saddest Story: A Biography of Ford Madox Ford.* New York: World.

Narmour, Eugene. 1977. *Beyond Schenkerism: The Need for Alternatives in Music Analysis.* Chicago: University of Chicago Press.
Neumann, John von, and Oskar Morgenstern. 1944. *Theory of Games and Economic Behavior.* Princeton: Princeton University Press.
Novitz, David. 1976: "Conventions and the Growth of Pictorial Style." *British Journal of Aesthetics* 16: 324-37.
——. *Pictures and Their Use in Communication: A Philosophical Essay.* The Hague: Martinus Nijhoff, 1977.
Nozick, Robert. 1974. *Anarchy, State, and Utopia.* New York: Basic Books.
Nussbaum, Martha. 1983. "Fictions of the Soul." *Philosophy and Literature* 7: 145-61.

Ohtaki, Toshio. 1989. "Das Literatursystem in Japan." Manuscript. University of Kanazowa.
Olson, Mancur, Jr. 1965. *The Logic of Collective Actions: Public Goods and the Theory of Groups.* Cambridge, Mass.: Harvard University Press.
Orléan, André. 1989. "L'économie des conventions." *Revue économique* 40: 241-72.
——. 1985. "Hétérodoxie et incertitude." *Cahiers du CREA* 5: 247-75.

Panofsky, Erwin. 1955. *Meaning in the Visual Arts: Papers in and on Art History.* New York: Doubleday, Anchor Books.
Pareles, Jon. 1990. "How Rap Moves to Television's Beat." *New York Times,* January 14, sec. 2.
Pavel, Thomas G. 1985. "Convention et interprétation." *Littérature* 57: 31-47.
——. 1986. *Fictional Worlds.* Cambridge: Harvard University Press.
——. 1988. *Le mirage linguistique: Essai sur la modernisation intellectuelle.* Paris: Editions de Minuit.
La philosophie analytique. 1962. Proceedings of the Royaumont Colloquium. Paris: Editions de Minuit.
Piatelli-Palmarini, Massimo, ed. [1979] 1980. *Language and Learning: The De-*

bate between Piaget and Noam Chomsky. Cambridge, Mass.: Harvard University Press.

Pileggi, Nicholas. 1987. *Wiseguy*. New York: Pocket Books.

Plato. [1961] 1973. *Cratylus*. Translated by Benjamin Jowett. In *The Collected Dialogues of Plato, Including the Letters*, edited by Edith Hamilton and Huntington Cairns, 421–74. Princeton: Princeton University Press.

Poincaré, Henri. [1908a] 1920. "L'invention mathématique." In *Science et méthode*, 43–63. Paris: Flammarion.

———. 1902. *La science et l'hypothèse*. Paris: Bibliothèque de philosophie scientifique.

———. [1908b] 1914. *Science and Method*. Translated by Francis Maitland. London: T. Nelson.

Popper, Sir Karl Raimund. 1972. "The Aim of Science." In *Objective Knowledge: An Evolutionary Approach*, 191–205. Oxford: Clarendon Press.

———. 1963. *Conjectures and Refutations: The Growth of Scientific Knowledge*. London: Routledge & Kegan Paul.

———. [1934] 1959. *The Logic of Scientific Discovery*. London: Hutchinson.

———. 1944, 1945. *The Open Society and Its Enemies*. Vols. 1, 2. London: Routledge & Kegan Paul.

———. 1983. *Realism and the Aim of Science*. Edited by W. W. Bartley III. Totowa, N.J.: Rowman & Littlefield.

Putnam, Hilary. "What Is Innate and Why: Comments on the Debate." In Piatelli-Palmarini 1979, 287–309.

Quine, Willard Van Orman. [1954] 1966. "Carnap and Logical Truth." In *The Ways of Paradox*, 107–32.

———. "Foreword." In Lewis 1969, xi–xii.

———. 1953. *From a Logical Point of View: Nine Logico-philosophical Essays*. Cambridge, Mass.: Harvard University Press.

———. 1969. "Ontological Relativity." In *Ontological Relativity and Other Essays*, 26–68. New York: Columbia University Press.

———. 1953. "On What There Is." In *From a Logical Point of View*, 1–19.

———. [1936; rev. 1964] 1966. "Truth by Convention." In *The Ways of Paradox*, 77–106.

———. 1953. "Two Dogmas of Empiricism." In *From a Logical Point of View*, 20–46.

———. [1961] 1966. "The Ways of Paradox." In *The Ways of Paradox*, 1–18.

———. [1966] 1976. *The Ways of Paradox and Other Essays*. Cambridge, Mass.: Harvard University Press.

———. 1960. *Word and Object*. Cambridge, Mass.: MIT Press.

Rabinowitz, Peter J. 1985. "The Turn of the Glass Key: Popular Fiction as Reading Strategy." *Critical Inquiry* 11: 418–31.

———. 1980. "'What's Hecuba to Us?' The Audience's Experience of Literary Borrowing." In *The Reader in the Text: Essays on Audience and Interpretation*, edited by Susan R. Suleiman and Inge Crosman, 241-63. Princeton: Princeton University Press.

Ramsey, F. P. [1926] 1960. "Truth and Probability." In *The Foundations of Mathematics*, edited by R. B. Braithwaite, 156-98. Paterson, N.J.: Littlefield, Adams.

Rawls, John. 1971. *A Theory of Justice*. Cambridge, Mass.: Harvard University Press.

Reeves, Charles Eric. 1986a. "'Conveniency to Nature': Literary Art and Arbitrariness." *PMLA* 101: 798-810.

————. 1982. "Convention and Literary Behaviour." In *The Structure of Literary Process: Studies Dedicated to the Memory of Felix Vodicka*, edited by P. Steiner, M. Cervenka, and R. Vroon, 431-54. Amsterdam: Benjamins.

————. 1986b. "The Languages of Convention: Literature and Consensus." *Poetics Today* 7: 3-28.

Ricoeur, Paul. [1983] 1984. *Time and Narrative*. Vol. 1. Translated by Kathleen McLaughlin and David Pallauer. Chicago: University of Chicago Press.

Riek, Miriam M. 1977. *The Golden Lands of Thomas Hobbes*. Detroit: Wayne State University Press.

Riffaterre, Michael. [1978] "L'illusion référentielle." In Barthes et al. 1980, 91-118.

Rorty, Richard. "Philosophy without Principles." In Mitchell 1985, 132-38.

Rosmarin, Adena. 1985. *The Power of Genres*. Minneapolis: University of Minnesota Press.

Roth, Alvin E. 1987. "Bargaining Phenomena and Bargaining Theory." In *Laboratory Experimentation in Economics: Six Points of View*, edited by Alvin Roth, 14-41. Cambridge: Cambridge University Press.

Rousseau, Jean-Jacques. [1762] 1966. *Du Contrat social*. Paris: Garnier-Flammarion.

————. [174.?, 175.?]; [1755] 1971. *Discours sur les sciences et les arts; Discours sur l'origine et les fondements de l'inégalité parmi les hommes*. Paris: Garnier-Flammarion.

————. [1781] 1968. *Essai sur l'origine des langues où il est parlé de la mélodie et de l'imitation musicale*. Edited by Charles Porset. Bordeaux: Guy Ducros.

Rusch, Gebhard. 1987. *Erkenntnis, Wissenschaft, Geschichte. Von einem konstruktivistischen Standpunkt*. Frankfurt am Main: Suhrkamp Verlag.

Saussure, Ferdinand de. [1916] 1969. *Cours de linguistique générale*. Paris: Payot.

Schelling, Thomas. 1984. *Choice and Consequence*. Cambridge, Mass.: Harvard University Press.

————. 1960. *The Strategy of Conflict*. Cambridge, Mass.: Harvard University Press.

Schenker, Heinrich. [1935; 1956] 1979. *Free Composition*. Translated and edited by Ernst Oster. New York: Longman.

————. [1906] 1954. *Harmony*. Edited by Oswald Jonas. Translated by Elisabeth Mann Borgese. Chicago: University of Chicago Press.

Schiffer, Stephen R. 1972. *Meaning*. New York: Oxford University Press.

Schiller, Friedrich. [1795] 1982. *On the Aesthetic Education of Man.* Translated by Elizabeth M. Wilkinson and L.A. Willoughby. Oxford: Clarendon Press.

Schmidt, Peter. 1980. "Buchmarkt, Verlagswesen und Zeitschriften." In *Deutsche Literatur: eine Sozialgeschichte,* vol. 5, edited by H. A. Glaser, 74–92. Reinbek: Rowohlt.

Schmidt, Siegfried J. 1980. "Fictionality in Literary and Non-Literary Discourse." *Poetics* 9: 525–46.

——. 1984. "The Fiction Is That Reality Exists." *Poetics Today* 5: 253–74.

——. 1982. *Foundations for the Empirical Study of Literature: The Components of a Basic Theory.* Translated by Robert de Beaugrande. Hamburg: Helmut Buske Verlag.

——. 1987a. "Der radikale Konstruktivismus: Ein neues Paradigma im interdisziplinären Diskurs." In *Der Diskurs des radikalen Konstruktivismus,* 11–88.

——. 1989. *Die Selbstorganisation des Sozialsystems Literatur im 18. Jahrhundert.* Frankfurt am Main: Suhrkamp Verlag.

——, ed. 1987b. *Der Diskurs des radikalen Konstruktivismus.* Frankfurt am Main: Suhrkamp Verlag.

Schotter, Andrew. 1981. *The Economic Theory of Social Institutions.* Cambridge: Cambridge University Press.

Schücking, Levin Ludwig. 1964. *Die puritanische Familie in literarisch-soziologischer Sicht.* Bern: Francke.

Searle, John. 1969. *Speech Acts: An Essay in the Philosophy of Language.* Cambridge: Cambridge University Press.

Selden, Raman. 1973. "Hobbes, Dryden, and the Ranging Spaniel." *N & Q* 20: 388.

——. 1974. "Hobbes and Late Metaphysical Poetry." *Journal of the History of Ideas* 35: 197–210.

Shakespeare, William. [1597] 1980. *Romeo and Juliet.* Edited by Brian Gibbons. London: Methuen.

——. [1597] 1984. *Romeo and Juliet.* Edited by G. Blakemore Evans. Cambridge: Cambridge University Press.

——. [1609] 1965. *Sonnets.* New Haven: Yale University Press.

Shapin, Steven, and Simon Schaffer. 1985. *Leviathan and the Air-Pump: Hobbes, Boyle, and the Experimental Life.* Princeton: Princeton University Press.

Shelley, Percy Bysshe. [1821] 1965. *A Defence of Poetry.* In *The Complete Works of Percy Bysshe Shelley,* edited by Roger Ingpen and Walter E. Peck, vol. 7, 105–40. London: Ernest Benn.

Shubik, Martin. 1982. *Game Theory in the Social Sciences: Concepts and Solutions.* Cambridge, Mass.: MIT Press.

Shusterman, Richard. 1986. "Convention: Variations on a Theme." *Philosophical Investigations* 9: 36–55.

——. 1981. "Evaluative Reasoning in Criticism." *Ratio* 23: 141–57.

——. 1978. "The Logic of Interpretation." *Philosophical Quarterly* 28: 310–24.

———. 1989. "Postmodernism and the Aesthetic Turn." *Poetics Today* 10: 605–22.

———. 1992. *Pragmatist Aesthetics: Living Beauty, Rethinking Art.* Oxford: Basil Blackwell.

———. 1988. *T. S. Eliot and the Philosophy of Criticism.* New York: Columbia University Press.

———. 1986. "Wittgenstein and Critical Reasoning." *Philosophy and Phenomenological Research* 47: 91–110.

Skinner, Quentin. 1972a. "Conquest and Consent: Thomas Hobbes and the Engagement Controversy." In *The Interregnum: the Quest of Settlement, 1646–1660*, edited by G. E. Aylmer, 79–98. London: Macmillan.

———. 1972b. "The Context of Hobbes's Theory of Political Obligation." In *Hobbes and Rousseau: A Collection of Critical Essays*, edited by Maurice William Cranston and Richard S. Peters, 109–42. New York: Doubleday.

———. 1966. "The Ideological Context of Hobbes's Political Thought." *Historical Journal* 9: 286–317.

Smith, John Maynard. 1982. *Evolution and the Theory of Games.* Cambridge: Cambridge University Press.

Spingarn, Joel Elias. 1908–9. *Critical Essays of the Seventeenth Century.* 3 vols. Oxford: Clarendon Press.

Springer, Sally P., and Georg Deutsch. 1981. *Left Brain, Right Brain.* San Francisco: W. H. Freeman.

Stachel, John. "Comments on 'Some Logical Problems Suggested by Empirical Theories' by Professor dalla Chiara." In Cohen and Wartofsky 1983, 91–102.

Stendhal [Marie Henri Beyle]. [1823] 1970. *Racine et Shakespeare.* Introduction by Roger Fayolles. Paris: Garnier-Flammarion.

———. [1827] 1948. *Le rouge et le noir.* 2 vols. Paris: Albert Guillot.

Stoll, Elmer Edgar. 1933. *Art and Artifice in Shakespeare.* Cambridge: Cambridge University Press.

Süßmilch, Johann Peter. 1741. *Die göttliche Ordnung in den Veränderungen des menschlichen Geschlechts.* Berlin: J. L. Spener.

Talmor, Sascha. 1984. *The Rhetoric of Criticism: From Hobbes to Coleridge.* New York: Pergamon Press.

Taylor, Charles. 1990. "Irreducibly Social Goods." In *Rationality, Individualism and Public Policy*, edited by Geoffrey Brennan and Cliff Walsh, 45–63. Canberra: Australian National University Press.

———. 1985. "Theories of Meaning." In Taylor, *Human Agency and Language: Philosophical Papers*, vol. 1, 248–92. Cambridge: Cambridge University Press.

Taylor, Michael. 1987. *The Possibility of Cooperation.* New York: Cambridge University Press.

Thomas, Keith. [1971] 1973. *Religion and the Decline of Magic: Studies in Popular*

Beliefs in Sixteenth- and Seventeenth-Century England. Harmondsworth: Penguin Books.

Thompson, Robert Farris. 1984. *Flash of the Spirit: African and Afro-American Art and Philosophy.* New York: Random House, Vintage Books.

Thorpe, Clarence de Wit. 1940. *The Aesthetic Theory of Thomas Hobbes.* Ann Arbor: University of Michigan Press.

Toop, David. 1984. *The Rap Attack: African Jive to New York Hip Hop.* Boston: South End Press.

Turner, Victor. 1981. "Social Dramas and Stories about Them." In *On Narrative,* edited by W.J.T. Mitchell, 137–64. Chicago: University of Chicago Press.

Urban, Greg. 1986. "Ceremonial Dialogues in South America." *American Anthropologist* 88: 371–86.

Vaihinger, Hans. 1924. *The Philosophy of "As If," a System of the Theoretical, Practical, and Religious Fictions of Mankind.* Translated by C. K. Ogden. London: K. Paul, Trench, Trubner.

van den Haag, Ernest. 1957. "Of Happiness and of Despair We Have No Measure." In *Mass Culture: The Popular Arts in America,* edited by Bernard Rosenberg and David Manning White, 504–36. Glencoe, Ill.: Free Press.

Ventura, Michael. 1986. *Shadow Dancing in the USA.* Los Angeles: J. P. Tarcher.

Vico, Giambattista. [1725; rev. 1744] 1974. *Scienza Nuova.* 2 vols. Edited by Fausto Nicolini. Rome: Laterza.

Walliser, Bernard. 1989. "Théorie des jeux et genèse des institutions." Manuscript.

Walton, Kendall. 1990. *Mimesis as Make-Believe: On the Foundations of the Representational Arts.* Cambridge, Mass.: Harvard University Press.

Watkins, John W. M. 1976. "The Human Condition: Two Criticisms of Hobbes." In *Essays in Memory of Imre Lakatos,* edited by Robert S. Cohen et al., 691–716. Dordrecht: D. Reidel.

Watson, George. 1955. "Hobbes and the Metaphysical Conceit." *Journal of the History of Ideas* 16: 558–62.

Weill, Alex, and François Terré. 1983. *Droit civil: Les obligations.* Paris: Dalloz.

Weitz, Morris. [1956] 1962. "The Role of Theory in Aesthetics." In *Philosophy Looks at the Arts,* edited by Joseph Margolis, 48–60. New York: Scribner.

Whitaker, Mark. 1988. "Hobbes's View of the Reformation." *History of Political Thought* 9: 45–58.

White, Hayden. 1987. *The Content of the Form: Narrative Discourse and Historical Representation.* Baltimore: Johns Hopkins University Press.

———. 1978. *Tropics of Discourse: Essays in Cultural Criticism.* Baltimore: Johns Hopkins University Press.

Willey, Basil. 1934. *The Seventeenth Century Background: Studies in the Thought of the Age in Relation to Poetry and Religion.* London: Chatto & Windus.

Wittgenstein, Ludwig. 1976. *Lectures on the Foundations of Mathematics.* Hassocks: Harvester Press.

———. [1953] 1958. *Philosophical Investigations.* Translated by G. E. M. Anscombe. Oxford: Basil Blackwell.

Wolin, Sheldon S. 1970. *Hobbes and the Epic Tradition in Political Theory.* Los Angeles: William Andrews Clark Memorial Library.

Wollheim, Richard. [1968] 1975. *Art and Its Objects: An Introduction to Aesthetics.* Harmondsworth: Penguin Books.

Wright, Georg Henrik von. 1971. *Explanation and Understanding.* London: Routledge & Kegan Paul.

———. 1966. "The Logic of Action—A Sketch." In *The Logic of Decision and Action,* edited by Nicholas Rescher, 121–36. Pittsburgh: University of Pittsburgh Press.

Zimmermann, Bernhard. 1988. "Lesepublikum, Markt und soziale Stellung des Schrifstellers in der Entwicklungsphase der bürgerlichen Gesellschaft." In *Propyläen Geschichte der Literatur,* vol. 4, 524–49. Berlin: Propyläen.

Note on Contributors

ALAIN BOYER is a member of the CREA, Ecole Polytechnique and "Maître de conférences" at Blaise Pascal University, Clermont-Ferrand. He is the author of *Karl Popper: Une épistémologie laïque?* (Presses de l'Ecole Normale Supérieur, 1978) and the co-translator of Karl Popper's *Realism and the Aim of Science*.

CLAUDIA BRODSKY LACOUR is associate professor of comparative literature at Princeton University. She is the author of a book on Kant and narrative representation, *The Imposition of Form: Studies in Narrative Representation and Knowledge* (Princeton University Press, 1987) and of articles on German, French, and English philosophy and literature.

PAUL DUMOUCHEL is associate professor of philosophy at the University of Quebec in Montreal. He is the co-author, with Jean-Pierre Dupuy, of *L'enfer des choses: René Girard et la logique de l'économie* (Editions du Seuil, 1979). He is the co-editor, with Dupuy, of *L'auto-organisation: De la physique au politique* (Editions du Seuil, 1983), and the editor of *Violence and Truth: On the Work of René Girard* (Athlone and Stanford University Press, 1988).

JON ELSTER teaches political science at the University of Chicago, having taught earlier at the universities of Paris and Oslo. His most recent books include *Psychologie politique* (Editions du Minuit, 1990), *The Cement of Society: A Study of Social Order* (Cambridge University Press, 1989), and *Nuts and Bolts for the Social Sciences* (Cambridge University Press, 1989). He is currently working on problems of constitution-making in Eastern Europe.

GÖRAN HERMERÉN is professor of philosophy at Lund University, Sweden; and, since 1988, president of the International Association for Aesthetics. He is the author of *Art, Reason, and Tradition* (Almqvist & Wiksell, 1991), *Aspects of Aesthetics* (Gleerup, 1983), *Influence in Art and Literature* (Princeton University Press, 1975), and *The Nature of Aesthetic Qualities* (Lund University Press, 1988).

METTE HJORT is assistant professor of English and director of the Cultural Studies Program at McGill University. She is the author of *The Strategy of Letters* (Harvard University Press, forthcoming 1993) and the translator of Louis Marin's *Food for Thought* (Johns Hopkins University Press, 1989).

PAISLEY LIVINGSTON is professor of English at McGill University. He is the author of *Ingmar Bergman and the Rituals of Art* (Cornell University Press, 1982), *Literary Knowledge: Humanistic Inquiry and the Philosophy of Science* (Cornell University Press, 1988), *Literature and Rationality: Ideas of Agency in Theory and Fiction* (Cambridge University Press, 1991), and *Models of Desire: René Girard and the Psychology of Mimesis* (Johns Hopkins University Press, 1992). He is also the editor of *Disorder and Order* (Anma Libri, 1984).

JOSEPH MARGOLIS is Laura H. Carnell Professor of Philosophy at Temple University. He is the author of a three-volume overview of philosophy, *The Persistence of Reality* (Blackwell, 1986, 1987, 1989), and of *The Truth about Relativism* (Blackwell, 1991). His most recent works, *The New Puzzle of Interpretation* and *The Flux of History and the Flux of Science,* are forthcoming.

PETER MCCORMICK is professor of philosophy and English literature at the University of Ottawa. He has published *Fictions, Philosophies, and the Problems of Poetics* (Cornell University Press, 1988), *Heidegger and the Language of the World: An Argumentative Reading of the Later Heidegger's Meditations on Language* (University of Ottawa Press, 1976), and *Modernity, Aesthetics, and the Bounds of Art* (Cornell University Press, 1990). He is the editor of *The Reasons of Art: Artworks and the Transformation of Philosophy* (University of Ottawa Press, 1986) and of *Roman Ingarden: Selected Papers in Aesthetics* (Catholic University of America Press, 1984).

THOMAS G. PAVEL is professor of comparative literature and Romance languages and literatures at Princeton University. He is the author of *The Feud of Language* (Blackwell, 1989), *Fictional Worlds* (Harvard University Press, 1986), *The Poetics of Plot: The Case of English Renaissance Drama* (University of Minnesota Press, 1985), and *La syntaxe narrative des tragédies de Corneille* (Klincksieck, 1976).

SIEGFRIED J. SCHMIDT studied philosophy, literature, linguistics, and art history. Since 1971 he has been professor of linguistics and literary theory at the universities of Bielefeld and Siegen. He was appointed director of the Institute for Empirical Studies in Literature and the Media in 1984, and was the editor of *Poetics* from 1980 to 1990. He is the honorary president of the International Society for the Empirical Study of Literature and a member of the Academia Europaea. He has published more than 300 books and articles in the fields of philosophy, literary theory, linguistics, and aesthetics, including *Foundation for the Empirical Study of Literature: The Components of a Basic Theory* (Helmut Buske Verlag, 1982) and *Die Selbstorganisation des Sozialsystems Literatur im 18. Jahrhundert* (Suhrkamp, 1989).

RICHARD SHUSTERMAN is associate professor of philosophy at Temple University. He is the author of *The Object of Literary Criticism* (Rodopi, 1984), *T. S. Eliot and the Philosophy of Literary Criticism* (Columbia University Press, 1988), and *Pragmatist Aesthetics: Living Beauty, Rethinking Art* (Basil Blackwell, 1992). He is also the editor of *Analytic Aesthetics* (Basil Blackwell, 1989).

CHARLES TAYLOR was for many years Chichele Professor of Social and Political Theory at Oxford, and now teaches in the Political Science Department at McGill University. He is the author of *The Explanation of Behaviour* (Routledge & Kegan Paul, 1964), *Hegel* (Cambridge University Press, 1974), *Hegel and Modern Society* (Cambridge University Press, 1979), *Patterns of Politics* (McClelland & Stewart, 1970), and *Sources of the Self: The Making of the Modern Identity* (Harvard University Press, 1989). He has also published a two-volume collection, *Philosophical Papers* (Cambridge University Press, 1985).

GEORGE M. WILSON is professor of philosophy at Johns Hopkins University. He is the author of two books: one on film, *Narration in Light: Studies in Cinematic Point of View* (Johns Hopkins University Press, 1986), and one on the theory of action, *The Intentionality of Human Action* (Stanford University Press, 1989). He has also written on the philosophy of language, the philosophy of mind, and aesthetics. He has taught at Princeton University, Harvard University, and the University of Pittsburgh.